March 2015

The San Francisco System and Its Legacies

In September 1951, Japan signed a peace treaty with forty-eight countries in San Francisco; in April 1952, the treaty came into effect. The San Francisco Peace Treaty is an international agreement that in significant ways shaped the post-World War II international order in the Asia-Pacific. With its associated security arrangements, it laid the foundation for the regional structure of Cold War confrontation: the "San Francisco System" fully reflected the strategic interests and policy priorities of the peace conference's host nation, the United States. The treaty fell far short of settling outstanding issues in the wake of the Pacific War or facilitating a clean start for the "post-war" period. Rather, critical aspects of the settlement were left equivocal, and continue to have significant and worrisome implications for regional international relations.

This book examines the key developments of the contentious political and security issues in the Asia-Pacific that share a common foundation in the post-war disposition of Japan, particularly the San Francisco Peace Treaty. These include both tangible and intangible issues, such as disputes over territories and "history" problems. Taking the San Francisco System as its conceptual grounding, the authors examine how these issues developed and have remained contentious long after the San Francisco arrangements. To provide bases for producing solutions, the chapters offer comprehensive accounts that explain and deepen our understanding of these complex regional issues and the San Francisco System as a whole.

By closely and systematically examining the legacy and various ramifications of the San Francisco System, this fascinating book adds to our understanding of current and growing tensions in the region. As such, it will be of great interest to students and scholars of Asian studies, history, international relations, and politics.

Kimie Hara is Professor and the Renison Research Professor at the University of Waterloo, where she is also the Director of East Asian Studies at Renison University College.

Asia's transformations
Edited by Mark Selden
Cornell University, USA

The books in this series explore the political, social, economic, and cultural consequences of Asia's transformations in the twentieth and twenty-first centuries. The series emphasizes the tumultuous interplay of local, national, regional and global forces as Asia bids to become the hub of the world economy. While focusing on the contemporary, it also looks back to analyze the antecedents of Asia's contested rise.

This series comprises several strands:

Asia's transformations
Titles include:

Asia's great cities

Each volume aims to capture the heartbeat of the contemporary city from multiple perspectives emblematic of the authors' own deep familiarity with the distinctive faces of the city, its history, society, culture, politics and economics, and its evolving position in national, regional and global frameworks. While most volumes emphasize urban developments since the Second World War, some pay close attention to the legacy of the longue durée in shaping the contemporary. Thematic and comparative volumes address such themes as urbanization, economic and financial linkages, architecture and space, wealth and power, gendered relationships, planning and anarchy, and ethnographies in national and regional perspective. Titles include:

1 **Bangkok***
   Place, practice and representation
   Marc Askew

2 **Representing Calcutta***
   Modernity, nationalism and the
   colonial uncanny
   Swati Chattopadhyay

3 **Singapore***
   Wealth, power and the culture of
   control
   Carl A. Trocki

4 **The City in South Asia**
   James Heitzman

5 **Global Shanghai, 1850–2010***
   A history in fragments
   Jeffrey N. Wasserstrom

6 **Hong Kong***
   Becoming a global city
   Stephen Chiu and Tai-Lok Lui

Asia.com

Asia.com is a series which focuses on the ways in which new information and communication technologies are influencing politics, society and culture in Asia. Titles include:

1 **Japanese Cybercultures***
   *Edited by Mark McLelland and
   Nanette Gottlieb*

2 **Asia.com***
   Asia encounters the Internet
   *Edited by K.C. Ho, Randolph
   Kluver, and Kenneth C.C. Yang*

3 **The Internet in Indonesia's
   New Democracy***
   David T. Hill and Krishna Sen

4 **Chinese Cyberspaces***
   Technological changes and
   political effects
   *Edited by Jens Damm and
   Simona Thomas*

5 **Mobile Media in the Asia-Pacific**
   Gender and the art of being mobile
   Larissa Hjorth

6 **Online@AsiaPacific**
   Mobile, social and locative media
   in the Asia-Pacific
   Larissa Hjorth and Michael Arnold

Critical Asian scholarship

Critical Asian scholarship is a series intended to showcase the most important individual contributions to scholarship in Asian Studies. Each of the volumes presents a leading Asian scholar addressing themes that are central to his or her most significant and lasting contribution to Asian Studies. The series is committed to the rich variety of research and writing on Asia, and is not restricted to any particular discipline, theoretical approach or geographical expertise.

The San Francisco System and Its Legacies

Continuation, transformation, and historical reconciliation in the Asia-Pacific

Edited by Kimie Hara

Routledge
Taylor & Francis Group

LONDON AND NEW YORK

First published 2015
by Routledge
2 Park Square, Milton Park, Abingdon, Oxon OX14 4RN

and by Routledge
711 Third Avenue, New York, NY 10017

Routledge is an imprint of the Taylor & Francis Group, an informa business

British Library Cataloguing in Publication Data
A catalogue record for this book is available from the British Library

Library of Congress Cataloging in Publication Data
The San Francisco system and its legacies: continuation, transformation and historical reconciliation in the Asia-Pacific / edited by Kimie Hara.
  pages cm. – (Asia's transformations; 45)
  Includes bibliographical references and index.
  1. Pacific Area–Foreign relations. 2. Asia–Foreign relations. 3. Security, International–Pacific Area. 4. Security, International–Asia.
  5. Conference for the Conclusion and Signature of the Treaty of Peace with Japan (1951: San Francisco, Calif.) I. Hara, Kimie, editor of compilation.
  JZ1980.S36 2014
  327.09182′3–dc23   2014019861

ISBN: 978-1-138-79478-8 (hbk)
ISBN: 978-1-315-75901-2 (ebk)

Typeset in Times New Roman
by Wearset Ltd, Boldon, Tyne and Wear

Printed and bound in Great Britain by
TJ International Ltd, Padstow, Cornwall

Contents

Illustrations

Figures

Tables

Contributors

John W. Dower is Emeritus Professor of History at the Massachusetts Institute of Technology. His books include *Empire and Aftermath: Yoshida Shigeru and the Japanese Experience, 1878–1954* (1979); *War Without Mercy: Race and Power in the Pacific War* (1986); *Embracing Defeat: Japan in the Wake of World War II* (1999); *Cultures of War: Pearl Harbor/Hiroshima/9–11/Iraq* (2010); and two collections of essays: *Japan in War and Peace: Selected Essays* (1994), and *Ways of Forgetting, Ways of Remembering: Japan in the Modern World* (2012).

Kimie Hara is Professor and the Renison Research Professor at the University of Waterloo, where she is also the Director of East Asian Studies at Renison University College. Her books include *Cold War Frontiers in the Asia-Pacific: Divided Territories in the San Francisco System* (2007, 2012); *Japanese–Soviet/Russian Relations Since 1945: A Difficult Peace* (1998, 2012); *Japanese Diplomacy Through the Eyes of Japanese Scholars Overseas* (2009, in Japanese); and *Northern Territories, Asia-Pacific Regional Conflicts and the Åland Experience: Untying the Kurillian Knot* (2009, 2013, edited with Geoffrey Jukes).

Scott Harrison is a PhD Candidate (ABD) at the University of Waterloo in global Indigenous and Cold War history. He is the author of *The Indigenous Ainu of Japan and the Northern Territories Dispute* (2008).

Hirofumi Hayashi is Professor of Politics at the Kanto Gakuin University, Japan. He is the author of several important books on Japanese war crimes during World War II (in Japanese). His English publications include; "Disputes in Japan Over the Japanese Military 'Comfort Women' System and Its Perception in History," *Annals of the American Academy of Political and Social Science*, 617 (May 2008); "Japanese Imperial Government Involvement in the Military 'Comfort Women' System," in Barbara Drinck and Chung-noh Gross (eds.), *Forced Prostitution in Times of War and Peace: Sexual Violence against Women and Girls* (2007); "The Japanese Movement to Protest Wartime Sexual Violence: A Survey of Japanese and International Literature," *Critical Asian Studies*, 33, No. 4 (December 2001); "British War

Crimes Trials of Japanese," *Nature–People–Society: Science and the Human-ities*, Kanto Gakuin University, No. 31 (July 2001); and "Japanese Comfort Women in Southeast Asia," *Japan Forum*, 10. No. 2 (1998).

Nong Hong is Director of Research Center for Oceans Law and Policy at the National Institute for South China Sea Studies (NISCSS). She received her PhD of interdisciplinary study of international law and international relations from the University of Alberta, Canada and held a Postdoctoral Fellowship in the University's China Institute. She was ITLOS-Nippon Fellow for Inter-national Dispute Settlement (2008–2009), and Visiting Fellow at the Center of Oceans Law and Policy, University of Virginia (2009) and at the Max Planck Institute for Comparative Public Law and International Law (2007). She is also a research fellow with China Institute, University of Alberta. Her recent publications include *UNCLOS and Ocean Dispute Settlement: Law and Politics in the South China Sea* (2012); *Recent Developments in the South China Sea Dispute* (co-edited with Wu Shicun, 2014).

Dong-Choon Kim is Associate Professor of Sociology at Sung Kong Hoe Uni-versity in Seoul, Korea. He served the Korean government as a standing com-missioner of the Truth and Reconciliation Commission, Republic of Korea (TRCK) from December 1, 2005 to December 10, 2009. He received his PhD from Seoul National University (1993). He specializes in historical sociology of Korean politics, working class formation, and the Korean War. He also has acted as an organizer of progressive academic movements since the 1980s and participated in several civil movements in South Korea (co-builder of PSPD in Korea). He has written articles on Korean War massacres and has organized concerned intellectuals and victims' families to settle the problem of massacres committed by South Korean authorities during the Korean War (1948–1953). He has written several academic articles and books, including *The Unending Korean War* (2009).

Seokwoo Lee is Professor of International Law, INHA University Law School, Korea. He is also Chairman of the Research Committee, SLOC (Sea Lanes of Communication) Study Group – Korea; and Chairman of the Foundation for the Development of International Law in Asia (DILA). He holds a DPhil (Oxford), LLMs (NYU, Minnesota, and Korea University), and LLB (Korea University). His representative publications in English are: *Asian Approaches to International Law and the Legacy of Colonialism and Imperialism: The Law of the Sea, Territorial Disputes and International Dispute Settlement* (edited with Jin-Hyun Paik and Kevin Y.L. Tan, 2012); *Dokdo: Historical Appraisal and International Justice* (edited with Hee Eun Lee, 2011); *Frontier Issues in Ocean Law: Marine Resources, Mari-time Boundaries, and the Law of the Sea* (edited with Harry N. Scheiber, 2008); "DOKDO: The San Francisco Peace Treaty, International Law on Territorial Disputes, and Historical Criticism," *Asian Perspective* (2011); "The 1951 San Francisco Peace Treaty and Its Relevance to the Sovereignty of Dokdo," *Chinese Journal of International Law* (2010) (with Jon M. Van Dyke).

Man-Houng Lin was mostly educated in Taiwan and received her PhD in history and East Asian languages from Harvard University in 1989. She has been a Senior Research Fellow at the Institute of Modern History, Academia Sinica since 1990 and Professor at the Department of History, National Taiwan Normal University since 1991. Lin's main area of research focuses on treaty ports and modern China, native opium of late Qing China, currency crisis and early nineteenth-century China, Taiwanese merchants' overseas economic networks, 1895–1945. She has published four books and about 80 papers in Chinese, English, Japanese, and Korean in these areas. Her book *China Upside Down: Currency, Society and Ideologies, 1808–1856* (2006) links China's topsy-turvy change from the center of the East Asian order to its setback in the modern period. From May 20, 2008 to December 16, 2010 she served as the president of the Republic of China's Academia Historica (State History Academy). Then she returned to Academia Sinica to finish her book, *Pacificbound: The Rise of the Taiwanese Merchants in the Asia-Pacific Commercial Network, 1895–1945*. It is in the research of this book that Lin encountered the Taipei Treaty signed in 1952 and its significance to Taiwan.

Gavan McCormack is Emeritus Professor at Australian National University. A graduate of the universities of Melbourne and London, he joined the ANU in 1990 after teaching at the Universities of Leeds (UK), La Trobe (Melbourne), and Adelaide. He was elected a Fellow of the Academy of Humanities of Australia in 1992. His three most recent books have been published also in Japanese and Korean, and two of them in Chinese; *Target North Korea: Pushing North Korea to the Brink of Nuclear Catastrophe* (2004, 2006); *Client State: Japan in the American Embrace* (2007, 2008); *Resistant Islands: Okinawa versus Japan and the United States* (with Satoko Oka Norimatsu, 2012, 2013). He was a co-founder of *Japan Focus* (2002) and is a coordinator of *The Asia-Pacific Journal – Japan Focus*.

John Price is Professor of History at the University of Victoria, British Columbia, Canada. He is the author of *Japan Works: Power and Paradox in Postwar Industrial Relations* (1997) and *Orienting Canada: Race, Empire and the Transpacific* (2011). He is currently working on a biography (with his collaborator in China, Ningping YU) of Victoria Cheung, the first Chinese Canadian to graduate from the University of Toronto Medical School and the longest-serving medical missionary to China. He is also researching the life story of Peter (Shinobu) Higashi, the founder of the *New Canadian* who left Canada in 1939 to work for the *Manchurian Daily News* in Harbin, China (then part of "Manchukuo"). These stories are part of his general research program focusing on the life stories of fifteen people with transpacific roots whose experiences will form the basis for a new publication on the history of Pacific Canada.

Konstantin Sarkisov graduated from St Petersburg (Leningrad) University with a PhD on Japan and the United Nations. He was formerly the Head of the Center for Japanese Studies and Vice-Director at the Institute of Oriental Studies of the Russian Academy of Sciences; President of the Russian Association of Japanology (1994–1998); member of NEACD (Northeast Asia Cooperation Dialogue, UC San Diego); Visiting Professor at the Hosei, Keio, and Hitotsubashi Universities, teaching Japanese policy in the Asia-Pacific; Professor in International Relations in the Asia-Pacific at the Postgraduate School, Department of Law, Yamanashi Gakuin University (2000–2010); and the Head of the Japan and Northeast Asia Studies Center at the Diplomatic Academy of Russia (2010–2011). He has written a number of books, parts of books, and articles on Russo-Japanese relations, Japan's foreign and internal policy, and international relations in Asia.

Mark Selden is Coordinator of *The Asia-Pacific Journal – Japan Focus*, and a Senior Research Associate in the East Asia Program at Cornell University. A specialist on the modern and contemporary geopolitics, political economy and history of China, Japan, and the Asia Pacific, his work has ranged broadly across themes of war and revolution, inequality, development, regional and world social change, and historical memory. His best-known books are *China in Revolution: The Yenan Way Revisited*; *Chinese Village, Socialist State* (with Edward Friedman and Paul Pickowicz); and *Censoring History: Citizenship and Memory in Japan, Germany and the United States* (with Laura Hein). Recent books include: *Chinese Society: Change, Conflict and Resistance* (third edition, with Elizabeth Perry), *Revolution, Resistance and Reform in Village China* (with Edward Friedman and Paul Pickowicz); *War and State Terrorism: The United States, Japan and the Asia-Pacific in the Long Twentieth Century* (with Alvin So); *The Resurgence of East Asia: 500, 150 and 50 Year Perspectives* (with Giovanni Arrighi and Takeshi Hamashita). He is the editor of book series at Rowman & Littlefield, Routledge, and M.E. Sharpe publishers.

Unryu Suganuma is Associate Professor in the College of Arts and Sciences at J.F. Oberlin University, Tokyo. After growing up and studying in China and Japan, he went to the United States for graduate studies, earning master's degrees at both St. John's University (in Chinese studies) and Syracuse University (in international relations), as well as a PhD (in geography) from the Maxwell School of Syracuse University. He is the author of *Sovereign Rights and Territorial Space in Sino-Japanese Relations* (2000) and *Rizhong Guanxi yu Lingtu Zhuquan* (History of Sino-Japanese Relations: Sovereignty and Territory) (2007).

Haruki Wada is Emeritus Professor at the University of Tokyo. He specializes in modern Russian history and North Korean history. Born in Osaka, he graduated from the Department of History of Western Countries, Philological Faculty, University of Tokyo, and became a Research Associate (1960), Lecturer (1966), Associate Professor (1968), Professor (1985), and the Director (1996) of the Institute of Social Science, University of Tokyo, and retired in March 1998. His main publications include: *Nikorai Rasseru: Kokkyo o koeru Narodoniki* (Nikolai Russel-Sudzhilovskii: A Russian Populist Who Went over the Borders of Countries) (2 vols., in Japanese, 1973); *Hoppo Ryodo Mondai o Kangaeru* (On the Northern Territories Problem) (in Japanese, 1990); *Kim Il Sung to Manshu Konichi senso* (Kim Il Sung and Manchurian Anti-Japanese Guerilla War) (in Japanese, 1992; Korean, 1992); *Kitachosen* (North Korea) (in Japanese, 1998; Korean, 2002); *Chosen Senso Zenshi* (A Complete History of the Korean War) (in Japanese, 2002); *Tohoku Aziya Kyodo no Ie* (Common House of Northeast Asia: A Regionalist Manifesto) (in Japanese, 2003; Korean 2004); *Aru Sengo Seishin no Keisei 1938–1965* (Birth of an Postwar Intellectual) (in Japanese, 2006); *Kitachosen Gendaishi* (A History of North Korea, 1932–2012) (in Japanese, 2012).

Acknowledgments

This book emerged from an international collaboration project and came to fruition thanks to the generous support of several organizations and individuals.

The project conference, *Sixty Years of the San Francisco System: Continuation, Transformation, and Historical Reconciliation in the Asia-Pacific*, was held in Waterloo, Ontario, Canada, on April 28, 2012, bringing together the authors from Korea, Japan, China, Taiwan, Russia, the United States, Australia, and Canada for extensive discussions. The conference, held exactly sixty years after the enactment of the San Francisco Peace Treaty, was supported by generous funding from the Northeast Asian History Foundation of Korea, as well as local funding and kind assistance from the Keiko and Charles Belair Centre for East Asian Studies of Renison University College, the Balsillie School of International Affairs, and the Japan Futures Initiative at the University of Waterloo. The project also benefited from research support from a Japan Foundation Fellowship and a grant from the Social Sciences and Humanities Research Council of Canada.

I would like to thank all of the project collaborators. Special thanks are due to all authors for their contributions. In addition to the authors, the workshop participants provided superb commentary and valuable insights. Many thanks to all of them: Joe-jeong Chung, Scott Harrison, Young Hwan Kim, James Manicom, Song Oh, Mark Selden, and David Welch. Young Hwan Kim also provided incredible logistical support for the project from its outset. The book received exceptional editorial support from Vicki Low and the Routledge editorial team, Hannah Mack and Stephanie Rogers in particular. My gratitude also goes to Laura Mackenzie, as well as friends and colleagues of Renison University College and the University of Waterloo, for their support and encouragement. Finally, I would like to express my personal thanks to my family – Hatski, Hugo, and Richard.

Kimie Hara

Introduction

The San Francisco System and its legacies in the Asia-Pacific*

Kimie Hara

Over sixty years have passed since the treaty of peace with Japan was signed (September 8, 1951) and came into force (April 28, 1952). With this post-war arrangement, widely known as the San Francisco Peace Treaty (SFPT) after the location of its signing ceremony, Japan returned to the international community. It then achieved remarkable post-war recovery – becoming the world's second-largest economy by the end of the 1960s. However, the treaty, which largely determined Japan's position in the post-war world, along with the US–Japan security treaty signed on the same day, also left negative legacies of "unresolved problems." Today, the countries and peoples of East Asia are still deeply divided by history, politics, and unsettled borders, even though they have become much closer in their economic, cultural, and other relations.

This introductory chapter provides the historical background to those "unresolved problems" in the context of the "San Francisco System." Paying attention to their common foundation, it suggests considering the solutions for these problems in a broader multilateral context beyond the immediate disputants, which could lead East Asia toward greater regional cooperation and community-building.

The San Francisco System: the Cold War and US dominant post-World War II order in the Asia-Pacific

The Cold War structure of the post-World War II world was often attributed to the Yalta System. This system originated from the US–UK–USSR agreements over the construction of the post-war international order made at Yalta in February 1945. However, with respect to the regional international order in the Asia-Pacific, the Yalta blueprint gave way to the San Francisco System. Following a series of East–West tensions, notably those centered on the communization of Eastern Europe and the division of Germany, the Yalta System was consolidated in Europe. The status quo received international recognition in the 1975 Helsinki Accord. By the early 1990s, however, the Yalta System had collapsed, accompanied by significant changes such as the democratization of Eastern Europe, the independence of the Baltic States, the reunification of Germany, and the demise of the Soviet Union. Since then, many have viewed the collapse of the Yalta System as synonymous with the end of the Cold War.

The Yalta System, however, was never established as an international order in the Asia-Pacific. The post-war international order was discussed and some secret agreements affecting Japan were concluded at Yalta. The terms "Yalta System" and "East Asian Yalta System" are sometimes used to refer to a regional post-war order based on those agreements.[1] But it was a blueprint that would have taken effect only if such agreements had been faithfully implemented. By 1951, when the peace treaty with Japan was signed in San Francisco, the Yalta agreements had been distorted or made equivocal. Under the new circumstances of escalating East–West confrontation that had begun in Europe, post-war Asia took a profoundly different path from that originally planned.

The San Francisco Peace Treaty was an international agreement that in significant ways shaped the post-World War II international order in the Asia-Pacific. With its associated security arrangements, it laid the foundation for the regional structure of Cold War confrontation: the San Francisco System fully reflected the strategic interests and the policy priorities of the peace conference's host nation, the United States. The system assured the dominant influence and lasting presence of the United States, or "Pax Americana," and brought Japan democracy and economic prosperity along with its peace constitution, but at the expense of lasting divisions among peoples and countries in East Asia.

The Cold War developed differently between the Atlantic and Pacific sides of the Eurasian continent. While falling short of "hot" war, it was "cold war" in Europe and the US–USSR context. By contrast, in Asia it was "hot" in places, and more complex. After the Japanese withdrawal, the post-war liberation and independence movements in some parts of the region turned to civil war over the governing principles for the new states, where competition over spheres of influence between the superpowers supervened. Instead of a direct clash between the United States and the USSR, Asian lands became surrogate battlefields between capitalism and socialism. In 1951, while failing to form a multilateral regional alliance like NATO in Asia, the United States signed a mutual defense treaty with the Philippines on August 30, a tripartite security treaty with Australia and New Zealand (ANZUS) on September 1, and a security treaty with Japan on September 8 on the same day as the peace treaty. The "San Francisco Alliance System" of US hub-and-spoke military alliances came into being.[2] (The United States made similar arrangements with South Korea in 1953, Taiwan in 1954, and Thailand in 1961.)

Along with political and military conflicts, significant elements within the Cold War structure in the Asia-Pacific are the regional conflicts among its major players. Confrontation over national boundaries and territorial sovereignty emerged from the disposition of the defeated Axis countries. Whereas Germany was the only divided nation in Europe, several Cold War frontiers emerged to divide nations and peoples in East Asia. The San Francisco Peace Treaty played a critical role in creating or mounting many of these frontier problems. Vast territories, extending from the Kurile Islands to Antarctica, and from Micronesia to the Spratlys, were disposed of in the treaty. The treaty, however, specified neither their final disposition nor their precise geographical limits, thereby sowing the seeds of multiple "unresolved problems" throughout the region.

Table I.1 shows the relationship between the San Francisco Peace Treaty and the major regional conflicts in East Asia, indicating the states that are party to these conflicts. The regional conflicts derived from the post-war territorial disposition of the former Japanese empire may be classified into three kinds: (1) insular territorial disputes such as those pertaining to the Northern Territories/ Southern Kuriles, Dokdo/Takeshima, Senkaku/Diaoyu, Spratly/Nansha, and Paracel/Xisha; (2) divided nations as seen in the Korean Peninsula and cross-Taiwan Strait problem;[3] and (3) status of territories as seen in Taiwan and the "Okinawa problem."[4] These problems did not necessarily originate solely in the San Francisco Peace Treaty. For example, a secret agreement to transfer the Kuriles and Southern Sakhalin from Japan to the USSR was reached at the Yalta Conference in February 1945. However, the problem emerged at San Francisco, since the peace treaty specified neither final designation nor precise boundaries of the territories that Japan renounced.[5] No peace treaty has yet been signed between the two countries, and the territorial issue is to this day the biggest obstacle to normalizing relations between Japan and Russia.

In addition to these tangible conflicts, the SFPT concerns other intangible issues of "history," such as war crimes, reparations, and their interpretation, which continue to divide Japan and its neighbors to this day. The treaty specified Japan's acceptance of the judgments of the International Military Tribunal for the Far East, the so-called Tokyo Tribunal (1946–1948). However, the tribunal overlooked the responsibility of the Japanese government for the torture and abuse of Chinese and Koreans in such matters as the Nanjing massacre, the use

Table I.1 The San Francisco Peace Treaty and regional conflicts in East Asia

Regional conflicts	San Francisco Peace Treaty (relevant articles)	Concerned states
Territorial disputes		
Dokdo/Takeshima	Article 2 (a) Korea	Japan, ROK
Senkaku/Diaoyu	Article 2 (b) Formosa (Taiwan) Article 3 (Ryukyu Islands)	Japan, PRC, ROC
Northern Territories/ Southern Kuriles	Article 2 (c) Kurile Islands/ Southern Sakhalin	Japan, Russia/USSR
Spratlys & Paracels	Article 2 (f) Spratlys & Paracels	PRC, ROC, Vietnam, Philippines, Malaysia, Brunei
Divided nations		
Korean Peninsula	Article 2 (a) Korea	ROK, DPRK
Cross-Taiwan Strait	Article 2 (b) Formosa	PRC, ROC
Status		
Okinawa	Article 3	Japan, USA
Taiwan	Article 2 (b)	PRC, ROC

Source: Kimie Hara, "The San Francisco Peace Treaty and Frontier Problems in the Regional Order in East Asia: A Sixty Year Perspective," *The Asia-Pacific Journal* 10, issue 17, no. 1 (2012).

of Korean and Chinese forced labor in Japanese mines and factories, and the forced prostitution of Korean, Chinese, and other nations' "comfort women" by the Japanese military. Instead, the tribunal "focused on Japanese actions that had most directly affected Western Allies: the attack on Pearl Harbor and the mistreatment of Allied prisoners of War."[6]

"Unresolved problems" in the San Francisco System

Close examination of the Allies' documents, particularly those of the United States (the main drafter of the peace treaty), reveals key links between the regional Cold War and the ambiguity of the Japanese peace settlement, particularly the equivocal wording about designation of territory; it suggests the necessity for a multilateral approach that goes beyond the framework of the current disputant states as a key to better understanding and conceptualizing approaches conducive to the future resolution of these problems.[7]

Prior to the final draft of the San Francisco Peace Treaty, completed in 1951 (six years after the Japanese surrender), multiple treaty drafts were prepared. Early drafts were, on the whole, based on the US wartime studies, and were consistent with the Yalta spirit of inter-Allied cooperation.[8] They reflected the "punitive" and "rigid" policy of the Allied Powers toward Japan, which was an enemy to be deprived of its conquered territories and weakened militarily and economically. As for the disposition of territories, those early drafts were long and detailed, providing clear border demarcations and specifying the names of small islands near the borders of post-war Japan, such as Takeshima, Habomai, and Shikotan, specifically to avoid future territorial conflicts.

However, against the background of the intensifying Cold War, which became "hot" in Asia with the outbreak of the Korean War in June 1950, the peace terms with Japan changed in sync with the new strategic interests of the United States. Specifically, Japan and the Philippines, soon to be the most important US allies in East Asia, were to be secured for the non-communist West with pro-US governments, whereas the communist states were to be contained.

In this context, drafts of the Japanese peace treaty went through various changes, eventually becoming simplified. The names of the countries that were intended to receive such islands as Formosa (Taiwan), the Kuriles, and other territories disappeared from the text, leaving various "unresolved problems" among the regional neighbors. The equivocal wording of the peace treaty was the result neither of inadvertence nor of error; instead, issues were deliberately left unresolved.[9] It is no coincidence that the territorial disputes derived from the San Francisco Peace Treaty – the Northern Territories/Southern Kuriles, Takeshima/ Dokdo, Senkaku/Diaoyu (Okinawa), Spratly/Nansha, and Paracel/Xisha problems – all line up along the "Acheson Line," the US Cold War defense perimeter of the western Pacific, announced in January 1950.

From north to southwest along the Acheson Line, territorial problems were left between Japan and its neighbors: the Northern Territories with the 100 percent communist USSR, Takeshima with half-communist "Korea," and

Senkaku (Okinawa) with mostly communist "China." These problems line up like "wedges" securing Japan in the Western bloc, or "walls" dividing it from the communist sphere of influence. The territorial problem between Japan and China originally centered on Okinawa (the Ryukyus),[10] as part of which the Sankakus were placed under US control, but after the reversion of administrative rights to Japan in 1972 the focus of the dispute shifted to the Senkakus.

With the outbreak of the Korean War, the United States altered its policy toward Korea and China, which it had once written off as "lost" or "abandoned," intervening in both nations' civil wars. However, in order to avoid further escalation of these regional wars, which could possibly lead to a nuclear war or the next total war, the "containment line" came to be fixed at the thirty-eighth parallel and Taiwan Strait, respectively. Thus, these containment frontiers could be perceived as double wedges from the viewpoint of Japanese defense, together with Takeshima and Senkaku (Okinawa) islands. On the other hand, viewed from the perspective of the United States' China policy, China's ocean frontier problems of Senkaku (Okinawa), the Spratlys, and the Paracels might be seen as wedges of containment, together with Taiwan (Figure I.1).

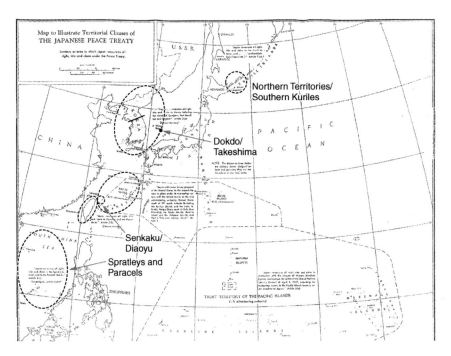

Figure I.1 Map to illustrate territorial clauses of the Japanese Peace Treaty (source: *United States, 82nd session, SENATE, Executive Report No. 2, Japanese Peace Treaty and Other Treaties relating to Security in the Pacific/Report of the Committee on Foreign Relations on Executives, A, B, C and D.* Washington: United States Government Printing Office, 1952, with related regional conflicts in East Asia marked by the author).

The Spratlys & Paracels, disposed of in Article 2(f) of the peace treaty and located in the South China Sea at the southwest end of the Acheson Line, may also be viewed as wedges to defend the Philippines, which was the core of US Cold War strategy in Southeast Asia. To varying degrees, Chinese ownership was considered for these territories in US wartime preparations for a post-war settlement. Their final designation was not specified in the San Francisco Treaty, not simply because it was unclear, but, more importantly, to prevent them from falling into the hands of China. Disputes over the sovereignty of these islands in the South China Sea existed before the war. However, the pre- and post-war disputes differ in terms of the countries involved and the nature of the disputes – that is, pre-war colonial frontiers were reborn as Cold War frontiers in Southeast Asia.[11]

Meanwhile, the United States tactically negotiated the terms of UN trusteeship for its advantage and secured exclusive control of its occupied islands, making the Pacific north of the Equator "an American Lake."[12] Among those islands, Micronesia, disposed of in the peace treaty's Article 2(d), was used for US nuclear testing, whereas Okinawa became one of the most important US military bases in the region.[13]

THE SAN FRANCISCO PEACE TREATY

CHAPTER II

Territory

Article 2

(a) Japan, recognizing the independence of Korea, renounces all right, title and claim to Korea, including the islands of Quelpart, Port Hamilton and Dagelet.

(b) Japan renounces all right, title and claim to Formosa and the Pescadores.

(c) Japan renounces all right, title and claim to the Kurile Islands, and to that portion of Sakhalin and the islands adjacent to it over which Japan acquired sovereignty as a consequence of the Treaty of Portsmouth of September 5, 1905.

(d) Japan renounces all right, title and claim in connection with the League of Nations Mandate System, and accepts the action of the United Nations Security Council of April 2, 1947, extending the trusteeship system to the Pacific Islands formerly under mandate to Japan.

(e) Japan renounces all claim to any right or title to or interest in connection with any part of the Antarctic area, whether deriving from the activities of Japanese nationals or otherwise.

(f) Japan renounces all right, title and claim to the Spratly Islands and to the Paracel Islands.

Article 3

Japan will concur in any proposal of the United States to the United Nations to place under its trusteeship system, with the United States as the sole administering authority, Nansei Shoto south of 29° north latitude (including the Ryukyu Islands and the Daito Islands), Nanpo Shoto south of Sofu Gan (including the Bonin Islands, Rosario Island and the Volcano Islands) and Parece Vela and Marcus Island. Pending the making of such a proposal and affirmative action thereon, the United States will have the right to exercise all and any powers of administration, legislation and jurisdiction over the territory and inhabitants of these islands, including their territorial waters.

Source: *Conference for the Conclusion and Signature of the Treaty of Peace with Japan, San Francisco, California, September 4–8, 1951, Record of Proceedings*, Department of State Publication 4392, International Organization and Conference Series II, Far Eastern 3, December 1951, Division of Publications, Office of Public Affairs, p. 314.

Besides the handling of territories, the US Cold War strategy was also reflected in other aspects of the peace settlement with Japan. In order to remake Japan as a pro-US nation, the peace terms to be presented by the United States had to be more liberal and attractive to Japan than those by the communist nations, which would attempt to estrange Japan from the United States. Accordingly, the peace settlement with Japan became "generous" rather than punitive, with the focus placed on democratization and economic recovery of post-war Japan. This "reverse course" led to the eventual return of conservative politicians, who were purged or prosecuted as war criminals during the occupation period.

With regard to the conflicts that stemmed from the Japanese peace settlement, it is noteworthy that there was no consensus among the states directly concerned. The Allied Powers, particularly the United States and United Kingdom, were divided over their recognition of "China," whereas Korea, a former Japanese colony, was not an Allied Power. As a result, neither of the governments of China (PRC or ROC) nor Korea (ROK or DPRK) was invited to the peace conference. The Soviet Union participated in the peace conference but did not sign the treaty. The Japanese peace treaty was prepared and signed multilaterally, making the forty-nine signatories the "concerned states." Except for Japan, however, none of the major states involved in the conflicts participated in the treaty. The result was to bequeath multiple unresolved conflicts to the countries directly concerned and to the region.[14]

The post-war peace treaty with Japan should have been a clear settlement to end the Pacific War and to start a "post-war" period. However, before the war could be so ended, Japan and the whole Asia-Pacific region became involved in the Cold War that had started in the Euro-Atlantic. The Japanese peace treaty was a by-product of the Cold War. The "unresolved problems" that share this common foundation were destined to continue to divide countries and peoples in East Asia.

Transformation and contemporary legacy of the San Francisco System

Over sixty years since the San Francisco agreement, the world has undergone significant transformations. After periods of East–West tensions and then their relaxation, such as the Cold War thaw of the 1950s and the détente of the 1970s, the Cold War was widely believed to have ended by the early 1990s.

In the Asia-Pacific, the Cold War developed differently from the bi-polar system in the Euro-Atlantic region. A tri-polar, United States–China–USSR system emerged following the Sino-Soviet split in the early 1960s. China had been targeted by the US containment strategy since its intervention in the Korean War. With its nuclear development in 1964 and its entry into the Indochina Wars, China came to hold an ever larger position in the Asian Cold War. Just as the emergence of nuclear weapons fundamentally changed the character of post-World War II international relations and became the biggest factor in defining the US–Soviet Cold War, United States–China confrontation became truly a "Cold War" in lieu of a direct military clash. Rather, surrogate wars were fought in the civil wars on China's periphery.

There is a view that the Cold War between the United States and China, and in Asia in general, ended with the series of Sino-US rapprochements and the normalization of their relations in the 1970s.[15] However, unlike the US–Soviet Cold War in Europe, which fundamentally ended with the collapse of the communist regimes, the Sino-US rapprochement was not an "end" of their Cold War. It was a rapprochement between two powers that do not share common values; it could take place only against the background of the Sino-Soviet dispute. During the détente of the early 1970s, the United States was improving its relations with the USSR as well as with the PRC. Furthermore, the United States continued its security commitment to Taiwan by introducing the Taiwan Relations Act, even after terminating their official diplomatic relations. There was never any general understanding that the "Sino-US Cold War" or the "Cold War in Asia" had ended, while the "US–USSR Cold War" or "Cold War in Europe" had not.

During the late 1980s and early 1990s, both US–Soviet and Sino-Soviet rapprochement was achieved. A remarkable relaxation of tension occurred in East Asia, where expectations soared for solutions to some of the most intractable frontier problems. In the late 1980s, serious deliberations began in Sino-Soviet/Russian border negotiations. The two countries finally completed their border demarcation by making mutual concessions in the 2000s. However, none of the unresolved problems that share their foundation in the SFPT reached a fundamental settlement. In fact, compared to the Euro-Atlantic region, where the wall dividing East and West completely collapsed, the changes that took place in the Asia-Pacific left intact fundamental divisions. Except for the demise of the Soviet Union, the regional Cold War structure of confrontation basically continues to exist. As of today, over twenty years hence and over sixty years after San Francisco, in addition to the above-mentioned territorial problems, China and Korea are still divided, with their communist or authoritarian sides still perceived as threats by their neighbors. Accordingly, the US military presence through the San Francisco Alliance System, along with associated issues such as the "Okinawa problem," continues in this region. Whereas ANZUS lost some validity as a trilateral alliance following New Zealand's anti-nuclear legislation and consequent US suspension of its security guarantee in the 1990s, its bilateral (USA–Australia and Australia–New Zealand) security relations remain strong. With the United States' other bilateral security alliances, the regional security system continues to operate, strengthening its bilateral features. Whereas the Warsaw Treaty Organization disappeared, and the North Atlantic Treaty Organization (NATO) lost its anti-communist focus when it accepted formerly communist countries in Eastern Europe as members, there are no indications that the remaining San Francisco Alliance System will embrace North Korea or China.

In the sense that the fundamental structure of confrontation remains, the dramatic relaxation seen in East Asia since the late 1980s can be viewed more appropriately as a kind of détente in, rather than an "end" to, the Cold War. The relaxation of tension seen in the Cold War thaw in the 1950s and détente in the 1970s in both instances gave way to subsequent deterioration of East–West relations. Similar phenomena have been observed in East Asia, for example, United States–China conflicts after the Tiananmen incident of 1989; military tensions across the Taiwan Strait and in the Korean Peninsula; disruption of negotiations between Japan and North Korea for normalizing their diplomatic relations; and political tensions involving Japan and its neighbors over territorial disputes and interpretation of history. Nonetheless, considering that the 1975 Helsinki Accords recognized the political status quo including the (then) existing borders in Europe, the political status quo in East Asia, where disputes over national borders continue, may not have attained the level of the 1970s détente in Europe.

Deepening interdependence in economic and other relations

Whereas countries and peoples in East Asia have been divided by politics, history, and unsettled borders, they nevertheless have become closely connected and have deepened their interdependence in economic, cultural, and other relations. With China's economic reform, it may be possible to consider that regional Cold War confrontation began to dissolve partially in the late 1970s. The economic recovery and transformation of East Asian countries for the last six decades from the ruins of war are in fact remarkable. Beginning with Japan in the 1950s, followed by the so-called newly industrializing economies (NIEs) in the 1970s and 1980s, and now with China's rise, East Asia, with the exception of North Korea, has become the most expansive center in the world economy. Economics is indeed the glue connecting the regional states, a glue that transcends old divides to make possible the incorporation of China and Indochina within the dynamic regional economy.

Economic-driven multilateral cooperation and multilateral institution-building have also developed in East Asia, especially since the 1990s. A broad regional framework has emerged in the Asia-Pacific, building on such foundations as the

Pacific Economic Cooperation Council (PECC), Asia-Pacific Economic Cooperation (APEC), and the Association of Southeast Asian Nations (ASEAN). In the wake of the global economic crises of 1997 and 2008, additional multilateral forums involving China (PRC), Japan, and South Korea (ROK) have emerged, such as ASEAN+3 (ASEAN plus the PRC, Japan, and the ROK) and the PRC–Japan–ROK Trilateral Summit, adding new dimensions to an emerging regionalism. In the meantime, Russia, which joined APEC in 1998 and hosted its meetings in Vladivostok in 2012, is also increasing its presence by enlarging investments in its Far East region and deepening economic ties with neighboring states in East Asia.[16]

Expanded regional cooperation and increased interaction have paved the way for confidence-building measures (CBMs) among neighboring states. Progress in CBMs since the 1990s, at both governmental and non-governmental levels, constitutes a leap beyond the Cold War era, particularly in non-traditional security areas such as the environment, food, energy, terrorism, and natural disasters. There have also been notable developments in conflict management and cooperation concerning disputed areas such as fisheries and continental shelves. Multilateral cooperation has been actively pursued in diplomatic and security dialogues as well, using forums such as those mentioned above. Nevertheless, while activities have multiplied, the depth of integration pales compared with that in Europe. While the European Community (EC) of the Cold War era has long since evolved into the European Union (EU), even the idea of an "East Asian Community" (not an "East Asian Union") is still a mere future aspiration. As yet, the East Asian countries do not have relations of sufficient mutual trust. Their countries and peoples are strongly connected economically, but they remain divided politically, and are still in dispute over the "unresolved problems" noted here, including those over territories and "history" issues.

Thus, even though global waves of "post-Cold War" transformations in international relations, such as globalization and regionalism, have reached East Asia, they do not necessarily negate the remaining structure of confrontation founded in San Francisco. More than six decades later, the so-called Acheson and Containment lines still divide countries and peoples of the region, toward which the United States is pivoting once more. In this new era, when the world is more closely connected by advanced technologies and deepened economic interdependence, the political and security situation of the Asia-Pacific evokes the conflicts embedded in the San Francisco System six decades ago.

Considering reconciliation in the Asia-Pacific

The Cold War has sometimes been called the period of "long peace," inasmuch as the balance of power was relatively well maintained and international relations were rather stable.[17] Such was the case in the US–Soviet and European contexts. However, in East Asia many regional conflicts emerged and international relations became highly unstable. These unstable circumstances continue today.

Interpretations of the "Cold War" and the "end of the Cold War" vary, as do those of the San Francisco System.[18] Regardless of these interpretations and no matter how neighborly relations improve, however, as long as these sources of conflict remain unresolved, many possibilities continue to exist for the resurgence of conflicts. Tensions over these conflicts have intensified periodically and will likely intensify again. Although efforts to enhance CBMs and prevent the escalation of conflicts are certainly important, CBMs alone do not lead to fundamental solutions. The road to peace ultimately requires the removal of principal sources of conflict. Complex threads of international relations cannot be easily disentangled. Yet, solutions to problems should not be considered impossible. Hence, to explore clues for solutions, there is need to gain comprehensive understanding of these problems and to disentangle their various threads.

The history of the past six decades seems to suggest that many problems in the Asia-Pacific are likely to remain unresolved, so long as they remain confined to the nations directly involved. Although there are numerous studies devoted to individual regional problems, few address their historical and political linkages originating in the early post-war arrangement with Japan.[19] In fact, there has been no in-depth, collective scholarly research on post-World War II developments tracing back to their common foundation in the San Francisco System. In East Asia, a time span of sixty years has special meaning, signifying the end of one historical cycle and the beginning of a new era. It is a good opportunity to remember the common foundation of many of the most intractable problems in the early post-World War II arrangements, to reflect on the history of the last sixty years and beyond, and to look for constructive ways to resolve these problems in a broader context of regional peace, reconciliation, and prosperity.

Thus, on April 28, 2012, the sixtieth anniversary of the enactment of the SFPT, an international conference was held in Waterloo, Ontario, Canada. This volume consists of revised conference papers and an additional chapter by the editor. The authors addressed the following overarching questions: How have major regional conflicts, the "unresolved problems" referred to above, developed over the last sixty years, and why do they remain contentious? What have been the notable developments in a region-wide perspective? What are the driving forces promoting, and obstructing, solutions to these issues? Has the nature of the issues changed, or evolved, over the years? If so, what new factors have led to change? And, how can these problems, or differences, be resolved?

The authors of this volume do not necessarily share a common interpretation of history or a common view concerning resolution of these problems. This was reflected in animated discussions in which participants – from Korea, Japan, Russia, China, Taiwan, the United States, Australia, and Canada – exchanged views. What they do share is a commitment to peaceful solutions to the intractable problems that challenge statesmen and citizens throughout the region and beyond.

Why Canada?

Readers of this volume may wonder why our conference was held in Canada. It is partly because the volume editor, who was also the conference organizer, is based in Canada, but also because Canada bears historical responsibility for major regional conflicts in East Asia. Although it is not widely known, Canada not only signed the SFPT, but also made a very important contribution to creating certain of the "unresolved problems" examined here. In the process of drafting the peace treaty, Canada proposed that the treaty not specify final designation of the territories. In 1950, after the Korean War broke out, the United States dropped "China" from its peace treaty draft as the country to receive Formosa (Taiwan), in order to make sure that the islands would not go to communist China. In the same draft, however, the USSR was still specified as the country to receive the Kurile Islands and Southern Sakhalin. When the draft was circulated, Canada suggested treating all former Japanese territories consistently, thus not leaving the way open for charges of discriminatory treatment; Canada proposed, in short, that the USSR be deleted from the relevant article and that no designation of territories should be specified.

The United States at first responded negatively to this suggestion, explaining that the situation was different for each territory, but eventually accepted it, realizing that this strategy could conveniently serve to meet its own geopolitical and strategic interests.[20] The peace treaty did not specify to which government or country these former Japanese territories belonged, sowing the seeds for various disputes.

Canada may have potential to become a peace-maker in East Asia. Canada fought in the region during World War II and in the Korean and Indochina wars, and provided uranium for the atomic bomb dropped in Japan, but it also has long been a strong advocate of multilateralism and international cooperation, making efforts to resolve international problems in collaboration with other nations. It has a reputation and record as an honest broker, peace-builder, and peace-keeper in various parts of the world, such as the Middle East, Rwanda, former Yugoslavia, and Afghanistan. However, Canada's presence in East Asia has been rather modest. Nevertheless, Canada now has vested interests in East Asia, which is important for its economy, especially where trade and investment are concerned. Many immigrants to Canada come from this region; they have become an important human resource in Canada. Building peace and stability in this region is in Canada's national interests. Considering its historical involvement and responsibility, as well as its current interests, Canada should play a more constructive role in East Asia. By hosting this project and its conference on the sixtieth anniversary of the SFPT, Canada might take a step in that direction.

Volume composition

The composition of the volume consists of this introduction and thirteen main chapters. Chapters 1–7 mainly deal with issues related to the territorial disposition of the former Japanese empire in the SFPT: (1) the Dokdo/Takeshima problem (Seokwoo Lee), (2) the Northern Territories/Southern Kuriles problem (Konstantin Sarkisov), (3) the Senkaku/Diaoyu problem (Unryu Suganuma), (4) the Spratlys & Paracels problem (Nong Hong), (5) Korea (Dong-choon Kim), (6) Formosa/Taiwan (Man-houng Lin), and (7) Okinawa (Gavan McCormack). Chapters 8–10 deal with issues of war crimes, responsibility, and reconciliation by shedding light on groups of people who were equally victims but for a long time neglected in the shadow of the San Francisco System: (8) comfort women (Hirofumi Hayashi), (9) Indigenous peoples (Scott Harrison), and (10) Asian immigrants in an Allied Power – Canada (John Price). (The Korean minorities in Japan are dealt with in Chapter 5.) Chapters 11 and 12 reflect the overall path of the San Francisco System and consider the future of the region: (11) "The San Francisco System: Past, Present, Future in United States–Japan–China Relations" (John Dower) and (12) "Historical Legacies and Regional Integration" (Haruki Wada). Chapter 13 explores ideas to resolve those problems, particularly the tangible territorial problems: "Preparing Ideas for the Future: Envisioning a Multilateral Settlement" (Kimie Hara). The epilogue is written by the book series editor, who also attended the conference (Mark Selden).

Chapter summaries

1 *Korea and Japan: The Dokdo/Takeshima Problem* (Seokwoo Lee). The 1951 SFPT ending World War II in the Pacific does not discuss sovereignty over Dokdo/Takeshima, the islets situated in the East Sea/Sea of Japan between Korea and Japan. Korea's independence was recognized in the treaty, and it gained other benefits from it. But the treaty's territorial clause does not purport to define Korea's boundaries in any detail, and does not assign ownership of the islets, thus sowing the seeds of Korea–Japan territorial conflict. The United States was clearly concerned with its own security interests during this period, including the challenges of the Cold War and the Korean War, and apparently sought to maintain some flexibility on this issue in case Korea was lost to the Communists. Determining the abstract legal question of sovereignty over Dokdo is one thing, but it is quite another to effectuate it in practice. Be that as it may, it is imperative that the disputants approach the issues through dialogue and a spirit of compromise. An all-or-nothing approach, which obviously does not reckon with the mutual interests of the disputants, will only aggravate an already precarious situation.

2 *Russia and Japan: The Algorithm of the Kuriles/Northern Territories Problem* (Konstantin Sarkisov). An algorithm in math and computer science is a step-by-step procedure for calculations. This chapter presents in a step-by-step fashion the main landmarks of the long history of territorial dispute between Russia and Japan, hoping it may be helpful to calculate possible approaches to its resolution. World War II, the Cold War, and transformations of the post-World War II international order are the main global factors that influenced the dispute. The origin of the Russia–Japan territorial

problem goes back to World War II, but its impasse derives from the Cold War. Stalin's refusal to sign the 1951 peace treaty with Japan was a strategic blunder though a natural product of Cold War logic. Gorbachev's "new political thinking" proved to be ineffective. Yeltsin's policy was driven by instinct rather than by a clear strategy derived from the uncertainties of his era. Putin tried to solve the dispute by a compromise, but failed too. Whether the "Chinese factor" helps to reach a compromise over this territorial problem under the new Putin presidency is a matter of calculation of factors given the algorithm of their change.

3   *Japan and China: Senkaku/Diaoyu and the Liuqiu/Ryukyu Problems* (Unryu Suganuma). The SFPT is a major reason for the Sino-Japanese territorial struggles in the East China Sea today. Nationalist viewpoints largely influence the Japanese handling of history, including pilgrimages to the Yasukuni Shrine by the prime minister and the building of a lighthouse on the disputed islands by conservative forces. The SFPT has been used by certain conservative circles in Japan as a perfect excuse for their nationalistic acts. Many unresolved issues, including territorial disputes, are the result of "landmines" set in the Asia-Pacific region by the United States. Meanwhile, China has steadily become one of the most powerful nations in the world. Given current geopolitical tensions in the region, the reconciliation of China and Japan appears very difficult; as a result, a Sino-Japanese collision over territorial borders may become unavoidable if both countries miscalculate and/or misjudge the situation.

4   *The South China Sea Dispute: A Review of History and Prospects for Dispute Settlement* (Nong Hong). The South China Sea dispute involves a variety of issues, one of which is the competing sovereignty claims over the Paracel Islands and the Spratly Islands. The bases of the disputant states' claims over territorial sovereignty vary from discovery and effective occupation to geographic adjacency or vicinity. One of the bases is directly relevant to the SFPT, but is subject to different interpretations. This chapter analyzes the impact of the treaty on the sovereignty dispute with special reference to the Paracel & Spratly Islands. The treaty has profound implications for contemporary maritime disputes in the South China Sea, one of which is the Island Regime of the United Nations Convention on the Law of the Sea (UNCLOS). Against the background of increasing tensions in the South China Sea since 2009, the prospects for dispute management are explored through the lens of claimant states.

5   *The San Francisco Peace Treaty and "Korea"* (Dong-Choon Kim). The interests of previous victims of Japanese colonialism, like those in Korea, were neither considered nor reflected in the SFPT. The historical task of reshaping the post-colonial order in East Asia was overshadowed by the atmosphere of the Cold War. Under the terms of the treaty, Japan was exempted from major responsibility for war crimes it committed before 1945. The persistence of war on the Korean Peninsula and the two Koreas' structural dependence on foreign forces, militarily and economically,

prevented the two nations from acting as fully autonomous subjects in international politics. The lack of Korean participation in the treaty highlights the question of who controls the Korean Peninsula, then and now. Without a breakthrough in the debacle of the national division as a de facto war system, the two Koreas have no choice but to remain peripheral subjects of the San Francisco System. As the United States sowed the seeds of current conflicts between two Koreas and Japan, only it can forge the conditions under which they can reconcile and overcome the legacy of colonialism. But thawing the Cold War confrontation and, accordingly, achieving reunification in the Korean Peninsula would be an epochal event toward the building of a workable system of peace in the Asia-Pacific region.

6 *Taiwan's Sovereignty Status: The Neglected Taipei Treaty* (Man-Houng Lin). When Taiwan's sovereignty status is discussed, it is often related to China's civil war or division. Today, the issue remains controversial. This chapter argues that, if we focus solely on Taiwan's sovereignty status per se, that is, ownership over and right of control of Taiwan, the question has actually already been settled by two international wars and treaties. The First Sino-Japanese War of 1894–1895 ended with the Shimonoseki Peace Treaty, in which Qing China ceded in perpetuity to Japan sovereignty over Taiwan. The Korean War that broke out in 1950 accelerated the organization of the San Francisco Peace Conference, leading to the SFPT, while the subsequent treaty of peace between the Republic of China (ROC) and Japan, the 1952 Taipei Treaty, transferred sovereignty over Taiwan from Japan to the ROC. The ROC had de facto ruled Taiwan since 1945 and its central government moved to the island in 1949. Taiwan had not been a part of the ROC when it was established in 1912, and it was still under Japanese rule when Kuomintang and Communist forces began their civil war in 1945. During the final phases of the civil war (1946–1949), Taiwan was not a battleground. After 1949, other than the islands of Jinmen and Mazu, held since 1912 as integral parts of China, ROC sovereignty over Taiwan was, furthermore, secured by international treaties. With effective government, a territory, a capacity to enter into relations with other countries, and a larger population than two-thirds of the countries of the world, the ROC in Taiwan is indubitably a country. It is the China-centric epistemology and its repercussions that have created the so-called Taiwan issue. The Pacific-centric historical perspective provided in this chapter highlights how politics affects knowledge, how knowledge causes political controversies, and how revised knowledge based on history is desperately needed to solve the issues.

7 *The San Francisco System at Sixty: The Okinawa Angle* (Gavan McCormack). The San Francisco Peace Treaty settlement divided Okinawa from the rest of Japan and instituted a system of systematic discrimination against it that has persisted for sixty years. The division between peace-constitution mainland and war-oriented Okinawa within the US-dominated Pax Americana regional order was maintained in substance despite the "reversion" of Okinawa to Japanese administration in 1972, the promised "reversion" of

Futenma Marine Air Station in 1996, and the various United States–Japan agreements on the realignment of US forces in Japan between 2005 and 2012. The Hatoyama government (2009–2010) promised to revise the Japanese relationship with the United States and to address Okinawan concerns, but pressure from Washington and from Japan's own national bureaucracy blocked it. Although post-Hatoyama Japan reverted to its "client state" posture of submission to Washington, the Okinawan opposition movement grew into a prefecture-wide resistance movement, the like of which had not been seen in modern Japan. This chapter considers the San Francisco System from an Okinawan perspective and poses the question of the possibility of a post-Pax Americana East Asian order.

8 *The Japanese Military "Comfort Women" Issue and the San Francisco System* (Hirofumi Hayashi). This chapter examines how the Japanese military "comfort women" issue has been dealt with under the San Francisco System. During the war crimes trials, the Allied nations regarded forced prostitution or the coercion of women into such a position as a war crime. Although a war crimes clause was inserted into the SFPT, it was not adhered to by the Japanese government. In addition, war compensation clauses in the treaty were modified in accordance with US policy during the Cold War. The "comfort women" issue was set aside in the process of negotiations and the implementation of compensation for victims of the war. The former "comfort women" were forced to keep silence until the 1990s, under the repression of undemocratic regimes in East Asian countries within the framework of the Cold War. Since then, campaigns have developed that support former "comfort women" and that demand a formal apology and individual compensation from the Japanese government. Such campaigns fostered grassroots international cooperation for the first time in East Asia.

9 *The Cold War, the San Francisco System, and Indigenous Peoples* (Scott Harrison). Examining Indigenous history in the Asia-Pacific through the lens of the Cold War and the San Francisco Peace Treaty offers a new dimension for understanding the last sixty years of the San Francisco System. Cold War structures, such as the San Francisco System, provide an often overlooked lens from which to view Indigenous history. This chapter looks at the historical relationship between the San Francisco System and the development of Ainu, Okinawan, Taiwanese aboriginal, and Marshallese identity as Indigenous peoples in relation to militarization, development, borders, and sovereignty. Modern pan-Indigenous movements and state recognition of Indigenous peoples in the region were closely related to the development of the San Francisco System; looking at these histories offers insights to resolving legacies associated with it.

10 *From and Beyond the Margins: Racism, the San Francisco System, and Asian Canadians* (John Price). The SFPT has largely been studied as an exercise in power politics and a reflection of the Cold War in East Asia. The ascent of transnationalism, Asian Canadian studies, and the growing recognition of racism as a factor in global politics offers new ways of approaching

the study of the treaty and the system that it engendered. This chapter examines the treaty as an exercise in racial exclusion, in which the racialized majority of Asia were denied any significant input into the treaty, and the concerns and rights of minorities in Japan and elsewhere were rendered invisible and sacrificed by the treaty. Racisms in this era allowed the remolding of Japan as a junior ally in a realigned white imperial alliance, with the United States replacing the British as the post-war global hegemon. Yet this transformation of Japan from enemy into ally did not lead to any changes in racist immigration quotas – the Japanese remained friends best appreciated from afar. The cultural (re)production of China from ally to communist enemy also had strong tinges of demonization of a type not dissimilar to pre-war racisms and justified the massive expansion, military and otherwise, of the United States in an emerging global coalition. This system proved to be inherently unstable, however, and required major changes in the late 1960s in order to secure and simultaneously obscure the intimate affinities between race and empire.

11 *The San Francisco System: Past, Present, Future in United States–Japan–China Relations* (John W. Dower). The United States–Japan security relationship forged in 1951–1952 bequeathed "eight problematic legacies" to Japan: (1) Okinawa and the "two Japans"; (2) unresolved territorial issues; (3) US bases in Japan; (4) rearmament; (5) the "nuclear umbrella"; (6) "history issues"; (7) containment of China and Japan's deflection from Asia; and (8) "subordinate independence." China's emergence as a major economic and military power challenges the strategic Pax Americana in Asia and has provoked a range of responses among US planners that extends to calls for an aggressive new high-tech containment policy, articulated most forcefully in the Air–Sea Battle concept. Japan's structural and psychological subordination to US policy, dating back to the creation of the San Francisco System, provides little reason for optimism that it will be able to play a genuinely independent and constructive role in this historic power shift.

12 *Historical Legacies and Regional Integration* (Haruki Wada). With the end of World War II, Japan's Fifty Years' War ended. But in East Asia, the New Asian Wars started with the Chinese Civil War. With the outbreak of the Korean War, the New Asian Wars entered a second phase, with the Cold War achieving deadly proportions. During this second phase of the New Asian Wars, the San Francisco Peace Treaty was concluded. This treaty, together with the United States–Japan Security Pact, defined Japan's position in the US camp for the New Asian Wars and the Cold War. The San Francisco System, supplemented by the Japan–ROK treaty, provided the framework for the United States to wage the Vietnam War. In 1975, the United States' defeat in Vietnam brought to an end the New Asian Wars. In 1991, the Cold War ended also and Soviet state socialism and the Soviet Union collapsed. But this was punctuated neither by peace conferences nor peace treaties. Therefore, we still face three historical legacies of past wars: the Japanese Wars of 1894–1945, the New Asian Wars of 1945–1975, and

the Cold War from 1945–1990. The main provisions of the San Francisco System remain in effect today. This forms the fourth historical legacy of our region. In order to overcome these historical legacies, we need a design for peaceful regional cooperation.

13   *Preparing Ideas for the Future: Envisioning a Multilateral Settlement* (Kimie Hara). At the conference, *Sixty Years of the San Francisco System: Continuation, Transformation, and Historical Reconciliation in the Asia-Pacific*, held on April 28, 2012, the participants did not necessarily share a common view of history or conflict resolution, but their lively exchanges generated significant inspirations for resolving disputes in a multilateral framework. The author discusses her ideas for conflict resolution, particularly the tangible territorial disputes, in East Asia. In addition to several possible multilateral frameworks, she proposes a settlement formula, "Mutual Concessions and Collective Gains," with some hypothetical but specific examples.

Notes

*   This project builds on the editor's earlier research, and accordingly this Introduction contains some overlapping content, particularly from the following publications. Kimie Hara, *Cold War Frontiers in the Asia-Pacific: Divided Territories in the San Francisco System* (New York: Routledge, 2012; first edition, 2007); "The San Francisco Peace Treaty and Frontier Problems in the Regional Order in East Asia: A Sixty Year Perspective," *The Asia-Pacific Journal* 10, issue 17, no. 1 (2012). A version of the latter paper also appears in Mikyong Kim, ed., *Routledge Handbook of Memory and Reconciliation in East Asia* (Routledge, 2015).

1   For example, see Akira Iriye, *The Cold War in Asia: A Historical Introduction* (Englewood Cliffs, NJ: Prentice Hall, 1974), 93–97, and Yoshihide Soeya, *Nihon gaiko to chugoku 1945–1972* [Japanese diplomacy and China 1945–1972] (Tokyo: Keio gijuku daigaku shuppan-kai, 1995), 33–38.

2   For details on the San Francisco Alliance System, see William T. Tow, T Russell B. Trood, and Toshiya Hosono, eds., *Bilateralism in a Multilateral Era: The Future of the San Francisco Alliance System in the Asia-Pacific* (Tokyo: Japan Institute of International Affairs, 1997).

3   The peace treaty alone did not divide China and Taiwan (Formosa). However, by leaving the status of the island undecided, it left various options open for its future, including possession by the People's Republic of China (PRC) or the Republic of China (ROC), or even its independence. The peace treaty also left the final designation of "Korea" unclear. Although Japan renounced "Korea" and recognized its independence in the treaty, no reference was made to the existence of two governments in the divided peninsula, then at war with each other. There was then, and still is, no state or country called "Korea," but two states, the Republic of Korea (ROK) in the south and the Democratic People's Republic of Korea (DPRK) in the north.

4   Okinawa (the Ryukyus), together with other Japanese islands in the Pacific, was disposed of in the treaty's Article 3. This article neither confirmed nor denied Japanese sovereignty, but guaranteed sole US control – until such time that the United States would propose and affirm a UN trusteeship arrangement over these islands. "Administrative rights," if not full sovereignty, of all the territories specified in this article were returned to Japan by the early 1970s, without having been placed in UN trusteeship. Yet, long after the "return," the majority of US forces and bases in Japan remain concentrated in Okinawa.

5 Hara, "The San Francisco Peace Treaty and Frontier Problems."
6 Gi-Wook Shin, "Historical Disputes and Reconciliation in Northeast Asia: The RUS Role," *Pacific Affairs* 83, no. 4 (December 2010), 664.
7 Hara, *Cold War Frontiers in the Asia-Pacific.*
8 Hara, "The San Francisco Peace Treaty and Frontier Problems."
9 Hara, *Cold War Frontiers in the Asia-Pacific.*
10 Chiang Kai-shek's Republic of China (ROC), representing "China" at the UN, was actively demanding the "recovery" of Ryukyus/Okinawa up to the early post-war years.
11 Before World War II, the countries involved in disputes in the South China Sea were China and two colonial powers, Japan and France. After the war, Japan and France withdrew; the islands came to be disputed by the two Chinas and the newly independent neighboring Southeast Asian countries. For details on the disposition of the Spratlys & Paracels in the SFPT, see Hara, *Cold War Frontiers in the Asia-Pacific,* chapter 6.
12 John W. Dower, "Occupied Japan and the American Lake," in *America's Asia,* edited by Edward Friedman and Mark Selden (New York: Vintage, 1971), 146–97. For Western imperial powers' control of the world's oceans, see Peter Nolan, "Imperial Archipelago," *New Left Review* 80 (March–April 2013).
13 For details, see chapters 4 (Micronesia) and 7 (the Ryukyus) in Hara, *Cold War Frontiers in the Asia-Pacific.*
14 Hara, "The San Francisco Peace Treaty and Frontier Problems."
15 For example, Kiichi Fujiwara, "Beichu reisen no owari to tonanajia," *Shakaigaku kenkyu* 44, no. 5 (1993), 35–47.
16 Russia and China are also the core members of the Shanghai Cooperation Organization (SCO), a Eurasian security organization that started as the Shanghai Five in 1996.
17 John Lewis Gaddis, *The Long Peace: Inquiries into the History of the Cold War* (New York: Oxford University Press, 1987); by the same author, *The United States and the Origins of the Cold War* (New York: Columbia University Press, 2000).
18 For relevant discussions, please see "Introduction: Rethinking the 'Cold War' in the Asia-Pacific" in Hara, *Cold War Frontiers in the Asia-Pacific,* 2–13. For the "San Francisco System," some use the term to indicate Japan's position in the post-war world based on the SFPT and the United States–Japan bilateral security alliance, whereas others see it in a broader context of the US-led post-war regional and Cold War order in the Asia-Pacific, as also seen in this volume. The term has also, but to a lesser degree, been used to refer to the US security alliance system in the region, the "San Francisco Alliance System" mentioned earlier in this chapter.
19 Kimie Hara, *Japanese–Russian/Soviet Relations since 1945: A Difficult Peace* (London: Routledge, 1998); Kimie Hara, "50 Years from San Francisco: Re-examining the Peace Treaty and Japan's Territorial Problems," *Pacific Affairs: An International Review of the Far East and Pacific Area* 74, no. 3 (2001), 361–82; Hara, *Cold War Frontiers in the Asia-Pacific*; Shin, "Historical Disputes and Reconciliation."
20 See Hara, *Cold War Frontiers in the Asia-Pacific,* 94–95.

1   Korea and Japan

The Dokdo/Takeshima problem

Seokwoo Lee

The territorial disposition of the San Francisco Peace Treaty and the legacy of US security interests in East Asia[1]

Since the conclusion of World War II, the legacy of Japanese militarism and colonialism in East Asia has left many unresolved conflicts, dividing the region. There are currently three territorial disputes over islands in East Asia in which Japan is a disputant: against Russia, Japan continues to claim sovereignty over the Southern Kurile Islands/Northern Territories; against China and Taiwan, Japan has claims over the Senkaku Islands (Diaoyudao); and against Korea, the claims are over Dokdo (Takeshima).[2] Deep-rooted historical bitterness between Japan and the other disputants impedes the resolution of these territorial disputes and still deeply influences international relations in this region.

Despite the fact that a very careful drafting of the territorial clauses of the San Francisco Peace Treaty (SFPT) in the early stages placed emphasis on ensuring that no islands would be left under disputed sovereignty, today, sixty years after its conclusion, the treaty has left an uncertain legacy in East Asia. This is partly because historical facts did not count as a major factor in post-World War II territorial dispositions in East Asia. Territorial dispositions by the SFPT were largely reflective of the Allied Powers' policy in post-World War II East Asia, which did not give serious consideration to the interests of local rival claimants over specific territories. The Allies were more concerned about their own geopolitical and strategic interests, a fact that resulted in outcomes perpetuating the current territorial disputes in East Asia.

These disputes involve intertwined political and legal issues. In other words, the three territorial disputes have multifaceted implications for the disputants, on the one hand, and for disputants and interested powers, notably the United States, on the other. For examples of US involvement in the territorial disputes of East Asia, one could look to the rivalry between the United States and the Soviet Union during the Cold War, and afterward with Russia; the United States' complicated stance toward cross-strait relations between China and Taiwan; and its hands-off policy toward the territorial disputes between Korea and Japan. In the larger context, regional stability in East Asia has largely been influenced by US security interests.

Geographically and geopolitically, the East Asian region has, notoriously, the most complex territorial and maritime disputes. Moreover, the legal issues of the East Asian region involve many aspects of the 1982 United Nations Convention on the Law of the Sea (UNCLOS). Given the exercise of maritime jurisdiction over territorial seas, contiguous zones, exclusive economic zones (EEZ), and the continental shelves of islands (and, in some cases, rocks), the outcome of maritime boundary disputes often depends on ownership and the classification of such issues as whether an island or a rock sustains human habitation or economic life. In sum, "territorial issues determine matters of maritime delimitation. Territorial disputes have their roots in the past whereas maritime delimitation is future-oriented once the territorial issues have been settled."[3]

Issues regarding the San Francisco Peace Treaty and the process of territorial disposition

The SFPT, concluded on September 8, 1951, between the victors of World War II and Japan, provided the basic legal mechanisms for determining the statehood of Japan. It further provided a basic interest structure for establishing relationships between Japan and states liberated from Japanese colonization. In the negotiations leading up to the conclusion of the treaty, general matters relating to the disposition of defeated states – territory, human rights, right to claims, and normalization of diplomatic relations among related states – had significant effects on Japan's statehood, its development, and the establishment of Korea–Japan relations.

Among several issues in the disposition of Japan's territory, we will discuss the legal justification for, along with the present-day implications of, the measures taken by the United States and Allied Powers regarding Japan following World War II, focusing mainly on the Supreme Commander for the Allied Powers (SCAP) and the SFPT.

Supreme Commander for the Allied Powers, war responsibility of the defeated State of Japan, and the legacy in the Far East

> I can only say that the majority of Japanese have no idea of the legacy of hatred they may have left behind them in South East Asia and that if I, or any other British official, were to tell them of it, we should probably be thought to be lying.[4]

In 1943, the Inter-Divisional Area Committee on the Far East was established under the US State Department. The United States' conciliatory policy, as evident in discussions of all matters related to post-war Japan, was again clear in the process of the disposition of Japan's territory. Criticism of this conciliatory policy was frequent even among the Allied powers.

Lacking a mature concern for the emotions felt toward Japan by its former colonies, the US policy also revealed a lack of awareness of history as well as of international legal justice. As a result of the excessive leniency shown with regard to the legal, psychological, and moral debts incurred by the now-defeated imperialist aggressor, a sense of deprivation with regard to historical understanding and international legal justice was produced in the states that had just suffered the painful consequences of Japanese colonialism.

That war crimes and atrocities (and subsequent obligations of the perpetrator for such acts) were not recognized in the Far East as in Europe can largely be blamed on the role taken by the United States and the Allied Powers in the post-war disposition process. That is, the US government "played a role in Japan's historical amnesia" by failing to confront the question of war guilt and responsibility for war crimes.[5] The United States also played a role in the extraordinarily generous and non-punitive nature of the right to claims and reparations in the SFPT.[6]

Ultimately, only when the pre-San Francisco history of Allied–Japanese relations is clarified can a resolution be proposed regarding Japan's relationship with its former colonies.

Following the declaration of absolute surrender on August 15, 1945, Japan signed the Instrument of Surrender on September 2, after which the Allied powers occupied Japan's territories. To enforce the occupation of Japan, the Allied Powers established the Far Eastern Commission, the SCAP, and the Allied Council for Japan.[7] Decisions made by the Far Eastern Commission, comprising the major victor states, materialized in the US government-issued directives to SCAP; in turn, SCAP issued individual orders to the Japanese government, thereby supervising the implementation of the occupation policy. SCAP actually issued numerous instructions directly to the Japanese government on the occupation's primary issues – demilitarization and post-war dispositions – in the form of "Supreme Commander of the Allied Powers Instructions," or SCAPINs. These SCAPINs contained information critical to the termination of the colonial relationship between Korea and Japan. In particular, SCAP dealt with matters such as the treatment of Koreans residing in Japan and Dokdo, an issue that continues to affect the relationship between the two countries to this day. The nature and substance of SCAPIN 677, through which SCAP determined the extent of Japan's administrative districts in the early days of occupation, is also an issue that never fails to come up in the sovereignty dispute between the two states.[8]

During the period of occupation over Japan, these SCAPINs were not decided independently; rather, it is noteworthy that there was agreement among the member states of the Far East Commission, as well as intimate cooperation among the US Departments of State, Defense, and the Navy.[9] In other words, during the occupation period of 1945 to 1952, SCAP functioned as the de facto government in nearly all areas for post-war Japan. US policy during the occupation period successfully protected Japan, the Japanese people, and Japan's post-war ruling class from the moral and political pressures of world public opinion.

In this context, the neglect regarding Japan's responsibilities greatly shaped the policy of the United States, the occupying power led by General MacArthur.

The US contribution to the historical amnesia of the Japanese government and people was not limited to its role in inserting an immunity clause in the peace treaty and concealing information about precedents of individual claims against Japan by US and other citizens, among other related matters. These actions and attitudes went on to form the entire structure of the US–Japanese relationship during the occupation period.[10]

Regardless of its accomplishments as an occupying power, the United States may be evaluated as having completely failed in notifying the Japanese government of the fact that other states did not regard post-war Japan or its moral responsibility in the same way General MacArthur did.[11]

In other words, while the economies of the Allied powers were barely recovering from the shock of the war, the Japanese did not understand "the abiding bitterness and anger with regard to how Japan had been treated so favourably and its economic reconstruction given so high a priority by the Americans."[12] British diplomat Sir Alvary Gascoigne also reported that Japan's prime minister, Yoshida Shigeru, "does not, or will not, appreciate that some time must pass before the British colonial subjects in the United Kingdom territories of South-East Asia overcome their hatred of the Japanese for the barbarous manner in which the latter behaved" during World War II.[13] Such misunderstanding and ignorance caused Japan to resist the imposition of responsibility for the stipulations regarding past war crimes. Japan's insensitivity toward the moral indignation felt by other countries and other peoples were concealed by MacArthur's directives and the firm position of John Foster Dulles regarding the non-punitive treaty, thereby nurturing "a mind-set that justified a refusal to come to terms with Japan's wartime past."[14] It was further strengthened by the United States' need for Japan's support when confronted with the Cold War, as part of a larger diplomatic package in aligning with the United States against the Communist bloc.[15]

The process of territorial disposition of Japan and evaluation under international law, prior to the conclusion of the San Francisco Peace Treaty

An international legal evaluation, in addition to a political and diplomatic evaluation, is very important for the formulation and transformation of the relationship between Korea and Japan after World War II, as well as that between the Allied Powers and the defeated state of Japan. A summary of the process of territorial disposition, with SCAP and the SFPT as the focus, follows.

The Cairo Declaration of December 1, 1943, in which heads of state from the United States, United Kingdom, and China gathered to determine the course of action after World War II, states that "Japan will also be expelled from all other territories which she has taken by violence and greed," and that "[t]he aforesaid three great powers, mindful of the enslavement of the people of Korea, are determined that in due course Korea shall become free and independent."[16]

The Potsdam Declaration of July 26, 1945 states in Article 8 that "The terms of the Cairo Declaration shall be carried out and Japanese sovereignty shall be limited to the islands of Honshu, Hokkaido, Kyushu, Shikoku, and such minor islands as we determine."[17]

According to Japan's Instrument of Surrender that followed on September 2, 1945,

> We [Japan] ... accept the provisions set forth in the declaration issued by the heads of the Governments of the U.S., China, and UK on 26 July 1945 at Potsdam, and subsequently adhered to by the Union of Soviet Socialist Republics, which four powers are hereafter referred to as the Allied Powers.... We hereby undertake for ... the Japanese Government and their successors to carry out the provisions of the Potsdam Declaration in good faith.[18]

Generally, a declaration under international law is a unilateral expression of intent and cannot be considered an international treaty; thus it is possible to argue that the Cairo and Potsdam declarations have, prima facie, no legal binding force under international law. However, in its Instrument of Surrender, Japan not only accepted the provisions in the Potsdam Declaration but also promised to carry them out in good faith. Thus, the Potsdam Declaration did not remain a unilateral act bearing mere declaratory effect under general international law; rather, it is properly viewed as having been transformed into an international document, or a document with legal binding force, as agreed to by the Allied powers and Japan. The legal nature of the Instrument of Surrender of September 2, 1945 was an acceptance by the defeated state of Japan of the offer made by the Allied Powers regarding post-war disposition through the two declarations. This is evident, as the instrument clearly uses the phrase "accept the provisions."

In the "Guiding Principles applicable to unilateral declarations of States capable of creating legal obligations" formulated by the International Law Commission (ILC) in 2006, it is stated that even declarations can result in legal binding force, creating legal rights or responsibilities.[19] In particular, Article 3 states, "To determine the legal effects of such declarations, it is necessary to take account of their content, of all the factual circumstances in which they were made, and of the reactions to which they gave rise."[20]

Thus, although the Cairo and Potsdam declarations are not unilateral declarations of any single state, thereby raising the question of whether they fall under the scope of the ILC guidelines, there is no reason to consider them any differently from the legal nature of state declarations merely because they were a joint declaration of the Allied Powers.

With regard to the contents, Article 8 of the Potsdam Declaration is a provision of dispositive nature regarding post-war Japanese territory. The expression "shall" in this article should not be interpreted as a mere political declaration regarding the future, based on Japan's Instrument of Surrender. Rather, it should be interpreted as creating legal rights or obligations as in international treaty usage. In other words, even if there had been no explicit acceptance of its terms in Japan's Instrument of Surrender, Article 8 is very specific, unlike the other provisions of the Potsdam Declaration; due to its dispositive nature and content, it has at the very least a binding effect upon the Allied powers. It further satisfies, in form, the publicity requirement.

By signing the Instrument of Surrender, Japan promised to carry out the declarations in good faith; thus, these related phrases must be interpreted as clearly binding upon the Allied Powers. Article 9 of the ICL guidelines, which deals with the issue of whether unilateral declarations can result in obligations for other states, requires clear acceptance of such declarations in order for legal obligations to be incurred.[21] Japan's signature of the Instrument of Surrender clearly indicates its intent to carry out the Potsdam Declaration in good faith; thus, the Cairo and Potsdam declarations are not only legally binding upon Japan but they also create the legal obligation to carry them out in good faith. The Chinese government, which is directly affected by both declarations, is of the position that both the Cairo and Potsdam declarations are documents of legal binding force.[22]

Further, Article 8 in both the Cairo and Potsdam declarations deals with the disposition of Japanese territory after the war, premised on the fact that Japan had lost the war. In general, victor states tend to acquire the right to dispose of the territory of defeated states; thus, because the relevant expressions of these declarations are the exercise of the dispositive powers of the Allies, the result binds the defeated state of Japan.

Article 8 of the Potsdam Declaration, which is legally binding, limits the sovereignty of Japan to the islands of Honshu, Hokkaido, Kyushu, Shikoku, and minor islands as determined by the Allied Powers, and requires that the provisions of the Cairo Declaration be carried out. The Cairo Declaration guaranteed the boundaries of Korea, while stripping Japan of all the islands in the Pacific that she had seized or occupied from the beginning of World War I in 1914, as well as guaranteeing that all the territories Japan stole from the Chinese between 1814 and 1895 following the Sino-Japanese War, such as Manchuria, Formosa, and the Pescadores, should be restored to the Republic of China. Japan was also to be expelled from all other territories that she had taken by violence and greed.

The third category of regions from which Japan was to be expelled, namely territories taken by violence and greed, is also relevant to the disposition of Korea. Thus, a determination of whether the territory at issue belongs to Korea or to the islands of Honshu, Hokkaido, Kyushu, Shikoku, and minor islands as determined by the Allied Powers, becomes an indicator of the appropriateness and legitimacy of the process.

The process of territorial disposition and evaluation under international law, after the conclusion of the San Francisco Peace Treaty

At the conclusion of the SFPT, the attitude of the United States in the disposition of Japan's territory shows that the clear distinction between Japan's inherent territories and the territories plundered in the process of imperialist expansionism was mishandled in the interests of the major victor states, to serve political and diplomatic convenience. Such abuse raises further questions regarding the authority behind the territorial disposition of defeated states by victor states, the legal basis for which has already been discussed.

In relation to the legal status of Dokdo in the SFPT, the now-released internal documents of the US State Department, as shown below, have significant implications for evaluating the legitimacy of the disposition. For example:

> Reference was made to the suggestions of Professor Reischauer of Harvard which have not yet been incorporated, stressing the proper psychological approach to the Japanese.[23]

> It may accordingly be questioned whether many of the terms of the [November 2, 1949] draft may not be too severe for a Japan which suffered total defeat, without offering us any conceivable advantage.[24]

> It is admitted that this Article offers a practical and convenient manner of describing the territories which Japan gives up and those which Japan retains. It is believed, however, that the method of delineation employed in this Article has serious psychological disadvantages. If possible, it is recommended that another method of description be employed which avoids circumscribing Japan with a line even if it is necessary to enumerate a large number of territories in an annex. We suggest that the practicability be explored of defining Japan territorially in positive terms.... In any event, the omission of ... the map is recommend[ed].... Articles 4 through 12. We suggest that in the treaty Articles 4 through 12 of the [November 2, 1949] draft be omitted, and that in a document subsidiary to the treaty among the signatories other than Japan the disposition of territories formerly under Japanese jurisdiction be agreed upon.[25]

> This report is based for the most part on Japanese language references available in the Department of State and the Library of Congress. Studies prepared within the Department of State and by the Japanese Foreign Office on some of the islands have also been consulted.[26]

As shown by various studies,[27] the disposition of Dokdo was an important issue; the various political conditions at the time – outbreak of the Korean War and the enhancement of the role of Japan in the Far East during the Cold War – caused the United States to view as a political priority the expeditious negotiation and conclusion of the treaty with Japan. As a result, much-debated issues were left out of the treaty draft. Dokdo was such an issue; in the final draft of the treaty, as we can see now, no mention of "Dokdo" or any relevant expression was made.

SCAP, the San Francisco Peace Treaty, and the formation of Korea–Japan diplomatic relations

Under international law, up to the signing of the peace treaty, SCAP was a belligerent occupying power, a legal subject responsible for carrying out the potential and limited roles of maintaining public order and restoring peace in the occupied state. During the occupation period, the expansion of the Soviet socialist powers and the economic burden of the United States in implementing the occupation policy led to changes in US and SCAP policies. Japan responded aggressively in order to preserve its sovereignty as much as possible before transitioning from a "de facto peace" to the conclusion of the peace treaty. Both the United States' changed policies and Japan's active efforts were also reflected in the treaty, resulting in a relatively moderate peace treaty compared to those of other nations.

In the territorial disposition of defeated states, the consideration and abuse of political administrative convenience has resulted in grave consequences, as has the application of post-historically conscious, functionalist, and opportunistic principles regarding territorial disputes and the so-called "colonial question" by the International Court of Justice (ICJ) and other international judicial bodies in their recent jurisprudence on territorial dispute resolutions. In this way, states newly freed from the colonial experience have faced a circular pattern of oppression, with judicial imperialism following political imperialism.

There is already a significant number of studies comparing the Korean–Japanese relationship with the French–German one with respect to the denial of past crimes. Such studies conclude that recognition of past faults at the state level is essential to the formation of trust and international harmony.[28] In that sense, it is possible to propose a better approach, which would acknowledge the harms done while looking forward.[29]

In concluding the 1905 Katsura–Taft Agreement,[30] US Secretary of War William Howard Taft, in negotiation with Japanese Prime Minister Katsura Taro, consented to Japan's domination over Korea in exchange for US domination over the Philippines. He mentioned that, although the US president could not officially carry out these promises without the consent of the US Senate, he was certain that the American people would accept such an exchange as a treaty obligation. Two days later, President Theodore Roosevelt sent a telegram stating that Taft's understanding was precise in every way, emphasizing that

> the establishment of a suzerainty over Korea by Japanese troops to the extent of requiring that Korea enter into no foreign treaties without the consent of Japan was the logical result of the present war and would directly contribute to permanent peace in the East.[31]

Taft, in his speech at the Japanese Chamber of Commerce in Tokyo in 1906, also stated plainly,

We are living in an age where the intervention of a stronger nation in the affairs of a people unable to maintain a government of law and order to assist the latter to better government becomes a national duty and works for the progress of the world.[32]

In the process of expanding territories in the imperialist era, state acts related to revealed national interests[33] resulted in the contemporary instability of the Far East – especially Korea–Japan diplomatic relations – while undergoing the SCAP and the peace treaty framework after World War II, largely due to the abuse of political administrative convenience.

This is the basis for the limited application in the Far East of the principle of intertemporal law,[34] often utilized in the process of defending acts committed in the territorial expansion of imperialist states. In reality, the past policies of Western imperialist states continue to be recognized today under the ideal of legal stability and the effect of intertemporal law, which is also clearly evident in recent ICJ jurisprudence. We can pose the question of whether the ideal of legal stability truly takes priority in the current situation of injustice. Contemporary international law is devoted to the ideals of legal stability, that is, to strengthening the utility of intertemporal law, and to the increased universal application of the functionalist/opportunist principle of *uti possidetis*.[35] Today, where international law factors in the law of the imperialist era, the validity of the formation of Korea–Japan diplomatic relations based on the SCAP and SFPT system must be re-evaluated, together with the historical background of the territorial pursuits of the United States in the Far East.

To effectuate the legal question of sovereignty in practice: the *Dokdo* case[36]

When the general understanding of what constitutes a valid claim to territory from the perspective of international law is applied to the determination of questions of sovereignty, the outcome of previous research indicates as follows.

By evaluating historical records and other evidence, it is reasonable to reach the conclusion that the historical evidence supporting the respective claims to Dokdo would indicate that Korea has probably made a better case, despite its virtual inaction over Dokdo during the material periods. When Japan agreed in Article 2 of the SFPT to renounce all right, title, and claim to Korea, the drafters of the treaty did not include Dokdo within the area to be renounced. In determining what course of action should be taken in the light of this development, the question arose of whether the SFPT left Dokdo to Korea or Japan. Therefore, the question of which claimant has lawful territorial sovereignty or ownership over Dokdo takes us back to the question of whether Dokdo belonged to Korea prior to Japan's alleged 1905 incorporation. In other words, again, it is the issue of the degree of probative value of historical evidence produced by Korea that outweighs that of Japan. To appreciate the nature of the territorial disputes over Dokdo, due consideration should be given to the historical relationship between

Korea and Japan. Japanese colonization of Korea commenced in 1904, a period that pre-dates Japan's official incorporation of Dokdo into Shimane Prefecture.

Determining the abstract legal question of sovereignty over Dokdo is one thing, but it is quite another to effectuate it in practice. Given the institutional void in the East Asian region insofar as the resolution of territorial disputes is concerned, and given the current political atmosphere in the region, one is skeptical that a feasible regional dispute resolution mechanism will emerge any time soon.

Recently, groups of scholars have proposed ideas for resolving the Dokdo issue based on their understanding of the dispute.[37] These proposals can be categorized into the following four approaches: first, a practical approach that includes the separation of the sovereignty issue from the allocation of maritime zones and other salient issues; second, an approach that looks to Japanese territorial disputes involving the Kurile and Senkaku islands; third, an approach that emphasizes the US role in the search for a resolution; and fourth, an approach that stresses the historical background of Japanese colonialism over Korea.

Separation of the sovereignty issue from the allocation of maritime zones and other salient issues[38]

This approach offers a moral perspective on the Dokdo issue that considers both law and the history of Japan's unjust treatment of Korea and the Korean people during the first half of the twentieth century. It notes that this treatment began with annexation and subsequent colonial rule and includes Japan's actions during World War II, including crimes against humanity.

From this perspective, two key elements of Japan's claim to Dokdo are evaluated. The first is the context and timing of Japan's seizure of Dokdo in 1904 and its eventual acquisition of the island, which, it is concluded, cannot be valid since Japan's conquest of Korea precluded any effective response from Korea. The second element is Japan's literalist interpretation of the 1951 SFPT. The argument that Japan's insistence that the treaty omitted Dokdo from among the territories it had to give up, and that any claims of reparations from those who suffered under Japanese rule were waived by the treaty, must be understood in light of the US government's interest in securing an early conclusion to its occupation of Japan and the Allied Powers' backing of a treaty that would be generous to Japan, in alignment with the US policies in the region during the Korean and Cold Wars. In this view, the treaty should be viewed not as providing the highest level of immunity, as Japan maintains, but setting forth the minimum set of obligations that Japan owes to Korea. In its conclusion, the study offers a compelling scenario whereby Japan would come to terms with its past by abandoning its claim to Dokdo in connection with a formal apology and restitution to those it harmed, while Korea would respond by agreeing to limit its claim to a territorial sea around Dokdo and compromise on fisheries and other resources in the EEZ.

Japanese territorial disputes involving the Kurile and Senkaku Islands[39]

This approach compares the two territorial conflicts over islands that Japan has with its neighbors in Northeast Asia: the Senkaku Islands dispute with China and the conflict over Dokdo with Korea. In both instances, Japan claims that the islands were *terra nullius*, discovered and effectively occupied by Japan – despite the historical evidence of discovery and administration of the island by China in the case of the Senkaku Islands and by Korea for Dokdo. Both islands were occupied by Japan through its colonialist and imperialistic actions during the 1895 Sino-Japanese War and the 1905 Russo-Japanese War. The attitude of the U.S. government differs with regard to the two disputes: it leans toward Japan with respect to the Senkaku dispute while taking a neutral stance on Dokdo. Another distinction is that Japan has actual control over Senkaku, whereas Korea has control over Dokdo.

The issue of sovereignty over these islands affects delimitation between Japan and China in the East China Sea as well as between Japan and Korea in the East Sea/Sea of Japan. Japan argues that its EEZ has full effect for Senkaku while China rejects that notion. Both Korea and Japan argue that their respective EEZs have full effect for Dokdo. This approach points out that Senkaku was first discovered by China, and Dokdo by Korea, adding that Senkaku is an appendage of Taiwan while Dokdo is an appendage of Ulleungdo. Ultimately, it concludes that Japan's allegation of prescription is legally untenable in both cases.

The row between Russia and Japan over the Kurile Islands illustrates a similar situation. Japan is unable to make concessions in the territorial disputes it has with its neighbors without affecting negotiations in other disputes, particularly in relation to the Kurile Islands. It contends that states under these circumstances are beleaguered and unable to take steps to resolve territorial disputes because of the linkages among them. If Japan surrenders one claim, its position over the others would be undermined. Thus, if Japan conceded its claim over Dokdo to Korea, it would lose all hope of obtaining the return of the Kurile Islands, which are significantly more important as homeland territory than Dokdo. This approach goes on to explain that public efforts by Korea to confront Japan on Dokdo are ignored and may in fact have the effect of strengthening Japan's resolve on the issue. An appreciation of the importance of the linkage between the Kurile Islands and Dokdo disputes for Japan would allow Korea to formulate a regional approach that may serve to remove the blockages in the Kurile Islands dispute and, in turn, help to resolve the Dokdo issue.

Another piece of analysis examines the potential role of economic interdependence and incentives to promote a resolution of the Dokdo dispute, using an analysis of Japan's respective disputes with China and Russia. The economic relationship between China and Japan was and is marked by a high level of economic interdependence. Economic incentives were utilized by Japan in an attempt to achieve a resolution of the Kurile Islands dispute. It suggests that, with respect to China, economic factors did not inspire the 2008 East China Sea settlement nor did it help to resolve the dispute over the Senkaku Islands. With respect to Russia, although the Japanese offered economic incentives, the Russians were not motivated to compromise.

Though Korea and Japan enjoy an extensive economic relationship, the political factors that animate the Dokdo dispute must be understood in order to facilitate a settlement of the issue. Each country should be keenly aware of the domestic and international political circumstances facing the other country, and make judgments as to how to approach negotiations based on the level of political capital of the ruling administration. A proper understanding of political realities may also lead to the use of economic incentives in a manner that encourages compromise. Political circumstances might be such that a deal potentially concluded between the two countries may not resolve all issues related to Dokdo. It warns that political leaders on each side must prepare their people and themselves for a possible backlash.

The US role in resolving the Dokdo issue[40]

Although Korea has a stronger claim to Dokdo, historically speaking, Korea has problems fully realizing its claim given the neutral position taken by other countries, especially the United States, and the absence of any reference to Dokdo in the SFPT. Thus, Korea appears to have three policy options. One is to focus on maintaining and strengthening its present physical control, anticipating that the current status quo will cause other nations to recognize Korea's claim and force Japan to abandon its own claim. Another option is to submit the dispute for settlement by third-party adjudication, such as through the ICJ. A third option is for a negotiated settlement between the two countries.

In choosing a particular policy option, Korea believes it will have to deal with instances of "Japan-bashing" at home. It notes the views of some Koreans that the Dokdo issue is part of a broader conflict with Japan, their belief that Japan has designs to invade Korea as it has done in the past, and the emotional reaction to any Japanese action in relation to Dokdo. These important elements have impacts not only upon Japan's approach on Dokdo and other issues related to its relationship with Korea, but also on the United States' attitude and perspective on the Dokdo issue, as well as Korean concerns about Japanese remilitarization.

Japanese colonialism over Korea and its linkage with the Dokdo issue

This approach has led to an understanding in Japan that, from Korea's perspective, the taking of Dokdo was the first step toward Japanese colonization and thus a potent symbol of Japan's conquest of the Korean Peninsula. In light of this, a group of Japanese scholars called for a more pragmatic approach on the part of the Japanese government toward resolving the Dokdo issue. They view Japan's claims over Dokdo as an impediment to Japan's attainment of a number of important foreign policy objectives related to North Korea, including the issue of Japanese citizens abducted by North Korea in the 1970s and 1980s, that country's nuclear program, and fishing rights around Dokdo. They see cooperation with Seoul as more important than pursuing Dokdo, which only provokes South Korea to the detriment of Japanese interests. Others want both countries to engage in dialogue as opposed to taking confrontational stances against each other. These scholars have also called for Japan to withdraw its claim to Dokdo and to recognize Korean sovereignty "in the spirit of repentance" for Japan's colonial rule over Korea.

These scholars generally accept the Korean view that Dokdo was wrongfully taken by Japan in 1905. By balancing the historical and legal arguments of both countries, these scholars seek to shift the nature of the dispute from the existing entrenched historical and legal arguments to a simpler, present-day calculation of cost and benefit. By doing so, the conclusion reached is that the dispute over Dokdo is not worth the cost to Japan. The insights offered by these Japanese scholars on the Dokdo issue add greatly to the approaches taken by others in understanding some of the complexities and challenges of this particularly vexing territorial dispute in East Asia.

The way forward

The ongoing territorial disputes in East Asia involve intertwined political and legal issues. Though it is not always easy to dichotomize politics and law in specific territorial disputes, it is also not impossible to reach a conclusion, based on international legal principles and sources, as to the strength of the competing claims to disputed territories.

Be that as it may, it is imperative that the disputants approach the issues through dialogue and a spirit of compromise. An all-or-nothing approach, which obviously does not reckon with the mutual interests of the disputants, will only aggravate an already precarious situation. Therefore, it is suggested that various confidence-building measures, including joint development of the disputed maritime zone for the mutual benefit of all the affected parties, should be engendered first, instead of a hasty emphasis on the question of sovereignty over the disputed territories. Finally, every effort should be made to determine the real worth of the disputed territories instead of placing undue reliance, as is presently the case, on exaggerated notions of what is at stake.

Though disputes over peripheral territory can usually be settled through negotiation and compromise, it should be pointed out that there are some disputes that have been elevated to the point of non-negotiability. Such is the case with Dokdo, which is in the complete and exclusive control of one party, that is, Korea.

Although this is an extreme position, insofar as it envisages that Japan would give up its claim *in toto*, the fact remains that it is the best solution for Korea. No doubt, a solution such as this is very difficult to bring to fruition; the opposing state would not be easily persuaded to give up its claim in view of domestic considerations. It is, however, possible if an imaginative set of ideas are considered by one state and put forward to the other.

Hence, a solution is fundamentally possible where (1) the *quid pro quo* being offered to the other state is of more importance to it than the current dispute over the island; and (2) the *quid pro quo* is of less importance to Korea than the disputed islands. Note that the *quid pro quo* does not have to be a single item; it can be a series of issues and matters, a regime, or a package of incentives. National pride on both sides could well be assuaged.

The Korean government needs to give very careful thought to the package of incentives that can be offered to the other state. While giving up some sovereign rights to gain or maintain territorial sovereignty can be a very attractive bargain, it does, nonetheless, constitute giving up something. The greatest advantage would be that a core issue could be settled in favor of Korea.

Notes

1 Refer generally to Seokwoo Lee, "Territorial Disputes in East Asia, the San Francisco Peace Treaty of 1951, and the Legacy of U.S. Security Interests in East Asia," in Seokwoo Lee and Hee Eun Lee (eds.), *Dokdo: Historical Appraisal and International Justice* (Leiden: Brill/Martinus Nijhoff Publishers, 2011), pp. 41–69.

2 The names of these territories are also subject to dispute: Russia refers to the islands as the "Kurile Islands," while Japan calls them the "Northern Territories"; China and Taiwan use the terms "Diaoyudao," "Diaoyutai," or "Diaoyu Islands," while Japan refers to the "Senkaku Islands"; finally, "Dokdo" is the Korean designation, while Japan refers to "Takeshima." Dokdo is also referred to by some as the Liancourt Rocks.

3 *Maritime Delimitation and Territorial Questions between Qatar and Bahrain*, Merits, Judgment, ICJ Reports 2001, p. 40, Kooijmans, J., sep. op., para. 4.

4 Harry N. Scheiber, "Taking Responsibility: Moral and Historical Perspectives on the Japanese War-Reparations Issues," *Berkeley Journal of International Law* 20, no. 1 (2002): 233–49 (citing dispatch of George Clutton at the UK Liaison Mission in Japan).

5 Ibid., p. 238. While Germany had thoroughly to bear responsibility for the war, Japan was relatively free from such burdens. One study points to the MacArthur administration, stating that the United States, in denying the emperor's responsibilities in order to take advantage of him, caused the Japanese people to become callous with regard to their war guilt. John W. Dower, *Embracing Defeat: Japan in the Wake of World War II* (New York: W.W. Norton, 1999), p. 727. The Korean translation of this book was published in 2009.

6 Scheiber, "Taking Responsibility," pp. 237–8.

7 Michael Schaller, *The American Occupation of Japan* (New York: Oxford University Press, 1985), pp. 60–1.

8 SCAPIN No. 677 of January 29, 1946, titled "Governmental and Administrative Separation of Certain Outlying Areas from Japan," provides: "The Imperial Japanese Government is directed to cease exercising, or attempting to exercise, governmental or administrative authority over any area outside of Japan, or over any government officials and employees or any other persons within such areas" (Art. 1); "For the purpose of this directive, Japan is defined to include the four main islands of Japan … and the approximately 1,000 smaller adjacent islands … and excluding … Liancourt Rocks" (Art. 3).

9 Eiji Takemae, *Inside GHQ: The Allied Occupation of Japan and its Legacy* (New York: Continuum International, 2002), pp. 201–12.

10 Scheiber, "Taking Responsibility," p. 240.

11 Ibid., p. 247.

12 Ibid.

13 Ibid. (Conversation between His Majesty's Ambassador and the Japanese Prime Minister: Sir. A. Gascoigne to Mr. Bevin [Received January 29, 1951], printed copy in FJ 10198/4 [19521], United Kingdom Public Records Office, Kew, UK.)

14 Ibid.

15 Ibid., pp. 247–8.

16 US Department of State (hereafter "USDOS"), *Foreign Relations of the United States: The Conferences of Cairo and Teheran* (Washington, DC: Government Printing Office, 1961), pp. 448–9; USDOS, *A Decade of American Foreign Policy: Basic Documents 1941–1949* (Washington, DC: Government Printing Office, 1950), p. 20.

17 USDOS, *Occupation of Japan: Policy and Progress*, Department of State Publication 2671, Far Eastern Series 17 (Washington, DC: Government Printing Office, 1946), p. 53; USDOS, *A Decade of American Foreign Policy: Basic Documents 1941–1949*, pp. 28–40.

18 USDOS, *Department of State Bulletin*, August 19, 1945, pp. 257–9 ("[Japan] … accept[s] the provisions set forth in the [Potsdam Proclamation]").

19 UN Doc A/CN.4/L.706, July 20, 2006. France's declaration that it would stop nuclear testing in 1974; Egypt's declaration on April 24, 1957, regarding the legal status of the Suez Canal; and Jordan's declaration to abandon rights to the West Bank are specific examples of unilateral declarations that give rise to legal obligations.

20 Ibid., para. 3.

21 Ibid., para. 9. "No obligation may result for other States from the unilateral declaration of a State. However, the other State or States concerned may incur obligations in relation to such a unilateral declaration to the extent that they clearly accepted such a declaration."

22 Wang Tieya, "International Law in China: Historical and Contemporary Perspectives," *Recueil des Cours* 221 (1990): 203.

23 1949/10/21 [USNARA/740.0011 PW (PEACE)/10-2149], US Department of State, "Notes on Discussion of Draft Treaty of Peace with Japan."

24 1949/11/19 [USNARA/740.0011 PW (PEACE)/11-1949], US Department of State, United States Political Adviser for Japan, "Comment on Draft Treaty of Peace with Japan."

25 Ibid. (Enclosure to Despatch No. 806 dated November 19, 1949, from Office of United States Political Adviser for Japan, Tokyo, subject: "Comment on Draft Treaty of Peace with Japan").

26 1950/4/19 [USNARA/Doc. No.: N/A], US Department of State, Division of Research for Far East, Office of Intelligence Research, "DRF Information Paper No. 326 (April 19, 1950): Notes on Certain Islands Adjacent to or Formerly Occupied by Japan (Unedited Draft)."

27 Seokwoo Lee, "The Resolution of the Territorial Dispute between Korea and Japan over the Liancourt Rocks," *Boundary and Territory Briefing* 3 (2002): 8; Seokwoo Lee, "The San Francisco Peace Treaty with Japan of 1951 and the Territorial Disputes in East Asia," *Pacific Rim Law & Policy Journal* 11 (2002): 63–146; see generally, Seokwoo Lee, *Territorial Disputes of East Asia and International Law* (Seoul: Jipmoondang, 2007) [in Korean].

28 For example, Jennifer Lind, *Sorry States: Apologies in International Politics* (Ithaca, NY: Cornell University Press, 2008).

29 Jennifer Lind, "The Perils of Apology: What Japan Shouldn't Learn From Germany," *Foreign Affairs* 88 (2009): 132, 146.

30 See, generally, Bruce W. Jentleson and Thomas G. Paterson (eds.), *Encyclopedia of U.S. Foreign Relations*, vol. 3 (New York: Oxford University Press, 1997), p. 24.

31 Harold Hak-Won Sunoo, *Korea: A Political History in Modern Times* (Columbia, MO: Korean-American Cultural Foundation, 1970), pp. 196–7.

32 The original materials were provided by the late law professor Jon M. Van Dyke of the University of Hawaii.

33 In relation to this, the cooperation between the United States and Japan in the process of annexing Hawaii reveals a facet of imperialist state practice seeking maximized national interest in territorial expansion. As Van Dyke observes,

> Japan also originally opposed the U.S. annexation of Hawaii, arguing in late 1897 that "the maintenance of the status quo in Hawaii was essential to the good understanding of the powers having interests in the Pacific" and that the rights and claims of Japanese subjects residing and working in Hawaii might be jeopardized.

This expression of Japanese concern was followed by US assurances to the Japanese government that Japanese subjects would be treated fairly and without discrimination in an annexed Hawaii. In December 1897, "Japan withdrew its protest against annexation and ultimately settled its difficulties with the Republic [of Hawaii] in return for an indemnity of $75,000, after Washington had exerted pressure to end the disagreement prior to annexation"; Jon M. van Dyke, "Reconciliation between Korea and Japan," *Chinese Journal of International Law* 5 (2006): 215, 223. The opposition to the US annexation of Hawaii voiced in the Canadian parliament was also very different from the approach and understanding of the same by Japan. Member of parliament N.F. Davin stated that "[t]o annex forcibly on the part of any power would be contrary to modern ideas of the obligations which control the actions of the great powers," while Alexander McNeill, MP, added, "If it be true that the native population is opposed to a change, any interference by the United States would be contrary to [the United States'] own principles." Jennifer M.L. Chock, "One Hundred Years of Illegitimacy: International Legal Analysis of the Illegal Overthrow of the Hawaiian Monarchy, Hawai'i's Annexation, and Possible Reparations," *University of Hawaii Law Review* 17 (1995): 463, 492 (quoting from "Canadians Don't Like It: They Think Annexation Would Mean Trouble for U.S.," *New York Times*, February 16, 1893, p. 1).

34 The principle of intertemporal law is related to the application of certain legal principles during a particular time regarding particular disputes. It refers to the application of existing law and principles at the time of the dispute as raised by the parties. The *Islands of Palmas Arbitration* defined the principle by stating:

> [as] regards the question which of different legal systems prevailing at successive periods is to be applied in a particular case (the so-called *intertemporal law*), a distinction must be made between the creation of rights and the existence of rights. The same principle which subjects the act creative of a right to the law in force at the time the right arises, demands that the existence of the right, in other words its continued manifestation, shall follow the conditions required by the evolution of law.

United Nations, "Island of Palmas Case (Netherlands, USA)," *Reports of International Arbitral Awards* 2, April 4, 1928, pp. 829, 845. For criticisms of intertemporal law, see Joshua Castellino, Steve Allen, and Jérémie Gilbert, *Title to Territory in International Law: A Temporal Analysis* (Burlington, VT: Ashgate, 2003), p. 3 ("a mere political handmaiden to the politics of power of the imperial states who set out on a worldwide conquest of territory"; "to prevent blind acceptance of past manipulations of a legal system that was created by, dominated by and imposed by imperial states upon the rest of the world").

35 There also needs to be further study regarding the concept of *uti possidetis*, its process of development, and the issue of application. In the case of South America under Spanish rule, the newly independent states declared that the internal administrative divisions of the colonial era became state frontiers. The same principle was later applied to regions of Asia, Africa, and even, more recently, the former Yugoslavia.

See, generally, Suzanne N. Lalonde, *Determining Boundaries in a Conflicted World: The Role of* Uti Possidetis (Montreal: McGill-Queens University Press, 2002); Steven R. Ratner, "Drawing a Better Line: *Uti Possidetis* and the Borders of New States," *American Journal of International Law* 90 (1996): 590; Surya Prakash Sharma, *Territorial Acquisition, Disputes, and International Law* (The Hague: Martinus Nijhoff, 1997), pp. 119–29.

36 This part is based on Seokwoo Lee and Hee Eun Lee, "Overview – Dokdo: Historical Appraisal and International Justice," in Lee and Lee, *Dokdo: Historical Appraisal and International Justice*, pp. 1–11.

37 Refer generally to Lee and Lee, *Dokdo: Historical Appraisal and International Justice*.

38 Harry N. Scheiber, "Legalism, Geopolitics, and Morality: Perspectives from Law and History on War Guilt in Relation to the Dokdo Island Controversy," in Lee and Lee, *Dokdo: Historical Appraisal and International Justice*, pp. 13–27.

39 Ji Guoxing, "Similarities and Differences between the Korean–Japanese Dokdo Disputes and the Sino-Japanese Diaoyudao Disputes," in Lee and Lee, *Dokdo: Historical Appraisal and International Justice*, pp. 189–207; Jean-Marc F. Blanchard, "Politics and Economics in the Resolution/Non-Resolution of the East China Sea/Diaoyu Islands and Northern Territories Issues: Feats, Failures, and Futures," in Lee and Lee, *Dokdo: Historical Appraisal and International Justice*, pp. 223–48.

40 Larry A. Niksch, "An American Assessment of South Korea's Policy Options Towards Its Claim to Dokdo and Its Relations with Japan," in Lee and Lee, *Dokdo: Historical Appraisal and International Justice*, pp. 177–88.

2 Russia and Japan

The algorithm of the Kuriles/Northern Territories problem

Konstantin Sarkisov

A misjudgment by Stalin

The origin of the Russia–Japan territorial dispute goes back to World War II, but its impasse derives from the Cold War. In September 1951, the Soviet Union did not sign the San Francisco Peace Treaty (SFPT). All the reasons why Stalin refused to sign the document at that time, history have proven to be illusory.

Stalin opposed the very idea of a peace conference without the participation of China, which at that time was already a Communist country. But in October 1950, things had seemed to be different. On October 23, Jacob Malik, the Soviet representative at the UN, agreed to discuss with John F. Dulles, the American representative, his seven-point proposal for the peace treaty. The Japanese daily *Yomiuri* mentioned it as a complete "turnaround" of the Soviet position.[1]

According to Hara, in October (26, 27) Dulles explained orally to Malik that "it could be assumed, that if the USSR were a party to the treaty, Japan would by the treaty, cede South Sakhalin and the Kuriles to the Soviet Union."[2]

Logically speaking, due to the Cairo Declaration provision, as territories gained by war, Taiwan (Formosa), as well as the southern part of Sakhalin and Korea, required the same approach, to be transferred back to their former master, that is, "China." In peace treaty drafts prepared in the United States earlier, that had actually been the case. However, after the outbreak of the Korean War in June 1950, US policy drastically changed. In exchange for recognizing Stalin's territorial gains at Yalta (Kurile Islands), Dulles tried to make a plain bargain – to get Stalin's signature on the treaty that ignored the existence of Communist China and left Taiwan without definite national residence.[3]

The document gives the strong impression that the Soviet side weighed this proposal carefully. Dulles thought the territories might be a good price for Stalin's consent on China. Negotiations were intensive and reflected hope on both sides for a compromise. But the deal did not take place, with the absence of Communist China in the peace settlement with Japan being the main obstacle. In secret testimony (January 21–25, 1952) before the United States Senate Committee on Foreign Relations (declassified on August 25, 2000), Dulles gives a list of reasons why the Soviets did not sign the treaty:

I negotiated at very considerable length with the delegates from the Soviet Union particularly Mr. Malik who was designated for that purpose. I met with him on three or four occasions. We discussed the prospective treaty.... We had negotiations ... which began October 1950 and carried on until February or March, 1951. At that time the Soviet Government announced that they would not carry on any further negotiations with me ... I would think that the principal reason ... why they did not go along with the treaty was because they, for political reasons, felt unable to go along and make a peace with Japan unless the Chinese Communist regime was also included in that peace. That was a position to which we objected adamantly.[4]

It is obvious why in March 1951 the Soviet side decided not to negotiate further. It was at the height of the war in Korea: Operation Ripper, just launched by US troops, was successful, and on March 14 Seoul was recaptured. Earlier that month, the anti-Soviet mood in the United States had reached a peak with the trial of Ethel and Julius Rosenberg. In September 1951, Japan signed the SFPT, by which it renounced Southern Sakhalin and the Kurile Islands, but the name of the country to which Japan renounced these territories (USSR) had been dropped. The treaty came into force in April 1952.

Stalin's refusal to sign the treaty proved to be a strategic mistake that created for Russia (the Soviet Union) a vicious circle of "peace negotiations" with Japan. But, ironically enough, the SFPT is a problem for both sides – for Russia because it did not sign the treaty, for Japan because it did. Russia did not get title over these territories and has had to negotiate bilaterally with Japan. Japan renounced its right to the Kuriles and has come to claim that all four islands it is claiming are not at all the same Kuriles that it abandoned in the SFPT.

The second half of the 1950s: the American factor and Article 26 of the SFPT

When Hatoyama Ichiro and his Democratic Party came to power on December 10, 1954, normalization of relations with the USSR had become a focal point of Japan's foreign policy, led at that time by a major political figure, Foreign Minister Shigemitsu Mamoru.

At least three problems were identified as urgent and could not be solved without a peace treaty with the USSR: UN membership, return of all Japanese POWs from Soviet camps, and a fisheries convention.[5] But negotiations were complicated by the territorial problem. Japan's claim on all the Kuriles and South Sakhalin gradually shrunk to four islands that had never belonged to Russia. In prolonged negotiations, the Soviet side suddenly proposed a compromise – the return of two islands, Shikotan and Habomai. This proposal caused a split inside the Japanese government, but finally Shigemitsu, then plenipotentiary representative, came to the conclusion that he was facing a dilemma: to agree with the two-island return proposal or to break off negotiations. He decided in favor of the former.

Worried that Japan might settle the territorial problem, Dulles hastily abandoned his former "hands-off" attitude.[6] The news that Dulles had actually blackmailed Shigemitsu reached Japan on August 24, appearing on the front pages of the evening editions of leading Japanese newspapers.[7]

A wave of protests in Japan forced the Americans to deny their blackmailing tactics. But later Dulles had to admit that

> he had reminded the Japanese Government that if it concluded a treaty with another Power on terms more favorable than those of the peace treaty with the United States, then, under the treaty, the United States would be entitled to claim "comparable benefits."[8]

The arm-twisting policy of the "closest ally" was portrayed in a cartoon that appeared in a Japanese newspaper.[9]

However, even after August 19, Shigemitsu did not abandon his efforts to "work" with the Americans to find a solution that could provide Japan with a treaty with Moscow.[10]

The clash between the two sides over the interpretation of Article 26 is clearly apparent from declassified materials of the State Department. On August 27, 1956, Shimoda Takezo, director of the Japanese Foreign Ministry Treaty Bureau, and Hogen Shinsaku, special assistant to the Japanese vice-minister of foreign affairs, visited the State Department in Washington to get American support for negotiations with Russia.

During the talk with William J. Sebald, deputy assistant secretary in charge of Far Eastern affairs, the Japanese officials made the point that Japan was facing three possible courses: (1) to accept the Soviet proposal; (2) to reject the Soviet proposal and face the possibility of an indefinite postponement of the re-establishment of normal relations; and (3) to ask the Allied Powers, especially the United States as the responsible country convening the San Francisco Peace Conference, to settle the territorial issue on an international plane. As Shimoda stressed, among these options the first was the only practical one.

Then discussion moved to Article 26. Asserting that the right of the United States to refer to Article 26 was "questionable," Shimoda referred to the three-year limitation in Article 26.[11] When Sebald objected that "the limitation was with respect to the first sentence of Article 26 and not the second," Shimoda protested that that "would be an assertion of the right to perpetual intervention in Japanese diplomacy by the Allied powers."

These negotiations with the State Department did not provide Japan with American approval, the lack of which seemed critical for a compromise with Moscow.

In Japan, it was widely believed that Hatoyama had instructed Shigemitsu, in the event of Soviet resistance to the "four islands" solution, to agree on the "two islands" solution. But after August 19, this turned out to be impossible. Besides, public opinion in Japan was very excited by heated debates over Article 26 and turned against the two-island compromise. Subsequently, the

Japanese government instructed Shigemitsu to reject the Soviet proposal of the return of the two islands.

As *The Times* informed readers on September 4,

> The Foreign Minister is reported to be bitter about Government's attempt to pull carpet from under his feet while the talks were in progress by instructing him to refuse the Russian terms when he was given full power to negotiate.[12]

Also,

> It is believed here that Mr. Hatoyama instructed Mr. Shigemitsu before he left that he might surrender the Southern Kuriles and sign the treaty if it was inevitable. But the Government took fright at the reaction of public opinion when the crucial moment arrived.[13]

The 1960s: new realities

Hatoyama volunteered to resign in December 1956. After a short-lived Ishibashi Tanzan government, Kishi Nobusuke came to power. Soviet–Japan relations reached a stalemate. In January 1960 the Kishi government concluded a new security treaty with the United States. In a memorandum of protest, the Soviet government insisted that the new military arrangement with the United States violated the 1956 Declaration, "wherein both countries agreed to cooperate in the interest of peace and security in the Far East." It was declared also that Moscow would not return the two islands as promised, unless all foreign troops had been withdrawn from Japan.

However, it was the USSR that took the initiative to unlock the stalemate. In August 1961, Vice-Prime Minister Mikoyan came to Tokyo to open the Soviet Trade Fair in Harumi, Tokyo. In a private conversation with Mikoyan's son, Sergo, he told the author that it was his father who had tried to go back to the "two-island" formula but ultimately abandoned the idea under pressure from the Soviet military. The second visit of Mikoyan to Tokyo on May 14, 1964, now in his capacity as Soviet president, marked a new stage in efforts to improve bilateral relations without a territorial solution. As a goodwill gesture, Soviet authorities released forty-eight Japanese fishermen arrested in disputed waters, in addition to 141 who had been freed in 1963.

In the midst of 1960s, the split with Beijing and a need to trade with Japan for Siberian exploration forced Moscow to turn toward Tokyo. In September 1964, just weeks before his resignation, Khrushchev suddenly proposed the two-island handover even without concluding the peace treaty, on condition that American troops withdrew from Okinawa.[14]

In Japan it was believed that the Soviet Union was playing a game "to give new ammunition to the local campaign against visits by American nuclear-powered submarines."[15] But the Soviet move could be also attributed to the

Chinese campaign of territorial claims. On September 2, 1964, the Russian Communist newspaper *Pravda* condemned China for questioning Soviet rights to 1,500,000 km² of Siberian territory. Questioned about his view on the Kurile Islands, Mao Zedong remarked that "the places occupied by Soviet Union are numerous."[16]

From that time onward, the territorial issue was influenced by escalated animosity between Moscow and Beijing, by the growing interest of the Japanese in Siberian resources, by Japanese eagerness to launch its first venture as an "honest broker" between the United States and Russia on Vietnam, and most of all by the issue of the return of Okinawa.[17] A visit by Prime Minister Sato to Moscow was an option. Andrei Gromyko's visit to Japan in July 1966 was the first-ever visit of a Soviet minister of foreign affairs. It took place in a rather relaxed atmosphere. Gromyko came with his wife and went sightseeing in Kyoto and Osaka. Discussions on territories were not in the schedule – only the issue of safe fishing in the area.

Things began to change when, in November 1969, an agreement on Okinawa's return was signed with the United States. The reaction of the Japanese Ministry of Foreign Affairs was quick. Foreign Minister Aichi Kiichi stated that the next objective would be the Northern Territories and that he was about to draw up a detailed diplomatic schedule for the return of all four South Kurile Islands.[18]

As part of the backdrop to the newfound Japanese assertiveness on the islands, there were unprecedented hostilities between Moscow and Beijing, with a military clash on Damansky Island in March 1969. The clash between Moscow and Beijing over certain territories was a strong argument for those in Japan who thought it was high time to make the territorial claims against the USSR a central point of bilateral relations. Besides, the "small war" over Damansky opened a dark age of unprecedented difficulties and problems of the Soviet state, which ultimately ended with its collapse.

In the beginning of the 1970s, booming Japanese heavy industry, which was facing the challenge of increasing resource nationalism centered in the Middle East, demonstrated a great interest in Siberian raw materials and oil resources. For a time it was a kind of preferences dilemma – "islands or resources?" The large, empty spaces in Siberia required huge capital injections, which the stagnating Soviet economy could not afford. The small war with China pressed Moscow to move troops and military infrastructure en masse into the region, which made investments not only desirable but critical.

However, the territorial issue remained. "If the Kuriles remain the live issue, Japan's business leaders may find it difficult to press the case for investing in Siberia. But the economic arguments seem certain to win in the end," argued the *Financial Times* in an assessment that turned out to be optimistic and premature.[19] In reality, political arguments prevailed.

The 1970s: China factor and Tanaka's visit to Moscow

When it was announced that President Nixon would make a journey to Beijing, relations with Japan for the Soviet Union seemed not only important but a key factor. The notion was simple. If Tokyo associated its interests with Beijing, the threat to Russian positions in the Far East would be ominous.

Mindful of this, Gromyko hastened to Tokyo. On January 23, 1972, his plane landed in Haneda. It had been eight years since his last visit to Japan. The atmosphere of the negotiations was in stark contrast with 1966, when the American failure in Vietnam had been a major factor shaping world and regional policy. Now, Japanese claims on the four islands dominated talks. "As time has passed, and Japanese confidence has filled out, the issue has become one over which all political parties in the country are united," elaborated the *Times* in an editorial.[20]

A communiqué signed at the end of Gromyko's visit included no mention of the Kurile Islands. But the decision to begin peace negotiations reflected the Kremlin's desire to discuss the matter in order to bring balance to the situation in the Far East, in light of the Sino-American rapprochement. It is proper to suggest that the outgoing Sato Eisaku government was also interested in improving relations not just for territories but to balance new Sino-American relations.

Tanaka Kakuei's victory over Fukuda Takeo in the Liberal Democratic Party (LDP) presidential election in July 1972, and his prompt visit to Beijing, where he was greeted as a hero, in September the same year, tempted him to use the Chinese card against Moscow. The vast Chinese market, with its huge, poor, and industrious population, was not less attractive to the Japanese than was Siberia. And Beijing, in supporting Japan's territorial claims against those of Russia, was not reluctant to lure Japanese capital from Siberia to China.

When Tanaka reached Moscow for three-day talks at the Kremlin on the evening of October 7, 1973, the timing was not good at all. The attention of Soviet leaders was distracted by a new war in the Golan Heights and Sinai. Though Brezhnev read secret telegrams from the Middle East from time to time, he did his best to tempt the Japanese with the abundant natural resources of the Soviet Far East. On his side, Tanaka stressed that he had come to make a peace treaty and to find a solution to the territorial dispute.[21]

He did not get what he had hoped for, but there was a "gift" from Brezhnev – the mention of an "unresolved question" in the joint communiqué. But when, after another five years, in January 1978 Foreign Minister Sonoda came to Moscow, he was told that there were no questions left unsettled. Instead, a large-scale military exercise took place in the seas off Japan.[22]

The Chinese card worked again. A treaty of peace and friendship signed in Beijing on August 12, 1978, with an anti-hegemony clause, was criticized by Moscow as an anti-USSR treaty. However, by contrast to 1960, when the United States–Japan security treaty was sharply criticized by Moscow, this time the Soviets behaved in a different manner. In February 1978, the blueprint of a Soviet–Japan treaty was handed directly to Fukuda. Though it was flatly rejected, the mainstream of Japanese political thought was in favor of so-called "all-direction peace diplomacy" (*zenpoi heiwagaiko*). This meant, first of all, balancing relations with China by improving relations with the Soviet Union. *Asahi*, in its editorial, suggested that this could be done on the basis of the situation in 1956.[23]

The 1980s: Gorbachev and "new political thinking" diplomacy

The chance to improve relations came in the mid-1980s. The decade began with a crisis in the Soviet Union that was due to a long period of stagnation. The economic and political stalemate during Brezhnev's era was aggravated by the invasion of Afghanistan in 1979, which gradually turned into a complete failure. Japan joined America and other countries in harsh criticism of the Soviet invasion, boycotting the Moscow Olympics in 1980.

Under these circumstances there was an unprecedented surge of Japanese government-sponsored campaigns for the return of all four islands. On January 6, 1981, a meeting of Japanese cabinet ministers decided to set up an annual celebration of Northern Territories Day on February 7. In an interview, the chief editor of *Pravda* stated that the confrontation "has brought Japan's relations with the Soviet Union to the lowest level since the Second World War."[24]

No dialogue on the peace treaty or the problem of borders could happen at all. Things started to change with the deaths, within a short space, of Brezhnev and two other general secretaries of the Communist Party of the Soviet Union (CPSU). With Prime Minister Suzuki's visit to Moscow for Brezhnev's funeral, the rounds of "funeral-attendance diplomacy" (弔問外交) began. When K. Chernenko died, Prime Minister Nakasone flew with great enthusiasm to Moscow to meet the new Soviet leader, Mikhail Gorbachev.[25]

At their meeting, when Nakasone touched on the territorial issue, he heard from Gorbachev, "You, Mr. Prime Minister, must be well aware that our position is consistent."[26] In his book, Gorbachev explained why he was so tough on the territorial issue:

> I must say we didn't have a considered policy toward Japan in the context of the "new thinking." There was only a desire to draw a line over the past and "begin from scratch." Initially I reiterated this idea to all my Japanese interlocutors without feeling the significance which had been given in Japan to the problem of the South Kurile Islands as a problem for the state, as a political, emotional, traditional, psychological and other sort of problem. In my first conversations I didn't even want to discuss this question, considering the postwar territorial divisions to be ultimate and not reversible. I didn't admit the very existence of this question. Due to the Gromykian formula, the territorial question, being a "result of the war," was solved, and therefore four islands lawfully belonged to Soviet Union, which was a big country but had "no land to spare." However, in the course of shaping the policy of new thinking and getting more knowledge about the gist of the matter and listening to the Japanese politicians' arguments, whom I met more and more often, I had to enter into discussions on the "territorial issue."[27]

Gorbachev's attempt to implement "new political thinking" about Japan encountered huge difficulties, since it had to be followed by territorial concessions that no one leader in office wants to preside over. He confessed: "The normalization of relations with this great neighboring country [Japan] has been my natural desire. And I said that in my speech at Vladivostok in summer 1986. *However I did underestimate the difficulties on the path to that.*"[28]

The logic of the Soviet diplomatic attitude at that time was easy to comprehend. After the 1972 China–Japan rapprochement, Gorbachev, like his predecessors, was not against considering a two-island solution, but he knew well that the Japanese side would not be happy with that and would definitely request the other two islands with more persistence. The author was told several times by a high-ranking Soviet diplomat that the Japanese had to suggest solving the problem by a recourse to 1956 conditions. Otherwise it was useless to confirm the two-island formula as a Soviet obligation since it could not provide a key to any solution at all.

While taking the same position, however, Gorbachev was seemingly different from his predecessors. He carefully listened to the Japanese, trying to understand their arguments. Japanese who met him knew what Thatcher, Reagan, and Mitterrand recognized in him as one "whom you can talk to."

In January 1986 Japan warmly welcomed Gorbachev's foreign minister, Shevardnadze, when he came to Tokyo, though they knew he was not ready to talk about the territories. After signing a joint communiqué with Abe, he told a press conference: "Our understanding of the historical and legal basis [of the territorial question] has not changed from previous times." Instead of territories, he put on the table a "broader agenda" – Gorbachev's initiative to eliminate all nuclear weapons until the beginning of the new century, the conclusion of the Agreement on Cultural Exchange and a Protocol on Political Consultations between the two governments, and the Long-Term Economic Cooperation Agreement.[29]

Abe Shintaro, who among high-ranking politicians enjoyed a reputation for being the most flexible person on the territorial issue, reached Moscow in June 1986 to sound out what concessions could be hoped for from the new Soviet leader. These turned out to be small but substantial. In 1986, after an eleven-year ban, former Japanese inhabitants of the disputed islands were permitted to visit the graves of their relatives, without passports or visas, in order not to harm the "principal position" the islands were Japanese. To save face, Gorbachev insisted on a "reciprocity principle," enabling Russians to also visit Russian graves without passports and visas.[30] The images of Japanese visiting the graves were widely shown on Soviet TV, underscoring the new era.[31]

In 1988 there was a new prime minister in Japan, but the approach to the territorial question remained the same. On February 7, 1988, in his speech at the Kudan Kaikan in Tokyo before 1,400 representatives of all political parties, Takeshita Noboru stressed that the four-island "all-at-once return" was the policy of his cabinet.[32]

But, later on, signals from the Kremlin demonstrated its desire to shift from "zero point." When Nakasone visited Moscow privately and talked with Gorbachev on July 22, 1988, the Soviet general secretary omitted for the first time mention that the problem did not exist or was solved – something that had been sacrosanct until this moment; however, he did casually mention the 1956 agreement. Alongside his appeal for joint ventures with Japanese companies, Gorbachev's behavior was perceived as a sign that the Soviet side had begun to think about what could be done with the territories in exchange for economic cooperation.[33] The shift was also noted by some well-informed observers, such as Zbigniew Brzezinski, who said in an interview in Japan, "It seems likely that the Soviets have begun to practically calculate in their heads what kind of gains could be hoped for in return if they gave back to Japan the Northern Territories."[34]

These rumors had their justification in the poor Soviet economy. During Perestroika, the economy moved downward. Oil prices fell in 1986. A prohibition campaign dealt a severe blow to the state budget when billions of rubles moved to the black market. The Chernobyl nuclear disaster in 1985 turned out to be a huge financial burden. Military expenses for the war in Afghanistan were enormous. And, symbolically, at the end of the 1980s Japan became the second-largest world economy, surpassing the USSR in nominal GDP.

In 1989 the dismal economic situation was aggravated by a rapidly developing political crisis of the entire Soviet system. The eventual collapse of the USSR was approaching. A number of complicated ethnic and border issues involving the republics of Armenia, Azerbaijan, and others erupted – in such a situation, territorial talks could not be welcomed by the Soviet people.[35] That same year, radical changes in Eastern Europe followed the erosion of pro-Soviet regimes in almost all countries, ending with the fall of the Berlin Wall on November 9, 1989.

The moment when the situation both within and without the Soviet Union crossed the red line was overlooked in Japan. The popularity and political attractiveness of Gorbachev and his Perestroika was dampened. From that time, he made only inevitable concessions like the withdrawal of Soviet troops from Germany; voluntary concessions, such as yielding the Kurile Islands to Japan in return for vague advantages, were beyond his reach.

However, Tokyo continued to hope for Gorbachev's flexibility and his desire for Japanese economic aid. In February 1989, Takeshita and Foreign Minister Uno Sosuke spoke with President George H.W. Bush in the American capital. Asked about relations with the Soviet Union, Uno bluntly said, "To conclude a peace treaty we need four islands.... The Soviet Union wants us to cooperate economically in Siberian development. But unless the territorial issue is solved we would not be able to do that."[36]

Gorbachev's visit to China in May 1989, followed by the normalization of Soviet–Chinese relations, seemed to be very helpful. Some analysts suggested that the trip to Beijing might pave the road to Tokyo.[37] The "Chinese factor" had been a strong one in the decision-making process in Moscow. However, at the time of Gorbachev's visit to Japan it did not help too much. The new relations with China were in their initial stage and, besides, China did not change its support of Japan's territorial claims.

The unwillingness to extend substantial economic aid to Gorbachev was revealed most conspicuously at the G7 Summit in Houston in July 1990. Foreign

Minister Nakayama Taro compared giving aid to a country "whose army is still occupying Japanese territory" to throwing money into a ditch. In a *Mainichi Shimbun* cartoon, the summit leaders were depicted dressed as chefs preparing something to serve an impatient-looking Gorbachev, waiting at his table in the background. In the same frame, the new Japanese Prime Minister Kaifu was told "You just pay the bill."[38]

The preparation for Gorbachev's visit to Japan took place under huge pressure from both internal and external imminent problems. It may be argued that, at this moment, Gorbachev already had a hunch that his visit to Tokyo was almost senseless. As a member of the group accompanying the Soviet leader in an unofficial capacity, the author had a strong feeling that, while in Tokyo, Gorbachev was mentally far from there. Nevertheless, he went on with his legendary optimism and tried to convince others that everything was fine.

A Japanese newspaper cheerfully reported: "Soviet President Mikhail Gorbachev indicated ... that he will try to solve all problems pending between Japan and the Soviet Union, including the Northern Territories issue, when he visits Tokyo next April."[39]

In the summer and fall of 1990, back-channel communications between Moscow and Tokyo began to take place, aimed at arranging a meeting between Ozawa Ichiro, then general secretary of the LDP, and Gorbachev. The purpose was to solve the territorial problem on a "business-like" platform. The conversation between the two general secretaries in Gorbachev's office at the Kremlin on March 25 was a long one. But the main portion of it was devoted to general topics without reaching the main point – territories. When time was up and Ozawa had to leave, he was upset. What he had come for – a plan of economic aid worth 28 billion dollars in return for territories – was not discussed at all.

Excited, he energetically requested one more meeting. "I was surprised and I didn't like it," commented Gorbachev. But he agreed, and this time Ozawa presented by himself his plan for a territorial solution. As Gorbachev described it, it consisted of three points to which the Japanese leadership hoped Gorbachev would agree:

1   That the 1956 joint declaration would be recognized as a document in legal force and make a starting point for all new negotiations on a peace treaty.
2   That from now on the "territorial question between the USSR and Japan" would be recognized as implying a decision on the fate of two other islands, Kunashir and Itourup.
3   That subsequent negotiations in the fall of the current year should determine the status of Kunashir and Itourup.

As a "stimulus," Ozawa hinted at the substantial economic aid that Japanese companies were ready to extend to the Soviet Union, recalled Gorbachev, adding, "I started from the last point and said that I categorically denied any bargaining as a way to make a deal. It was completely unacceptable not only in a dialogue between Japan and Soviet Union but in principle."[40]

Gorbachev's narration gives the impression that he was caught offguard and that all he heard from Ozawa surprised and infuriated him. But this cannot be true. Despite the confidentiality of the back-channel communications, the gist of them had appeared regularly in newspapers. On March 21, three days before Ozawa came to Moscow, *Yomiuri* had published an article with full coverage of the economic aid package that Ozawa was going to propose "officially." It comprised a list of several economic projects worth 28 billion dollars (3.6 trillion yen). The package was much bigger than what the Germans had given Gorbachev in return for his cooperation in East Germany (12.5 billion dollars). The Japanese package included a manufacturing plant in Bryansk, a petrochemical plant in Tobolsk, oil and natural gas projects in Sakhalin, and so on. As to territories, *Yomiuri* reported that Ozawa planned to suggest a flexible solution: recognition of Japanese sovereignty over the four islands, the immediate return of Habomai and Shikotan, and, after a certain period, the other two. All these proposals were transmitted beforehand to the Moscow authorities, through Arkadi Volsky.[41]

After the complete failure of Ozawa's back-channel mission, the Japanese government through an anonymous source reaffirmed its readiness to consider a "two-phased return."[42] But this fell on deaf ears. The Ozawa mission proved that nothing drastic could be expected of a visit by itself. In a joint communiqué signed on April 18, all four islands were mentioned by name and it was stated that a peace treaty between the two countries should be a document of final, post-war normalization, including a solution to the territorial problem.[43]

In an interview in 2011 Gorbachev confessed that he had discussed a "possibility under certain conditions to hand over two islands as it was determined by the bilateral agreements of the mid-1950s."[44]

Gorbachev's questionable ability to make bold decisions was further undermined by the intentional subversive activity launched against him by his political foes. Among them, the most powerful was his arch-rival, Boris Yeltsin. Yeltsin visited Japan on January 14, 1990. In a speech at the National Press Club in Tokyo, he presented a five-step solution to the territorial dispute, in which the resolution of the territorial question was named as the fifth step, while the signing of a peace treaty was named as the fourth. Apparently, the concept was hastily prepared for the occasion and revealed a practical ignorance of the issue, despite his assurances that he had studied the issue from its history in the nineteenth century. Gaimusho commented that the proposal was "pointless" (「拍子抜け」), and aimed at postponement of the solution.[45]

Nevertheless, Yeltsin's lectures and comments demonstrated his desire to settle the issue. But his intentions drastically changed when, in August the same year, he visited Kunashiri Island. After the trip, he told the Russian media that "my views on the Kuriles changed completely," saying, "I had thought it would be a terrible place to visit, but this is a wonderful island which can be developed as a resort. We should not abandon this island. We should rather encourage more people to live here." He insisted that Gorbachev "should not hurry in solving the northern territorial dispute with Japan" and that "the issue should be left for future generations to solve." He suggested that the islands should remain under Soviet control for at least fifteen to twenty years and that they should be under the dominion of the Russian Federation, of which he was president.[46]

The 1990s: Yeltsin and the territories

After the aborted coup against Gorbachev in August 1991 and the fall of Communist Party rule, real power in the Soviet Union shifted to Yeltsin. Worried about the forthcoming economic nightmare, the new ruler sent messengers to major developed countries, calling for help. Ruslan Khasbulatov, acting chairman of the Russian Supreme Soviet, came to Tokyo. On September 9, 1991, he handed Kaifu a letter from Yeltsin.

Reiterating what was in the letter, Khasbulatov said that the Russian Federation had recognized the existence of the territorial issue and showed respect for Japanese public opinion, which was calling for the return of Habomai, Shikotan, Kunashiri, and Etorofu. He suggested that some proposals included in Yeltsin's five-stage plan, which provided measures like the recognition of the existence of the dispute, establishment of a free economic zone on the islands, and demilitarization of the islands, had already been carried out. He expressed the intention to build up bilateral relations not as "between a winner and a loser of World War II," but on the basis of "equality and peace in accordance with international laws."

He asked for emergency aid, which by his words could be consistent with Japan's principle of connecting political and economic issues.[47] Khasbulatov's visit left an impression in Tokyo that Yeltsin was stuck on his five-stage plan and sincerely believed that the territorial solution might be pushed to the last stage.

In November 1991, Kaifu's government resigned. Miyazawa Kiichi as prime minister and Watanabe Michio as foreign minister became the fresh new actors dealing with the territorial question. Though the Japanese should have known that Yeltsin was completely different from Gorbachev – more expansive and less predictable – they trusted his "democratic beliefs" and abided by the same tactics, pushing for the return of all four islands as a precondition for any substantial economic aid (with a two-phase return as the limit of flexibility). In February 1992, Miyazawa said he was determined to solve the prolonged territorial dispute "all at once" in September, when Yeltsin planned to visit Japan. He suggested that the most crucial topic was how the current residents of the islands would be treated in the event of the islands' return to Japan. "We must not make the residents of the islands feel uncertain about their future. Granting residency should be considered, as well as securing housing for those who will be evacuated (from the islands in the event they are returned to Japan)," Miyazawa said.[48]

This notion of the "most crucial topic" was rather strange, as it was not even clear that Yeltsin would agree even on the two-island plan of return. All available documents and further developments prove that the decision-making process under Yeltsin was rather erratic and undermined by the lack of a clear understanding of political goals, being influenced by the unpredictability of the main actor – Yeltsin himself.

This unpredictability was perfectly demonstrated by his behavior before his visit to Japan in September 1992, when he not once but many times gave assurances that he had several options for a solution to the territorial question. Finally, it appeared that he in fact did not have any solutions at all. All speculation was ended by the abrupt and clumsy cancellation of his state visit to Japan. The next year in October, several days after the bloody suppression of an attempted coup against him during which time it seemed that he could not go even ten meters from the Kremlin walls, he flew 8,000 km to Tokyo to sign the Tokyo Declaration. In his book he confessed that it had not been possible "to disappoint the whole people of Japan twice in a row."[49]

It was assumed that, during his visit to Japan, Yeltsin did recognize the 1956 joint declaration. "It is needless to say this [1956] declaration is included [in all international commitments by my Soviet predecessors]," he said, at a joint press conference with Prime Minister Hosokawa Morihiro. However, the dispute would be solved only after Japan and Russia had developed closer ties and narrowed the "psychological gaps" that existed between the peoples of the two nations. "It cannot be settled in one breath," he stated.[50]

In the Tokyo Declaration, signed in 1993, these notions were expressed indirectly:

> The Prime Minister of Japan and the President of the Russian Federation ... have undertaken serious negotiations on the issue of where the islands of Etorofu, Kunashiri, Shikotan and Habomai belong. Both sides agree that negotiations towards an early conclusion of a peace treaty through the solution of this issue on the basis of historical and legal facts and based on the documents produced with the two countries' agreement as well as on the principles of law and justice should continue, and that the relations between the two countries should thus be fully normalized. In this regard, the Government of Japan and the Government of the Russian Federation confirm that the Russian Federation is the State retaining continuing identity with the Soviet Union and that all treaties and other international agreements between Japan and the Soviet Union continue to be applied between Japan and the Russian Federation.[51]

It was, obviously, a fundamental document that was similar in name to the 1956 declaration but without its legally binding force. It was all Yeltsin could do on the issue. The hope for something more proved to be illusory. Afterwards, the dispute resolution process again fell into a state of lethargy. Yeltsin was preoccupied by internal problems and did not respond to signals from Tokyo. The Foreign Minister Kono Yohei tried in 1994 to appeal to his Russian counterpart in a most eloquent way at the UN headquarters in New York, saying that the post-World War II era had ended in Europe on August 31, 1945, but in Asia, the war's aftermath lingered on, particularly with regard to relations between Russia and Japan. In light of this, he suggested, the countries should go ahead with talks on the status of the Northern Territories.[52]

Russia compensated for the lack of progress on the territorial question with some political gestures proving its friendship and desire to cooperate in other spheres. In March 1995, Foreign Minister Andrei Kozyrev declared that Russia would support Japan's efforts to join the UN Security Council.[53]

In 1996 one person ascended the political stage in Japan who seemed eager to turn the tide – Prime Minister Hashimoto Ryutaro. Hashimoto tried to look at bilateral relations from a "broader perspective," and managed to establish close personal relations that could be summed up in the phrase "Boris and Ryu." He well understood that it was a flawed tactic to be too persistent and aggressive. Besides, 1996 was a very hard year for Yeltsin: the presidential elections required all his mental and physical resources, and he had to have heart surgery. Hashimoto was very attentive in sending Yeltsin regular telegrams.

The same year, the Russian foreign ministry had a new chief, Yevgeni Primakov, who was a great master of conflict resolution. His first idea was joint exploration of the islands. As to legal questions, they must be studied, he said.[54] Japan's reaction was, for the first time, positive.

After recovering from surgery, "Boris" met "Ryu" twice in Krasnoyarsk in November 1997 and at Kawana. On July 24, 1997, before his meeting with Yeltsin in Krasnoyarsk, Hashimoto presented his three principles of policy to Russia – trust, mutual benefit, and long-term perspective. He believed that the controversy over the islands "can be overcome only by these concepts."[55]

It was an obvious departure from the long-standing position of "inseparability of policy and economy." It was well received by Moscow alongside Hashimoto's concept of "Eurasian diplomacy," declared in Japan's Diet on September 29 as a balanced position implying a solution of the dispute in a framework of improved bilateral relations.

Both Krasnoyarsk (November 1–3, 1997) and Kawana (April 18–19, 1998) were informal meetings. In relaxed ("without neckties") and frank conversations, both leaders agreed that the problem should be resolved before the end of the twentieth century. In Kawana, Hashimoto proposed the idea of "residual sovereignty" over the four islands, wherein the territories were conceded by Russia to be Japanese but stated to be returned in a certain period, in exchange for very broad economic cooperation. As one of the most experienced Russian experts on the matter put it, Hashimoto's proposal was trumpeted as new when revealed, but it "struck experts as being about as new as a steam engine."[56]

Nevertheless, Hashimoto's sudden resignation in July 1988 was a shock for those who thought his personal relations with Yeltsin might produce a solution.[57]

In order not to lose the momentum and warmth that had been built between Hashimoto and Yeltsin, Obuchi Keizo, who became the new prime minister of Japan at the end of July 1998, flew to Moscow in November. A very long, all-encompassing document called the "Moscow Declaration on Establishing a Creative Partnership between Japan and the Russian Federation" was signed on November 13, but did not comprise anything "creative" in terms of a territorial resolution. Later on, it appeared that, subsequent to the Kawana summit talks, the Japanese had allegedly proposed (1) drawing the Japan–Russia border in the Etorofu Strait, between Etorofu and Urup, and the Soya Strait between Sakhalin and Hokkaido, and (2) entrusting Russia with administrative authority over the Northern Territories – Etorofu, Shikotan, Kunashiri, and the Habomai group of islets – for the present.

For its part, the Russian side pledged (1) to incorporate into a peace treaty a statement of determination by both nations to resolve the territorial issue and their intention to separately establish a procedure for its settlement, and (2) to put in place a special legal system for joint economic activities on the islands.

As a newspaper wrote, "the negotiating positions of both countries were revealed, even though the release of such information was not authorized by either side."[58]

Meanwhile, by allowing former Japanese residents to visit the islands freely, Russia pushed its idea of a special legal status for the islands. This proposal met with a positive response from the Japanese government. Some unidentified officials called it Japan's "partial gain of administrative power" over the Northern Territories.[59]

Discussions about the results of Obuchi's November 1998 visit to Moscow stretched into the next year. Some newspapers reported that, during negotiations, Yeltsin had proposed to conclude a "peace, friendship, and cooperation" treaty with a commitment by both countries to resolve the Northern Territories issue, but in a separate treaty.[60]

The new century: Putin and the algorithm of conflict

The algorithm of the conflict could be presented figuratively in the form of a gauge, with Japan and Russia at opposite ends, and with two cursors moving toward each other from their respective extreme values – Japan "4," Russia "0" – to a point where they might eventually meet. Calibrated by numbers, the gauge is evenly divided, but calibrated by size of territory, the distances between "2" and "4" are hugely disproportionate.

In Stalin's period, both cursors were stuck at their extreme points. In the mid-1950s both cursors moved to mark "2" but did not touch. On the Soviet side, mark "2" remained as the meeting point of the cursors. But Khrushchev in 1960 imposed new conditions on the promise to return two islands, which made it in de facto terms defunct. Brezhnev tried to get back to "2" in 1972, but the position was never fixed and remained very uncertain. Gorbachev weighed "2" as an option but finally rejected the idea. Yeltsin elaborated on his own algorithm of resolution. But it proved to be a political game aimed at covering his reluctance to make any concessions at all.

Putin was the first Russian leader directly to recognize the validity of the 1956 Soviet–Japanese joint declaration. He was enthusiastic about a peace treaty with Japan. Being an emotional leader, he highly valued his personal relations with Prime Minister Mori Yoshiro. From Mori, the author heard a story about his father's grave in the Mori family cemetery at Kanazawa. Visiting with Putin, Mori told him about the will of his father, who had spent a lot of time in a Siberian prison as a prisoner of war. Mori's father asked for his ashes to be divided and for one part to be buried in the cemetery of a little village near Baikal Lake where he had spent his term as a prisoner. By that, he wanted to express his gratitude to those Russians who had helped him during the hard times. When Putin heard the story, Mori recounted, "tears welled up in his eyes."[61]

At the same time, Putin was quite rational. He begun cautiously by confirming only what had been achieved by his predecessors. In September 2000 he signed with Mori a statement on the issue of a peace treaty. Both sides agreed to continue negotiations for working out a treaty "through the solution of the issue of where the islands of Etorofu, Kunashiri, Shikotan and Habomai belong."[62] In March 2001 Putin signed the Irkutsk Statement, which confirmed that the Soviet–Japanese joint declaration was a legal document and the basis and start of negotiations on the Northern Territories issue.

Things turned in a negative direction when Mori stepped down and Koizumi took power. When it appeared to Putin that he had lost the thread of personal communications with Japanese leaders in order to reach a compromise on mutually acceptable terms, he decided to settle on a two-island return as his utmost condition and waited patiently for a move from the Japanese side. On November 15, 2004, during the Russian cabinet ministers' meeting, he officially stated his intention to solve the problem on a two-island return basis.[63] The plan was confirmed on November 17 by the Russian Minister of Foreign Affairs Lavrov, to his counterpart, Machimura.[64] All further developments around the territorial issue, particularly during the symbolic presidency of Medvedev, have represented a steep decline in the dynamics of the search for resolution.

Putin's return to the Russian presidency in February 2012 may be a new (or last?) chance to resolve the territorial dispute by escaping the vicious circle created by previous algorithms of searching for a resolution when the two cursors could not move to the point where they can meet. Logic suggests that a possible compromise may be found in the space between "2" and "4," not in quantitative but qualitative terms, such as joint exploration of the other two islands with a special legal system, which could provide the Japanese side with a feeling, as mentioned earlier, that they have got a "partial gain of administrative power" over the territories.

Notes

1 *Yomiuri Shimbun*, October 23, 1950.
2 Kimie Hara, *Cold War Frontiers in the Asia-Pacific: Divided Territories in the San Francisco System* (New York: Routledge, 2007), p. 90.
3 *Foreign Relations of the United States* (*FRUS*), 1950, Vol. 6, p. 1332.
4 Ibid., p. 60.
5 Toshikazu Kase, "Japan's New Role in East Asia," *Foreign Affairs* 34, no. 1 (October 1955): 40–9.
6 *The Times*, August 27, 1956.

7 *Asahi Shimbun*, August 24, 1956, evening edition.

8 *The Times*, September 13, 1956.

9 *Yomiuri Shimbun*, August 30, 1956.

10 *The Times*, August 27, 1956.

11 Article 26:

> Japan will be prepared to conclude with any State which signed or adhered to the United Nations Declaration of January 1, 1942, and which is at war with Japan, or with any State which previously formed a part of the territory of a State named in article 23, which is not a signatory of the present Treaty, a bilateral Treaty of Peace on the same or substantially the same terms as are provided for in the present Treaty, but this obligation on the part of Japan will expire three years after the first coming into force of the present Treaty. Should Japan make a peace settlement or war claims settlement with any State granting that State greater advantages than those provided by the present Treaty, those same advantages shall be extended to the parties to the present Treaty.

12 *The Times*, September 4, 1956.

13 Ibid.

14 *The Times*, September 18, 1964.

15 Ibid.

16 *Pravda*, September 2, 1964.

17 *The Times*, January 14, 1966.

18 *The Times*, December 1, 1969.

19 *The Financial Times*, February 10, 1970.

20 *The Times*, January 25, 1972.

21 *Asahi Shimbun*, October 9, 1973.

22 Chalmers Johnson, "The New Thrust in China's Foreign Policy," *Foreign Policy*, Fall 1978 (www.foreignaffairs.com/articles/29933/chalmers-johnson/the-new-thrust-in-chinas-foreign-policy?page=show [accessed September 5, 2013]).

23 *Asahi Shimbun*, September 16, 1978.

24 *The Times*, February 9, 1981.

25 *Asahi Shimbun*, March 13, 1985.

26 Ibid.

27 Mikhail Gorbachev, *Жизнь и реформы. Книга 1*. "Глава 26. Япония. Официальный визит президента СССР" [Life and Reform, book 1, "Chapter 26, Japan. The official visit of the president of the USSR"] (www.gorby.ru/gorbachev/zhizn_i_reformy [accessed September 5, 2013]).

28 Ibid. Emphasis added by author.

29 *Asahi shimbun*, January 20, 1986.

30 *Asahi Shimbun*, June 7, 1986.

31 *Yomiuri Shimbun*, September 4, 1986.

32 *Asahi Shimbun*, February 8, 1988.

33 *Asahi Shimbun*, June 26, 1988; *Yomiuri Shimbun*, August 3, 1988.

34 *Asahi Shimbun*, September 18, 1988.

35 *Yomiuri Shimbun*, July 27, 1990.

36 *Asahi Shimbun*, February 3, 1988, evening edition.

37 *Financial Times*, April 4, 1989.

38 Hugo Dobson, *Japan and the G7/8: 1975 to 2002* (New York: Routledge, 2004), p. 85.

39 *Yomiuri Shimbun*, December 6, 1990.

40 Gorbachev, "Life and Reform."

41 *Yomiuri Shimbun*, March 21, 1991.

42 *Yomiuri Shimbun*, April 11, 1991.

43 Japanese–Soviet Joint Communiqué (1991) (www.mofa.go.jp/region/europe/russia/territory/edition92/period6.html [accessed September 5, 2013]).

44 *Russian Information Network*, February 21, 2011 (http://news.rin.ru/news/285826 [accessed September 5, 2013]).

45 *Mainichi Shimbun*, January 17, 1990.

46 *Yomiuri Shimbun*, August 28, 1990.

47 *Yomiuri Shimbun*, September 10, 1991.

48 *Yomiuri Shimbun*, February 4, 1992.

49 Boris Nikolayevich, Yeltsin, *Записки Президента* [Notes of the president] (Moscow: ROSSPEN, 2008), p. 177.

50 *Yomiuri Shimbun*, October 14, 1993.

51 "Tokyo Declaration on Japan–Russia Relations (Provisional Translation)," Ministry of Foreign Affairs of Japan website (www.mofa.go.jp/region/europe/russia/territory/edition01/tokyo.html [accessed September 5, 2013]).

52 *Yomiuri Shimbun*, October 1, 1994.

53 *Yomiuri Shimbun*, March 4, 1995.

54 *Mainichi Shimbun*, November 16, 1996.

55 *Yomiuri Shimbun*, July 25, 1997.

56 Georgy Kunadze, "How enigmatic is Russo-Japanese puzzle?" *Yomiuri Shimbun*, February 28, 1999.

57 *Mainichi Shimbun*, July 14, 1998.

58 *Yomiuri Shimbun*, November 25, 1998.

59 *Yomiuri Shimbun*, November 14, 1998.

60 *Yomiuri Shimbun*, January 23, 1999.

61 Personal conversation with the author in 2010.

62 "Statement by the Prime Minister of Japan and the President of the Russian Federation on the Issue of a Peace Treaty (Provisional Translation)," (www.mofa.go.jp/region/europe/russia/territory/edition01/statement.html [accessed September 5, 2013]).

63 *Asahi Shimbun*, November 16, 2004.

64 *Asahi Shimbun*, November 18, 2004, evening edition.

3 Japan and China

Senkaku/Diaoyu and the Okinawa/ Liuqiu problems

Unryu Suganuma[1]

Introduction

When Hatoyama Yukio took office in the fall of 2009 after the Democratic Party of Japan (DPJ) won the lower house elections, relations between Japan and China improved. However, this state of affairs did not last for long. As discussed in an article by Hatoyama, published in the Japanese monthly journal *Voice*,

> due to the historical and cultural conflicts existing between the countries of the region, in addition to their conflicting national security interests, we must recognize that there are numerous difficult political issues. The problems of increased militarization and territorial disputes, which stand in the way of regional integration, cannot be resolved by bilateral negotiations between, for example, Japan and South Korea or Japan and China.[2]

Hatoyama refers to the territorial conflicts between Japan's neighbors and proposes a "fraternity foreign policy," in particular the creation of an "East Asian Community," to resolve these disputes. In addition to this article, Hatoyama has publicly discussed his idea of "the fraternity of the sea" on other occasions. Yet, the response from Beijing is relatively slow and unclear. China appears to have lingering concerns about other issues over which the two countries have been at loggerheads, such as visits to Yasukuni Shrine[3] by Japanese prime ministers, honoring the nation's war dead (including those whom China may see as war criminals) from World War II.

As discussed by Hatoyama, Japan has three border disputes with its neighbors today: (1) the Northern Four Islands/Kuriles with Russia in the north; (2) Takeshima/Dokdo with Korea in the west; and (3) Diaoyu/Senkaku Islands[4] with China in the south. As China overtook Japan in 2010 to be the world's second-largest economy and expanded its influence in the international community, the Diaoyu Island dispute between Japan and China came to receive frequent media attention. This continued in April 2012, when Tokyo governor Ishihara Shintaro made top news in both China and Japan by declaring that the Tokyo metropolitan government would "purchase" the Diaoyu Islands.[5] As Japan's ambassador to China, Niwa Uichiro, told the *Financial Times* on June 6, 2012: "If Mr. Ishihara's plans are acted upon, [they] will result in an extremely grave crisis in relations between Japan and China.... We cannot allow decades of past effort to be brought to nothing."[6] The ambassador's comments were rebuked by the Japanese government as "personal opinions"; many politicians from both the ruling party, DPJ, and opposition parties (e.g., the Liberal Democratic Party, or LDP) asked that the ambassador be fired. In addition, most in the Japanese media criticized Niwa's comments. However, Niwa's views symbolized current geopolitical tensions between Japan and China, in particular inside Japan, which is struggling to retain its territory in the East China Sea (ECS). Niwa was removed from his position in December 2012.

Over the years, two major approaches have formed with respect to issues relating to the Japan–China border: the "international law" approach and the "historical evidence" approach, even though both are interwoven with each other. On the one hand, scholars such as Park Choon-ho, Chiu Hungdah, Ma Ying-Jeou, Okuhara Toshio, and Victor H. Li seek a resolution of the dispute based upon an international law approach, which in turn depends heavily upon historical evidence. Others, including Inoue Kiyoshi, Murata Tadayoshi, Huang Yangzhi, Ma Tingying, Yabuki Susumu, and Midorima Sakae rely upon historical evidence to prove the sovereignty issue of the Diaoyu Islands. While scholars following the historical evidence approach rely heavily on historical developments and facts to show that either China or Japan has ultimate sovereignty over the Diaoyu Islands, researchers following the international law approach base their arguments upon international legal norms, which is a new approach to Sino-Japanese territorial disputes.

This chapter examines developments in the Sino-Japanese territorial disputes over the Diaoyu Islands and the related issues of Sino-Japanese relations. Following the overview of the territorial dispute since it erupted in the late 1960s and early 1970s, it evaluates the historical position of the Diaoyu Islands up to the end of World War II, especially in relation to treatment of the Liuqiu (Ryukyu) Kingdom. It then considers major obstacles to the solution of these problems, paying close attention to domestic factors in Japan and their relations to the "San Francisco System." The chapter concludes with the author's warning that war might be inevitable between Japan and China if both governments mismanage their diplomatic relations regarding these territorial disputes, which in turn have been directly influenced by the San Francisco System.

Overview of Sino-Japanese territorial disputes

The Diaoyu Islands are located in the ECS, about 120 miles northeast of Taiwan, approximately 180 miles west of Okinawa, Japan, and approximately 250 miles east of China's mainland. The islands are a set of eight uninhabited islets, including three barren rocks,[7] which are claimed by the People's Republic of China (PRC), Taiwan (Republic of China, or ROC),[8] and Japan. Currently, Japan controls these islands administratively, which are "officially" under the jurisdiction of Ishigaki City of Okinawa Prefecture. Until 1968, the Diaoyu Islands were essentially "worthless" islets for both China and Japan, and neither country appreciated their value. This changed in 1968. As soon as the Committee for Co-ordination of Joint Prospecting for Mineral Resources in Asian Offshore Areas (CCOP), under the auspices of the Economic Commission for Asia and the Far East, reported substantial petroleum deposits under the area of the Diaoyu Islands in the ECS, both Japan and China claimed sovereignty of these islets, which are estimated to contain between 10 and 100 billion barrels of oil.[9] In 1994 Japan's Ministry of Economy, Trade, and Industry (METI) estimated that deposits of oil and natural gas in the ECS measure 500 million kiloliters in crude oil volume, ten times Japan's crude oil stockpile and equivalent to Japan's oil consumption for two years.[10] However, according to Selig Harrison,

> Chinese estimates of potential East China Sea gas reserves on the entire shelf range from 175 trillion to 210 cubic feet in volume (Saudi Arabia has "proven and probable" gas reserves of 21.8 trillion cubic feet and the United States, 117.4 trillion). Foreign estimates of potential oil reserves on the shelf have gone as high as 100 billion barrels (Saudi Arabia has "proven and probable" oil reserves of 261.7 billion barrels and the United States 22 billion).[11]

To date, neither China nor Japan has actually drilled oil and gas in the disputed area. Nor has an international solution been possible, since neither party is willing to submit the dispute to the International Court of Justice (ICJ).

In the current debates, two competing views have emerged. China's claim emphasizes the use of historical evidence, from the archives of the Ming (1368–1644) and Qing (1644–1911) dynasties. Japan's claim is based upon the "discovery" theory in international law, arguing that the Japanese "rediscovered" these islands in 1884, as *terra nullius* (unadministered territory, or no man's land). During the post-World War II period, the pro-Japan irredentist view claimed that the Diaoyu Islands were not included in the territory that Japan renounced under the San Francisco Peace Treat (SFPT) with Allied nations. Rather, these disputed islets were controlled by the United States.[12] In accord-ance with the agreement signed on June 17, 1971, between Japan and the United States of America concerning the Ryukyu Islands and the Daito Islands, the pro-Japan irredentist group claims that the Diaoyu Islands are part of the Liuqiu Islands (Okinawa), which were explicitly returned to Japan. In reality, the Diaoyu Islands have become "hostage" to the disputants since the 1970s.[13]

Held "hostage" since the 1970s

The Cold War changed the geopolitical landscape of the East Asian region. In the Sino-Soviet split, the PRC ended its alliance with the Soviet Union in 1960. As tensions between the two Communist nations reached their peak in 1970, the United States capitalized on the conflict to shift the balance of power in favor of the West. In what would later be known as playing the "China card," President

Richard Nixon purposefully improved relations with the PRC to gain a geopolitical advantage over the Soviet Union. China successfully entered the United Nations in October 1971; President Nixon became the first American president to visit "Red" China in February 1972. The "China card" shocked Japan. In response, Prime Minister Tanaka Kakuei (1918–1993) rushed to establish diplomatic relations with the PRC, despite opposition by some pro-Taiwan and nationalist politicians in his ruling LDP. On September 29, 1972, Chinese Premier Zhou Enlai (1898–1976) and Tanaka signed a Joint Communiqué of the Government of Japan and the Government of People's Republic of China (the first key bilateral document between the two countries). By agreement, the communiqué did not address or even mention the issue of disputed territories; Article 5 in the communiqué stated that the PRC "declares that in the interest of the friendship between the Chinese and the Japanese peoples, it renounces its claim to war reparations from Japan." This basically shut down any Chinese lawsuits against the Japanese, including civil claims regarding World War II issues.[14]

The "Protect the Diaoyutai" Movements

In October 1970 some overseas Chinese, in particular Chinese students in North America, along with people in Taiwan and Hong Kong, joined hands to form the Bao Diaoyutai Yundong, or "Protect the Diaoyutai Movement" (hereafter Bao Diao Movement), headquartered at the University of Chicago. The current leader of Taiwan, Ma Ying-Jeou, was part of this movement as a student at Harvard University. During this period, mainland China was relatively quiet on the question as a result of Beijing's international isolation and apparent unwillingness to let the dispute stand in the way of the normalization of relations with Japan, which took place in September 1972.

On August 12, 1978, Japan and China signed the Sino-Japanese Treaty of Peace and Friendship – the second key bilateral document – despite the opposition of some LDP members. Deng Xiaoping (1904–1997) made a special trip to Tokyo to celebrate the treaty with Prime Minister Fukuda Takeo (1905–1995). Both governments, however, failed to solve the disputed islands issue.[15] During the press conference in Tokyo, Deng Xiaoping publicly stated that the Diaoyu Islands issue should be "left to posterity" when a Japanese reporter inquired about the sovereignty issue relating to these islets.[16] Furthermore, neither Japan nor China was willing to work out a solution to the disputed islands when Jiang Zemin visited Japan for his first state visit as president of China (not as secretary-general of the Chinese Communist Party) in November 1998. When Jiang pressed the historical issue of Sino-Japanese relations during a banquet with the Japanese emperor, there was a rise in neo-nationalist pressure not to compromise with China on any issue. The visit resulted in the third key bilateral document – the Japan–PRC Joint Declaration on Building a Partnership of Friendship and Cooperation for Peace and Development – which was signed by Jiang Zemin and Prime Minister Obuchi Keizo (1937–2000). This document also failed to address the issue of the Diaoyu Islands. As a result, since 1972, each of the three important documents signed by Japan and China has "shelved" the Diaoyu Islands dispute.

While both Tokyo and Beijing have been willing to postpone the final settlement of the territorial boundaries in the ECS, activists in both countries, including private citizens, have been eager to fight for the sovereignty of the Diaoyu Islands. In 1996, overseas Chinese, in particular in Taiwan and Hong Kong, once again joined forces to provide momentum to the Bao Diao Movement after Japanese conservatives "repaired" a lighthouse on the disputed islands. This time, the movement involved not only the first generation of the Bao Diao Movement, dominated by Taiwan, Hong Kong, and overseas Chinese, but also radical Mainland Chinese nationalists. The movement spread all over the world: some 20,000 people marched in San Francisco in its support. This was the so-called Di'er Bao Diaoyutai Yundong, or the "Second Protect Diaoyutai Movement." Gordon Mathews has discussed in detail how Chinese people in Hong Kong have tried to protect the Diaoyu Islands since 1996.[17] A climactic event was the sending of a ship of activists from Hong Kong to Diaoyu in an attempt to "assert" Chinese sovereignty, but it was marred by the drowning of one activist, 45-year-old David Chan, who fell into the sea while trying to climb up onto one of the disputed islets, in a clash with the Japanese Marine Self-Defense Force (SDF).[18] Yet, during this Bao Diao Movement, the Japanese and Chinese governments both tried to downplay the territorial issues in order to avoid escalation of Sino-Japanese tensions.

The Chunxiao Oil/Gas Field Agreement in the ECS

At the turn of the new century, the territorial disputes in the ECS increasingly bedeviled Sino-Japanese relations. In October 2002, for example, the Japanese government registered, and flaunted, its rental of three of the five disputed islands (Diaoyu Dao/Uotsuri Jima; Beixiao Dao/Kita Kojima; Nanxiao Dao/Minami Kojima) for the period of April 1, 2002 through March 31, 2003, under a 22 million Japanese yen contract.[19] In fact, the Japanese government considers itself the owner of one island in the group, the Chiwei/Taisho islet, while the others are privately held.[20] This move by the Japanese government sparked protests from China, Taiwan, and Hong Kong. Eventually, Chinese resentment against Japan, resulting in the so-called "anti-Japanese movement" which erupted inside China during the Asian Football Cup in 2004. Massive attacks by Chinese individuals throwing stones and splattering colored ink on the Japanese consulates in Shanghai and Beijing, as well as other large cities, were reported in April 2005. By the end of 2005, the Diaoyu Islands had turned into a heated issue of contention between Tokyo and Beijing.

On May 28, 2004, a bombshell was dropped by the Japanese media on the already shaky Sino-Japanese relationship. The media reported that, starting in August 2003, China had begun to develop a natural gas field exploration project in the ECS, in the Chunxiao/Shirakaba oil/gas fields in Chinese territory (not part of territorial disputes between Japan and China), four kilometers west of the exclusive economic zone (EEZ) border claimed by Japan. Tokyo considered that Beijing had used the Chunxiao islet, located outside Japan's unilaterally drawn center line in the ECS, to "suck out Japan's natural resources with a straw."[21] The Japanese government worried that this drilling would enable the Chinese to siphon off the 1.6 trillion cubic feet of precious natural gas buried under their side of the Diaoyu Islands.[22]

Starting in May 2004, Japan and China held several rounds of bureau chief-level talks and occasional informal negotiations. Basically, the Chunxiao oil/gas field is under Chinese sovereignty; however, Japanese requests are to hand over any data from Chunxiao or to suspend drilling. Even though the Chinese side made a proposal for joint development of the disputed territory in the eastern section of the ECS, the Japanese side insisted on its sovereignty over the Diaoyu Islands and refused the joint development proposal. On the other hand, Japan made a proposal to jointly develop four oil fields: Chunxiao, Duanqiao/Kusu-noki, Tianwaitian/Kashi, and Longqing/Asunaro, which are only tens of kilo-meters northeast of the Diaoyu Islands. This proposal was rejected in turn by the Chinese. As the Japanese government argued, one of the four oil fields crosses the median line claimed by Japan, while the remaining three are completely inside Japan's EEZ. Yet Beijing has refused to accept the median line set by Tokyo. Instead, China has argued that its own EEZ extends to the far reaches of its continental shelf, which ends west of the Okinawa Prefecture. Hence, Japanese and Chinese sovereignty claims overlap over a large section of maritime territory in the ECS.

A major breakthrough occurred when the two East Asian superpowers finally reached an agreement after several events: Chinese President Hu Jintao visited

Table 3.1 Sino–Japanese consultation concerning the ECS, Bureau Chief level

Round	Place	Date
1st round of the Sino–Japanese Consultation	Beijing	October 25, 2004
2nd round of the Sino–Japanese Consultation	Beijing	May 30–31, 2005
3rd round of the Sino–Japanese Consultation	Tokyo	September 30–October 1, 2005
4th round of the Sino–Japanese Consultation	Beijing	March 6–7, 2006
5th round of the Sino–Japanese Consultation	Tokyo	May 18, 2006
6th round of the Sino–Japanese Consultation	Beijing	July 8–9, 2006
7th round of the Sino–Japanese Consultation	Tokyo	March 29, 2007
8th round of the Sino–Japanese Consultation	Beijing	May 25, 2007
9th round of the Sino–Japanese Consultation	Tokyo	June 26, 2007
10th round of the Sino–Japanese Consultation	Beijing	October 11, 2007
11th round of the Sino–Japanese Consultation	Tokyo	November 14, 2007

Source: compiled by the author using data from Reinhard Drifte, "From 'Sea of Confrontation' to 'Sea of Peace, Cooperation and Friendship'? Japan Facing China in the East China Sea," *Japan Aktuell* (March 2008): p. 41. Unryu Suganuma, "The Diaoyu/Senkaku Islands: A Hotbed for a Hot War?" in *China and Japan at Odds*, edited by James C. Hsiung (New York: Palgrave Macmillan, 2007), p. 162.

Japan in May 2008, after holding the ministerial meeting in Beijing on December 1, 2007; Fukuda made his trip to China during December 27–30, 2007; and the Sino-Japanese strategic dialogue meeting (in Beijing) was opened on February 22–23, 2008. During the summit meeting in Tokyo, both Fukuda Yasuo and Hu Jintao emphasized that the ECS should be a "Sea of Peace, Cooperation and Friendship." On June 18, 2008, both Tokyo and Beijing simultaneously announced the pact of the Chunxiao oil/gas field. Two major developments are contained in this accord: to jointly explore the 2,700 km² area south of the Longjing oil field, which stretches across the Japanese-claimed median line, and to allow Japanese corporations to invest in the Chunxiao oil/gas field under Chinese law.[23] A Chinese scholar has claimed that this Sino-Japanese agreement utilizes a Chinese compromise model similar to the one used in the solution to a Sino-Vietnamese territorial dispute in the South China Sea (SCS).[24] By 2009 China had completed its drilling facilities in the Chunxiao oil/gas field, according to the Japanese media.[25] No further joint development of the ECS has been reported since both sides reached the agreement in June 2008.

Liuqiu Kingdom and the Diaoyu Islands

The Diaoyu Islands' geographic location in the ECS is extremely important for determining who has owned the territory during various periods of history. The Liuqiu Kingdom, an independent country until Japan annexed it in 1879, was a tributary nation for both the Chinese empires since Ming times and the Japanese shoguns since Qing times over the years. The Liuqiu Kingdom is positioned south of mainland Japan, while Taiwan is situated south of the Liuqiu Kingdom (see Figure 3.1). The Diaoyu Islands are located between Taiwan and Liuqiu. Based upon a historical timeline, the ownership of the Diaoyu Islands may be determinable for certain periods of time. Importantly, the status of the Liuqiu Kingdom, whether the Diaoyu Islands are treated as part of the Liuqiu Kingdom or not, is deeply and directly impacted by the San Francisco System, which ultimately created the territorial issues between Japan and China. As the Russian media have stated, the American government "deliberately" set up territorial "landmine" problems in the Asian region, including both the Diaoyu Islands and Dokdo after the Korean War started.[26] Furthermore, the San Francisco System offered by the United States has provided a golden opportunity for conservative Japanese forces to legitimize, or quasi-legitimize, Japanese war crime activities in the Asian region. As a result, Japanese conservatives have openly expressed radical historical views of World War II.

Discovery of the Diaoyu Islands to the annexation of the Liuqiu Kingdom in 1879

According to *Shunfeng Xiangsong* (May fair winds accompany you!), which dates back to 1403 and is the oldest historical record on the region known to exist today, it is undeniable that the Chinese first discovered the Diaoyu Islands.

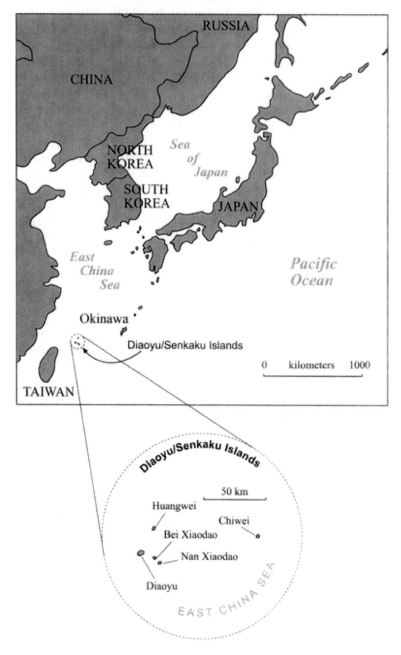

Figure 3.1 The geographical location of the Diaoyu and Liuqiu Islands (source: Suga-numa, *Sovereign Rights and Territorial Space in Sino-Japanese Relations*, 164).

During the Ming and Qing dynasties, the Chinese government dispatched at least twenty-four *cefeng* (investiture) missions to the Liuqiu Kingdom; the last mission was led by Zhao Xin in 1866. During the more than 500 years of relations between the Liuqiu Kingdom and the Ming and Qing dynasties, both the Chinese and the Liuqiuans recorded the name "Diaoyu Islands" in historical documents. Importantly, Chinese envoys recorded the name of the Diaoyu Islands in the *Shilu*, or *Shi Liuqiu Lu* (The record of the mission to the Liuqiu Kingdom), which contained travel records of the Liuqiu Kingdom, maps, and scholarly works.[27] At the same time, officials from the Liuqiu Kingdom often visited the Middle Kingdom; for instance, in Ming times the number of tributary missions to the Middle Kingdom reached over 300. In other words, both the Liuqiuans and Chinese acknowledged the existence of the Diaoyu Islands, which were used as navigational aids, employing the name of "Diaoyu" in Chinese-language records. No other descriptions of the Diaoyu Islands in any other language, including both English and Japanese, existed during this time; thus the name "Senkaku" significantly post-dates that of "Diaoyu."

Under the Pax Sinica, the Liuqiu Kingdom was a tributary nation of the Chinese empire. Since Japan is located north of the Liuqiu Kingdom, which was an independent nation, it is at least clear that Japan did not historically own the Diaoyu Islands, which are located south of the Liuqiu Kingdom. Under the 500-year-long Pax Sinica, there were no territorial disputes involving the Diaoyu Islands between China as suzerain and the Liuqiu Kingdom as tributary.[28] This continued until Japan annexed the kingdom in 1879. Since the name "Diaoyu" was given by the Chinese and used by other nations, including the Liuqiu Kingdom, the Chinese appear to have stronger ground for claiming "inchoate" title, according to international law.

From 1879 to the Shimonoseki Treaty of 1894–1895

Japan won the first Sino-Japanese war of modern history in 1894–1895. When China and Japan signed the Shimonoseki Treaty in 1895, Japan ultimately had sovereignty of the Diaoyu Islands. Only after the Japanese won the war in 1894 did the Japanese allow Koga Tatsushiro to develop these islands – meaning Japan was confident that the Chinese would not confront Japan regarding the Diaoyu Islands.

According to the Shimonoseki Treaty, China ceded Taiwan to Japan as part of war reparations in 1894–1895. It is not clear whether the Diaoyu Islands were then part of the Liuqiu Kingdom or part of Taiwan. However, since the Liuqiu Kingdom was annexed by the Japanese in 1879, and Taiwan was ceded to Japan in 1895, almost all major islands in the ECS basically fell under the Japanese empire. There is no way that only the Diaoyu Islands may be singled out as non-Japanese territories. Nonetheless, as Jean-Marc F. Blanchard pointed out, strictly speaking, "the islands were not transferred to Japan pursuant to the Treaty of Shimonoseki."[29]

Some serious questions need to be addressed during this period. First, on January 14, 1895 the Japanese government adopted a cabinet-level decision that placed the Diaoyu Islands under the jurisdiction of the Okinawa Prefecture by erecting a territorial landmark.[30] Interestingly, the Japanese cabinet decision does not bear the name of "Senkaku," and the landmark on the Diaoyu Islands was not actually erected by the Japanese government in May 1969. The Japanese government, furthermore, merely translated the Chinese name of "Diaoyu" (meaning "to go fishing" in Chinese) into "Uotsuri"; the word "Senkaku" might not be considered as a "legal" term.

Second, when Koga Tatsushiro, a native businessman from Fukuoka Prefecture, "rediscovered" in 1884 both Diaoyu Island and Huangwei/Kuba Jima Island, two of the eight islets of the Diaoyu Islands group, he requested that the Japanese government allow him to develop these islands. However, the Japanese government repeatedly denied his requests. Koga did not get the permission from the central government in Japan until the country won the war in 1894–1895. If Japan had confidence that the Diaoyu Islands were *terra nullius* as some pro-Japan irredentist scholars claim, why did the government deny Koga's requests continually for over a decade? The reason is simple. When Koga repeatedly asked to possess the Diaoyu Islands starting in 1884, the Japanese government continued to record these islands in its national archives under their Chinese name – "Diaoyu Islands" – fearing a backlash from the Chinese media.[31] Japan was trying to avoid "military" conflict with China. Furthermore, Japan made no "public announcement" of the acquisition of the Diaoyu Islands "legally" to entitle itself with the ownership of the "*terra nullius*" islands.[32]

Given these facts, however, if the Chinese government had given up its sovereignty of the Diaoyu Islands by 1879, Japan, according to international law, had the right to claim "rediscovery" of these islands. Ironically, both Koga and the Japanese government had repeatedly used the Chinese name of the "Diaoyu" Islands, not "Senkaku," for years.

From the Shimonoseki Treaty to World War II in 1945

During this period, Japan invaded almost all territories in the Asian region, while Nazi Germany dominated European countries. By the end of World War II, Japan fundamentally controlled all territories in the ECS and SCS, including Taiwan, Liuqiu, and the Diaoyu Islands.

The Japanese high-school teacher Kuroiwa Hisashi, who published his article in 1900, named the Diaoyu Islands "Senkaku," which for the first time appeared in the history textbook. Yet the Japanese government officially adopted the name "Senkaku" (meaning "pinnacle") from a British naval document (*The British Battleship Samarang Survey in 1843*), and recorded it into a historical archive only as late as the 1950s.[33] That is, the Japanese government did not create its "own term" to describe the Diaoyu Islands. It was not until the twentieth century that the Japanese government recognized this name and acknowledged the existence of these islands in the ECS.

Meanwhile, Koga had started a new business collecting tortoise shells and other kinds of shells, guano, and albatross feathers; he continued until World

War II, when the United States embargoed petroleum exports to Japan.[34] According to international law, Japan has thereby demonstrated its "will" to possess the Diaoyu Islands.

From 1945 to the SFPT in 1951

Most territorial disputes in the Asian region originated in this period based upon the San Francisco System. It is one of the most controversial eras in the study of current geopolitics, and can be divided into two periods: prior to 1949 and 1950–1951. In the first phase, the Allies, headed by the United States, mainly concentrated on how and when Japan should "unconditionally surrender." The aim of the Allies, however, changed once mainland China became a Communist state in October 1949; they intervened in the Korean War in 1950. China may have had a chance to receive sovereignty over the Diaoyu Islands at least until then, but Japan's chance to claim the Diaoyu Islands increased after 1950 due to the SFPT and American "strategic ambiguity."

According to the Cairo Declaration on November 27, 1943,

> The three Great Allies [i.e., the United States, ROC, and the United Kingdom] are fighting this war to restrain and punish the aggression of Japan.... Japan shall be stripped of the islands in the Pacific which she has seized or occupied since the beginning of the First World War in 1914, and that all the territories Japan has stolen from the Chinese, such as Manchuria [Northeast China], Formosa [Taiwan], and the Pescadores [Penghu], shall be restored to the Republic of China. Japan will also be expelled from all other territories which she has taken by violence and greed.

From this document, at least two points can be made: (1) Japan must return all territories seized since 1914, the beginning of World War I. In other words, the Liuqiu Kingdom, which was annexed by Japan in 1879, cannot be in this category of territories that Japan had "taken by violence and greed." (2) The declaration mentioned Manchuria, Taiwan, and Penghu, but not the Diaoyu Islands at all.

Moreover, in the Yalta Agreements of February 11, 1945, which dealt with the division of territories from Germany and Japan, Stalin did not invite China (that is, Chiang Kai-shek). Meanwhile, President Roosevelt was extremely sick and could not bargain with the USSR at all, so Stalin was able to get the territories he wanted.[35] The only sentence in Article 3 of the Yalta Agreement regarding the Chinese territories is that "the agreement concerning Outer-Mongolia and the ports and railroads referred to above will require concurrence of Generalissimo Chiang Kai-shek." Basically, Stalin had stolen Chinese territories, including Outer Mongolia (the present-day Mongolian People's Republic) and others. The agreement did not mention anything about the Diaoyu and Liuqiu Islands.

The third document relating to Japan's unconditional surrender is the Potsdam Declaration of July 26, 1945. Article 8 of the Potsdam Declaration states: "The terms of the Cairo Declaration shall be carried out and Japanese sovereignty shall be limited to the islands of Honshu, Hokkaido, Kyushu, Shikoku and such minor islands as we determine." Two points are relevant here: (1) The Liuqiu Islands are not mentioned. The words "such minor islands" might not include the Liuqiu Islands, which are not "minor islands" at all. If the words "such minor islands" do not embrace the Liuqiu Islands, it is difficult to imagine that they would contain the Diaoyu Islands. Since the Diaoyu Islands are located south of the Liuqiu Islands, Japan cannot possess the Diaoyu Islets' territories without first owning the Liuqiu Islands. Therefore, it is extremely difficult for Japan, through the Potsdam Declaration, to claim sovereignty of not only the Diaoyu Islands, but also the Liuqiu Islands. (2) The words "we determine" are crucial for the Chinese case. "We," according to Article 1 of the Potsdam Declaration, includes "the President of the United States, the President of the National Government of the Republic of China, and the Prime Minister of Great Britain." As a result, the Chinese (that is, the ROC) also have a say in defining "such minor islands as we determine."

Furthermore, on August 10, 1945, the Japanese government was

> ready to accept the terms enumerated in the Joint Declaration which was issued at Potsdam on July 26th, 1945, by the heads of the Governments of the United States, Great Britain and China ... Declaration does not comprise any demand which prejudices the prerogatives of His Majesty as a sovereign ruler.[36]

Thus, Japan did not have any chance to possess the Diaoyu Islands prior to 1949. In fact, Historical evidence demonstrates that "war committees" in Washington including the SWNCC (State-War-Navy Coordinating Committee) negatively impacted the sovereignty of the Diaoyu Islands by including it as part of Okinawa as "Nansei Shotō south of 29° North latitude" because the United States used the 1939 Japan map which was created before the American troops landed on Okinawa.

As Hara's analysis shows, in addition, Chiang Kai-shek wanted the Liuqiu Islands to be an integral part of Chinese territory.[37] Nonetheless, when the Cold War started, and the Yalta Agreement was replaced by the San Francisco System, the American geopolitical strategy toward the Asian region totally changed. Japan, once a former enemy, came to be considered an American "unsinkable aircraft carrier" in the region. In fact, Article 3 (regarding the Liuqiu) and Article 2(b) (regarding the Taiwan Islands) of the SFPT "concerns the origins of various regional conflicts." As Hara observes: "The treaty did not specify to which country Japan renounced its former territories, nor did it define the precise limits of these territories; this has created various 'unresolved problems' in the region."[38]

General Douglas MacArthur, "Japan's new emperor," feared that socialist and communist forces might dominate Japanese politics; he completely changed his policies, which had prohibited both war criminals and leaders of business conglomerates from entering politics. MacArthur released a number of conservatives and war criminals, such as Kishi Nobusuke (1896–1987) and Shoriki Matsutaro (1885–1969), allowing them to enter Japanese politics. Furthermore, the priority for Washington, especially John Foster Dulles, focused on potential domination by the communist expansion or prevention of any "domino effect" in the Cold War. Therefore, by not clearly defining territorial disposition in the SFPT, there remained a potential source of discord among Japan and its neighbor countries.[39]

Even in the early planning stages of the SFPT, Japanese Prime Minister Yoshida Shigeru expressed his support for having Communist China at the San Francisco conference; Yoshida's request was rejected by both MacArthur and the US Congress, which loathed the communist ideology.[40] Ironically, both Russian soldiers and American army forces had been shoulder to shoulder in fighting against both Nazi Germany and imperialist Japanese. By 1950, however, the Russians and Americans became deadly enemies.

Meanwhile, the PRC has consistently rejected the SFPT.[41] Even among the Western nations there was, according to Ross and Yoshitsu's analysis, disagreement regarding how to deal with the PRC.[42] Without the attendance of the Soviet Union, neither the government of the PRC nor that of the ROC was invited to the peace conference, owing to a difference of opinion between the British government (which wanted to recognize the PRC) and the American government (which favored continued recognition of the ROC). The only beneficial outcome from this disagreement within the West was for Japan, especially conservative elements, who had their own view or interpretation of World War II.

In addition, Article 14 of the SFPT basically waived most Japanese war reparations because "the resources of Japan are not presently sufficient." As a result, radical Japanese views of the war were fundamentally legitimized by the United States. This set the way for a Class-A criminal like Kishi, grandfather of Abe Shinzo, to become prime minister, and shaped the architecture of the United States–Japan Security Treaty in the 1960s. Even today, conservative Tokyo governor Ishihara Shintaro has publicly proclaimed that "If Japanese hadn't fought the white people, we would still be slaves of the white people. There would have been colonization. We changed that."[43] It is unthinkable that this kind of radical voice could be heard in present-day Germany, where it is considered illegal, but it has become normal in Japanese society and even a part of "mainstream" Japanese politics.[44] The San Francisco System provided legitimacy for the rising right wing in Japan, especially with the creation of the LDP in 1955. The "1955 system," in which two conservative parties, the Liberals and Democrats, merged to form a large ruling party in opposition to the socialist parties, was established.[45]

As primary documents reviewed by Hara in her early study discuss, American policy regarding Liuqiu (in 1943) and the Dulles peace draft (in 1950) were influenced by Cold War politics.[46] When the trawler incident at the Diaoyu Islands occurred in 2010, some Chinese media in Hong Kong and Taiwan claimed that a "secret note" between the United States and the ROC regarding the status of the

Liuqiu Islands existed when Japan surrendered. If any "secret notes" existed, however, Ma Ying-Jeou, who was in the vanguard of the Bao Diao Movement in his student days, would be in a position to know of such a note. However, no further information has come out of Taiwan. Nevertheless, according to the United States' declassified documents, during the meeting of President Roosevelt and Generalissimo Chiang Kai-shek, the American president asked if China should play the leading role in the post-war military occupation of Japan:

> Generalissimo Chiang believed, however, that China was not equipped to shoulder this considerable responsibility, that the task should be carried out under the leadership of the United States and that China could participate in the task in a supporting capacity should it prove necessary by that time. The Generalissimo also took the position that the final decision on the matter could await further development of the actual situation.[47]

In the other words, the ROC gave up a chance to occupy the Liuqiu Islands, even though President Roosevelt made the offer to China repeatedly. Because of space limitations, this issue will not be discussed further in this chapter, but explored on another occasion.

Continuing major obstacles

The complexity of the territorial disputes in the ECS is further linked to many other issues, such as the Yasukuni Shrine and the Japanese view of World War II history. The fact of the matter is that, unlike the Nuremberg Trials in Germany, the Tokyo Trials were a farce managed by the United States.[48] Many issues, such as Unit 731, chemical and biological weapons, sex slaves, and so on, were completely ignored at the trials; not a single Japanese war criminal was punished, and no one in Japan takes any responsibility for these issues, even today. The San Francisco System effectively provided an opportunity for revitalizing Japanese conservative methodology in both society and politics. For China (though not for the United States), it is inconceivable for the ongoing territorial dispute to be settled without addressing these historical issues.

It is true, nonetheless, that in order to understand the state of Sino-Japanese relations during the Koizumi administration, when they reached their lowest point since World War II, two main issues need to be reviewed: the rising Japanese neo-nationalist movements and Koizumi's Yasukuni Shrine pilgrimage. Sadly, no official from the White House, including George W. Bush, denounced Koizumi's pilgrimages to the Yasukuni Shrine. Chiefly, Washington was blindsided by the Yasukuni issue, which became a major and contentious issue between Japan and China during Koizumi's term of office. However, the "peaceful rise" of China, which overtook Japan in 2010 as the second-largest economy in the world, has become a serious concern for the White House.

Since World War II the United States has moved Japan about like a chess piece for its foreign policy purposes, as a balance against China. In other words,

Japan has been played and used by American "national interests." At the same time, Japanese foreign policy has never been "independent (i.e., based on Japanese national interests as expressed by Ozawa Ichiro)"[49] from the American Asian strategy, even today.

Japan's neo-nationalist movements since the 1990s

Many Japanese had hoped that the heightened economic and political ties following Emperor Akihito's successful trip to China in October 1992 would serve to further friendship between the two countries. This hope was furthered when Prime Minister Hosokawa Morihiro acknowledged in 1993 that the war was a mistake and that it was "a war of aggression," after the LDP lost majority control of the Diet, ending thirty-eight years of single-party domination in Japanese politics. Hosokawa was the first Japanese prime minister ever to extend heartfelt and meaningful apologies to the countries that had been victims of Japanese aggression. Any gains on the international level by these admissions were frustrated by the backlash in domestic politics.

Hosokawa was almost killed by a radical conservative member in an enraged reaction to his apologies. Moreover, the apology speech was seized upon by Japanese conservative politicians as an opportunity to revise the course of Japanese political history. Soon after Hosokawa took office on August 9, 1993, one of the seven coalition partners in the Diet, the Japan Socialist Party (JSP), began "secret negotiations" with the LDP in December 1993.[50] In August 1993 a group within the LDP formed the Rekishi kento iinkai (Committee on history and screening), with 105 members, to examine Hosokawa's apology. The aim of the Rekishi kento iinkai was to call for a more patriotic awareness of Japan's past and to revise history. Subsequently, the Rekishi kento iinkai produced a summary of the Japanese war in Asia; their findings were published in book form as *Daitoa senso no sokatsu* [The comprehension of the Greater East Asia war] on August 15, 1995, to coincide with the fiftieth anniversary of Japan's defeat in World War II. The summary had four major points:

> that the Greater East Asia War was one of self-defense and liberation; that the Nanjing Massacre and stories about comfort women were fabrications; that a new textbook drive was necessary to correct the wrongful acknowledgement of invasion and damage [caused by Japan] in recent textbooks; and that a national movement was needed to disseminate the historical view put forward in the first two points.[51]

The Rekishi kento iinkai invited conservative intellectuals from all over Japan, such as Fujioka Nobukatsu, to take note and reflect on these points in their speeches and writings. Later, more intellectual members of the Rekishi kento iinkai became members of today's well-known right-wing organization, Atarashii kyokasho o tsukuru kai (Japanese society for history textbook reform).[52]

The tumultuous state of Japanese politics, a result of the failure of LDP dominance in 1993, provided another golden opportunity for the conservative groups to gather strength. At the end of the JSP–LDP "secret negotiation," the LDP agreed to support the installation on June 30, 1994, of a socialist, Murayama Tomiichi, as Japan's eighty-first prime minister, ending the ephemeral era of Hosokawa. On August 15, 1995, Prime Minister Murayama gave a speech "on the occasion of the 50th anniversary of the war's end," in which he publicly apologized for Japanese atrocities during World War II. In reaction, junior politicians in the LDP, such as Nakagawa Shoichi and Abe Shinzo, created a networking group known as Nihon zendo to rekishi kyoiku o kangaeru wakate giin no kai (Junior congresspersons' committee on thinking about history education and the future of Japan). The purpose of this committee is to examine historical events and issues, such as comfort women, in the history textbooks. The Japanese neo-nationalists have developed two powerful channels through which a formidable conservative coalition is assembled in Japanese society. The Nihon zendo to rekishi kyoiku o kangaeru wakate giin no kai mobilizes conservative politicians, while the Atarashii kyokasho o tsukuru kai rallies conservative intellectuals. Together with the conservative media – the Fuji Sankei group (including *Sankei Shimbun, Bungei Shunju,* Fusosha publishing company, and Fuji TV)[53] – these two forces and other right-wing groups share the common goal of justifying or revising World War II history according to their own terms, and of rewriting the Japanese constitution (especially Article 9). In the end, Japanese politicians voted for resolutions marking the fiftieth anniversary of the end of the Pacific War (Japan's defeat) that rejected apologetic concessions, even offering justifications for the rejection.

In 2001 the Japanese right wing found someone who could speak for them – Koizumi Junichiro. It did not take long, however, for Chinese leaders to figure out Koizumi's political agenda. Koizumi dashed Beijing's hopes for better relations when he fired Tanaka Makiko as foreign minister and repeatedly visited the Yasukuni Shrine on August 13, 2001; April 21, 2002; January 14, 2003; January 1, 2004; October 17, 2005; and August 15, 2006. By visiting Yasukuni during the last year of his office (2006) on August 15, the date Japan surrendered in World War II, the Japanese right wing, as the Chinese foreign ministry stated, was challenging international justice and trampling on the conscience of mankind. It was an absolute insult to all the countries that defeated the German Nazis, Japanese Imperialists, and Italian Fascists in World War II.[54] As mentioned above, no official from the White House, including George W. Bush, denounced Koizumi's visits to the Yasukuni Shrine.

In order to conceal his "real" political beliefs, Koizumi put on a political show during his visit to China in October 2001, visiting the Marco Polo Bridge as well as the War of Resistance Museum in Beijing. He also offered a "*shudao*" (heartfelt apology) to the Chinese.[55] His "heartfelt apology," however, lacked sincerity and meaning for the Chinese people, who viewed it as "lip service" and did not buy Koizumi's claims that the pilgrimages were simply part of "Japanese culture."[56]

In sum, conservative forces have come to dominate Japanese society. Their dominating network not only has political control of the Japanese Diet, but also controls media propaganda, including racial books and *manga* (comics) to influence the younger generation and radical conservative scholars in the academic world creating their own interpretations of World War II history. Consequently, Japanese society has been strongly shaped by right-wing neo-nationalism. Many people know Japan is a democratic nation, but not so many people know that the fundamental principles of democracy and freedom of speech today have been terrorized by hawkish nationalists in Japan.

During the nadir of Sino-Japanese relations, as Koizumi repeatedly visited Yasukuni, some people in Japan questioned his acts. The home of Fuji Xerox chief executive and Chairman Kobayashi Yotaro was targeted by handmade firebombs after he criticized Koizumi's Yasukuni visits. Kobayashi received death threats – he travels with bodyguards, which is extremely unusual in Japan. Similarly, after Japanese LDP senior politician Kato Koichi had criticized Koizumi's decision to visit Yasukuni, Kato's parental home was burned down by a radical extremist on August 15, 2006.[57] Today, Japanese society has gradually become a 1930s-type militarist-terrorized society, in which emperor-worship and "thought control" are moving into more mainstream circles.

One major reason for this rising power of the Japanese right wing is the San Francisco System, which was ambivalent not only on territorial issues, but also on World War II responsibility. As a result, the radical right wing in Japan believes that the United States has "acquiesced" to Japanese war activities. This has led conservative politicians such as Koizumi to keep visiting the Yasukuni Shrine and conservative scholars to continue rewriting the history of World War II.

These radical right-wing groups not only ignore historical facts of World War II that are widely accepted by the international community, but they have also started to hijack Japanese foreign policy toward China, including pressing for there not to be diplomatic compromise on the Diaoyu Islands territorial dispute. Since Koizumi, all incumbent Japanese prime ministers, whether belonging to the LDP (and including the radically right-wing Abe Shinzo-I)[58] or DPJ, have avoided pilgrimages to Yasukuni during their terms of office; the issue of Yasukuni Shrine has not been top news in either Japanese and Chinese media. As long as incumbent Japanese prime ministers do not make pilgrimages to Yasukuni Shirine, Beijing will not publicly criticize Tokyo.

In August 2012, even though Noda himself did not go, two of his cabinet members, Matsubara Jin and Hata Yuichiro, made a "private" pilgrimage to the Yasukuni Shrine. The editorial of the *People's Daily* denounced their visit.[59] August 15 is a special day for many people in the Asian region, especially Chinese and Koreans; it is the day the Japanese emperor announced unconditional surrender, ending Japanese aggression in World War II. However, in Japan today, all, including the media and the government, refer to this day not as *haisen* (losing the war) but rather as *shusen* (ending the war). On August 15, 2012, a group of Chinese nationalists successfully landed in the Diaoyu Islands. After fourteen Chinese were deported to Hong Kong, ten Japanese radicals landed without governmental permission in the Diaoyu Islands a few days later, leading to massive anti-Japanese demonstrations in over twenty-five Chinese cities. Even some Japanese-made Chinese police cars were destroyed by radical Chinese. "Defend the Diaoyu Islands to the death," one banner wrote. Another stated, "Even if China is covered with graves, we must kill all Japanese."[60] Once again, both Yasukuni and territorial issues have complicated Sino-Japanese relations, on the fortieth anniversary of the normalization of relations between Japan and China (September 29, 2012). As a result, many celebration events for this anniversary in China and Japan were cancelled or postponed indefinitely. In addition, Japanese Prime Minister Noda Yoshihiko and Chinese premier Wen Jiabao skipped exchanging congratulatory messages, symbolizing the nadir of Sino-Japanese relations since 1972. This cancellation of the congratulatory message was the first time since Sino-Japanese normalization.

China's "peaceful rise" in the twenty-first century

Today, China's "peaceful rise" is one of the most significant phrases used in the study of contemporary international politics. After the Tiananmen incident in 1989, the Chinese government under Jiang Zemin's leadership heavily endorsed "patriotic" education in the schools, in order to avoid another situation of internal "chaos" like the "June Fourth Movement." This has been one of many things at the root of anti-Japanese and anti-American sentiment in present-day China. The second major factor for the "patriotic" movement is globalization and the popularity of the internet among individual citizens. Sina Weibo, for instance, China's most widely used microblogging service (like a Chinese version of Twitter), has provided a golden opportunity for normal citizens to express their opinions, including on the Diaoyu Islands issue. Chinese politics has a more democratic structure than ever before in Chinese history; therefore, Chinese public opinion cannot be ignored by leaders in Beijing, no matter who becomes the leader in China. As the *New York Times* described in an article entitled "Islands Reflect Japanese Fear of China's Rise," the right wing in Japan has realized that the Chinese are going after them.[61]

In 1990, however, the conservative research institute of the SDF launched the "China threat" theory in a conservative magazine.[62] Subsequently, around the world the "China threat" has become one of the hottest topics of academic discussion; *The Coming Conflict with China*, published in 1997 by Richard Bernstein and Ross H. Munro,[63] symbolizes the currency of the "China threat," not only in academic circles but also in the mass media.

Interestingly, as 2005 approached, a number of scholars began to pay serious attention to the Chinese economy. Beijing also realized that it was important to let the West know what the Chinese government thought. In the fall of 2005, Zheng Bijian, a mentor of Hu Jintao, published his essay in *Foreign Affairs* titled "China's 'Peaceful Rise' to Great-Power Status," which shocked many readers, especially neo-conservatives in the United States.[64] Zheng wrote:

> Since ... 1978, the Chinese leadership has concentrated on economic development. Through its achievements so far, China has blazed a new strategic path that suits its national conditions while conforming to the tides of history. This

path toward modernization can be called "the development path to a peaceful rise." Some emerging powers in modern history have plundered other countries' resources through invasion, colonization, expansion, or even large-scale wars of aggression. China's emergence thus far has been driven by capital, technology, and resources acquired through peaceful means.[65]

As Zheng indicated to the West, in particular the United States, China will follow "the development path to a peaceful rise," not colonization or aggression. Beijing has publicly assured the West:

China will not follow the path of Germany leading up to World War I or those of Germany and Japan leading up to World War II, when these countries violently plundered resources and pursued hegemony. Neither will China follow the path of the great powers vying for global domination during the Cold War. Instead, China will transcend ideological differences to strive for peace, development, and cooperation with all countries of the world.[66]

Still, China, according to Zheng, is a developing country with a massive population, along with a number of serious issues that need to be dealt with, including the environment and pollution. In 2005, he observed,

China's economy ... [was] still just one-seventh the size of the United States' and one-third the size of Japan's. In per capita terms, China remains a low-income developing country, ranked roughly 100th in the world. Its impact on the world economy is still limited.[67]

On the surface, the West, including both Japan and the United States, has welcomed Chinese pledges. In reality, the humble and obsequious tone of the Beijing regime is doubted by both the United States and Japan. In fact, Vice-President Joe Biden stated during his visit to China in August 2011 that "a rising China will fuel economic growth and prosperity and it will bring to the fore a new partner with whom we can meet global challenges together."[68] As China overtook Japan to become the second-largest economy in 2010, President Barack Obama openly said, during his State of the Union speech, that the United States does not want to be "second place" after China. By the middle of 2010, Secretary of State Hillary R. Clinton proclaimed that the United States was going to "return to Asia" in the ASEAN forum. The geopolitics of the East Asian region has become steadily more complex; Japan and China are on a collision path. It is the first time in 2,000 years of human history that both a "strong Japan" and a "strong China" co-exist. Since the seventh century, when the Chinese empire was in a "strong" period, Japan had been "weak." Conversely, when the Qing dynasty went through a "weak" era, experiencing 150 years of humiliation, Japan was "strong," culminating with the Meiji Restoration in the nineteenth century. As Robert Fogel, the 1993 Nobel laureate in economics, stated, "Today, the notion of a rising China is, in Chinese eyes, merely a return to the status quo."[69] China has been the globe's top economy for eighteen of the past twenty centuries. Will Japan accept a "strong" China in the twenty-first century? While China has enjoyed economic expansion since 1978, Japan is still attempting to reverse its economic stagnation since the bursting of its bubble economy in the 1990s. Japan is facing its third "lost decade" right now.

Conclusion

In the end, the San Francisco System has affected many war-related issues. It has stymied the efforts of those seeking judicial compensation against the Japanese government on issues such as comfort women, POW slavery, kidnapping, chemical and biological weapons, and Unit 731. The reason is simple: Article 14(b) of the SFPT states,

> Except as otherwise provided in the present Treaty, the Allied Powers waive all reparations claims of the Allied Powers, other claims of the Allied Powers and their nationals arising out of any actions taken by Japan and its nationals in the course of the prosecution of the war, and claims of the Allied Powers for direct military costs of occupation.

As a result, almost all lawsuits filed against the Japanese government regarding World War II crimes have been thrown out of court. This has further strengthened the claims about and interpretations of World War II by the Japanese conservative forces. The younger generations since World War II have grown up ignorant about the factual history of World War II. It is true that Japanese leaders, including both the emperor and several prime ministers, have expressed on many occasions their "regret" regarding World War II. However, these efforts have come to be seen as mere "lip service" by people in the Asian region, because Japanese politicians will not completely stop making their pilgrimages to Yasukuni Shrine. Two things might provide an opportunity for reconciliation between Japan and China: (1) like Chancellor Willy Brandt of West Germany, who spontaneously knelt down at the monument for victims of the Warsaw Ghetto Uprising in December 1970, the Japanese leaders could sincerely *apologize* in front of the monument to the People's Heroes in Beijing; and (2) as with the Berlin Holocaust Memorial, Memorial to the Murdered Jews of Europe, in Germany, as an example, the Japanese government could allow the building of a "Rape of Nanjing" museum in the center of Tokyo. Big gestures like this are needed. Until events of this type occur, reconciliation between Japan and China is almost impossible. However, it seems impossible for today's Japanese leaders to extend their hands to the Chinese people.

Furthermore, the San Francisco System has resulted in fundamental territorial problems for both Japan and China, as Washington deliberately left the language of the SFPT vague.[70] The issue of the Diaoyu Islands in the ECS seems unlikely to change. While Japan has control over these islets, it is yet unable to develop any natural resources. Meanwhile, Chinese nationalists, surveillance ships, and patrol planes are likely to continue their attempts to enter the Diaoyu Islands, whereas the Japanese coast guards will continue to prevent them from doing so. If both Japan and China miscalculate, collision will become unavoidable. There exists strong potential for the flames of war to be ignited in the ECS.

Notes

1 Chinese and Japanese personal names are given in the text in the customary order of family name first. Works published in English by Chinese and Japanese authors, however, are given in the Western order of putting the surname last. This chapter is a revised and expanded version of a part of a paper "The Sino-Japanese Geopolitical Confrontation in the East China Sea-I," originally published in the *Journal of J. F. Oberlin University: Studies in Humanities* 3 (March 2012): 31–49. The author has corrected some errors in the previous version.
2 Hatoyama Yukio, "'Subsidiarity' Society's True Path," *Japan Times*, September 9, 2010, p. 3.
3 The Yasukuni Shrine is located in Tokyo, enshrining bodies of Japanese war criminals, including Class-A criminals as well as 2.4 million other war dead.
4 For purposes of convenience, the islands will be referred to as the Diaoyu Islands, their Chinese name, rather than by their Japanese name, Senkaku Islands. This is not intended to suggest that the Chinese claim is "correct."
5 On September 7, 2010, in response to the Chinese fishing trawler collision incident in the ECS, Prime Minister Kan Naoto totally denied the existence of the territorial border issue with China. In doing so, Japan violated the bottom line of the unspoken Sino-Japanese "implicit agreement," surprising not only leaders of Beijing, but also leaders of Korea and Russia. Immediately, on November 1, 2010, in response to the fishing boat accident with China, Russian president Dmitry Medvedev took an unprecedented trip to the Northern Territories. In July 2012, Medvedev visited the disputed territories once again. On August 10, 2012, South Korean President Lee Myung-Bak made his unprecedented visit to Dokdo. Because of space limitations, this chapter will not discuss the conflict over the Chinese trawler that occurred in September 2010. It will be explored on another occasion.
6 Mura Dickie, "Tokyo Warned over Plans to Buy Islands," *Financial Times*, June 6, 2012.
7 Japan does not have unified names for these islands and often uses Chinese, English, or Japanese names. Unryu Suganuma, *Sovereign Rights and Territorial Space in Sino-Japanese Relations: Irredentism and the Diaoyu/Senkaku Islands* (Honolulu: Association for Asian Studies and University of Hawaii Press, 2000), p. 95. The group of eight small islets are named below: 1–5 are five small islets and 6–8 are three rocks:

    1 Diaoyu Dao/Diaoyu Yu/Diaoyu Tai/Gyocho Sho/Chogyo Sho/Uotsuri Jima
    2 Huangwei Yu/Kobi Sho/Kuba Jima
    3 Chiwei Yu/Sekibi Sho/Taisho Jima/Kuba Akashima
    4 Beixiao Dao/Kita Kojima
    5 Nanxiao Dao/Minami Kojima
    6 Nan Yu/Oki no Minami-iwa
    7 Bei Yu/Oki no Kita-iwa
    8 Feilai Yu/Tobise.

8 Taiwan is not currently a member of the United Nations and is claimed by mainland China as a renegade province. This chapter addresses only two parties, Japan and China.
9 The Japanese government conducted its survey (twice) immediately following the 1968 UN reports that there were well over 94.5 billion barrels of oil trapped in the

ECS. Erica Strecker Downs and Phillip C. Saunders, "Legitimacy and the Limits of Nationalism: China and the Diaoyu Islands," *International Security* 23, no. 3 (Winter 1998/1999): 124.

10 Kensuke Nakazawa, "Government Slow to Wake up to Potential of EEZ," *Daily Yomiuri*, August 27, 2004.

11 Selig Harrison, "Seabed Petroleum in Northeast Asia: Conflict or Cooperation?" in *Seabed Petroleum in Northeast Asia: Conflict or Cooperation?* edited by Selig Harrison (Washington, DC: Woodrow Wilson International Center for Scholars, 2010), p. 5. (This book can be downloaded from the web at www.wilsoncenter.org/publication/seabed-petroleum-northeast-asia-conflict-or-cooperation-selig-s-harrison [accessed July 31, 2012]).

12 The United States government has consistently insisted on a neutral position regarding the Diaoyu Islands. As late as August 15, 2012, spokesperson of the Department of State Victoria Nuland noted,

> With regard to the incident [Chinese Nationalists landed in the Diaoyu Islands on August 15], with regard to the general issue of this set of territorial disputes, we talked about it at some length yesterday, and we also talked about it on Monday. We don't take sides in these things. We want to see people work it out.

See Department of State, daily press briefing, August 15, 2012 (www.state.gov/r/pa/prs/dpb/2012/08/196509.htm [accessed August 22, 2012]).

13 Suganuma, *Sovereign Rights and Territorial Space in Sino-Japanese Relations*, p. 2. Regarding the irredentist claims by China and Japan, see chapters 2 and 3.

14 Ming Jin, "The 'Waiver of Right' Issue in Chinese Civil Claims for War Reparations from Japan," *Law China* 5, no. 1 (2010): 1–26.

15 Phil Deans, "The Diaoyutai/Senkaku Dispute: The Unwanted Controversy," *Kent Papers in Politics and International Relations* 6, no. 1 (1996): 7–8.

16 Li Enmin, *"Nitchu heiwa joyaku" kosho no seiji katei* [The political process of the negotiation in the "Sino-Japanese Treaty of Peace and Friendship"] (Tokyo: Ochanomizu Shobo, 2005), 143–4. Also see Unryu Suganuma, *Zhongri guanxi yu lingtu zhuquan* [History of Sino-Japanese relations: Sovereignty and territory] (Tokyo: Kyohosha, 2007), p. 179.

17 Gordon Mathews, "A Collision of Discourses: Japanese and Hong Kong Chinese during the Diaoyu/Senkaku Islands Crisis," in *Globalizing Japan: Ethnography of the Japanese Presence in Asia, Europe, and American*, edited by Harumi Befu and Sylvie Guichard-Anguis (London: Routledge, 2001), pp. 154–75.

18 Urano Tatsuo, "Dainiji hocho undo ni kansuru chugokugawa shiryo" [Materials regarding the Chinese claim in the second protect the Diaoyutai movement], *Hogaku Kiyo* [Bulletin of law] 41 (2000): 605–75. Bert Eljera, "Chinese Protest Japanese Land Grab," *Asia Week*, October 3, 1996. "In Death, Island Protester Becomes Martyr," *CNN News*, September 27, 1996. Regarding the 1996 matter, see Dan Xiao and Wang Fan, *Baowei Diaoyu Dao* [The protection of the Diaoyu Islands] (Hong Kong: Zhonghua wenhua chuban youxian gongshi, 1996); *Diaoyutai – Zhongguo de lingtu!* [The Diaoyu Islands – Chinese territory!] (Hong Kong: Mingbao chubanshe youxian gongshi, 1996).

19 Regarding the history of the issue of rental of the Diaoyu Islands, see Suganuma, *Sovereign Rights and Territorial Space in Sino-Japanese Relations*, pp. 96–9, 118–19.

20 "China Protests over Senkaku Isles," *Daily Yomiuri*, January 6, 2003. Also see "Japan Leasing Disputed Southern Island for U.S.," *Reuters*, January 8, 2003; and "Government's Island Tactic Shows Soft Approach," *Daily Yomiuri*, January 3, 2003.

21 James C. Hsiung, "Sea Power, Law of the Sea, and a Sino-Japanese East China Sea 'Resource War,'" in *China and Japan at Odds: Deciphering the Perpetual Conflict* (New York: Palgrave Macmillan, 2007), p. 140.

22 "Asian Powers Edging Toward an Energy War," *Edmonton Journal*, October 1, 2005.

23 "Joint Press Conference by Minister for Foreign Affairs Masahiko Koumura and

Minister of Economy, Trade and Industry Akira Amari (Regarding Cooperation between Japan and China in the ECS), Ministry of Foreign Affairs of Japan," June 18, 2008, www.mofa.go.jp/mofaj/area/china/higashi_shina/press.html (accessed April 13, 2010). Regarding this issue, see James Manicom, "Sino-Japanese Cooperation in the East China Sea: Limitations and Prospects," *Contemporary Southeast Asia* 30, no. 3 (2008): 455–78.

24 Regarding the Sino-Vietnamese territorial dispute, see Zhang Zhirong, *Zhongguo duiwai guanxi xinlun* [Chinese foreign relations: New perspectives on geopolitics and the good neighbor policy] (Hong Kong: Lizhi chuban she, 2008), pp. 265–81.

25 Hidemichi Katsumata and Ryuhei Yoshimura, "Upgrade of Brigade Target China Threat," *Daily Yomiuri*, April 8, 2010.

26 "Ni-chu-kan no ryodo arasoi wa beikoku ga umeta 'jirai;' jiyu boekiken koso mo hakushi no kiki – roshia medeia" [The landmine of the territorial confrontation among Japan, China, and Korea is set up by the United States; their FTA may be in the crisis – Russian media], *Record China*, August 7, 2012, www.recordchina.co.jp/group.php?groupid=63553 (accessed August 11, 2012).

27 Suganuma, *Sovereign Rights and Territorial Space in Sino-Japanese Relations*, chapter 2.

28 Ibid., pp. 27–8.

29 Jean-Marc F. Blanchard, "The U.S. Role in the Sino-Japanese Dispute over the Diaoyu (Senkaku) Islands, 1945–1971," *China Quarterly* 161 (March 2000): 102.

30 Yoshiro Matsui, "International Law of Territorial Acquisition and the Dispute over the Senkaku (Diaoyu) Islands," *Japanese Annual of International Law* 40 (1997): 16.

31 Murata Tadayoshi, *Senkaku retto/Uotsuri jima wo do miruka* [How to understand the issue of the Diaoyu/Senaku Islands] (Tokyo: Nihon kyoho sha, 2004), pp. 28–40. Murata analyzed this period thoroughly. His latest book is *Nitchu ryodo mondai no kigen* [The origins of Sino-Japanese territorial issue] (Tokyo: Kadensha, 2013).

32 Japan is required to make the announcement "publicly" by the acquisition of the Diaoyu Islands, which it is continuing to occupy "steadily and peacefully," according to L. Oppenheim, *International Law: Peace*, 2nd edn., vol. 1 (New York: Longmans, Green, 1912), p. 309.

33 Suganuma, *Sovereign Rights and Territorial Space in Sino-Japanese Relations*, p. 96.

34 Ibid., p. 97.

35 S.M. Plokhy, *Yalta: The Price of Peace* (London: Penguin Books, 2010). Also see Kimie Hara, "50 Years from San Francisco: Re-examining the Peace Treaty and Japan's Territorial Problems," *Pacific Affairs* 74, no. 3 (fall 2001): 364.

36 Communications exchanged in connection with surrender, note of the Japanese government of August 10 regarding their acceptance of the provisions of the Potsdam declaration.

37 Kimie Hara, *Cold War Frontiers in the Asia-Pacific: Divided Territories in the San Francisco System* (London: Routledge, 2007), p. 161.

38 Hara, "50 Years from San Francisco," p. 362.

39 Ibid., p. 373.

40 Michael M. Yoshitsu, *Japan and the San Francisco Peace Settlement* (New York: Columbia University Press, 1982), pp. 25–38.

41 Caroline Ross, *Sino-Japanese Relations: Facing the Past, Looking to the Future?* (London: RoutledgeCurzon, 2005), pp. 43–44.

42 Yoshitsu, *Japan and the San Francisco Peace Settlement*, pp. 69–74. Ross, *Sino-Japanese Relations*, pp. 43–4.

43 Audrey McAvoy, "Racist or Realist, Ishihara Vents His Spleen," *Japan Times*, October 6, 2004, p. 3.

44 Jeff Kingston, *Japan's Quiet Transformation: Social Change and Civil Society in the Twenty-First Century* (London: RoutledgeCurzon, 2004), pp. 12–15, 225–46.

45 Hara, "50 Years from San Francisco," p. 367.

46 Hara, *Cold War Frontiers in the Asia-Pacific*, pp. 162–71.
47 *Foreign Relations of the United States: The Conferences at Cairo and Tehran, 1943* (Washington, DC: Government Printing Office, 1961), pp. 323–4. The document can be downloaded at http://digital.library.wisc.edu/1711.dl/FRUS.FRUS1943CairoTehran (accessed on December 30, 2012).
48 "Tenno no na no motoni: Nankin daigyakusatsu no sinso [In the name of the emperor: Rape of Nanjing]," VHS War documentary, directed by Christine Choy and Nancy Tong, written by Nanette Burstein and Nancy Tong, 1998.
49 Ozawa Ichiro, *Ozawaizumu* [Ozawaism] (Tokyo: Shueisha, 2009), pp. 144–62.
50 Gerald L. Curtis, *The Logic of Japanese Politics: Leaders, Institutions, and the Limits of Change* (New York: Columbia University Press, 1999), p. 270.
51 Ross, *Sino-Japanese Relations*, p. 53.
52 Takahashi Tetsuya, "Outo no shippai" [The failure of response], *Gendai Shiso* [*Revue de la pensé d'aujourd'hui*] 33, no. 6 (June 2005): 49.
53 Right-wing media began to publish racial *manga* (comic books), magazines, and books in an attempt to sway public opinion.
54 *Xinhua News*, August 15, 2006.
55 Suganuma, *Zhongri guanxi yu lingtu zhuquan*, 209.
56 Koizumi's father built an airfield in Kagoshima, which was used for *kamikaze* (suicide) missions during World War II; his cousin died on such a mission. According to Koizumi, his visit was to respect the war dead, not to endorse any political stance or movement to remilitarize. It is a familiar tactic of Japanese politicians to point to "Japanese culture" when the Japanese government is trying to persuade the international community regarding controversial policies. Japan, for example, has also tried to explain that eating whales is a part of "Japanese culture" at the annual meeting in the International Whaling Commission (IWC).
57 Steven Clemons, "The Rise of Japan's Thought Police," *Washington Post*, August 27, 2006. Also see Linus Hagström, "Sino-Japanese Relations: The Ice That Won't Melt," *International Journal* (Winter 2008–2009): 237.
58 But in his second term Abe visited Yasukuni in December 2013.
59 Zhong Sheng, "Bayueshiwuri bushi riben zhengke shua xiao congming de rizhi" [August 15th is not a date for the Japanese politician to be smart], *Renmin Ribao* [People's daily], August 14, 2012.
60 Keith Bradsher, Martin Fackler, and Andrew Jacobs, "Anti-Japan Protests Erupt in China Over Disputed Islands," *New York Times*, August 19, 2012.
61 Martin Fackler, "Islands Reflect Japanese Fear of China's Rise," *New York Times*, August 22, 2012.
62 Murai Tomohide, "Shin Chugoku 'Kyoi' ron" [The new theory of the China threat], *Shokun* [Bunshun opinion magazine] (May 1990): 186–97.
63 Richard Bernstein and Ross H. Munro, *The Coming Conflict with China* (New York: Alfred A. Knopf, 1997).
64 Robert D. Kaplan, "The Geography of Chinese Power," *Foreign Affairs* (May/June 2010): 22–41.
65 Zheng Bijian, "China's 'Peaceful Rise' to Great-Power Status," *Foreign Affairs* (September/October 2005): 19–20.
66 Ibid., p. 22.
67 Ibid., p. 19.
68 Department of Defense, *Annual Report to Congress: Military and Security Developments Involving the People's Republic of China 2012* (Washington, DC: Office of the Secretary of Defense, 2012), p. 12.
69 Robert Fogel, "123,000,000,000,000," *Foreign Policy* (January/February 2010): 75.
70 Kimie Hara, "Cold War Frontiers in the Asia-Pacific: The Troubling Legacy of the San Francisco Treaty," *Japan Focus* (September 2006), (www.japanfocus.org/-Kimie-HARA/2211 [accessed April 21, 2013]).

4   The South China Sea disputes

A review of history and prospects for dispute settlement

Nong Hong

Introduction

The South China Sea is a semi-enclosed sea defined by Article 122 of the United Convention on the Law of the Sea (UNCLOS),[1] with an area of 648,000 square nautical miles.[2] There are hundreds of small islands in the South China Sea: uninhabited islets, shoals, reefs, banks, sand bars, cays, and rocks.[3] They are distributed widely in the form of four groups of islands and underwater features: the Pratas Islands (Dongsha Qundao), the Paracel Islands (Xisha Qundao), the Macclesfield Bank (Zhongsha Qundao), and the Spratly Islands (Nansha Qundao).[4]

The South China Sea dispute is regarded as the most complex and challenging ocean-related regional conflict in East Asia, sources of which include historical claims on sovereignty, contention over energy sources, significance of geographic location, threats to maritime security, and overlapping maritime claims under the newly established maritime regimes authorized by UNCLOS.

The matter of maritime boundary delimitation in the South China Sea is especially problematic, primarily because the present situation is as a configuration of overlapping unilateral claims to sovereignty over an assortment of semi-submerged natural formations scattered throughout the region. China, Taiwan,[5] and Vietnam contest each other's claims to sovereignty over the Paracels and the Spratlys.[6]

The Spratly Islands are situated in the southern reaches of the South China Sea and consist of some 170 low-lying features. The total land area of the tiny islands is not more than 2–3 km[2] in an ocean area covering over 200,000 km[2]. The dispute over the Spratly Islands is the most complicated, since it has been going on for a long time and involves as many as six parties. China, Taiwan, and Vietnam claim the entire archipelago, while the Philippines, Malaysia, and Brunei claim sovereignty over portions of the Spratlys. Except for Brunei, all the claimant countries have established a military presence in the Spratlys.[7] There is no evidence so far to prove that the islands can sustain a permanent population or any lasting economic activities, but are now the focus of intense competition and conflicting claims.[8]

The growing dispute over the sovereignty of the Spratly Islands has arisen over the past few decades. China, Vietnam, Malaysia, the Philippines, and

Taiwan have established a continuous human presence on different islands and at some of the key reefs. Their military outposts and other facilities serve to demonstrate the seriousness of their sovereignty claims.[9] This competitive occupation of key features has grown sporadically over the past five decades, as one country and then another has staked out its territorial and maritime claims to the Spratly Islands.

The basis of the disputant states' claims over territorial sovereignty varies from discovery and effective occupation to geographic adjacency or vicinity. One of these legal grounds is directly relevant to the San Francisco Peace Treat (SFPT), since these states adopt different interpretations of some articles of the treaty to help justify their claims.

The San Francisco Peace Treaty and its relevance to the Paracel Islands and Spratly Islands

The Treaty of Peace with Japan, commonly known as the SFPT, between Japan and several of the Allied Powers, was officially signed by forty-nine nations on September 8, 1951, in San Francisco, and came into force on April 28, 1952. This treaty, along with the Security Treaty signed the same year, is said to mark the beginning of the San Francisco System. In this document, Japan renounces Korea, Formosa (Taiwan), the Pescadores (Penghu), Southern Sakhalin, the Kurile Islands, the Spratly and Paracel Islands, Micronesia, and Antarctica.[10] There is also some ambiguity regarding over which islands Japan renounced sovereignty. This has led to disputes over Takeshima/Dokdo, the Northern Territories/Kurile Islands, the Diaoyu/Senkaku Islands, and the Paracel and Spratly Islands.

China and the San Francisco Peace Treaty[11]

During World War II, Japan invaded the Spratlys and the Paracels. The 1943 Cairo Declaration had clearly stated that Japan must return the territories it had seized from China, and the Potsdam Declaration that Japan accepted at the time of its surrender in 1945 stated "the terms of the Cairo Declaration shall be carried out." To protest against Western countries, such as the United States and Britain, that attempted to exclude China from negotiations with Japan on the SFPT, Zhou Enlai, the foreign minister of the newly established People's Republic of China, stated on August 15, 1951, that

> the draft treaty stipulates that Japan should renounce all right to Nan Wei Island (Spratly Island) and the Xi Sha Islands (the Paracel Islands), but again deliberately makes no mention of the problem of restoring sovereignty over them: As a matter of fact ... the entire Nan Sha Islands, Zhong Sha Islands and Dong Sha Islands, Xi Sha Islands and Nan Wei Islands have always been China's territory. Although they had not been occupied by Japan for some time during the war of aggression waged by Japanese

imperialism, they were all taken over by the then Chinese government following Japan's surrender. The Central People's Government of the People's Republic of China hereby declares: Whether or not the United States–British draft treaty obtains provisions on this subject, and no matter how these provisions are worded, the inviolable sovereignty of the People of China over Nan Wei Island (Spratly Island)[12] and Xi Sha Islands (the Paracel Islands) will not be in any way affected.[13]

The Soviet Union expressed vigorous and vocal opposition to the draft treaty text prepared by the United States and the United Kingdom. The Soviet delegation made several unsuccessful procedural attempts to stall the proceedings through a lengthy September 8, 1951 statement by Gromyko.[14] One of the Soviet concerns was that Communist China was not invited to participate, despite being one of the main victims of Japanese aggression.

After the SFPT, Japan and the Republic of China (ROC) signed the Sino-Japanese Peace Treaty (Treaty of Taipei) on April 28, 1952 – the same day the SFPT came into force. This treaty was necessary, because neither the Republic of China nor the People's Republic of China had been invited to sign the SFPT. According to Article 2 of this treaty, "Japan has renounced all right, title, and claim to Taiwan (Formosa) and Penghu (the Pescadores) as well as the Spratly Islands and the Paracel Islands."[15] Although this article did not specify to which country or government Japan renounced these territories, it could be understood that the Spratlys and Paracels were treated in the same way as Formosa and the Pescadores, as Japan at that time recognized the ROC (Taiwan) as the legitimate government of China. This can be understood as meaning that both Taiwan and the South China Sea islands were regarded as territories of "China," provided "China" means the ROC.[16]

The nature of the Sino-Japanese Peace Treaty indicated that the titles to the renounced islands, including the Paracel and Spratly islands, were to be handed over to China.[17] While the 1951 Peace Treaty clearly mentioned five categories of sovereignty issues, the 1952 Treaty of Taipei mentioned only land features mentioned in 2(b) and 2(f) of the SFPT, which implies that both countries consider sovereignty of the Paracels and the Spratlys to be a bilateral issue between them. Since Japan, by Article 2(b), handed the sovereignty of Taiwan and Penghu to China, sovereignty over the Spratlys and the Paracels should also be handed over to the same signatory, namely the ROC and, later, the PRC, as the successor. The 1952 Sino-Japanese bilateral treaty, and the bilateral process leading to the treaty, shows Japan's tacit recognition of China's claims over the two island groups in the South China Sea.[18] Article 3 of the 1972 China–Japan joint communiqué reinstated Japan's compliance with Article 8 of the Potsdam Declaration, in which Taiwan and the Pescadores were returned to China. Samuels concluded that, through the two bilateral treaties, Japan recognized China's sovereignty over the Paracels and the Spratlys.[19]

Apart from the SFPT, two other documents also play an important role with relevance to the Paracels and Spratlys, namely the Cairo and Potsdam declarations. One of the purposes of the Cairo Declaration was to establish that all the territories that "Japan has stolen from the Chinese, such as Manchuria, Formosa, and the Pescadores, shall be restored to the Republic of China."[20] Article 8 of the Potsdam Declaration reaffirmed the content of the Cairo Declaration. It is the combination of the 1951 SFPT and the 1952 Sino-Japanese Peace Treaty that offered ideal opportunities for allocating sovereign ownership, including of the Spratlys.[21]

Vietnam and the San Francisco Peace Treaty

Although the SFPT did not mention to which country Japan renounced the Spratlys and the Paracels, the Vietnamese government has tried to justify its claims over these two island groups through its own interpretation of Article 2(f).

Article 2(f) states: Japan renounces all right, title, and claim to the Spratlys Islands and to the Paracel Islands.

In the Republic of Vietnam's (ROV) 1975 white paper, further reinforced by the three white papers issued by the Socialist Republic of Vietnam (SRV) after the country's unification, Vietnam claimed that, by the 1951 SFPT, Japan was obliged to renounce the right over the two island groups, the Paracels and the Spratlys. According to Vietnam, first, although the SFPT itself does not specify which countries were to recover which specific territories renounced by Japan, further reading of Article 2 shows that each sub-paragraph is relevant to the rights of one particular country and sub-paragraph (f) refers to the rights of Vietnam.[22] Second, the Cairo (1943) and the Potsdam (1945) declarations, which are the basic documents for post-war territorial settlements, contained no clause contrary to the sovereignty of Vietnam over both archipelagos. Therefore, Tran Van Huu, head of the South Vietnam (pro-Western) delegation to the San Francisco Conference, declared Vietnam's sovereignty over the Paracel and Spratly Islands.[23] Communist North Vietnam supported Chinese claims.[24]

Vietnam's interpretation is that, by referring to previous paragraphs, Article 2(f) implied that the receiving nation of sovereignty over the Paracels and Spratlys should be Vietnam. Vietnam further stated that its representative at the San Francisco Peace Conference reaffirmed Vietnam's sovereignty over the Paracel and Spratly islands and that no participating country protested. However, neither the PRC nor the ROC was invited to participate in the peace conference.[25]

The above interpretation overlooks several factors. First, the SFPT is only one of a series of international documents regulating Japan over the issue of giving up the territories specified in the treaty. Attention should also be given to relevant bilateral documents in which Japan is a party. The sovereignty issue of the Spratlys should be interpreted in consideration of all these interconnected documents, including the 1943 Cairo Declaration, the 1945 Potsdam Declaration, the 1945 Instrument of Surrender by Japan, the 1951 SFPT, the 1952 bilateral treaty between Japan and Chinese Taipei, and the 1972 joint communiqué on normalization of bilateral relations between the PRC and Japan.[26]

Second, at the San Francisco Conference, the leader of the Soviet delegation, Andrei Gromyko, recognized that these islands were China's "alienable territory."[27] Although neither the PRC nor the ROC was present, before the conference on August 15, 1951, Chinese Premier Zhou Enlai had stated:

> The draft [of the SFPT] intentionally arranged that Japan was denounced of all the rights to the Spratly and the Paracels without mentioning the issue of sovereignty return. In fact, just like the entire Nansha Islands, Zhongsha Islands and Dongsha Islands, both the Spratly and the Paracels have long been China's territory. They were occupied by Japan during the imperialist invasion and should be returned to China after Japan's surrender.[28]

The Philippines and the San Francisco Peace Treaty

The Philippines claims most of the Spratly islets. Its claim is more recent than that of China and Vietnam, and is based on a theory that the islets are adjacent or contiguous to the main Philippines islands, that this region is vital to the country's security and economic survival, that the islets were *res nullius*, or "abandoned," after World War II, and that the recent Philippine occupation of some of the islets gives it title either through "discovery" or "prescriptive acquisition."[29]

The *res nullius* claim stems from the "discovery" and "occupation" of the Spratlys by a Filipino businessman and lawyer, Tomas Cloma, who claimed the islets in 1947 and established settlements there.[30] Another branch of the *res nullius* claim is based on the 1951 SFPT, after which – according to the Philippines – the Spratlys were "de facto under the trusteeship of the Allied Powers."[31] According to the Philippine view, the status of the islands as "trusts" nullified any previous ownership of them, and justifies its occupation of the features. The Philippines also argues that the Spratlys were "abandoned" during 1950–1956, when no nation paid any attention to them.[32] It asserts that Japan had acquired the islands but renounced its sovereignty over them at the time of 1951 SFPT without ceding them to any other country. The Philippines has reinforced its *res nullius*/occupation claims by sanctioning drilling off the Reed Bank area since 1971[33] and occupying eight of the features since 1978.[34]

The position of the Philippines is rather weak. In the document "Shinnan Gunto (Spratly and Other Islands)," prepared by the US State Department in May 1943 (T-324), these islands were "definitely beyond the boundary of the Philippines as established by the treaty of December 10, 1898."[35] Another document with the same title (CAC-310), prepared within the US government by the Inter-Divisional Area Committee on the Far East, on December 19, 1944, carried the sentence, "Shinnan Gunto is beyond the boundary of the Philippines," but preceded it with "The United States has made no claims to the islands either for itself or for the Philippines islands."[36]

Contemporary implications of the San Francisco Peace Treaty on the South China Sea dispute

The South China Sea dispute involves a variety of issues, for example, competing sovereignty claims, maritime delimitation, and historical claims versus modern claims under the UNCLOS framework. The core element is the competing sovereignty claims over the Paracels and the Spratlys. Maritime delimitation can only proceed after territorial sovereignty is determined. Thus, the "regime of islands" under UNCLOS becomes an important issue for debate.

Regime of islands

For decades, the regime of islands has been an issue of great interest, given special attention during UNCLOS III. After nine years of negotiations, the conference adopted a single provision concerning islands, Article 121 of UNCLOS:[37]

Regime of Islands
1. An island is a naturally formed area of land, surrounded by water, which is above water at high tide.
2. Except as provided for in paragraph 3, the territorial sea, the contiguous zone, the exclusive economic zone and the continental shelf of an island are determined in accordance with the provisions of this Convention applicable to other land territory.
3. Rocks which cannot sustain human habitation or economic life of their own shall have no exclusive economic zone or continental shelf.

Three core issues remain in the case of South China Sea islands – the sovereignty of islands, the islands' granted maritime zones, and the delimitation of EEZs and continental shelves. First, with regard to sovereignty, each claimant state must realize that its claim may not ultimately or completely prevail if the dispute were to be referred to arbitration. Thus, and because of widespread distrust of Western-dominated international law, some claimants may prefer the status quo, seek a military solution, or attempt to resolve the dispute through bilateral or multilateral negotiations. It is highly unlikely that they would be willing to risk all in a third-party tribunal ruling that may create winners and losers.

The second issue relates to the maritime zones granted to the islands or other features in the South China Sea. Applying Article 121(3) to the South China Sea islands sounds extremely difficult. In regard to the Spratly features, it seems that none of the features can at present be said to have been proven capable of sustaining by themselves human habitation or economic life. It thus seems quite likely that, if some of the claimant states should succeed in their quest for sovereignty, they would gain little from the victory in terms of recognized maritime zones. Elferink elaborates two scenarios.[38] If the islands in the South China Sea are excluded in establishing the extent of the EEZs, there remains a considerable area of high seas in the central part of the South China Sea.[39] It seems likely that at least part of this area might be claimed as part of the legal continental shelf of the mainland coasts under Article 76 of UNCLOS.[40] If all the islands under consideration in the present analysis were to generate an EEZ, it would appear that no areas of high seas would be left in the South China Sea. Moreover, the EEZs of the islands would, to a considerable extent, overlap with the EEZs of the mainland coasts surrounding the South China Sea. The fact that all the coastal states of the South China Sea, except Indonesia, claim one or more of the Spratly Islands makes this the most complex dispute in terms of territorial sovereignty and claims to maritime zones.

Beckman argues that all the parties other than China would not apply the regime of islands to their occupied features in the Spratlys.[41] This assumption is based on the text of the Joint Submission of Malaysia and Viet Nam,[42] and the Submission of Viet Nam. In his paper, Beckman argues that "The submissions were also significant because Malaysia and Viet Nam claimed an EEZ only from the baselines along their mainland. They did not claim an EEZ from any of the islands they claimed in the Spratly Islands."[43] In the author's view this is only a scholarly assumption, and does not necessarily represent the official positions of these states. It seems that none of the claimant parties have made it clear whether they would apply the regime of islands to their occupied features. At least some of the islands in the South China Sea, which are larger and able to sustain by themselves human habitation and economic life, are entitled to claim an EEZ and continental shelf; for example, the Itu Aba (Taiping Dao). Other insular formations can almost certainly be considered as rocks or other features that are not entitled to claim an EEZ and continental shelf by themselves, as provided by Article 121(3) of UNCLOS.

The third issue is related to the maritime delimitation of EEZs and continental shelves. The parts of the maritime zones of the islands that do not overlap with those of the mainland coasts cannot be the subject of delimitation. In areas where the EEZs and continental shelves of the islands overlap with those of the mainland coasts, there is on the other hand a need for delimitation. Elferink claims that delimitation between these zones of the islands and the mainland coasts should, in any case, not result in a boundary that coincides with the 200-nautical-mile limit of the mainland coast, leaving the islands only the remaining maritime areas.[44] In other words, in the situation of maritime delimitation between the mainland coast and an island, it would not be fair for an island to enjoy only the maritime zones left after the full maritime zone of 200 nautical miles had been given to the mainland coast. International law (that is, state practice and international jurisprudence) is clear that, where a maritime space is to be delimited between a mainland and an island, the island is unlikely to receive full effect; the smaller and more insignificant the island, the less that effect will be – the treatment of the Channel Islands and St. Pierre et Miquelon are pertinent examples.

If it is possible to claim a continental shelf beyond 200 nautical miles under Article 76 of UNCLOS, a number of complications would arise. The rules of procedure of the United Nations Commission on the Limits of the Continental Shelf (CLCS) seem to exclude any submission from being considered without the prior consent of all states involved in the disputes concerning the South China Sea. The existence of a continental shelf beyond 200 nautical miles would not lead to substantially different outcomes of maritime delimitation between the islands and the mainland coasts. However, there could be a divergence between the EEZ and continental shelf boundaries in certain areas, implying that one state may have jurisdiction over the water column (EEZ) and another state may have jurisdiction over the seabed and its subsoil (continental shelf).

Post-2009 development of the South China Sea dispute

In November 2002, China and the ten members of the Association of Southeast Asian Nations (ASEAN) adopted a Declaration on the Conduct of Parties in the South China Sea (DOC), laying a political foundation for possible future commercial cooperation between China and ASEAN countries, as well as for long-term peace and stability in the region. Though the DOC has been criticized for a number of weaknesses – it is neither a binding treaty nor a formal code of conduct – the signing of this document helped keep the South China Sea quiet for a couple of years, at least before 2009.

The year 2009 saw several major developments that stirred up controversy in the South China Sea all over again, and highlighted the difficulties of maintaining stability in the region. In mid-February, the Philippines Congress passed a territorial Sea Baseline Bill, laying claim to Scarborough Shoal (sovereignty of which is also claimed by China) and a number of islands in the South China Sea. Another event was the clash on March 8 between Chinese vessels and the US ocean surveillance ship *Impeccable* in China's EEZ.[45] On May 6, 2009, Malaysia and Vietnam lodged a joint submission with the United Nations CLCS. Vietnam also lodged a separate submission in relation to the northwestern part of the central South China Sea. These extended continental shelf submissions have served to highlight existing disputes and appear likely to add an extra dimension to them. Indeed, there are already indications that the tension is being heightened.

The year 2010 witnessed the escalation of the controversy in the South China Sea, with an increasing US presence in the region, and a series of Sino-American spats over the South China Sea. In March, as first reported by Japanese media and then by US media, Chinese officials told two visiting senior Obama administration officials that China would not tolerate any interference in the South China Sea, now part of China's "core interest" of sovereignty. In July, US Secretary of State Hillary Clinton made a statement at the tenth ASEAN Regional Forum (ARF) that the disputes over the highly sensitive South China Sea were a "leading diplomatic priority" and now "pivotal to regional security."[46] This backdrop certainly contributed to increasing concerns in Beijing, which saw Clinton's statement as a signal that the United States would change its neutral position on the South China Sea dispute and back other claimant states, especially Vietnam.

The tension in the South China Sea continued to escalate in 2011. In May, Vietnam accused China of cutting the exploration cables of an oil survey ship. In June it claimed a Chinese fishing boat had "intentionally rammed" the exploration cables of another of its boats. Yet China insisted that in the incident its fishing boats were chased away by armed Vietnamese ships. According to China's foreign affairs spokesman, the fishing net of one of the Chinese boats had become entangled with the cables of a Vietnamese oil-exploration vessel, which was operating in the waters claimed by China, and was dragged for more than an hour before it was cut free. China accused Vietnam of "gravely violating" its sovereignty and warned it to stop "all invasive activities." In June, Vietnam held live-firing exercises in the South China Sea amid high tensions with China over disputed waters. Chinese state media denounced the exercises as a military show of force to defy Beijing.

Standoffs also took place in 2011 between Chinese and Philippine vessels. In March, two Chinese maritime surveillance ships reportedly ordered a Philippine survey ship away from an area called Reed Bank. As argued by China, the Philippine survey ship was in China's jurisdictional waters. The Philippines later sent in military aircraft.[47] Philippine president Benigno Aquino's office said on June 13, 2011, that it was renaming the South China Sea as the "West Philippine Sea," as tensions with Beijing mounted over the disputed area. Starting from May 2011 the Philippines Navy removed foreign marker posts that were placed on reefs and banks that are part of the much-disputed Spratly group of islands. The tension between China and the Philippines over Scarborough Shoal, which started on April 10, 2012, again proves the difficulty of maritime dispute management in this region.[48]

Prospects for dispute settlement among the claimant states

The disputes and conflicts contained in the South China Sea cover almost every aspect of UNCLOS – for example, maritime delimitation, historical title, territorial sovereignty, use of force, military activities, fishing, marine scientific research, freedom of navigation, marine environment protection, and deep seabed mining. The South China Sea dispute involves a rising maritime power like China, archipelago states like Indonesia and the Philippines, strait states like Malaysia and Indonesia, and user states like the United States, Japan, and others, reflecting the many dimensions of the users of UNCLOS. Approaches to settlement vary according to the nature of these disputes. For the purpose of this chapter, the following discussion on dispute settlement will focus only on the claimant states.

Bilateral efforts

To manage their disputes, China and Vietnam have formalized a highly structured and extensive mechanism of talks and discussions. From top to bottom, the system consists of four tiers: high-level talks between presidents, prime ministers, and secretaries-general of the communist parties of China and Vietnam; foreign minister-level talks; government-level talks involving deputy or vice-ministers; and expert-level talks.[49] While each tier has its unique function in bilateral dispute management, every tier contributes to the success of the entire system.

During the exchange visit by China's then party secretary-general Jiang Zemin to Vietnam in November 1994, the two leaders signed a communiqué in which the two sides "reaffirmed" that they would "persist" in peaceful negotiations to solve their boundary and territorial issues, and that, pending the settlement of the territorial disputes, they would refrain from taking actions that would "complicate or enlarge the disputes" and would also refrain from using, or threatening to use, force.[50]

The most recent exchange visits took place in 2011, when Vietnam's party Secretary-General Nguyen Phu Trong visited Beijing in October and China's Vice-President Xi Jinping visited Vietnam in December. The key outcome of the first visit was the signing of a six-point agreement on the guiding principles for negotiation of sea-related issues between the two countries. The countries also signed a joint statement during the summit, in which both sides expressed their "political will and determination to settle disputes through friendly negotiation and talks in order to maintain peace and stability" in the South China Sea.[51]

Although bilateral efforts have helped achieve progress in dispute resolution, as exemplified by the delimitation agreement in 2000 and the guiding principles in 2011, challenges remain. Little progress has been achieved with regard to the competing sovereignty claims to the Paracels and Spratlys, as well as the overlapping claims to waters and continental shelf areas. Although expert-level talks have been initiated, the two parties have yet to agree on which disputes to include on the agenda. Vietnam has been pushing for the Paracel Islands to be included as an agenda item alongside the Spratlys, whereas China wants to discuss only the latter.

After the Mischief Reef incident in 1995,[52] China and the Philippines decided to repair their bilateral relations. Between 1996 and 2000, the two countries conducted low-key but frequent high-level contacts and official visits, including President Joseph Estrada's state visit to Beijing in May 2000. During his visit, the two countries signed the Joint Statement on the Framework of Bilateral Cooperation in the 21st Century, which laid down the strategic direction for bilateral cooperation in defense, trade and investment, science and technology, agriculture, education and culture, the judiciary, and other areas. The visit normalized bilateral diplomatic relations between the two countries.[53]

In September 2004, China and the Philippines (and, later, Vietnam) signed an agreement called Joint Marine Seismic Undertaking (JMSU) in the disputed waters of the South China Sea. In 2005 the three countries conducted their first joint marine seismic survey of the South China Sea, a milestone in joint development in the disputed areas of the South China Sea.[54] This agreement was terminated in 2008 when the Philippines pulled out under domestic political pressures.

At the seventeenth Foreign Ministry Consultations held in Beijing on January 15, 2012 both China and the Philippines agreed to implement the consensus reached at the highest level during the state visit of President Benigno Aquino III to China, and to promote comprehensive cooperation in the areas of energy and maritime cooperation, among others.[55]

China and Malaysia signed the Joint Declaration of Future Bilateral Cooperation Framework in 1999, which states that "both sides should maintain the peace and stability of the South China Sea, and resolve disputes through friendly bilateral consultations under the International Law and 1982 UNCLOS."[56] On December 15, 2005, Premier Wen Jiabao and Prime Minister Abdullah Badawi signed the Joint Communiqué between the People's Republic of China and Malaysia, stating that, together with other ASEAN countries, both sides will follow the DOC in order to maintain the peace and stability of the South China Sea. Both sides welcomed concrete cooperation in disputed waters of the South China Sea.[57] In 2011, several Malaysian officials proposed joint development at multilateral meetings or other diplomatic events. Kohilan, the deputy minister of foreign affairs, indicated in April 2011 that the dispute in the South China Sea should be resolved bilaterally at the table, in the spirit of the DOC and with mutual trust. He also mentioned that joint development will be an ad hoc solution to all claimants with overlapping claims.[58] At the Shangri-la Dialogue in June 2011, the defense minister, Hamidi, stated a much clearer blueprint for joint development, pointing out that Malaysia plans to establish an institution with members from all claimant states negotiating economic activities in this region, and that hopefully all nations involved in the dispute can share the abundant natural resources.[59]

Since the early 1990s, Brunei has supported multilateral efforts to resolve the dispute; Sultan Bolkiah has referred to the November 2002 ASEAN–China Declaration on the Conduct of Parties in the South China Sea as "a big step forward" in managing the situation. When he met Chinese President Hu Jintao during a visit to Beijing in September 2004, the two leaders declared that ASEAN and China should move toward a formal code of conduct for the South China Sea. During his visit to Brunei in April, President Hu was reported by the *China Daily* as stating that priority should be given to the joint development of resources "on the basis of mutual respect, equality and mutual benefit and in an open and flexible manner." In addition, China and Brunei have been discussing projects on joint oil exploration in the South China Sea since 2010. In 2011, during his visit to Brunei, Premier Wen Jiabao held bilateral talks with the sultan. The two sides signed an agreement on energy cooperation, including cooperation on offshore oil and natural gas exploration.[60]

Role of a third-party forum under UNCLOS

Except for Cambodia, the coastal states of the South China Sea – China (including Taiwan), Vietnam, the Philippines, Malaysia, Indonesia, Thailand, Singapore, and Brunei – have all ratified UNCLOS. UNCLOS provides an integrated legal framework on which to build sound and effective regulations for the various uses of the ocean.[61] It does not specify in detail when and how fishers can harvest living resources in the EEZs of coastal states or what the terms of leases for deep seabed mining would be. What it does do, however, is to create (sometimes contentious) procedures for arriving at collective decisions about such matters. It is the principal legal instrument providing a framework for the public order of the oceans and seas.[62]

None of the South China Sea claimant states have made a declaration under Article 287 choosing a forum for compulsory settlement procedures. This means, according to Annex VII, that any disputes occurring among these states (assuming none of them makes a declaration under Article 298 in the event of an incident) would be brought before the arbitration tribunal, unless the states involved make a declaration on the choice of forums in the future. While China is the only state that has made a declaration under Article 298 excluding disputes from compulsory settlement procedures, Malaysia, the Philippines, and Vietnam made separate declarations when ratifying UNCLOS. Worth mentioning is that the Philippines' declaration[63] encountered objection from Australia, Belarus, and Russia. The objection mainly focused on three aspects. First, the mentioned states considered that the statement made by the Philippines upon signature, and then confirmed upon ratification of UNCLOS, contains in essence reservations and exceptions to the convention, which is prohibited under Article 309.[64] Second, the discrepancy between the Philippine statement and the convention can be seen, *inter alia*, from the affirmation by the Philippines that "The concept of archipelagic waters is similar to the concept of internal waters under the Constitution of the Philippines, and removes straits connecting these waters with the economic zone or high sea from the rights of foreign vessels to transit passage for international navigation."[65] Moreover, the statement emphasizes more than once that, despite its ratification of the convention, the Philippines will continue to be guided in matters relating to the sea not by the convention and the obligations under it, but by its domestic law and by agreements already concluded that are not in line with the convention. Thus, according to these countries, the Philippines

> not only is evading the harmonization of its legislation with the Convention but also is refusing to fulfill one of its most fundamental obligations under the Convention namely, to respect the régime of archipelagic waters, which provides that foreign ships enjoy the right of archipelagic passage through, and foreign aircraft the right of over flight over, such waters.[66]

As discussed earlier, UNCLOS is not intended to address disputes over sovereignty. Under Article 298 of Part XV, states may declare that they do not accept third-party settlement for disputes concerning the interpretation or application of articles concerning the delimitation of the territorial sea, the EEZ, the continental shelf, or those involving historic bays or historic title. However, such disputes may be submitted to conciliation if one party so wishes, except for those disputes involving the concurrent consideration of any unsettled dispute concerning sovereignty or other rights over territory. China has made a declaration excluding all disputes listed in Article 298. Hence, any disputes in the South China Sea concurrently involving a dispute concerning sovereignty or other rights over territory appear to be excluded from the reach of the compulsory dispute settlement provisions of the convention.

The South China Sea dispute is complex; settlement is challenging. Can the disputes settlement regime under Part XV of UNCLOS play a critical role in this game? The regime of islands is the core issue in the various disputes. Klein argues that third-party settlement forums still have a role to play in disputes related to the regime of islands.[67] To the extent that the status of islands is part of the overall settlement of territorial seas, EEZs, and/or continental shelf boundaries, disputes over the qualification of certain landforms as islands will be subject to the same procedures as specified in Article 298(1)(a). Article 298 does not prima facie exclude disputes over the interpretation or application of Article 121 from compulsory procedures entailing a binding decision, if a state has otherwise so elected.[68] A state may try to raise the specific question of whether a particular feature is a rock or an island under Article 121 without asking a tribunal or court to be involved in the actual maritime delimitation. Such a decision could then be used by a state in negotiations over the boundary.

The desire to avoid compulsory procedures entailing binding decisions is obviously understandable. The conciliation process in Article 298(1)(a) returns states to negotiation. The inclusion of an optional exception for disputes relating to Articles 15, 74, 83, and historic bays and titles thus retains the emphasis on state decision-making and agreement. However, the legal regimes for straight baselines and for islands do require compulsory dispute settlement. Article 7 sets out the criteria for drawing straight baselines. While some external review is possible under Article 16 in the process of registering and publicizing baselines used for maritime delimitation (or perhaps through the work of CLCS), states could well interpret the language of UNCLOS somewhat loosely in order to augment their exclusive maritime space. Where this action impacts on areas that would otherwise constitute high seas, all states have an interest in ensuring that legal standards are maintained and upheld. Mandatory jurisdiction plays an essential role in this regard. Articles 7 and 121 should color the characterization of a dispute that may otherwise be excluded from mandatory jurisdiction by means of another exception or limitation.[69]

Confidence-building from DOC to COC

China and ASEAN signed the Declaration on the Conduct of Parties in the South China Sea (DOC) in 2002, confirming the intention to promote pragmatic cooperation and, ultimately, to reach a code of conduct in the South China Sea. The establishment of a Code of Conduct (COC) with legal binding force is called for.

At present, it is of equal importance to implement the DOC. The year 2011, particularly, witnessed positive progress and significant achievement in the implementation of the DOC. In July, China and the ASEAN countries adopted the Guidelines for the Implementation of the DOC, which paved the way for advancing practical cooperation in the South China Sea. In the Joint Statement of the fourteenth ASEAN–China Summit to Commemorate the 20th Anniversary of Dialogue Relations, held in Bali in November 2011, China reiterated its efforts to work together with ASEAN countries toward the eventual adoption, on the basis of consensus, of a code of conduct in the South China Sea, so as to further contribute to peace, security, stability, and cooperation in the region.[70]

At the moment, China is stepping up coordination with ASEAN countries to implement a number of projects within the framework of the DOC. Premier Wen Jiabao made a very important statement at the fourteenth China–ASEAN Summit in November 2011,[71] stating that China will establish a three-billion-yuan China–ASEAN maritime cooperation fund. The cooperation may start with marine research, environmental protection, connectivity, navigation safety, search and rescue, and the combating of transnational crimes, gradually expanding into other fields, with the goal of developing multi-tiered and all-round maritime cooperation between China and ASEAN. China also proposes that the two sides set up a mechanism to study the initiative and work out a plan for cooperation. In November 2011, the Workshop on the Regional Oceanography of the South China Sea was held in Qingdao, as the first cooperation project of all parties under the framework of the DOC. The Seminar on "Implementing DOC: Maintaining Freedom and Safety of Navigation in the South China Sea" was held in the same month, representing another major step forward in cooperation under the DOC.

Conclusion

The SFPT has profound implications for current maritime disputes in the South China Sea. The South China Sea has become and will continue to be a hot spot in the international security spectrum in the twenty-first century. Since 2009 these troubled waters have been stirred up again after being calm since 2002, when the DOC was signed. It remains an open question whether the submission on the outer limits of the continental shelf to CLCS has helped clarify claims or if it has made the situation even worse; in other words, whether this new dimension of the disputes represents progress or a setback to regional cooperation in the South China Sea.

Prospects for dispute management in the South China Sea vary according to the nature of the disputes. Among the claimant states, UNCLOS should be used as a legal framework for dispute settlement. Bilateral negotiations should be held between claimant states either in institutionalized format or through less formal arrangement, but consensus has yet to be reached on this. Third-party forums under UNCLOS should have a certain role in the settlement process. The efforts of China and ASEAN on developing a code of conduct in the South China Sea bring hope for easing the current tension. In the meantime, it is of equal importance to implement the cooperation projects based on the Guidelines for the Implementation of the DOC.

Notes

1 UNCLOS, Article 122.
2 J.R.V. Prescott, *The Maritime Political Boundaries of the World* (London: Methuen, 1985), p. 209.
3 Hungdah Chiu, "South China Sea Islands: Implications for Delimitation of the Seabed and Future Shipping Routes," *China Quarterly* 72 (1977): 756.
4 Zou Keyuan, *Law of the Sea in East Asia: Issues and Prospects* (Leiden: Martinus Nijhoff, 2005), p. 47.
5 For the purpose of this chapter, China refers to the People's Republic of China (PRC). Taiwan, which China regards as part of its territory, refers to the Republic of China (ROC) before 1949, when the Kuomintang left the Chinese mainland for Taiwan Island.
6 Christopher C. Joyner, "The Spratly Islands Dispute in the South China Sea: Problems, Policies, and Prospects for Diplomatic Accommodation" (www.southchinasea.org/docs/Joyner,%20Spratly%20Islands%20Dispute.pdf [accessed May 5, 2012]).
7 See Cheng-yi Lin, "Taiwan's South China Sea Policy," *Asian Survey* 37 (1997): 324.
8 Mark J. Valencia, Jon Van Dyke and Noel Ludwig, *Sharing the Resources of the South China Sea* (The Hague: Kluwer Law International, 1997), p. 7.
9 Scott Snyder, *The South China Sea Disputes: Prospects for Preventive Diplomacy, A Special Report of the United States Institute of Peace* (Washington, DC: United States Institute of Peace, 1996), p. 5.
10 Article 2 of the SFPT.
11 Neither the ROC nor the PRC was invited to the San Francisco Peace Conference; neither were parties to the SFPT. The ROC concluded a separate Treaty of Peace with Japan in 1952.
12 FO 371/92583, PRO, cited in Kimie Hara, "The Spratlys and the Paracels: The South China Sea Dispute," in Kimie Hara, *Cold War Frontiers in the Asia-Pacific: Divided Territories in the San Francisco System* (Abingdon: Routledge, 2007), p. 154.
13 Ibid.; see also Wu Shicun, *Origin and Development of Spratly Disputes* (Beijing: China Economic Publishing, 2009).
14 Text of Gromyko's Statement on the Peace Treaty, *New York Times*, September 9, 1951, p. 26.
15 Article 2 of the Treaty of Taipei.
16 Hara, *Cold War Frontiers*, p. 155; Wu, *Origin and Development of Spratly Disputes*.
17 John K.T. Chao, "South China Sea: Boundary Problems relating to the Nansha and Hsisha Islands," *Chinese Yearbook of International Law and Affairs 1991*, (Baltimore, MD: Chinese Society of International Law – Chinese (Taiwan) Branch of International Law Association), p. 88.
18 Marwyn S. Samuels, *Contest for the South China Sea* (New York: Methuen, 1982; reprinted by Routledge, 2005), p. 80.
19 Ibid., p. 80.
20 *Cairo Communiqué, December 1, 1943.*
21 Lee. G. Cordner, "The Spratly Islands Dispute and the Law of the Sea," *Ocean Development and International Law* 25, no. 1 (1994): 69.
22 *The 1975 White Paper of Vietnam 1–2.*
23 *The 1975 White Paper of Vietnam 3*, p. 16.
24 Hara, *Cold War Frontiers*, p. 156.
25 Hungdah Chiu and Choon-ho Park, "Legal Status of the Paracel and Spratly Islands," *Ocean Development and International Law Journal* 3, no. 1 (1975): 14.
26 Japan recognized the PRC and terminated official diplomatic relations with the ROC.
27 Chao, "South China Sea," p. 88.
28 Wu, *Origin and Development of Spratly Disputes*, p. 45.
29 See, generally, Haydee B. Yoroc, "The Philippine Claim to the Spratly Islands

Group," *Philippine Law Journal* 42 (1983): 58; Mark Valencia, "Spratly Solution, Still at Sea," *The Pacific Review* 6, no. 2 (1993): 155–70.

30 R. Haller-Trost, "International Law and the History of the Claims to the Spratly Islands," paper presented at South China Sea conference, American Enterprise Institute, September 7–9, 1994, pp. 21–2; Cordner, "The Spratly Islands Dispute and the Law of the Sea," p. 66.

31 Jon M. Van Dyke and Dale L. Bennett, "Islands and the Delimitation of Ocean Space in the South China Sea," *Ocean Yearbook* 10 (1993): 74; Cordner, "The Spratly Islands Dispute and the Law of the Sea," p. 66.

32 Valencia *et al.*, *Sharing the Resources of the South China Sea*, p. 34.

33 Van Dyke and Bennett, "Islands and the Delimitation of Ocean Space," p. 75.

34 Ibid., p. 58.

35 RG59, Records of Harley A. Notter, 1939–45; quoted in Kimie Hara, "The Spratlys and the Paracels: The South China Sea Dispute," in Hara, *Cold War Frontiers*, p. 146.

36 Microfilm T1221, roll 5, NA, cited in Hara, *Cold War Frontiers*, p. 147.

37 UN Doc. A/CONF.62/122, (1982), United Nations, Official Text of UNCLOS with Annexes and Index.

38 Ibid., p. 171.

39 See Valencia *et al.*, *Sharing the Resources of the South China Sea*, p. 264, Plate 11, which indicates the 200-nautical-mile limit in the South China Sea without taking into account the Paracel Islands, the Spratly Islands, and Scarborough Reef; see also Alex G. Oude Elferink, "The Islands in the South China Sea: How Does Their Presence Limit the Extent of the High Seas and the Area and the Maritime Zones of the Mainland Coasts?" *Ocean Development & International Law* 32 (2001): 171.

40 Article 76(1) of UNCLOS reads:

> The continental shelf of a coastal State comprises the seabed and subsoil of the submarine areas that extend beyond its territorial sea throughout the natural prolongation of its land territory to the outer edge of the continental margin, or to a distance of 200 nautical miles from the baselines from which the breadth of the territorial sea is measured where the outer edge of the continental margin does not extend up to that distance.

41 Robert Beckman, "The South China Sea Dispute: An International Lawyer's View," paper presented at CIL Conference on Joint Development and the South China Sea, June 16–17, 2011, Singapore.

42 On May 6, 2009, Malaysia and the Socialist Republic of Viet Nam submitted jointly to the CLCS, in accordance with Article 76, paragraph 8, of UNCLOS, information on the limits of the continental shelf beyond 200 nautical miles from the baselines from which the breadth of the territorial sea is measured in respect of the southern part of the South China Sea.

43 Robert Beckman and Tara Davenport, "Joint Development of Hydrocarbon Resources in the Spratly Islands: International Legal Framework," paper presented at the CIL International Conference on Joint Development and the South China Sea, June 16–17, 2011, Singapore.

44 Elferink, "The Islands in the South China Sea," p. 182. This conclusion may be somewhat surprising in view of the considerable number of articles arguing against such an outcome. A partial explanation may be that certain dicta and precedents of the case law have been transposed to the South China Sea without the implications being considered of a different factual background.

45 USNS *Impeccable* (T-AGOS-23) is an Impeccable-class ocean surveillance ship acquired by the US Navy in 2001 and assigned to Military Sealift Command's Special Missions Program. On March 5, 2009, the *Impeccable* was in the South China Sea monitoring submarine activity when it was approached by a People's Liberation Army Navy (PLAN) frigate, which crossed its bow at a range of approximately 100 yards

without first making contact. This was followed less than two hours later by a Chinese Y-12 aircraft conducting eleven flyovers of the *Impeccable* at an altitude of 600 feet (180 m) and a range from 100–300 feet (30–90 m). The frigate then crossed *Impeccable*'s bow again, this time at a range of approximately 400–500 yards. China and the United States both maintain the rightfulness of their actions based on competing interpretations of UNCLOS. For more on the interpretation of freedom of navigation, read Nong Hong, "Charting a Maritime Security Cooperation Mechanism in the Indian Ocean: Sharing Responsibilities among Littoral States and User States," *Strategic Analysis* 36, no. 3 (2012): 400–12.

46 Ernest Z. Bower, "Hillary Clinton: A Secretary of State Fluent in ASEAN," July 20, 2010, CSIS (http://csis.org/publication/hillary-clinton-secretary-state-fluent-asean [accessed September 1, 2011]).

47 "An Encounter in Reed Bank," *Manila Times* (www.manilatimes.net/opinion/philippines-and-china-%E2%80%93-an-encounter-in-reed-bank [accessed April 5, 2013]).

48 For more information on the Scarborough Shoal tension in 2012, read Shicun Wu, "The Huangyan Island Standoff: A Review of the Claims and the Prospects for the Future," *China–US Focus*, May 5, 2012 (www.chinausfocus.com/peace-security/the-huangyan-island-standoff-a-review-of-the-claims-and-the-prospects-for-the-future [accessed April 5, 2013]).

49 Ramses Amer and Nguyen Hong Thao, "Vietnam's Border Disputes: Assessing the Impact on Its Regional Integration," in *Vietnam's New Order: International Perspectives on the State and Reform in Vietnam*, edited by Stéphanie Balme and Mark Sidel (Basingstoke and New York: Palgrave Macmillan, 2007), pp. 74–6.

50 Ibid.

51 Li Jianwei and Ramses Amer, "Recent Practices in Dispute Management in the South China Sea," in *Maritime Energy Resources in Asia: Legal Regimes and Cooperation*, edited by Clive Schofield, Special Report No. 37, pp. 79–113 (February 2012) (Seattle: National Bureau of Asian Research), p. 101.

52 The Mischief Reef (Meiji Jiao) incident refers to a political confrontation that took place between China and the Philippines in 1995. The Mischief Reef incident marked the first time China and the Philippines engaged in a military confrontation.

53 Renato Cruz De Castro, "The US–Philippine Alliance: An Evolving Hedge against an Emerging China Challenge," *Contemporary Southeast Asia* 31, no. 3 (December 2009): 399–423.

54 Ibid.

55 Department of Foreign Affairs of Republic of the Philippines 2012.

56 CNMFA, The Joint Communiqué of People's Republic of China and Malaysia, 2005 (www.fmprc.gov.cn/chn/pds/ziliao/zt/ywzt/2005year/wjbzlfw/t226666.htm [accessed January 29, 2013]).

57 Ibid.

58 "Parliament: Malaysia Favours Peaceful Resolution to Maritime Boundary Dispute," *Bernama*, April 6, 2011 (http://maritime.bernama.com/news.php?id= 576829&lang=en [accessed March 1, 2012]).

59 "Malaysia Proposes Sharing Resources in the South China Sea," *Qianfeng Bao*, June 6, 2011.

60 Embassy of the People's Republic of China in Negara Brunei Darussalam (http://bn.china-embassy.org/chn/sgxw/t880975.htm [accessed January 29, 2012]).

61 Oran Young, "Commentary on Shirley V. Scott, 'The LOS Convention as a Constitutional Regime for the Ocean,'" in *Stability and Change in the Law of the Sea: The Role of the LOS Convention*, edited by Alex G. Oude Elferink (Leiden: Martinus Nijhoff Publishers, 2004), p. 42.

62 Rainer Lagoni, "Commentary," in *Stability and Change in the Law of the Sea: The Role of the LOS Convention*, edited by Alex G. Oude Elferink (Leiden: Martinus Nijhoff Publishers, 2004), p. 51.

63 For the declaration of the Philippines, see www.un.org/Depts/los/convention_agree-ments/convention_declarations.htm#Philippines%20Understanding%20made%20 upon%20signature%20(10%20December%201982)%20and%20confirmed%20 upon%20ratification (accessed April 5, 2013).

64 Article 309 (Reservations and Exceptions) provides: "No reservations or exceptions may be made to this Convention unless expressly permitted by other articles of this Convention."

65 Ibid.

66 Ibid.

67 Natalie Klein, *Dispute Settlement in the UN Convention on the Law of the Sea* (Cambridge: Cambridge University Press, 2005), p. 276.

68 Ibid.

69 Klein, *Dispute Settlement*, p. 279.

70 Full text of Premier Wen's statement at the fourteenth China–ASEAN Summit is at http://english.gov.cn/2011-11/18/content_1997716.htm (accessed May 5, 2012).

71 Ibid.

5 The San Francisco Peace Treaty and "Korea"

Dong-Choon Kim

Prologue

The San Francisco Peace Treaty (SFPT) was signed by the forty-eight Allied nations and Japan in the September 1951 conference. SFPT was an international agreement that structurally determined the post-war political order in the Asia-Pacific, the most crucial part of which was Japan's status in the region after World War II:

> Whereas the Allied Powers and Japan are resolved that henceforth their relations shall be those of nations which, as sovereign equals, cooperate in friendly association to promote their common welfare and to maintain international peace and security, and are therefore desirous of concluding a Treaty of Peace which will settle questions still outstanding as a result of the existence of a state of war between them;
>
> *Article 8*(a) Japan will recognize the full force of all treaties now or hereafter concluded by the Allied Powers for terminating the state of war initiated on 1 September 1939, as well as any other arrangements by the Allied Powers for or in connection with the restoration of peace.

Though it officially proclaimed the "end of war" between Japan and the Allied nations, the treaty laid the foundation for the regional defense structure of another conflict: the Cold War. The SFPT granted the United States the right to keep its armed forces and military bases in Japan, which in turn promised to provide facilities and services in support of any US military action in the Far East. In exchange for Japan's unilateral dependency on US military protection, it was absolved of the need to bear any moral responsibility for its wartime actions or to provide material remuneration to its former colonies.

It was quite ironic that the treaty was signed when another full-fledged war, in Korea, had just broken out. One crucial piece of the background of this war was the attempt to create a unified post-colonial nation-state, a process that gained momentum as the war continued.[1] Its binding force as a "peace treaty" then proved quite dubious when some significant stakeholders in the Asia-Pacific order – Korea and China – were left out of the treaty. While it denied a role to

Japan's former colonies, Article 1(b) recognized post-war Japan as enjoying "full sovereignty." As a "system" for confronting the new Cold War, it seemed that SFPT sanctioned the past wrongdoings of Japanese imperialist power by alienating its past victims, Korea and China. Under the slogan of "ending the war" between the Allied Forces and Japan, the problem of how SFPT would liquidate Japanese colonialism and make sustainable peace between Japan and its other neighbors remained unresolved. Could peace between Japan and the Allied nations guarantee peaceful relations between Japan and its former colonies who had suffered most from Japanese occupation? The answer may be found in the enduring conflicts between them.

These defects of SFPT arose as it was geared mainly toward the interests of the United States, which wanted to establish a new foothold in East Asia by reviving the Japanese economy and bilateral alliances with other East Asian countries. The politico-ideological cause of these limitations may stem from the fact that the main actors of the treaty – the United States, the United Kingdom, and Japan – were devoid of the "problematic of colonialism" like their predecessors at the Treaty of Versailles in 1919. Since then, Western powers had used their language of "war" in quite a restricted sense when confronting claims to self-determination and sovereignty of the colonies. The term "war" in SFPT excluded the military operations waged by Japan to conquer and suppress its colonial peoples on the Korean Peninsula and in Manchuria before 1939. This is especially clear in the case of the United Kingdom, which opposed the United States' plan to include the Republic of Korea (ROK) as a member of the treaty while retaining its own colonies at the time of signing the SFPT. So the insensitivity toward the issue of colonialism is reflected in the concrete terms and content of the articles of SFPT by which the reconfiguration of post-World War II status of Japan and its relations with neighboring countries was anticipated.

We may attribute Korea's exclusion from SFPT to the inability of Koreans to drive out Japanese colonialism on their own, which resulted in the divided military occupation of the peninsula by the United States and the Soviet Union. In contrast to Europe, where Germany was divided as a punishment for its past war crimes, in the Asia-Pacific, Korea was divided instead of Japan. The division of Korea also prevented it from issuing one powerful voice in the negotiation process for the treaty.

As the Korean War stimulated the prompt signing of SFPT by the United States and Allied Powers, its durability or applicability was affected by the division of Korea. The spirit of SFPT presupposed a "national division" or "state of war" on the Korean Peninsula. The initial shortcomings of SFPT have inhibited the building of a future-oriented regional community in the Asia-Pacific. The United States still deploys its troops in numerous places across this region. As "the San Francisco System" is still a working reality, a way of overcoming it and achieving permanent peace should be sought by examining the very nature and defects of both the treaty and the system from Korea's standpoint.

Korea's exclusion from SFPT and its implications

There are strong connections between SFPT and the United States' post-war policies on Japan, the preservation of the Showa emperor system, and the pretense of prosecuting Japanese war criminals in the International Military Tribunal in the Far East (Tokyo Tribunal). These linkages were transparent for the Koreans and Chinese, who, having suffered the most from Japanese aggression, were eager to remove the colonial past through the Tokyo Tribunal and SFPT. Korea was neither represented by judges in the Tokyo Tribunal, nor invited to join as members of the treaty. Korea's exclusion from the peace conference in September 1951 went hand in hand with Japan's newly recognized status as a sovereign independent country and a base of US-led anti-communist containment policy in East Asia.

Originally, US Secretary of State John Foster Dulles had wanted to invite the ROK to the conference as the legitimate government of Korea, but the United Kingdom and Japan stubbornly refused, because Korea had not been an Allied nation in World War II. The United Kingdom suggested the possible parties of SFPT should be restricted to the "Allied and associated powers and other United Nations with whom Japan provoked the state of war."[2] Japan was at that time afraid of the property claims and voices of one million Japanese-Koreans if Korea participated in the conference. The Korean ambassador to the United States, Yang Yu Chan, defended the right of the ROK to attend.[3] The US ambassador to Korea, John Muccio, also remarked,

> We are strongly of the view the ROK should be included in some capacity among nations participating in the Japanese peace treaty…. Another consideration persuading us toward Korean participation is our feeling that Japanese Korean problems can be better resolved through an international forum than through bilateral negotiations.[4]

Meanwhile, "patriotic" organizations that supported Rhee Syngman organized a mass meeting against the proposed draft of the treaty and demanded that the ROK be allowed to participate. Their appeal fell on deaf ears. Using popular anti-Japanese sentiment for political gain, President Rhee expressed his anger and frustration against the United States, but he could not refuse the United States–Japan contract while the destiny of the ROK was heavily dependent on US military assistance. Before and during the conference, separate talks were conducted between the ROK and Japan, with US mediation. At first, Rhee ordered Ambassador Yang to do his best to enlist the ROK in the conference.

While Dulles took a different position on Korean minorities in Japan from Japan and the United Kingdom, he eventually accepted their argument. In a discussion with Japanese Prime Minister Yoshida Shigeru on this issue, on April 23, 1951, Dulles told Yoshida that he had heard the Japanese government objected to Korea being a signatory to SFPT. Yoshida responded that "the Government would like to send almost all Koreans in Japan to their homes because it had long been concerned by their illegal activities."[5] Dulles stated that he could see the wisdom of "Korean nationals in Japan, mostly Communists … not obtain[ing] the property benefits of the treaty." Furthermore,

> Dulles suggested that many of these Koreans were undesirables, being in many cases from North Korea and constituting a center for communist agitation in Japan. He believed that probably a legitimate Japanese fear of certain of these Koreans was involved in any action taken against them by the Japanese authorities.[6]

The war in Korea, which began on June 25, 1950, transformed the US policy on East Asia by consolidating US–Japan relations, which affirmed the interdependence of Japan and the ROK's security interests. The US State Department sought an immediate, non-punitive peace treaty with Japan, despite Moscow and Peking's obstructionism. The strategic role of Japan in American security interests in the Asia-Pacific was thus enhanced; the ROK in South Korea, as a battlefield of the East Asian anti-communist bloc, was supposed to be a partner of Japan. The Korean War rendered Japan readily available as a vital support area for US military activities in Korea. Following the United States–Japan Mutual Defense Treaty of 1952, the United States–ROK Mutual Defense Treaty took effect in November 1953. In exchange for US protection, the ROK lost the opportunity to be a subject at the international table, where it could have asked for reparations from Japan for wrongs committed during its colonial past.

In historical perspective, the Dulles–Yoshida decision to exclude Korea from the conference repeated the old contract between the United States and Japan, the secret Taft–Katsura Agreement of 1905, following which Korea and the Philippines were colonized. The concept of "peace" referred to in the forum meant first ending the war between the United States and Japan, and second between Japan and the other Allies. American policy-makers sought to establish and maintain an international economic order open to US trade and investment, especially in the industrialized countries of Western Europe and Japan.[7] Reconstruction of the devastated Japanese economy was needed, not only for strengthening it against possible conquest or intimidation by the Soviet Union but for guaranteeing US economic interests. In terms of economic development and market size, Japan's status in American policy considerations was quite different from that of other Asia-Pacific countries. As US policy placed more weight on the national interest of building an anti-communist bloc in the Asia-Pacific, it inevitably gave a privileged position to Japan, which was seen as geopolitically and economically more important than the ROK. Therefore, all the articles of SFPT inevitably show the American consideration of Japanese interests.[8] Despite its self-imposed role of an onlooker, the United States intended to directly influence the relationship between Japan and both Koreas thereafter.

The US decision to exclude Korea from the forum was originally based on an assessment of the capacity of the Korean independence movement under Japanese colonial rule. US officials judged that:

The Japanese Annexation of Korea by treaty in 1910 was recognized by almost all countries, including the U.S., and no general recognition was given any Korean state or government until 1948. Resistance to Japanese rule within Korea was restricted to localized or belief disorders, the people generally accepted the rule of the Japanese Governor-General. The rival Korean nationalist organizations outside Korea … were not given any formal international recognition and appear to have had very little force in the homeland. Only for a time during the World War II, as a consequence of pressures of the Chinese government, did the Korean Provisional Government in China hold the united loyalties of even the Korean forces in China.[9]

Even if grounded in its justification of Korea's past annexation to Japan, this biased assessment, or the American underestimation of the Korean independence movements against Japan, seemed to contribute greatly to its post-World War II policy on Korea.[10]

The ROK's failure to participate in the conference could be explained by the fact that it took place at a time of life-and-death struggle with the Democratic People's Republic of Korea (DPRK) in the north, but is mainly attributable to the non-recognition by the Allied Powers of Korea's provisional government in China during the period of Japanese colonial rule, which allowed Japan to argue that Korea was simply one of its territories. Korea's exclusion reflected its hugely disadvantageous position as a post-colonial country, when we take into consideration Japan's active role in finalizing the treaty.

The Korea-related articles in SFPT

Territorial issues

As another chapter in this collection deals with the territorial issue of Dokdo/Takeshima, I will not mention that here. Instead, I examine the basic logic of the articles of the treaty.

> *Article 2*(a) Japan, recognizing the independence of Korea, renounces all right, title and claim to Korea, including the islands of Quelpart, Port Hamilton and Dagelet.

If Japan renounced its "right" to Korea, was its occupation of Korea from 1910 to 1945 legitimate according to international law? The treaty did not specify to which country Japan renounced its former territories.[11] If a country occupies another country's territory by force, to the extent that any open resistance is crushed and rebellious groups massacred, can that constitute a peaceful relation between the oppressor and the oppressed and can the occupier's "right" to rule the occupied be advocated? This treaty article presupposes that the Japanese occupation of Korea was conducted without violence and that Koreans willingly accepted Japanese rule. In this article, the former colonized people's position was not reflected.

Just after the Japanese surrender, the Korean Peninsula was jointly occupied by the United States and the Soviet Union. But the status of Korea after the Japanese surrender remained unclear: After August 15, 1945, was it still Japanese territory or a territory occupied by Allied Forces?[12] In particular, the United States' ambiguous position on Korea reflected its occupation policy until 1948, when the ROK's sovereign statehood was established following the general election in South Korea and the recognition of its legitimacy at the General Assembly of the United Nations. However, the ROK government was not necessarily entitled to be an entity authorized to ask Japan to return all the territories and properties seized after annexation, because another government (DPRK) was also established on the other side of the 38th parallel, receiving recognition from the USSR and its satellites.

The issue of reparations

The most controversial chapter in the treaty would be the issue of reparations between Japan and other victim countries.

> *Article 14*(a) It is recognized that Japan should pay reparations to the Allied Powers for the damage and suffering caused by it during the war. Nevertheless it is also recognized that the resources of Japan are not presently sufficient, if it is to maintain a viable economy, to make complete reparation for all such damage and suffering and at the same time meet its other obligations.

As stipulated in this article, Japan should pay reparations "only" to the Allied Powers for the damage and suffering caused by it "during the war." So it had no need to pay reparations to Korea for damage and suffering caused by it "before the war." As far as its obligation was restricted to "war-related" damages and suffering, Japan could clear itself from responsibility for suffering caused through its occupation policy over its colonial subjects. Additionally, Article 14 also stated that:

> Japan will promptly enter into negotiations with Allied Powers so desiring, whose present territories were occupied by Japanese forces and damaged by Japan, with a view to assisting to compensate those countries for the cost of repairing the damage done, by making available the services of the Japanese people in production, salvaging and other work for the Allied Powers in question.

In accordance with this agreement, the Philippines and South Vietnam received compensation in 1956 and 1959, respectively. Burma and Indonesia were not original signatories, but they later signed bilateral treaties in accordance with Article 14.

Article 14(b) Except as otherwise provided in the present Treaty, the Allied Powers waive all reparations claims of the Allied Powers, other claims of the Allied Powers and their nationals arising out of any actions taken by Japan and its nationals in the course of the prosecution of the war, and claims of the Allied Powers for direct military costs of occupation.

After SFPT, all lawsuits filed in Japan were either thrown out or left unresolved. The Japanese Supreme Court has regarded SFPT as the legal ground on which to avoid compensating colonialism-related victims.[13] By this article, however, Japan would bear only moral obligation to Korea, which was settled in 1965 by a comprehensive agreement to resolve all past issues. From the standpoint of Japan, all colonialism- and war-related issues were expected to be settled by SFPT; bilateral agreement with concerned countries thereafter would finalize them. But the Korean people, including the victims of Japanese colonialism who had been alienated by the treaty and mutual agreements before 1965, never thought that colonialism-related issues with Japan had been resolved.

Based on the logic of SFPT, Japan also demanded the transfer of its people's assets and property in Korea to Japan. In Article 14, "each of the Allied Powers shall have the right to seize, retain, liquidate or otherwise dispose of all property, rights and interests of 'Japan and Japanese nationals.'" In accordance with Article 14, Allied forces confiscated all assets owned by the Japanese government, firms, organizations, and private citizens, in all colonized or occupied countries except China. (China repossessed all Japanese assets in Manchuria and Inner Mongolia, which included mine works and railway infrastructure.) Consequently, it is considered that Korea was also entitled to the rights provided by Article 21, which stated, "Notwithstanding the provisions of Article 25 of the present Treaty, China shall be entitled to the benefits of Articles 10 and 14(a)2; and Korea to the benefits of Articles 2, 4, 9 and 12 of the present Treaty." In the so-called Rusk documents (the official diplomatic correspondence sent by Dean Rusk, then assistant secretary of state for Far Eastern Affairs, to Yang You Chan) on August 10, 1951, the negotiating position of the United States was that "Japan has no obligation to compensate for damage to private property owned by Koreans that was damaged in Japan during the war."

Japan insisted until the end of 1957 that it had the right to demand compensation for the property in Korea, even though it had acquiesced by signing the treaty to the measures taken by the US military government in Korea, which expropriated all Japanese public and private property in Korea and later transferred them to the ROK. In response to Japan's demand, President Rhee announced that the ROK government was claiming eight billion won for gold and art objects taken from Korea by the Japanese government during the occupation, to compensate for the forced labor imposed on Koreans. Japan's "demand" ignited anti-Japanese sentiment in Korea.[14] But this conflict signified that Korea's problems with Japan, such as offshore fishing rights, the status of Korean residents in Japan, war reparations, and questions of sovereignty over disputed islands, were still pending resolution. When ROK–Japan diplomatic negotiations began after the military coup of 1961, Japan offered fifty million dollars for the cause of "aiding" Korean economic development, an amount hardly equivalent to that owed in reparations for the damages and suffering caused by Japanese colonization.

Japan's basic stance on the issue of reparations for South Korea originated from Article 14, according to which Japan had no need to apologize to or compensate Korea. But with national division and the necessity of economic development, South Korea's military leaders were eager to make up for their illegitimacy with economic growth by any means, which also served to legitimize Japan's non-reparation policy and even removed room for individual victims claiming reparations.

Zainichi Koreans (Korean minorities in Japan)

The status of Korea in the forum that preceded SFPT was directly connected to the status of Zainichi Koreans (Korean minorities in Japan). As the Allied occupation of Japan ended on April 28, 1952, with the treaty entering into force and Japan formally abandoning its territorial claim to the Korean Peninsula, Zainichi Koreans formally lost their Japanese nationality. Before the treaty, in December 1945, the Japanese government had stripped Koreans residing in Japan of their right to vote. In 1947, Koreans residing in Japan became subject to the Alien Registration Ordinance. The basis for this treatment was that Koreans who did not have their *koseki* (family registration) in Japan were not seen as "true" Japanese, even though they were Japanese nationals. When the treaty came into effect on April 28, 1952, the Japanese government unilaterally stripped Korean residents of their Japanese nationality. They did not even give Korean residents the option to choose between Japanese or Korean nationality.

The problem of Zainichi Koreans was the main reason why the Japanese government lobbied to exclude the ROK from the conference. In replying to Dulles during their July 19 meeting, Yang defended the ROK's right to attend the peace conference by explaining that the Japanese government, still smarting over its loss of Korea, was discriminating against the 800,000 Koreans still residing in Japan.[15] To this,

> Dulles suggested that many of these Koreans were undesirables, being in many cases from North Korea and constituting a center for communist agitation in Japan. Dulles believed, therefore, that probably a legitimate Japanese fear of certain of these Koreans was involved in any action taken against them by the Japanese authorities.[16]

Moreover, as it obtained independence from the Allied nations' control, the Japanese government awarded compensation to war veterans and the families of those who died in combat. However, no compensation was awarded to those Korean veterans who had been conscripted into the Japanese military during World War II or to their families. This was on the grounds that they were not

Japanese nationals when the laws were established, even though they had been forced to serve as Japanese soldiers and guards during the war.

In addition, Koreans employed into the Japanese army were given orders by their superiors to abuse captives of the Allied Forces. These Koreans were penalized and executed as war criminals even after they were stripped of their Japanese nationality. The Japanese government and the Japanese Supreme Court rejected Korean protests relating to this unfair treatment, stating that, despite the fact that they were no longer Japanese nationals, those Koreans forced to commit war crimes would be found guilty as "Japanese nationals," and there would be no exemption from punishment.[17]

Even before SFPT, hundreds of thousands of people of Korean descent were excluded from the benefits that other Allied civilians received. Furthermore, the discriminatory mindset shared by US and Japanese leaders had an immediate impact even prior to the signing of SFPT. The Japanese government, either under orders from the Supreme Commander of the Allied Forces (SCAP) or with its approval, issued a number of anti-Korean ordinances, forcing all people of Korean descent to register as "aliens," closing Korean-run schools, and adopting a plan to deport all Koreans.

The lack of protection for Korean nationals allowed the Yoshida government to announce on April 19, 1952, that all former colonial subjects, of whom 90 percent or more were of Korean descent, would lose their Japanese nationality when the treaty came into effect on April 28.[18] Although some Zainichi Koreans volunteered to participate in the Korean War, President Rhee did nothing about the legal disenfranchisement of Koreans in Japan. Like Yoshida, Rhee also feared many of them had been "infected" with communist ideology in Japan.

Rhee's unpreparedness with regards to the treaty had serious defects from today's vantage point. The ROK government restricted the definition of damage brought by colonialism to tangible properties like gold. It did not estimate the unpaid wages of forced labor or place a value on the loss of life and inhumane treatment by Japanese. Furthermore, the ROK government did not claim compensation for forced labor or wartime "military sexual slaves," and never investigated the numerous massacres committed by Japanese troops on the Korean Peninsula and in Manchuria before and after annexation, which constituted the prehistory of the Nanjing massacre. As life-and-death civil war, the Korean War, was being waged at that very time, Koreans had little room to appeal to the United States regarding "past" atrocities or inhumane violence committed by the Japanese during the colonial period. It was the worst time for Koreans to bring their concrete demands to the United States and lobby systematically in the preparation for the treaty.

Even though he proclaimed the "Rhee Line" and arrested Japanese fishermen in Korean waters in response to Japan's "shameless" demand and unwillingness to apologize, Rhee himself manipulated popular anti-Japanese feelings in order to stabilize his regime rather than resolve past wrongs.[19] The United States sought to rearm Japan, but the ROK and other neighboring countries strongly opposed this policy. On July 18, 1951, Yang issued a press statement warning that the Japanese government could not be trusted. For example, on January 12, 1951, upon hearing that the United States was rearming Japan and hoping to send Japanese troops to fight in Korea, Rhee said to the press, "On this occasion I declare to the world that we will fight the Japanese before we expel the Chinese." The US policy confirmed its lack of sensitivity about the Korean fear of possible Japanese invasion and the sense of humiliation that had been created by thirty-five years of colonial rule. Under the DPRK's attack, Rhee could not resist the United States' policy of establishing a regional defense pact that would include Japan. Nevertheless, that Rhee resorted to such statements reflected the deep antipathy that many Koreans held against Japanese imperialism.

Korea after SFPT: de facto war under the umbrella of "peace"

It has been postulated that the security of the ROK was essential for the security of Japan, and that American bases in Japan were necessary for supporting the security of the ROK. The Korean War supplied a cause or justification for the United States' anti-communist policy, in which Japan would be a keen partner of the United States in securing American interests in the region. The United States' prompt intervention in the Korean conflict showed its commitment to the security of Japan on the assumption that the communist seizure of South Korea would pose a threat to the security of Japan in particular and the Asia-Pacific in general. The "peace treaty" with Japan was necessitated by the outbreak of "war" in Korea. No other country in the Asia-Pacific found itself situated in such a para-doxical position within the San Francisco System. "Peace" for the Japanese and Americans could mean lasting "war" for Koreans. The Cold War, which has been referred to as the "long peace,"[20] was a time of war against both external and internal enemies: the DPRK in the north and anti-system movements.

With the effectuation of SFPT, the United States and Japan jointly victimized Okinawa and the ROK. In Okinawa, a peripheral Japanese territory, the US military stationed its troops permanently. In the ROK, US troops were stationed in more than 100 bases with the approval of the pro-American ROK government. The United States made unequal partnerships with these two "allies," but the character of their respective relationships was strikingly different. While Japan could launch economic development under the US defense umbrella, the ROK, as a forward base of the US-led East Asian defense system, sustained itself as a "garrison state," ruled first by National Security Law and former Japanese-trained police and, eventually, the military.[21] President Rhee used anti-Japanese rhetoric openly, but he was heavily dependent on the pro-Japanese elites and never opposed the US post-war policy of remaking Japan as a new partner.[22]

Even after the ceasefire of 1953, the ROK's ruling class secured its power and earned its legitimacy mainly from the US-sponsored anti-communist system – a cornerstone of SFPT. As anticommunism in the ROK presupposed the national division, it had suppressed the argument of the nationalists pursuing reunification, which posed a threat to its regime. When President Rhee's dictatorship ended, a great wave of reunification movements swept through the ROK. Park Jung-hee's military *coup d'état* on May 16, 1961 reflected the fears of the power bloc in the ROK that regarded the democracy movements and national reunification activities as serious threats to their vested interests. The most pressing task for the military leaders was the normalization of diplomatic relations with Japan. With all strong opposition from students and intellectuals, Park Jung-hee succeeded in building diplomatic relations with Japan in 1965. The ROK's military leaders, who lacked legitimacy by coming to power through a military *coup d'état*, secretly negotiated and signed a "normalization" treaty.

The two countries signed a full range of treaties and agreements to resolve all colonial issues. Not as a token of Japanese colonial responsibility, but to aid the South Korean economy, Japan provided 500 million dollars in soft loans and 300 million in grants to the ROK, which meant the "liquidation" of all burdens Japan had borne for the 1910–1945 occupation, leaving many colonial, territorial, and property issues unresolved, including the issue of wartime military sexual slavery (the "comfort women" issue).[23] The amounts were given to the ROK not as reparation or compensation but as "economic aid" in the form of soft loans.[24]

Park Jung-hee's policy of economic development and normalization of relations with Japan showed his accommodation of the US-controlled "regional integration" policy and the San Francisco System. The United States also oversaw these policies from the inception of Park's presidency. In order to compensate for his lack of legitimacy in seizing power, he put more emphasis on economic development, which required economic aid from Japan. As president of the ROK, Park announced that overwhelming economic superiority over the DPRK would automatically bring about national reunification. His policy line coincided eventually with the basic design of SFPT, in strengthening the capitalist economies of Japan and the ROK in defense against the communist bloc.

The DPRK's belligerence in the late 1960s gave justification for Park's anti-communist stance in the 1970s. While détente at the turn of the 1970s pushed the two Koreas into secret dialogue over their survival, this resulted in a hardened Cold War system: the Yusin system in the ROK (1972) and Juche socialism in the DPRK.[25] The relaxation of tension in the global Cold War system, paradoxically, justified the consolidation of the two country's existing political system – authoritarianism and communism. But the ROK's economy ran ahead of the DPRK's, becoming closely connected to the economies of Japan and other countries.

Whereas the ROK paved the way for economic development and democracy in the 1980s as a representative case of the newly industrializing countries (NIEs) in East Asia, the DPRK's economy stagnated and became further isolated. The collapse of the Soviet Union and the opening of the Chinese economy dealt a fatal blow to the DPRK, which drove it to develop nuclear weapons as part of its survival strategy. Internal democratization and the external freeze of the Cold War transformed the ROK's traditionally tough stance against the DPRK. Kim Dae-jung's "Sunshine Policy" toward the DPRK and the ROK–DPRK joint declaration on June 15, 2000, marked an epochal transformation in the history of national division. Though the basic system of confrontation between the two Koreas remained unchanged, the feasibility of peaceful coexistence and future reunification was revealed briefly with the declaration, until the ensuing North Korean nuclear crisis reversed the situation. The North Korean nuclear crisis testified to the fact that the problems of the Korean Peninsula cannot be resolved through bilateral dialogue between the two Koreas. Without receiving the United States' firm guarantee for its existence, the DPRK will not relinquish its will to develop nuclear weapons. The resolution of South–North confrontation and DPRK's belligerence must be sought in a multilateral framework.

As the concept of "peace" in SFPT included "confrontation" with the communist bloc from the beginning, the cornerstone of the San Francisco System must be revised or re-examined in order to settle the problem of the Korean Peninsula. While the belligerence of North Korea has been exploited as a justification for the persistence of the system, the self-defensive strategy of North Korea should not be exaggerated as a threat to the East Asian security system. As we have seen a stall in the Six-Party Talks over the North Korean nuclear crisis, the United States should take a more active role in resolving the debacle, because it oversaw SFPT and remains stationed in South Korea and therefore continues to have an influence over all DPRK-related issues.

The crisis in South–North Korean relations increases regional instability in the Asia-Pacific, which urges a revision of South Korea and Japan's defense alliance with the United States. As the Korean War gave America good cause to station its troops in Japan and South Korea, in the name of defending these countries against the communist threat, bringing the Korean War to an end would add significant momentum for the transformation of this sixty-year-old system into a multilateral security system.

Redressing the colonial past and Korea–Japan reconciliation

The SFPT may be regarded as a final decision by the Allies on Japan's post-war status as a sovereign state. It was the final form of the order, beginning with the Tokyo Tribunal and the enactment of the Japanese constitution, of exonerating old war criminals and making them new partners in the Asia-Pacific Cold War, which meant rebuilding Japan without making an apology to or compensating for the worst exploited of its colonies, China and Korea. The Tokyo Tribunal and SFPT also constituted the post-World War II framework of Japanese relations with new nation-states that were Japanese colonies before 1945. But, from the beginning, the United States and Allies focused only on Japanese war crimes that had been committed after its attack on China and the United States. Compared to the trials conducted outside of Japan against Class-B and Class-C criminals, where thousands of these criminals received death sentences, only seven Class-A war criminals were executed as a result of the Tokyo Tribunal. The decision was too lenient to be effective in making Japan a truly democratized or peace-minded country. It showed that the main interest of the United States was not to punish Japan but to rebuild it as a new geopolitical and economic partner. This remission is reflected by the fact that, without remembering anything about their past inhuman treatment and violence against Koreans and Chinese, most ordinary Japanese people still ask "Why did we lose the war?"

In SFPT's definition of war crimes, Japan's military actions before its war with the Allied Powers were not taken into consideration. While Japan's war of aggression took place in China and Korea before 1941, the Tokyo Tribunal and negotiations for SFPT did not examine this point. Japan had already colonized Taiwan and Korea long before its open military campaign against China in 1937; in the course of colonization in the late nineteenth century, the Japanese military also massacred rebellious civilians and committed numerous "crimes against humanity." None of the inhumane treatment of colonized peoples was discussed or considered in the conference. The infamous Unit 731's biological weapons experiments, which might be considered the most heinous of war crimes, were also left outside the jurisdiction of the trials. As the damages to and suffering of Asian peoples that occurred before the start of the war against the Allied Powers in 1939 were omitted from consideration, responsibility for conquering and causing suffering to these peoples was also neglected. As the Tokyo Tribunal has been described as a typical case of "victor's justice," SFPT that followed might be called "peace without justice" for those who had suffered from war and colonialism in the Asia-Pacific.

The US policy in the Tokyo Tribunal had major repercussions for the collective Japanese memory. The tribunal was understood to be taking place because Japan was defeated and occupied by the Allied Forces. But the "crimes against humanity" that imperial Japan committed against Chinese and Korean civilians were never reckoned in judging the war criminals. So the tribunal could not make the Japanese reflect on their misdeeds from before 1945. SFPT consolidated the Japanese self-image of victimhood without burdening a sense of responsibility for its misdeeds as an imperialist aggressor before its open invasion of mainland China and Southeast Asia. Both the ROK and DPRK demanded apologies for what they view as the brutal, unjust occupation of the Korean Peninsula. Some liberal Japanese cabinet members have made apologies. However, Japanese prime ministers and officials, including the Japanese ambassador to Seoul, have made statements either whitewashing or justifying Japanese occupation.

The weakness of SFPT was grounded in an anti-communist coalition by which the task of decolonization was ignored or submerged. Without confirming the past misdeeds of Japan, the Cold War simply froze them and left room for the chronic aggravation of old wounds and revival of painful memories. Keeping pace with French and British colonialism in other parts of Asia, the United States also secured another form of "satellite" country in East Asia. The San Francisco System as an exoneration of Japan's responsibility to its neighboring countries created the conditions in which "the past" continues to haunt the present in East Asia. Under the anti-communist alliance of SFPT, the ROK could secure its survival, but at the cost of the victimization of the Korean minority in Japan and settlement of the Japanese colonial legacy.

When formerly imperialist Japan became an important partner of America's global containment policy, formerly colonized peoples, like Koreans, could ask for an apology and compensation from their old occupier by employing remedial measures such as invoking Japan's moral or political responsibilities; the deep-seated antagonism toward Japan, however, could not be settled. But the normalization in 1965 of diplomatic relations between the ROK and Japan was an opportunity to resolve this colonial legacy, as I mentioned.

Even after the normalization of diplomatic relations in 1965, Japan and the ROK have occasionally run into conflict over the past issues. Japan's unapologetic stance toward their past has invigorated Koreans; every newly elected ROK president's repeated calls for an apology have annoyed the Japanese people, who think Japan fully recognized its responsibility by signing and honoring SFPT and by providing economic assistance at the normalization of diplomatic relations with the ROK. Certainly, the ROK government never raised the "past issues" like that of the "military sexual slaves" during diplomatic normalization talks before 1965. And the ROK delegates also removed the possibility of individual lawsuits against Japan in the agreements. So a large part of the responsibility should be attributed to the ROK military leaders who neglected past issues with Japan in exchange for economic assistance.

All post-war issues were first resolved when Japan signed a full range of treaties and agreements with the ROK in 1965. But, contrary to Japan's point of view, which regarded all issues related to World War II and colonization settled with SFPT and normalization of diplomatic relations with the ROK, the legal settlement between the states did not cover all colonialism-related issues. From moral, political, and historical points of view, Japan offered minimum things to those neighboring countries that had suffered most by Japanese occupation for some forty years. Since 1965, the ROK government and people have been asking for an official apology and necessary compensation for victims of colonialism, like the "military sexual slaves," because the issue was never brought up during diplomatic dialogues. The lasting conflict between these two countries over this historical issue signifies the limitations of SFPT, which omitted Japan's responsibilities to those who suffered most, like the Koreans and Chinese.

On August 15, 1995, Japanese prime minister Murayama finally issued a statement concerning past Japanese wrongdoings, using the term "colonial rule and aggression," which was the most straightforward recognition of history that a Japanese prime minister had ever made. Although his statement functioned as a policy guideline for successive prime ministers in diplomatic relations with neighboring countries, it led to a harsh attack from the right wing. Japanese politics eventually drifted to the right in issues of historical memory.[26] Prime Minister Koizumi Junichiro's annual visit to the Yasukuni Shrine angered the Koreans and Chinese.[27]

Following the Murayama statement, Koizumi and the DPRK's Kim Jong-il issued the Pyongyang Declaration on September 17, 2002, after the first Japan–DPRK summit meeting. The declaration stipulated their intention to normalize diplomatic relations between the two countries, based on Japan's apology for its colonization of the peninsula:

> Both leaders confirmed the shared recognition that establishing a fruitful political, economic and cultural relationship between Japan and the DPRK through the settlement of the unfortunate past between them and the outstanding issues of concern would be consistent with the fundamental interests of both sides, and would greatly contribute to the peace and stability of the region.[28]

For Japan, the relation with the DPRK is one important exception in terms of resolving all its post-war issues. The Japan–DPRK dialogue had already been initiated in the early 1990s in order to normalize relations. The negotiations were aided by Tokyo's support of a proposal for simultaneous entry into the United Nations by both the ROK and the DPRK; the issues of international inspection of North Korean nuclear facilities and the nature and amount of Japanese compensation, however, proved more difficult to negotiate. Japan preferred the package deal, a precedent set when Japan had normalized relations with the ROK, while the DPRK's primary motives appeared to be a quest for relief from diplomatic and economic isolation.

But these talks also failed to develop further due to the North Korean nuclear crisis and the problem of abductions of Japanese citizens. When normalization talks resume between the two countries, the issue of the colonial past will come to the fore again. It may signify an opportunity for reviewing not only all past issues between Korea and Japan that were neglected in the SFPT and System, but the US-controlled defense system in the Asia-Pacific as well.

Epilogue

While the SFPT was signed between Japan and forty-eight other countries, past victims of Japanese colonialism like those in Korea and Taiwan, whose post-World War II national interests were heavily dependent on the result of SFPT, were neither considered nor reflected in SFPT itself. Following this, the historical task of reshaping the post-colonial order in East Asia was overshadowed by the atmosphere of the Cold War. Issues of sovereignty and territory that were ambiguous in SFPT became the roots of regional conflict. But a much more serious issue than these has been Japan's stance toward those neighboring countries who suffered most from Japanese invasion or colonization. Under the terms of SFPT, Japan was exempted largely from all accountability for those war crimes it committed before 1945.

The persistence of war on the Korean Peninsula and the two Koreas' structural dependence on foreign forces, militarily and economically, have prevented the two nations from acting as fully autonomous "subjects" in international politics. The lack of Korean participation in SFPT highlights the question of who controls the Korean Peninsula, then and now. Without a breakthrough in the debacle of the national division as de facto war system, the two Koreas have no choice but to remain peripheral subjects of the San Francisco System. As the United States sowed the seeds of current conflict between the ROK and Japan, only the United States can forge the conditions under which the ROK and Japan can reconcile and overcome the legacy of colonialism. But as the civil war in the Korean Peninsula prevented the two warring Koreas from intervening in the building of the system, both nations must make all efforts to end the Korean War by peaceful means.

The collapse of communism and the rapid economic growth of China in the late 1980s and 1990s weakened the validity of the Cold War model of United States–Japan defense relations. Both nations have been forced to acknowledge that the global deployment of forces, which was the strategic underpinning of the United States–Japan Security Treaty, is no longer necessary to meet the threats now most likely to emerge in the Asia-Pacific region. This has forced Japan to consider seriously, with at least the tacit blessing of the United States, a revision of its peace constitution that would allow the country to become a more "normal nation" – equipped to defend itself aggressively against military threats and, most importantly, to work with its allies in collective security efforts. The potential for Japan to become a "normal nation" reminds Koreans of the nightmare of the Japanese invasion of the Korean Peninsula. But a nationalistic China would also alarm Korea, together with other countries along China's periphery. South Koreans are afraid that the possibility of a new Cold War between the United States and China would make Korea's national division an everlasting one.

As the full-fledged Korean War changed the dynamics of SFPT process, the peaceful relation or reunification of the two Koreas by significant changes in the DPRK may threaten the *raison d'être* of the San Francisco System. Japan's central role as a US base in the Korean conflict may be fundamentally re-examined when the possibility of military confrontation on the Korean Peninsula disappears. It has been said that "as the System was created as a by-product of unprecedented rupture in world history, replacing it would also require a major crisis."[29] In any event, the representation of Russia, China, and Korea would be the precondition for resolving lasting conflicts in the Asia-Pacific region. As both Japanese and South Korean top political leaders lack sufficient political capital to overcome the hurdles to regional harmony, the United States should act as the most crucial broker of the multilateral system for East Asian peace. But thawing out the Cold War confrontation and, accordingly, achieving reunification in the Korean Peninsula would be an epochal event in the building of a workable system of peace in this region.

Notes

1 The violent civil conflicts after Liberation in South Korea were mostly related to the issue of removing the legacies of colonialism and punishing Japanese collaborators. Although the DPRK's military invaded South Korea under the sponsorship of China

and the Soviet Union, the Korean War may be regarded as a final form of civil conflict that had focused on building a unified nation-state after colonialism.

2 Originally, the first draft by the United Kingdom read:

> Whereas Japan under the military regime became the part to the tripartite pact with Germany and Italy, undertook a war of aggression and thereby provoked a state of war with all the Allied and Associated Powers and United Nations, and bears her share of responsibility for the war.

3 Yang demanded of Dulles that Korea should be included in the Allied Powers against Japan. US Department of State, *Foreign Relations of the United States* (thereafter *FRUS*), 1951, Vol. 6, Part 1, p. 1204. And see also *Donga Ilbo*, July 22, 1951.

4 1949/12/3, "Incoming Telegram by Mr. Muccio" (US Ambassador in Korea), US NARA/740.0011 PW(PEACE)/12-349.

5 US Department of State, *FRUS*, 1951, Vol. 6, Part 1, p. 1007.

6 Ibid.

7 Benjamin O. Fordham "Economic Interests, Party, Ideology in Early Cold War Era U.S Foreign Policy," *International Organization*, 52, no. 2 (1998).

8 In Article 14 "it is also recognized that the resources of Japan are not presently sufficient, if it is to maintain a viable economy, to make complete reparation for all such damage and suffering and at the same time meet its other [obligations]."

9 1949/12/12, US Department of State, Division of Research for Far East, "Participation of the Republic of Korea in the Japanese Peace Settlement."

10 The United States might be uninformed about or have underestimated the Korean guerrilla forces in Manchuria and underground organizations like the Alliance for Nation-building in Seoul and other regions. Korea's Provisional Government in China also proclaimed war against Japan after 1919.

11 Kimie Hara, "50 years from San Francisco: Re-examining the Peace Treaty and Japan's Territorial problems," *Pacific Affairs* 74, no. 3 (2001): 362.

12 The US position on Korea was seen in MacArthur's General Proclamation No. 1 on September 9, 1945. The proclamation stated that Korean territory was occupied by a "victorious military force" and all (Korean) "persons will obey promptly all my [MacArthur's] orders and orders issued under my authority. Acts of resistance to the occupying forces or any acts which may disturb public peace and safety will be punished severely." The rights that should have been accorded to Koreans as citizens of a liberated country were denied from the beginning.

13 Gi-Wook Shin, "Historical Disputes and Reconciliation on North-east Asia: The U.S. Role," *Pacific Affairs* 83, no. 4 (2010).

14 Chong-sik Lee, "Japanese–Korean Relations in Perspective," *Pacific Affairs* 35, no. 4 (Winter 1962–1963).

15 US Department of State, *FRUS*, 1951, Vol. 6, Part 1, p. 1204.

16 Ibid. "As of December 1953, three quarters of the Koreans in Japan registered themselves as citizens of the People's Republic (North Korea) while only a quarter did so as citizens of Republic of Korea (South Korea)." Lee, "Japanese–Korean Relations," p. 319.

17 Aiko Utsumi, "Chosenjin BC Kyu Senpan no Kiroku" [Documentary: Korean B-C class war criminals] (Tokyo: Keiso-shobo, 1982).

18 John Price, "A Just Peace? The 1951 San Francisco Peace Treaty in Historical Perspective," JPRI Working Paper No. 78, June 2001 (www.jpri.org/publications/workingpapers/wp78.html [accessed April 5, 2013]).

19 Jung Sung Wha, *The Politics of Anti-Japanese Sentiment in Korea: Japanese–South Korean Relations under American Occupation, 1945–1952* (New York: Greenwood Press, 1991).

20 Gaddis called the Cold War era the "long peace." But this is an America-centric point of view. During the Cold War, there occurred numerous "low intensity wars" in the

114   *D.-C. Kim*

Third World in addition to two big "hot wars" in Korea and Vietnam. John Lewis Gaddis, *Long Peace: Inquiries into the History of the Cold War* (New York: Oxford University Press, 1987).

21 Lasswell and Stanley have pointed to Manchuria under Japanese rule as a typical case of a garrison state. Independent, "democratic" South Korea inherited the system in terms of law, way of rule, and composition of elites. Harold D. Laswell and Jay Stanley, *Essays on the Garrison State* (New Brunswick, NJ, and London: Transaction Publishers, 1997).

22 When Rhee met MacArthur in Japan on February 16, 1949 he even reiterated the necessity of the South Korea–Japan alliance in supporting the United States' policy in East Asia. This speech possibly narrowed his policy options in the US-led discussion over SFPT, because as long as he followed the United States' "regional integration" policy, South Korea's concern for burying the colonial past could be victimized.

23 In January 2005, the South Korean government disclosed 1,200 pages of diplomatic documents that recorded the proceedings of SFPT. The documents, kept secret for forty years, recorded that South Korea agreed to demand no further compensation, either at the government or individual level. However, the South Korean government used most of the loans for economic development and failed to provide adequate compensation to victims.

24 When South Korea was alienated from SFPT, it lost the right to ask for reparations or compensation from Japan at the international table. The terms of the compensation issue used in the process of diplomatic normalization between South Korea and Japan changed from "reparation" to "claim" and from "claim" to "economic aid." Even though these nominal changes in the compensation issue happened, there were no critical discontinuities in reckoning the colonial past between South Korea and Japan. Officially, Japan bore no legal or political responsibilities for Korea over its forty-year occupation of Korea. Chang Bak-jin, "An Analysis on the Change Processes in the Negotiations for Compensation in the South Korea–Japan Normalization Talks," *Academic of Korean Studies* [*Jungsin Munwha Yeongu*] 110, no. 3 (2008): 209–41.

25 The "Yushin System" was a highly centralized and authoritarian regime established by President Park Chung-hee in South Korea between 1972 and 1979, regulated by the Yushin Constitution, adopted in October 1972 and confirmed in a referendum on 21 November 1972. From 1972 to 1979, power was monopolized by Park Chung Hee and his Democratic Republican Party. The DPRK's "Juche idea" officially appeared in parallel with the ROK's Yushin System. The Juche Idea, sometimes spelled *Chuch'e* (주체, 主體), is a political thesis formed by Kim Il-sung that states that the Korean masses are the masters of the country's development. It also means "main body" or "mainstream," and is sometimes translated in the DPRK as "independent stand" or "spirit of self-reliance."

26 Kasuhiko Togo, "Development of Japanese Historical Memory: The San Francisco Peace Treaty and Murayama Statement in Future Perspective," *Asian Perspective* 35 (2011): 337–60.

27 The Yasukuni Shrine contains the remains of 1,068 convicted war criminals. Visiting Yasukuni means not just honoring the spirits of Japanese war dead, but paying tribute to the war criminals.

28 Ministry of Foreign Affairs of Japan, Japan–DPRK Pyongyang Declaration (www.mofa.go.jp/region/asia-paci/n_korea/pmv0209/pyongyang.html [accessed April 5, 2013]).

29 See Youngshik Daniel Bong, "Past is Still Present: The San Francisco System and a Multilateral Security Regime in East Asia," *Korean Observer* 41, no. 3 (2010).

6 Taiwan's sovereignty status

The neglected Taipei Treaty

Man-houng Lin

Introduction

Before Japan's rule over Taiwan (including Taiwan's main island, Penghu, and subordinate islands hereafter, unless in quotations) began in 1895, Taiwan's relationship with mainland China had been strengthening. The opening to international trade of two of Taiwan's main ports following the Treaty of Tianjin (1858) enabled Taiwan to purchase more goods from mainland China; this expanded international trade mostly passed through mainland ports.[1] More Chinese bureaucratic, military, and cultural establishments were built in Taiwan.[2] Emma Teng's *Taiwan's Imagined Geography* explains why and how Taiwan moved from being disposable land in the early Qing to become a coastal bastion in the late Qing.[3]

In the introduction of the May 2005 special issue of the *Journal of Asian Studies* on Taiwan, Robert Eskildsen expressed puzzlement over the fact that Japan had occupied Taiwan as a result of the Sino-Japanese War of 1894–1895, even though the war had taken place outside of Taiwan.[4] This puzzlement neglects Japan's attempt to extend its defensive line to include Taiwan from the late Bakufu era onward, when Japan, smaller in size than China, was shocked by China's defeat by England in the Opium War of 1839–1841 and the US Admiral Commodore Matthew Perry's forced opening of trade in 1853. On the eve of the 1894 war, Japan had not attempted to take Taiwan, but after the unexpectedly prompt victory, Japan sent an expedition to Penghu on March 23, 1895, and took it in three days. This prepared the way for Japan's request for Taiwan's inclusion in the Shimonoseki Treaty, signed on April 17 and taking effect on May 8, 1895.[5]

In negotiations for the Shimonoseki Treaty, John Watson Foster had helped Japan to obtain Taiwan.[6] In what would prove to be an odd quirk of history, Foster inspired his grandson, John Foster Dulles, to step into international politics.[7] It was Dulles who drafted both the San Francisco Peace Treaty (SFPT) and the Taiwan Peace Treaty (TPT), two crucial treaties for Japan's transfer of sovereignty over Taiwan to the Republic of China (ROC). This chapter will delineate how cooperation between the United States and Japan in the Shimonoseki Treaty, the SFPT, and the TPT turned Taiwan from a defensive bastion of China, particularly after 1874–1884 when Taiwan was invaded by Japan and France, into one of Japan and/or the United States for more than a century.

Many cases examined in this book, such as the Kurile Islands, Dokdo/Takeshima, Senkaku/Diaoyutai, and the South China Sea, have arisen because of the unclear arrangements in the SFPT regarding their sovereignty status. Taiwan, by contrast, will be shown to have a clear sovereignty status under the SFPT system. Yet, as we shall see, this status has been blurred by the epistemological neglect of Taiwan's shift from the periphery of China to the periphery of Japan and/or the United States.

This chapter starts with more than a century of history of the Asia-Pacific region, in order to shed light on the shifts in Taiwan's formal sovereignty status in 1895 and in 1952. It then refers to international laws as well as to the archives of the ROC's Ministry of Foreign Affairs, stored at the Academia Historica and the Institute of Modern History of Academia Sinica, to explain the relationship between the SFPT and the TPT for Taiwan's sovereignty status. Finally, this chapter investigates textbooks, diplomatic rhetoric, political magazines, and newspapers from the angle of cultural history, to understand how the epistemological construct, intertwined with the "imaginary territory" of the ROC shaped by the Cold War, has made Taiwan's sovereignty status blurred and controversial.

The Asia-Pacific world around the first Sino-Japanese War

The United States became an Asia-Pacific country after California became a state in 1848/1849. In addition, Hawaii and the Philippines were subsumed under US governance in 1898. Similarly, Japan enhanced its position in the Asia-Pacific region in the decades following the Meiji Restoration. The Panama Canal, opened in 1914, symbolized the rise of Pacific Ocean steamship navigation for connecting Asia and the larger world, in the same way that navigation across the Atlantic had been stimulated by the opening of the Suez Canal in 1869.[8]

After US power was extended to the Pacific in the mid nineteenth century, the US became interested in Taiwan. In the Treaty of Tianjin, signed in 1858, the United States asked for international ports on Taiwan to be opened; before the US Civil War, it had even discussed purchasing Taiwan.[9] Following its withdrawal from the Far East due to its domestic conflict and the Meiji Restoration, the United States cozied up to Japan to maintain a balance of power against European intervention in the China market.[10] The former US consul in Xiamen, Charles Le Gendre, supported Japan's invasion of Taiwan during the Botan/Mudan Tribe Incident in 1874. Le Gendre also supported the cession of Taiwan to Japan. The Americans supplied Japan with arms during the First Sino-Japanese War, and a US war journalist even acted as a guide for Japanese soldiers taking over Taiwan.[11]

US policy toward China in the latter half of the nineteenth century was, on the one hand, on par with that of the British, French, and Russians in acquiring and maintaining privileged status. On the other hand, it was different from that of the European powers in extending friendship to China. When China suffered horrible defeat in the Sino-Japanese War of 1894–1895, the United Kingdom's attempt to mediate cooperatively with the United States, Russia, Germany, France, and others was abandoned, because each of those countries feared that the United Kingdom would negotiate to its own advantage. In 1894 the representative of the Qing dynasty requested urgent mediation from the United States in the Qing–Japan quarrel; US Secretary of State Walter Q. Gresham responded with a proposal for ceasefire talks to the Japanese ambassador in the United States. After Japan agreed, the United States was deeply involved in peace negotiations, with John Watson Foster as the key player.[12]

Foster, born in 1826, was appointed in 1880 as US ambassador to Russia. There, he became acquainted with the Qing ambassador to Russia, Zeng Jize; this became the foundation of his close relationship with China for the next thirty years. Foster helped the United States sign a series of commercial and duties agreements with various countries. At the completion of his short term as secretary of state in 1892, he went to China and became a VIP guest of the Qing premier, Li Hongzhang, who was later responsible for the Shimonoseki talks. On December 23, 1894, Foster received China's invitation to be a consultant for these negotiations.[13] He persuaded Japan to reduce the amount of war reparations and the number of Chinese ports to open for trade. On the other hand, he convinced China to upgrade its diplomatic representatives and to relinquish peripheral Taiwan to Japan, so as to dispel further threats of imminent war on the capital at Beijing.[14]

The Asia-Pacific world at the time of the Korean War

More than a half-century later, the establishment of the People's Republic of China (PRC) on October 1, 1949, and the retreat of the ROC's central government to Taiwan was a setback to the United States in the Cold War environment. The US Department of State announced on August 5, 1949, in a foreign relations white paper, its policy of non-interference in the Chinese civil war. The United States created a defensive perimeter to prevent the expansion of the Union of Soviet Socialist Republics (USSR), which extended from the Aleutian Islands through Japan and Okinawa to the Philippines, without including Taiwan.[15]

On the eve of the outbreak of the Korean War, US attitudes regarding Taiwan were still in a state of vacillation. The so-called China Lobby, consisting of pro-KMT factions, Republicans, and military figures such as Douglas MacArthur, asserted that Taiwan was an important strategic location in the west Pacific Ocean. During World War II, Taiwan supported Japan's economy and provided a military bulwark against China, Southeast Asia, and the southwest Pacific. The China Lobby argued that if Japan and Taiwan's post-war trade relations could be enhanced, then war-torn Japan could be stabilized to prevent the spread of communism in that country. But President Truman felt that providing Chiang Kai-shek with additional military aid might increase cooperation between the Chinese Communists and USSR against Chiang.[16]

On June 25, 1950, North Korea crossed the 38th parallel; in October, the PRC joined the war. The United States recognized a growing communist threat in need of containment. Truman's stance toward Taiwan changed accordingly. On January 5, 1950, he had announced that the Cairo and Potsdam declarations had decided the transfer of Taiwan to Chiang Kai-shek's government; that in the past every country had recognized China's sovereignty over Taiwan; and that the United States had no intention of interfering with the issue of Taiwan.[17] However, on June 27, 1950, two days after the outbreak of the Korean War, Truman's "Basic Principles against Disorder" clearly stated: "Determination of the future status of Formosa [Taiwan] must await restoration of security in the Pacific, a peace settlement with Japan or consideration by the United Nations."[18]

Under these circumstances, the United States became enthusiastic about the much-delayed peace treaty with Japan, hoping to terminate the occupation of the Allies in that country and to enable Japan to develop peaceful relationships with most of the Allied nations. The multilateral SFPT was signed in this state of mind on September 8, 1951.[19]

When the Allies signed the treaty with Japan at the San Francisco Peace Conference, the issue of whether the ROC or the PRC should represent China surfaced between the two organizing countries: the United States and the United Kingdom. The United Kingdom wished to maintain its commercial interests in Hong Kong and China through friendship with the PRC, and was afraid that the United States would unite with Japan and the ROC on Taiwan to threaten its commercial interests in Southeast Asia.[20] The United States, eyeing the ongoing Korean War and wishing to contain communist power, did not want to invite the PRC, though it did not insist on inviting the ROC.[21] In the end, the SFPT specified Japan's renunciation of "Formosa (Taiwan)," but without final designation (ownership) of the island. Furthermore, neither the PRC nor the ROC were invited to the peace conference.[22] Nevertheless, a Taipei Treaty was arranged by the United States during the conference, to be stipulated in the future.

On the eve of signing that TPT, then ROC premier (or chief of the Executive Yuan), Chen Cheng, said that the US policy toward Taiwan could be divided into three stages:

> First, when we lost in China, the US took the wait-and-see approach, saying that it was a matter to be self-determined by the Chinese. Second, when the Korean War erupted, the Seventh Fleet was sent to Taiwan, and Taiwan became needed. But our government had not necessarily become needed, that is, the US needed the territory, but not the people. Third, the current stage is the one wherein the US understands that Taiwan must not be lost to Communist hands; hence they must maintain our political power.

At this stage, the United States was able to dispatch only 300,000 soldiers to the Far East for battle. Korea, Vietnam, and Tibet all required military support. Chiang Kai-shek's army of 300,000–600,000 had suddenly become essential to the whole anti-communist endeavor.[23]

The SFPT and the TPT

Because the ROC reported to the United States on signs that Japan was establishing diplomacy with the PRC,[24] President Truman asked John Foster Dulles, who had helped create the SFPT, to indicate to Japan, which was then wavering, that if Japan's choice of counterpart for the peace treaty was the PRC rather than the ROC, the US Senate might not approve the SFPT. If that treaty did not go into effect, Japan would still be occupied by the Allied Forces and would not recover its sovereignty over its own territory.[25] Japanese Prime Minister Yoshida therefore indicated to Dulles, through the so-called Yoshida Memo, Japan's intention to sign the peace treaty with the ROC. For the integrity of the US Asia-Pacific defensive perimeter, it was only after the negotiation of the TPT began on February 19, 1952, that the US Senate approved the SFPT on March 20 of the same year;[26] only seven-and-a-half hours after the TPT was signed at Taipei Guest House at 3:30 p.m., April 28, 1952, the SFPT came into effect.[27] Covers of the TPT in various languages may be seen in Figure 6.1.

Figure 6.1 Covers of the TPT in English, Chinese, and Japanese (source: photographed by Ms. Shen Huaiyu at the Ministry of Foreign Affairs, ROC).

Article 4(b) of the SFPT reads: "Japan recognizes the validity of dispositions of property of Japan and Japanese nationals made by or pursuant to directives of the US Military Government in any of the areas referred to in Articles 2 and 3." Taiwan had been renounced by Japan in Article 2 of the SFPT. Previously, Chiang Kai-shek's military takeover of Taiwan on October 25, 1945 was based on General MacArthur's Order No. 1.[28] However, MacArthur's order only conferred de facto control, because Taiwan had been ceded to Japan by a treaty, therefore only another treaty could further alter sovereignty over Taiwan. Article 26 of the SFPT stated that:

> Japan will be prepared to conclude with any State which signed or adhered to the United Nations Declaration of 1 January 1942, and which is at war with Japan ... which is not a signatory of the present Treaty, a bilateral peace treaty on the same or substantially the same terms as are provided for in the present Treaty.

The ROC was exactly in that situation and perfectly fit that requirement.

Further sovereignty change after the Shimonoseki Treaty

As a subsidiary treaty of the SFPT, the TPT has as its Article 2:

> It is recognized that under Article 2 of the Peace Treaty which Japan signed at the city of San Francisco on 8 September 1951, Japan has renounced all right, title, and claim to Taiwan (Formosa) and Penghu (the Pescadores) as well as the Spratly Islands and the Paracel Islands.

The legal basis for Japan's right, title, and claim over Taiwan and Penghu was Article 2 of the Treaty of Shimonoseki (Figure 6.2), written in its English version as "China cedes to Japan *in perpetuity and full sovereignty* [italics by author] the following territories [including the island of Formosa and the islands appertaining or belonging to the said island of Formosa, and the Pescadores Groups] together with all fortifications, arsenals and public property thereon."[29]

The three versions – Chinese, Japanese, and English – of the Shimonoseki Treaty differ somewhat: from "right" in the Chinese version, to "sovereignty" in the Japanese version, to "full sovereignty" in the English version. The special provision of this treaty noted: "In the event of disagreement between the Japanese and Chinese versions of the Treaty hereafter, the English version shall be referred to and apply."[30]

Change in sovereignty goes together with change in nationality. In relation to the nationality of the Taiwanese, according to Article 5 of the Treaty of Shimonoseki,

> The inhabitants of the territories ceded to Japan who wish to take up their residence outside the ceded districts shall be at liberty to sell their real property

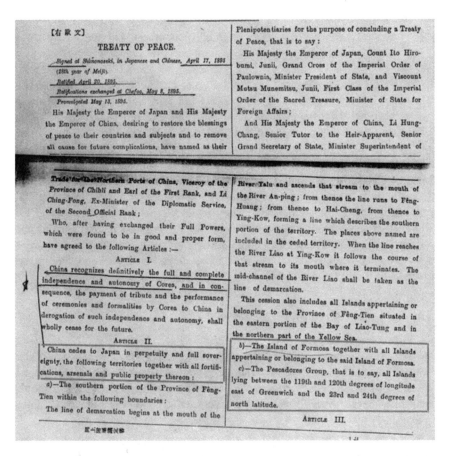

Figure 6.2 Article 2 of the Treaty of Shimonoseki for China's ceding Taiwan to Japan (source: Gaimushō hensan, *Nihon gaikō bunsho* [Japan's diplomatic documents] (Tokyo: Nihon kokusai rengōkai, 1960)).

and retire. For this purpose a period of two years from the date of the exchange of ratifications of the present Act shall be granted. At the expiration of that period those of the inhabitants who shall not have left such territories shall, at the option of Japan, be deemed to be Japanese subjects.

On January 12, 1946, following Japan's surrender, the ROC government declared that the people of Taiwan were nationals of that country, with effect from October 25, 1945.[31] Yet from August 31, 1946, to December 23, 1949, the British and the US correspondence to the ROC continued to state that, though they agreed to hand over Taiwan to the ROC based on the Cairo Declaration, a treaty between Japan and the ROC would still be needed to finalize matters of sovereignty and citizenship.[32] Similarly, *International Law*, by Yamamoto Sōji, points out:

The time when nationality changes, according to general practice, is not when the sovereignty of the territory is changed, such as when the territory is ceded, merged, renounced, returned, and others, but the day when a Treaty formally recognizing such relation becomes effective.[33]

In this light, Japan's Superior Court of Tokyo in 1959 and 1960 deemed the Taiwanese in Japan to be nationals of the ROC, and ROC sovereignty over Taiwan was established from the effectuation date of the TPT on August 5, 1952.[34] In 1980, this court again pointed out that the Japan–ROC peace treaty with signing party as the ROC not only confirmed that Japan had renounced its right over Taiwan and Penghu, but also could be explained as establishing that Taiwan had been transferred to the target country of this treaty – the ROC (Figure 6.3).[35]

Furthermore, Yeh Kung-chao, the ROC representative for signing the TPT, explained at the Legislative Yuan on July 16, 1952, that Article 10 of the TPT – which stipulates that all inhabitants, including old and new natural persons and juridical persons in Taiwan, by going through the laws of the ROC, were turned into nationals of the ROC – "has been absent from the SFPT" and "is of great importance to this country."[36]

The ROC continued and transformed

In the process of early negotiations for the TPT during February 19–26, 1952, the Japanese government was of the view that, since there had been no war between Japan and the ROC government in Taiwan, there was no need to enter into a peace treaty between the two countries from a state of war; Japan should enter into a treaty with Taiwan as it did with India.[37] However, the ROC took a

Figure 6.3 The exchange of the ratified versions of the TPT by the representatives of the ROC and Japan (source: provided by the Ministry of Foreign Affairs, ROC).

different view. Yeh Kung-chao pointed out that "In fact, Mr. Dulles has from the beginning insisted that this bilateral peace treaty strictly follow the format of the SFPT." At the non-official meeting for the TPT held on February 27, the Japanese side formally expressed its consent to revise the name of the meeting from "Japan–China Treaty Meeting" to "Japan–China Peace Treaty Meeting."[38]

The TPT itself confirmed the ROC position in Article 1, which says, "The state of war between Japan and the ROC is terminated as from the date on which the present Treaty enters into force." Obviously, the ROC government that signed the treaty was the old ROC government established in 1912, which had declared war against Japan with the Allied Forces in the Cairo Declaration announced on December 1, 1943. The ROC government that entered into the TPT with Japan merely differed from the ROC government on the Chinese mainland by the territories they governed in practice; the two were nevertheless connected by "continuity" and were "identical."[39]

Underlying the negotiations for the TPT were prior wartime agreements between some of the Allies. The Cairo Declaration states that "all territories Japan had stolen from China such as Manchuria, Taiwan, and the Pescadores (Penghu), shall be restored to the ROC."[40] Article 8 of the Potsdam Declaration, signed on July 26, 1945, emphasized that "the terms of the Cairo Declaration shall be carried out." The Japanese government's proposed exchange of notes for surrender was issued on August 10, 1945; the surrender announcement was issued by the Japanese emperor on August 12, 1945; the imperial rescript was issued on August 15, 1945; and the surrender order was issued by the Japanese emperor on September 2, 1945. All these edicts confirmed: "the Japanese government is ready to accept the provisions announced at the Potsdam Declaration."[41]

According to international law, war is not just the use of force but a legal status in which force is used to exercise legal rights (state of war), the commencement and termination of which requires determination.[42] The transfer of territories caused by international war must be agreed upon in a peace treaty executed between transferor on the losing side and transferee on the winning side to confirm legal and valid governance.[43] The SFPT and the TPT were both treaties aimed at entering into peace between Japan and the Allies and for the transfer of territories, based upon the Allies' Cairo Declaration of war against Japan.

Japanese leaders subsequently explained why it was necessary to reach a peace settlement with the ROC. On May 9, 1970, Japanese Prime Minister Satō Eisaku, in answering interpellation from a member of the Senatorial Diplomatic Committee, said: "Japan was at war with the government of President Chiang Kai-shek, it is only natural that one enters into a Peace Treaty with one's war opponent."[44] Prime Minister Yoshida Shigeru, who had led Japan in signing the TPT, wrote of Japan's reasons for signing with the ROC:

> The Japanese government had always hoped to mend its diplomatic and trade relations with the ROC. At the same time, it wanted to avoid having to deny the PRC, due to its close relationship with the ROC. Japan, however,

was aware that the ROC had always been the counterpart in war to Japan, whose status in the UN was extremely important. In addition, for the safe return of Japanese soldiers and nationals when the war ended, the ROC government could not be ignored as the party to reach peace with. Since the US Senate was still concerned, even though our relationship with PRC was also very important, it would have been unbearable to hamper the approval of the SFPT. Hence it was necessary to state clearly our position and the counterpart with which to negotiate peace, and Japan had no choice but to choose the ROC.[45]

In the TPT, the ROC was considered to represent the whole of China, with one key qualification. The treaty itself had three main effects: it ended the war with Japan, transferred Taiwan's sovereignty from Japan, and nullified all former treaties between China and Japan. On the other hand, as Exchange of Notes No. 1 of the TPT stipulated: "All articles of this Treaty *with respect to ROC shall apply to territories currently or which may hereafter be under the control of its government* [italics by author]" (Figure 6.4). This means the treaty applied to Jinmen and Mazu, still held by the ROC in 1952, as well as to Taiwan, which the ROC obtained from Japan. Therefore, the TPT, as an international treaty, asserted the continuity of the ROC state, previously established on the Chinese mainland in 1912, and transformed into the state of the ROC on Taiwan (Figure 6.5).

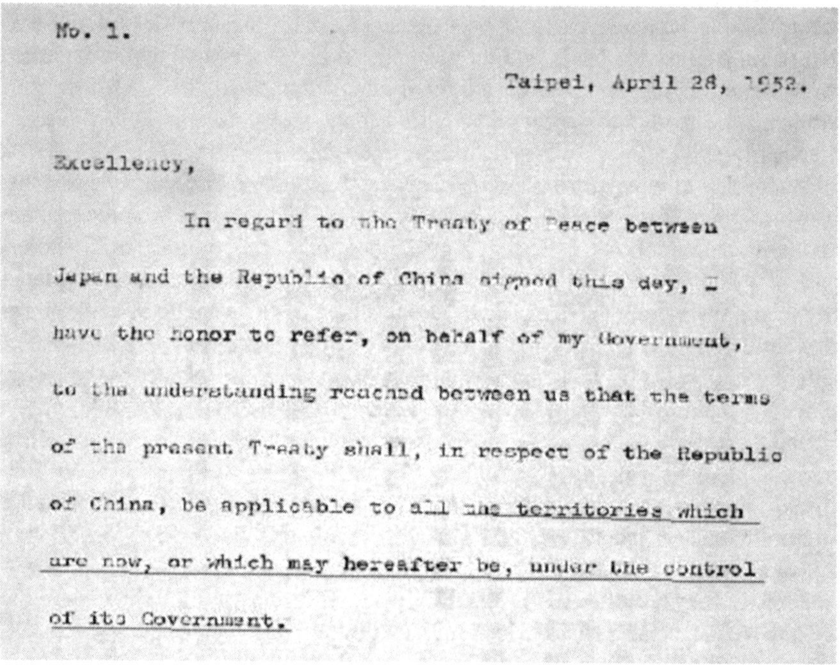

No. 1.

Taipei, April 28, 1952.

Excellency,

In regard to the Treaty of Peace between Japan and the Republic of China signed this day, I have the honor to refer, on behalf of my Government, to the understanding reached between us that the terms of the present Treaty shall, in respect of the Republic of China, be applicable to all the territories which are now, or which may hereafter be, under the control of its Government.

Figure 6.4 Exchange of Notes No. 1 for the Area of Effective Control of the ROC (source: photographed by Ms. Shen Huaiyu at the Ministry of Foreign Affairs).

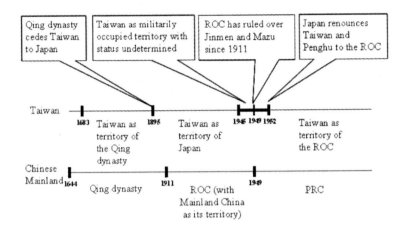

Figure 6.5 Movement of the ROC from the Chinese mainland to Taiwan.

This Exchange of Notes of the TPT has been compatible with the amendments to the ROC constitution since 1991, based on a division between "free land" (*ziyou diqu*) and "mainland China land" (*dalu diqu*). The introduction of the constitution speaks of "the necessity of unification," and Article 11 of the amendment states: "rights and obligations and other matters of the people of mainland China land may be stipulated otherwise in law." Two key clauses of the original constitution – "The autonomy of Mongolia's localities shall be stipulated by law" and "Tibet's autonomy shall be warranted" – remain in the amended versions.[46]

The various versions of the Korean constitution could provide us with some references with which to understand these points. The Korean version claims its territory to "have consisted of" the whole Korean Peninsula, while its English version states "*shall* [italics added] consisted of." The English version reflects more the reality, while the Korean version reflects more the intention. Similarly, the articles on the relationship between Taiwan and the Chinese mainland in the constitutions of the ROC and of the PRC reflect intention rather than reality. The constitution of the PRC claims "Taiwan is part of the sacred territory of the PRC. It is the inviolable duty of all Chinese people, including our compatriots in Taiwan, to accomplish the great task of reunifying the motherland." The phrase "may hereafter be under the control of ROC government" in Exchange of Notes No. 1 of the TPT could therefore be compatible with the intention of the ROC constitution.

Impact of Japan–PRC diplomacy in 1972

When Japan and the PRC established diplomatic relations in 1972, Japan's foreign minister, Ohira Masayoshi, announced the unilateral termination of the TPT in a press conference. But international law specialist L. Oppenheimer took the view that a treaty consists of executory articles and executed articles. Alliances, trade, administration, and extradition belong to the former, while boundaries, cession, and transfer of territory belong to the latter. Once executed, the terms of the treaty become permanent; if the parties to the treaty do not sign new treaties for amendment, the status quo must persist.[47] The termination of the TPT in 1972 by Japan canceled the executory articles related to trade, fisheries, and diplomacy, but not the articles related to the state of peace, the shift of sovereignty over Taiwan, and the nullification of old treaties, including the Shimonoseki Treaty.

In 1972 the PRC and Japan issued a Japan–China Joint Declaration. On September 30, 1972, Ohira vehemently stated at the headquarters of the Liberal Democratic Party (LDP) that:

> On the issue of the sovereignty over the territory of Taiwan, 'China' claims that it is inalienable from the territory of PRC, but Japan has taken the stance of understand and respect but not recognize such claim ... both the two countries have demonstrated perpetual disagreement.

In addition, Director-General Takashima of the Department of Treaties, who was involved in this negotiation, also stated as Japan's stance: "even though 'China' views Taiwan as a part of 'China,' such admission cannot be made in law."[48]

In practice, much of the old status quo does remain. Japan still permits entry as before to Taiwanese with ROC passports that satisfy requirements for disembarkation. The Asia-Pacific department of the ROC's Ministry of Foreign Affairs thereby noted that "Taiwanese" refers to nationals of the ROC, not merely nationals of the province of Taiwan.[49] It was also because of the executed articles of the TPT that "peace" in the Treaty of Peace and Friendship between Japan and the PRC in 1978 emphasized only enhancement of cooperation and covered no discussion about the termination of the state of war, or war compensation, or the sovereignty of Taiwan.[50]

The Taiwanized ROC's statehood

One can then ask what the legal status of ROC statehood has been since the 1952 TPT. The first article of the Montevideo Convention of 1933 defines a state as having a permanent population, a defined territory, a government, and the capacity to enter into relations with other states. Article 3 stipulates that statehood is independent of diplomatic recognition by other states. The definition used by the European Union for what constitutes a state is based on this convention.[51]

The process by which numerous countries opened relations with the PRC held conflicting implications for the ROC. When these nations issued "joint communiqués" with the PRC, announced while severing their diplomatic relations with the ROC, they implied that they no longer recognized the ROC state. However, as Canada first maintained, these international arrangements *did not mean denying* that the ROC was a state.[52]

Furthermore, the communiqués did not go through the process of ratification in the home countries, nor was there an exchange of the ratified versions, as is required with treaties. For example, the TPT was ratified in Japan by the Showa emperor on July 9, 1952, after the ratifications by the House of Representatives on June 7, the Senate on July 5, and the Cabinet on July 8; in Taiwan it was ratified by Chiang Kai-shek, the president of the ROC, on August 2, after ratifications by the Executive Yuan on April 30 and the Legislative Yuan on July 31. The exchange of the ratified versions was made on August 5, 1952, at Taipei, when the TPT took effect.[53]

Both international and domestic ROC law emphasizes that ratified and registered treaties carry legal weight. Chapter 16, Article 102 of the UN Charter recognizes only treaties registered at the UN. The TPT was duly registered as No. 1858 of the 1952 treaty series.[54] Hence, the TPT is not only an international treaty between the ROC and Japan. It carries much broader international significance. The ROC constitution says that treaties signed by its government are deemed as domestic law,[55] to be proclaimed by the president. Chiang Kai-shek proclaimed the TPT on August 9, 1952, with the appended order to the Executive Yuan mentioning not only the UN registration, but also the establishment of Japan's embassy in the ROC (Figure 6.6).

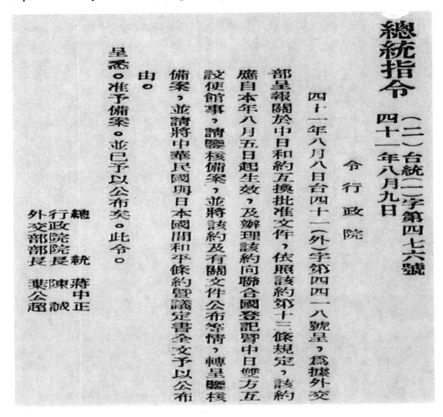

Figure 6.6 The proclamation of the TPT as domestic law (source: *Presidential Gazette of the Republic of China*, No. 359, p. 2, published on August 12, 1952).

With the effectuation of the TPT, Japan set its new embassy up in Taipei on August 5, 1952.[56] This act illustrated that Taipei had become the capital city of a Taiwanized ROC. The location of this embassy, on Section Two of Zhongshan North Road, is almost the same as that for the ROC consulate established in Taipei during the Japanese colonial period, between April 6, 1931 and February 1, 1938.[57] The flag that flew in front of this ROC consulate in Taipei is the national flag of the Taiwanized ROC today. These changes also show the relevance of the TPT for the shift of Taiwan's sovereignty from Japan to the ROC.

A neglected treaty

Despite the great importance that the TPT holds in regard to Taiwan's status in both international and domestic law, it has been very much neglected by diplomats and scholars both inside and outside of Taiwan. Instead, they have looked at other statements to determine Taiwan's sovereignty.

Though the Cairo Declaration was not a ratified treaty, before 2000 both the PRC and the ROC cited it rather than the TPT as the legal basis for Taiwan's status. The PRC's white paper on "the Taiwan issue and China's unification," issued in 2000, argued that the "China" to which "Japan shall return territories" in Article 8 of the Potsdam Proclamation and its predecessor, the Cairo Declaration, was China, and the international societies recognize only one China, the PRC. The second Koo–Wang meeting, held on October 13, 1998, has been the only face-to-face meeting for both sides that touched upon the Taiwan sovereignty issue.[58] Koo, on the side of the ROC, also referred to the Cairo Declaration and the Potsdam Proclamation as bases for Taiwan's legal status and stressed that the declaration clearly stipulated that it was the ROC rather than the PRC to which Japan should return Taiwan.[59] However, Koo did not emphasize the fact that the ROC continues to exist as a legal entity in Taiwan with the TPT. This left the PRC room to claim that it had fully replaced the ROC.

Since 1993 the Ministry of Foreign Affairs of the ROC has trumpeted the "UN for ROC" proposal. This proposal also quotes the Cairo Declaration and Potsdam Proclamation rather than the TPT:

> Upon the ROC receiving Taiwan and Penghu pursuant to the Cairo Declaration and Potsdam Proclamation in 1945, the PRC was not yet established. Since the PRC's establishment in 1949, its governing territory has never reached Taiwan, Penghu, Jinmen and Mazu.[60]

Nor was the TPT mentioned by the daring two-China theorists during the authoritarian Chiang Kai-shek period in early post-war Taiwan. The September 1959 issue of *Free China*, published in Taipei, echoed the Conlon Report of the US Senate Committee on Foreign Relations. *Free China* stated that, once the US recognized the PRC, there should be considered to be "two Chinas" or "one China, one Taiwan";[61] this article also did not refer to the TPT. In 1960 the chief editor of *Free China*, Lei Zhen, was arrested. After his release in 1971 he suggested replacing the ROC by the Republic of Chinese Taiwan (Zhonghua Taiwan minzhuguo).[62] Again, he did not refer to the ROC's legal status already consolidated in the TPT.

President Lee Teng-hui's "two states theory" was not based on the TPT either. Formulations of the "ROC on Taiwan," "the special state-to-state relations," or the "two states" incrementally proposed by Lee between 1991 and 2000 were based upon various amendments to the ROC constitution since 1991, in which the election of the central-level representatives and the president and vice-president of the ROC was limited to Taiwan and which admit the legality of the PRC's governance over mainland China by abolishing the Mobilization and Rebels Pacification Provisional Acts issued in 1948.[63] However, the stipulation that the head of state shall be elected by the people does not necessarily mean that the state has territorial sovereignty. Therefore, with respect to the referendum on UN membership, proposed by the Democratic Progressive Party (DPP) government in 2008, Lee, who was elected by the people as ROC president, thought that Taiwan's international legal status remained undetermined.[64]

Nor did Taiwan's high-school history textbooks refer to the TPT for Taiwan's sovereignty. From 1957 to 1999, the single version of the textbook published by the National Textbook Compilation Bureau emphasized that the Cairo Declaration confirmed the abolition of the Treaty of Shimonoseki, announced in the ROC government's initiation of war with Japan in 1941, and had supported the restoration of Taiwan to the ROC.[65] The textbooks did mention the TPT, but only in light of the re-establishment of diplomacy between Japan and the ROC. Between 2000 and 2006, high-school history textbooks expanded into six versions, published privately. Yet their theories on Taiwan's sovereignty extended from the earlier versions. After almost fifty years of taking the Cairo Declaration as the basis for Taiwan's sovereignty status, between 2006 and 2012 the six or seven high-school history textbooks produced have the unsettled theory or the self-determination theory, rather than the TPT, as the basis of Taiwan's sovereignty status.[66]

Therefore, we must ask: Why has the TPT not been linked to theories of Taiwan's sovereignty in important political debates or history textbooks?

Politics and knowledge

A direct answer may be found in Chiang Kai-shek's attitude toward this treaty. Zhou Hongtao, Chiang's secretary and confidant between 1943 and 1958, wrote in his diary that, even though President Chiang had indicated that Taiwan would be retrieved through the treaty between the ROC and Japan, he also stated: "Our policy may be so, but *in terms of public opinion, we should still insist on the decision made by the Cairo Conference* [italics added]."[67] Chiang's directives, issued on April 17, 1952, for engaging the TPT carry a similar message: "As for the legal status of Taiwan and Penghu, since they have been restored and ruled by us, there is no need to contend over the nominal matters."[68]

The unsettled position of Taiwan's legal status, expressed in textbooks published since 2006, comes also from an administrative order. On February 6,

2006, the Ministry of Foreign Affairs replied to the Executive Yuan with respect to its question, sent on January 8, about whether the Cairo Declaration had returned Taiwan to China: "concerning Taiwan's sovereignty shift after the end of World War II, the SFPT is regarded as the most authoritative treaty, yet neither the nationalist government nor the Communist government was invited to attend this conference." The ambiguity of this statement became the basis for new textbooks later that year when, on October 30, the Ministry of Education of the ROC sent correspondence to the National Textbook Compilation Bureau requesting it to forward the Ministry of Foreign Affairs' correspondence to textbook reviewers and publishers.[69]

These two administrative orders have been intertwined with some "metageography" shaped in Taiwan. "Metageography" denotes a set of spatial structures through which people order their knowledge of the world and which becomes their history, sociology, anthropology, economics, political science, and even their basic natural science.[70] Under the leadership of a political goal, a certain map, rather than an external truth, is drawn to change the reality perceived in that society.[71] Figure 6.7 is an example of the map drawn for Taiwan with the national goal of counter-attacking the Chinese mainland. This map was printed in 1976 at the center of an award certificate for the study of the history of Taiwan at a national youth center led by staff members of then Premier Chiang Ching-kuo, when he commenced leading the ROC on a path toward localization. Even though the study of Taiwan was starting to be encouraged, in the map on the

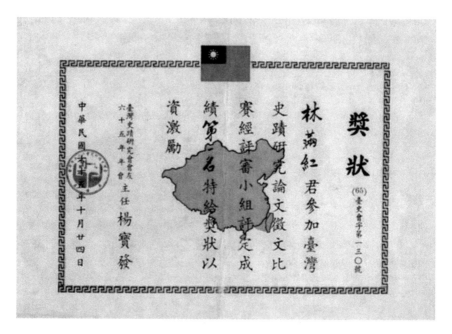

Figure 6.7 China map given by the ROC government in 1976 for awarding Taiwan studies.

certificate Taiwan was in fact so closely connected to the Chinese mainland that the Taiwan Strait ceased to be visible.

Considering a map like this, it can be seen how the study of ancient Chinese history, which explores the origins of Chinese identity, was a much encouraged form of historical study in the ROC on Taiwan. In 1992, when a historian of Taiwan's origins obtained the highest ROC award for historical research with an outstanding study on ancient Chinese history, he suddenly exclaimed that what he had learned before was completely disconnected from the society in which he resided.[72] In 2004 he became the minister of education, after the DPP defeated the KMT a second time in the presidential elections. In order to break away from the above metageography of Taiwan, he began encouraging the adoption of a Taiwan map that featured a ninety-degree rotation to the left.[73] However, neither of these maps showed the structural transformation of Taiwan from the periphery of China to the periphery of the Asia-Pacific world. This was the same minister who issued the correspondence regarding the unsettled status and self-determination for Taiwan's sovereignty mentioned above for textbook compilation.

Despite the advent of this sort of thinking, the China map still lingered, under the political persuasion of the DPP during its leadership between 2000 and 2008. The DPP affirms the Treaty of Shimonoseki, but opposes the TPT on the basis that the ROC had been succeeded by the PRC and that to continue to refer to the country as the ROC would lead to the PRC's eventual control over Taiwan.[74] Such rhetoric feeds into the myth that the ROC always denotes the idea of a China that includes the mainland, disregarding the possibility that state succession need not always be "complete succession," meaning that the original territory has been entirely replaced by another state. There is also "partial succession," such as the PRC's succession to the ROC of its territory other than Jinmen and Mazu; Japan's succession of only Taiwan from Qing China; and the ROC's succession to only Taiwan from Japan.[75]

Although the DPP theorists have some legal basis upon which to question the Cairo Declaration argument taught by the KMT, as it was not a treaty signed with Japan, they simply noted Article 2 in both the SFPT and the TPT, regarding Japan's renunciation of Taiwan without target. They neglected to read into Articles 4 and 26 of the SFPT and Articles 1, 3, 4, 10, and Exchange of Notes No. 1 of the TPT, regarding Taiwan's sovereignty status.

The 2006 correspondence from the Ministry of Education used Chen Longzhi's theory of self-determination after the "unsettled" assertion. From the 1960s onward, Chen had felt that there was a problem with his assertion about Taiwan's "unsettled" sovereignty status; in the late 1990s he began to promote the theory of effective governing based on two lines of reasoning. In this theory, Taiwan could be treated as no man's land (*terra nullius*), an area in which status has become determined through fifty years of effective governance. Furthermore, since the 1990s, Taiwan began a process of liberalization, democratization, and Taiwanization. This transition manifests the Taiwan people's exercise of the right of self-determination in international law.[76]

However, both of Chen's points had weaknesses. The premise of *terra nullius* is no man's land; or the lack of governmental organization over human habitation; or human habitation with organization that is not categorized as civilized international society; or land abandoned by civilized countries.[77] Taiwan since 1945 does not satisfy any of these criteria. Furthermore, the series of democratic revolutions carried out what constitutional scholars call "popular sovereignty," but not "territorial sovereignty" in international law.[78] Self-determination, in international law, according to Wilson's principles, is for colonized territories, but the ROC government that rules Taiwan, though relocated from mainland China, was in fact not a colonizer as it does not have a real motherland. Paragraph 2 of Article 1 of the Charter of the UN, which Chen has cited for making self-determination the basis of statehood, says: "[The UN should] develop friendly relations among nations based on respect for the principle of equal rights and self-determination of peoples, and to take other appropriate measures to strengthen universal peace." This provision applies, however, to states that are already UN member nations, rather than establishing that self-determination is a premise for being a UN nation. The UN also recognizes only its member nations that have applied the self-determination principle to change its national title.[79]

The Cold War and Taiwan's China mythology

The Cold War is an important context for both the signing of the TPT and the creation of Taiwan's China mythology. Statements made on the eve of the signing of the TPT by Chiang Ting-fu, ROC representative to the UN from 1947 to 1962, serve as an example of the mentality of mainlanders who relocated to Taiwan but had their hearts in China:

> If our nation were willing to preserve merely Taiwan and give up mainland China, we would foresee no future for China, and no safety for the Far Eastern world, our personal life would also become meaningless; the signing of the Treaty with Japan was a way to obtain cooperation with the US.... With respect to the status of Taiwan, the UN's General Assembly decided to adopt the proposal from the US and maintain its status quo. No parties shall use arms. On principle, our government can accept this, but we make a broad reservation about our retrieving mainland China. We understand that the proposal is an emergency measure for keeping peace, which shall not affect our right to maintain the integrity of our territory; hence we reserve our position in this regard for expedient overall review.[80]

This mindset from a minority population dominated Taiwan's politics and government throughout the Cold War period. In 1992 the Ministry of the Interior Administration announced that the mainlander migrants living in Taiwan constituted 13 percent of the population.[81] How could the mentality and hope of this 13 percent have such a strong influence for such a long time in the society to which they had relocated? The United States' reliance upon the ROC government's political-military power for resisting the Communists, as Chen Cheng said, has been a crucial factor.

With the support of the United States and other countries, the ROC on Taiwan represented all of the China that ended the war with Japan. The foreign minister of Japan, Aichi Kiichi, said in 1971 that

> we always hoped to normalize relations with the PRC, but on the other hand we must remind everyone that the nation we surrendered to after World War II was the ROC. From our perspective, the ROC has the legitimacy to represent the people of China at the UN.[82]

The government of a state can normally only represent the territory and people it actually governs, but, before 1971, the ROC on Taiwan represented the territory and people it used to govern. This sometimes happens in international law for governments-in-exile.[83] However, when the ROC National Assembly member stated in 1971 that "Japan signed the treaty with our state, recognizing the sovereignty our state has over the whole of China,"[84] the argument jumped from "right of representation" to "sovereignty."

While the KMT government on Taiwan did not accept the coexistence of the ROC and the PRC, US national policy did not admit this reality either, until 1971.

Although US national policy did not accept the coexistence of the ROC and the PRC, both officials and private citizens proposed the recognition of such a situation. Dulles, who drafted the TPT, supported the "One China, One Taiwan" policy in 1953. His proposal consisted of (1) support for the membership of the PRC in the UN; (2) cancelation of the embargo against the PRC; (3) establishment of the Republic of Taiwan; (4) transference of Security Council membership at the UN to the PRC; (5) continuation of the promise to safeguard Taiwan; and (6) retreat of the ROC army from Jinmen and Mazu. Such a position was seen as radical in a period of anti-communism. As Eisenhower did not want the PRC to join the UN, this proposal was not adopted.[85] During Kennedy's presidency (1961–1963), advisers such as John K. Fairbank proposed on Dulles' theory dual representation in the UN, but the dual representation proposal was not made owing to the history of McCarthyism, Kennedy's narrow victory in the presidential campaign, and the high anti-communist sentiment of the United States.[86]

The US-led Security Council in the UN deferred discussion about the issue of the PRC's entry right up to 1960. From 1961 to 1970, the discussion of this issue in the UN was treated as one requiring a two-thirds majority approval.

Public opinion in the United States shifted dramatically on the issue of PRC membership in the United Nations. According to the Gallup polling agency, the proportion of citizens approving the PRC's entry to the UN reached a high point of 35 percent in September 1970, with those disapproving being 49 percent.[87] The Harris poll on June 2, 1971 found that approval of the PRC's entry to the UN had risen by nearly five times to 48 percent from 10 percent in 1964. Opposition was reduced from 73 percent to 27 percent. The poll went on to say that it was one of the most drastic recent changes in the attitudes of US citizens.

At the time, 50 percent of the people approved the two-China proposal, 22 percent opposed it, and 18 percent had no opinion. It also said that support for the two-China proposal had continued to increase over the previous five years.[88]

Several reasons explain the American people's reluctance before 1970 to allow the PRC to enter the UN. Many Americans had been killed by Chinese Communists in the KMT–Communist war and the Korean War.[89] The expansion of the communist forces in Southeast Asia had always been manipulated by the PRC. At the same time, the United States cited the violence of PRC domestic campaigns, including the Three Antis Campaign (1951), the Five Antis Campaign (1952), the Great Leap Forward (1958–1960), and the Cultural Revolution (1966–1969 or 1976) as not satisfying the requirement for a "peace-loving nation," as demanded by the UN Charter.

However, numerous shifts in the late 1960s provided the context for changing opinions. The Cultural Revolution eased after 1969. At the same time, the Vietnam War reached a stalemate. China had successfully developed nuclear and hydrogen bombs. It also changed its diplomatic stance and began to cooperate with capitalist countries. In addition, China provided a balance against the USSR. The UN grew to see the PRC as a necessary member for maintaining international peace.[90] Prior to 1971, accepting the PRC was a social taboo in the United States, but an editorial in the *People's Weekly* (February 4, 1971) commented on Republican senator McGowen's proposal to allow the PRC to be a permanent member of the Security Council: "It has taken 20 years for one person to honestly, logically, and bravely say something in public almost everyone agreed on privately during the Dulles era."[91]

Not until later in 1971 was the Kissinger proposal along this line of dual representation formally made. Due to a delay in sending the proposal, it was scheduled after the Albania Resolution, which forced the ROC to leave the UN.[92]

Western neglect of Taiwan's Pacific ties

Even beyond the end of the Cold War in 1991, there remains an epistemological neglect of Taiwan's Pacific ties in the Western world. Current discussions in the United States on Taiwan's sovereignty still continue the 1970s trend of viewing Taiwan as a part of China.

In January 1971, at a seminar attended by the Massachusetts Democratic senator Edward Kennedy and many members of Congress, as well as academic scholars, Edwin O. Reischauer, former US ambassador to Japan and long-time professor of the history of Japan at Harvard University, supported the theory of "One China, One Taiwan." He pointed out that, in consideration of the circumstances in China, the majority of the people on Taiwan did not wish to be merged into China. Taiwan and China have been two separate political entities for more than half a century, except for a short period of four years.[93] US scholars on China urged the passage in 1979 of the Taiwan Relations Act, which demonstrated US intentions to help defend Taiwan from a PRC invasion, to deem Taiwan as a foreign country by US law, and not to exclude Taiwan from international organizations.[94] However, they also thought that, for the sake of engaging the PRC in the global community, the Chinese unification belief held by Chinese Communist leaders and Chiang Kai-shek's followers needed to be given attention.[95] Some recent American works on the Taiwan issue have carried these views, in examining Taiwan in the framework of Chinese history,[96] rather than arguing from Reischauer's Pacific perspective.

Conclusion

Prior to the eve of the severance of diplomatic relations between the ROC and Japan in 1972, and also in the 1980s, some theorists of the TPT appeared in Taiwan. They did not discuss, as does this chapter, the Montevideo Convention, a century of history in the Asia-Pacific, historical memory, or the English version of the Treaty of Shimonoseki with respect to ceding "in perpetuity and full sovereignty" of Taiwan, and the profound significance of the applicable scope of the TPT to the effective governing of territory.[97] Nevertheless, some scholars, including Chen Zhishi, Qiu Hongda, and Lin Jinjing, mentioned that the TPT is tremendously important to Taiwan's status and sovereignty. However, these writings have had no resonance with the national status theories of the KMT or the DPP.

After the SFPT was signed on September 8, 1951, Zhou Enlai, the premier and PRC minister of foreign affairs, declared the treaty illegal and ineffective. On May 5, 1952, Zhou issued a statement resolutely opposing the "Japan–Chiang Peace Treaty."[98] On May 7, 1952, Zhou further announced a formal statement of opposition to these two treaties.[99] It is a deep, historical irony that the KMT government disregarded the SFPT and the TPT from 1952 to 2000, and the DPP government from 2000 to 2008 placed emphasis on the SFPT but denied the TPT. Both have caused denial of Taiwan's sovereignty status, as did Zhou Enlai.

However, it is noteworthy that the diplomatic ties made between the PRC and Japan in 1972 implied the PRC's recognition of the SFPT, as this treaty was a prerequisite for Japan to retain its sovereignty and was a condition for Japan in winning post-war diplomatic recognition. It is also important to know that the Treaty of Peace and Friendship between Japan and the PRC, signed in 1978, implied the recognition of the TPT as an executed treaty because issues such as the end of the war between China and Japan, the transfer of Taiwan's sovereignty, and the abolition of the treaties between China and Japan prior to the TPT were not dealt with between the PRC and Japan.

People living in Taiwan have long been baffled by the country's national status. An illustrative example of this is the grand justice's interpretation of note No. 328, which states that the territorial issue in the ROC constitution is a political rather than a juridical issue under the grand justice's responsibility.[100] Due to the DPP leaders' attempt to change the official name of the country from the Republic of China to the Republic of Taiwan and to stipulate a new constitution, the TPT appeared more frequently in the mass media in the years 2006–2008, as a solution for a divided and puzzled Taiwan.[101] The documents related to the

TPT have been exhibited at the visitors area in the presidential office since December 31, 2008 by the KMT government that took office on May 20, 2008. Since April 28, 2009 bronze statues of the representatives who signed the TPT have been made visible to visitors coming to the Taipei Guest House, where the TPT was signed.[102] The new versions of history textbooks for senior high-school used from September 2012 onward have elaborated on the role of the TPT for establishing Taiwan's sovereignty status.[103] However, the general public remains largely ignorant of this treaty, as the Taiwan sovereignty status issue has continued to be viewed as taboo.

In the present book evaluating the SFPT arrangement, the question might be raised as to whether it has been fair that Japan made peace with the Taiwan-based ROC rather than with the PRC. Japan's Sato Eisaku has answered this question by arguing that the war was led by the ROC government. Without the ROC government's alliance with the Allies in the Cairo Declaration, China might not have been on the winning side. However, because war is a nation-to-nation relationship, the sacrifice of the Chinese people on the mainland has indeed not been dealt with, without the PRC's participation in the San Francisco Peace Conference. But the PRC's admission as a permanent member of the Security Council in the UN in 1971 was a way to repay the Chinese people's sacrifice in the war. Furthermore, the ODA of US$46.5 billion, rendered from Japan to the PRC between 1978 and 2007, has also been deemed as tacit war compensation.[104]

Just as we are concerned about the people on the Chinese mainland under the rule of the PRC government, we should also be concerned with the people of Taiwan under the rule of the ROC government since 1945. Too much emphasis has been put on the relationship between the ROC government and the PRC government concerning the Taiwan issue. As Reischauer pointed out, the Taiwanese people have really not been ruled by the PRC government. The relationship between the ROC and the PRC has actually been quite different from the situations in Korea and Germany, where the territory of one nation was divided into two nations. The Taiwanized ROC obtained its principal territory from another nation, Japan.

For Taiwan's post-war settlement, we should bear in mind that the war was not only an engagement between China and Japan, but between the Allies and Japan. According to international custom, the control over the defeated country's territory is often determined by a few major countries. For example, in 1945 the United States, United Kingdom, France, and the USSR controlled Germany. In 1951 the United States designed the SFPT according to its own priorities. These traditions have been based upon the fact that the major countries bear heavy responsibilities, and they contributed much toward the end of the war.[105]

Developments across the Taiwan Strait since the SFPT and the TPT also help us to evaluate the post-war settlement for Taiwan. The joint effort of the ROC and the United States halted further expansion of the Chinese Communists to Taiwan. Although there was no serious military conflict after the PRC bombardment at Jinmen in 1958, the US Seventh Fleet still embargoed the strait until

January 1, 1979, when the United States established diplomatic relations with the PRC. US protection has helped Taiwan to build a Chinese democratic society on quite a sound economy.

After 1979 both governments of the PRC and the ROC began gradually to lift their restrictions and facilitate cross-strait relations. The PRC became the ROC's top trading partner in 2001, as it did for both Japan and Korea. In this exchange these countries under the US Asia-Pacific defense line provide a flow of knowledge and intellectual capital to the PRC, in striking contrast to the inflow of these commodities from China in earlier periods. At present, six of the top ten exporters in the PRC are Taiwanese merchants. At the same time, the PRC still has 1,300 missiles trained on the ROC. Taiwan purchased military weapons amounting to US$13.1 billion from the United States in the years 2008–2010.[106]

For most people in Taiwan it has been over 100 years since the division of sovereignty across the Taiwan Strait. However, most people in Taiwan speak some dialect of Chinese, and Taiwan has retained the more positive aspects of Chinese culture.[107] Even though the PRC government has never forsaken the idea of conquering Taiwan by arms, with the rapid development of commercial and cultural exchanges across the Taiwan Strait after 1979, people from Taiwan certainly look forward to the "peaceful rise of China," as claimed by the PRC.

Article 1 of the UN Charter demonstrates the primary purpose of the UN: "in conformity with *the principles of justice and international law* [italics added], adjustment or settlement of international disputes or situations which might lead to a breach of the peace." The Treaty of Peace and Friendship between Japan and the PRC in 1978 also stressed observation of the UN Charter.

With a territory consisting of 36,000 km^2 and a population of twenty-three million, the ROC on Taiwan had in 1970, the year prior to its withdrawal from the UN, a population larger than two-thirds of the countries of the world.[108] The ROC on Taiwan has been without representation in the UN since 1971, as was the PRC between 1950 and 1970. However, the PRC was not seen as a *peaceful* country by the UN during these twenty years, while the ROC on Taiwan in the forty years since 1971 has been consistently considered to be a peace-loving country.

Based on the Montevideo Convention, the SFPT, the TPT, and the UN Charter, the UN General Assembly could renew discussion of the Albania Resolution made in 1971, which discussed only the representation of mainland China but not the representation of Taiwan.[109] The recovery of the membership rights and obligations that the ROC on Taiwan should have assumed since 1971 would benefit peace in East Asia and assist the peaceful rise of China. The ROC's constitution still leaves unification with the mainland as a choice for Taiwan. If this choice is to be taken, another treaty should be made by the ROC to replace the TPT.

Notes

1 Man-houng Lin, "Economic Ties between Taiwan and Mainland China, 1860–1895: Strengthening or Weakening?" in *Tradition and Metamorphosis in Modern China,*

edited by Hao Yan-ping (Taipei: Institute of Modern History, Academia Sinica, 1998), pp. 1067–89.

2 Li Guoqi, *Qingdai Taiwan shehui zhi zhuangxing* [The transformation of Taiwan society in the Qing dynasty] (Taipei: Jiaoyubu shehui jiaoyusi, 1978).

3 Emma Teng, *Taiwan's Imagined Geography: Chinese Colonial Travel Writing and Pictures, 1683–1895* (Cambridge, MA: Harvard University Press, 2004).

4 Robert Eskildsen, "Taiwan: A Periphery in Search of a Narrative," *Journal of Asian Studies* 65, no. 2 (2005): 290–1.

5 Liang Huahuang, "Riben bingtun Taiwan de yunniang ji qi dongji [Fermentation and motive of Japan's occupation of Taiwan]," *Guoli Chenggong daxue lishi xuexi xuebao* (Bulletin of the Department of History, Chenggong University) 1 (1974): 141, 161.

6 Huang Jiamo, *Meiguo yu Taiwan* [The US and Taiwan] (Taipei: Zhongyang yanjiuyuan jindaishi yanjiusuo, second printing, 2004), pp. 411–22.

7 "John Foster Dulles" (www.spartacus.schoolnet.co.uk/USAdulles.htm [accessed March 22, 2008]).

8 Man-houng Lin, "Taiwan, Hong Kong, and the Pacific, 1895–1945," *Modern Asian Studies* 44, no. 5 (September 2010): 1053–80.

9 Huang, *Meiguo yu Taiwan*, pp. 127–58, 166.

10 Xu Naili, "Yuehan Fusite yu jiawu zhanzheng qianhou zhi Zhong-Mei guanxi [John Watson Foster and Sino-American relations around the First Sino-Japanese War]," *Jiawu zhanzheng yibai zhounian jinian lunwenji* [Collected Papers for the centennial commemoration of the First Sino-Japanese War] (Taipei: History Department, National Taiwan Normal University, 1994), p. 31.

11 Huang, *Meiguo yu Taiwan*, pp. 411–22.

12 Xu, "Yuehan Fusite," pp. 21–2.

13 Ibid., pp. 24–6.

14 Ibid., pp. 29–32; Huang, *Meiguo yu Taiwan*, p. 420.

15 Liao Hongqi, *Maoyi yu zhengzhi: Tai-Ri jian de maoyi waijiao (1950–1961)* [Trade and politics: The trade diplomacy between Taiwan and Japan, 1950–1961] (Taipei: Daoxiang chubanshe, 2005), p. 46.

16 Robert Accinelli, *Crisis and Commitment: US Policy Toward Taiwan 1950–1955* (Chapel Hill, NC and London: University of North Carolina Press, 1996).

17 "US Policy Toward Formosa: Statement by President Truman and Extemporaneous Remarks by Secretary Acheson," *The Department of State Bulletin* 22, no. 550 (January 16, 1950): 79.

18 Irie Keishirō, *Nihon kōwa jōyaku no kenkyū* [A study of Japan's peace treaty] (Tokyo: Itagaki shoten, 1951), pp. 63–9.

19 Lin Jinjing, *Zhanhou ZhongRi guanxi yu guojifa* [Postwar relations between ROC and Japan], trans. by Sun Keying (Taipei: Caituan faren ZhongRi guanxi yanjiuhui, 1987), p. 65.

20 Yu Heqing, "Zhong-Ri heping tiaoyue zhi yanjiu [A study of the Taipei treaty]" (Taipei: MA thesis, Japan Institute, Chinese Cultural University, 1970), p. 13.

21 Lin Man-houng, *Wanjin shixue yu liangan siwei* [Historical contemplations on relations between Taiwan and Chinese Mainland] (Taipei: Maitian Press, 2002), p. 95.

22 Zhang Shuya, "Dulesi yu duiRi gouhe zhong de Taiwan wenti [John F. Dulles and the Taiwan issue in peace talks with Japan]," *Zhonghua Minguoshi disanjie taolunhui zhuanti lunwenji* [Conference proceedings on specific topics of the history of the Republic of China] (Taipei: Guoshiguan, 1992), p. 4.

23 Archive of the Ministry of Foreign Affairs, ROC (hereafter AMOA), category No. 036.012/6.

24 AMOA, archive number 012.6.

25 Article 2 of the US Constitution confers on the president power, by and with the advice and consent of the Senate, to make treaties, provided two-thirds of the senators present concur. Article 1 of SFPT states:

The state of war between Japan and each of the Allied Powers is terminated as from the date on which the present Treaty comes into force between Japan and the Allied Power concerned as provided for in Article 23. The Allied Powers recognize the full sovereignty of the Japanese people over Japan and its territorial waters.

26 Liao, *Maoyi yu zhengzhi*, pp. 73–4.
27 AMOA (Asia-Pacific section), archive No.: 012.1/89001, W-5, vol. 1, 1972.8.8–1972.10.31. The Taipei Guest House was the residence of Japan's governor-general in Taiwan before Japan's surrender.
28 Supreme Commander for the Allied Powers General Order No. 1: "a. The senior Japanese commanders and all ground, sea, air and auxiliary forces within China (excluding Manchuria), Formosa and French Indo-China north of 16 north latitude shall surrender to Generalissimo Chiang Kai-shek."
29 For the various versions of the Treaty of Shimonoseki, see Gaimushō hensan, *Nihon gaikō bunsho* [Japan's diplomatic documents] (Tokyo: Nihon kokusai rengōkai, 1960), vol. 1, pp. 362–75. The original version may be seen at Taipei's Palace Museum or Tokyo's Archive Center for Diplomatic Historical Materials.
30 Zheng Hailin, "Taiwan de lingtu zhuquan wuyi shuyu Zhongguo [There is no question that Taiwan's sovereignty belongs to China]," *Haixia pinglun* [Strait Forum], 190 (October 2006): 53.
31 Tang Manzhen and Wang Yu, *Taiwan shidian* [Dictionary of Taiwan's historical events] (Tianjin: Nankai daxue chubanshe, 1990), p. 508.
32 AMOA (East Asia section), No. 5449; AMOA (East Asia section), East 35, No. 304; Irie Keishirō, *Nihon kōwa jōyaku no kenkyū*, pp. 63–9.
33 Yamamoto Sōji, *Kokusai hō* [International law] (Tokyo: Yūhikaku, 1994), p. 333.
34 Qiu Hongda, "Pingshu yige Zhongguo baipishu [A comment on the One China white paper]," *Lianhebao* [United Daily], February 23, 2000; Qiu Hongda, "Yige Zhongguo yuanze yu Taiwan de falu diwei [One China principle and Taiwan's legal status]," *Faling yuekan* [Law monthly] 52, no. 2 (Taipei, February 2001): 52–75; Qiu Hongda, "Taiwan Penghu falu diwei de yanjiu [The legal status of Taiwan and Penghu]," *Dongfang zazhi* [Oriental journal] 4, no. 12 (1971): 55.
35 Chen Hongyu, "Taiwan falu diwei zhi yanbian [The change of Taiwan's legal status]," in *Taiwan 1950–1960 niandai de lishi shengsi* [A historical retrospect of Taiwan in the 1950s–1960s] (Taipei: Academia Historica, 2007), p. 134, note 54, cited from *Somu getsuho* [Monthly bulletin of lawsuits], of the lawsuits and plans section of Japan's Ministry of Justice, 26: 11, 2, 025-2, 030.
36 Zhonghua Minguo waijiao wenti yanjiuhui, *Zhonghua Minguo dui Ri heyue* [Taipei Treaty] (Zhonghua Minguo waijiao wenti yanjiuhui, 1966), pp. 348–9.
37 Huang Zijin, "Zhanhou Taiwan zhuquan zhengyi yu 'Zhong-Ri heping tiaoyue' [Taiwan's sovereignty controversy and the Taipei Treaty]," *Zhongyang yanjiuyuan Jindaishi yanjiusuo jikan* [Bulletin of the Institute of Modern History, Academia Sinica] 54 (December 2006): 90; Zhonghua Minguo waijiao wenti yanjiuhui, *Zhonghua Minguo dui Ri heyue*, p. 2.
38 "Dui Ri heyue an" (Taipei treaty), AMOA (Asia-Pacific section), archive No.: 070 (012/6) (1952.2–1952.3), pp. 115–16.
39 "Ge buhui dui Zhong-Ri duanjiao yingbian jihua jiqi ni jiaoshe shixiang" [The response plan and negotiation details after the severance of diplomatic relation between ROC and Japan proposed by various ministries], AMOA (Asia-Pacific section), archive No.: 12.1/89001 (1972.8.8–1972.10.31).
40 Tōyō keizai shinpōsha, Gaimushō shiryōshitsu [The special materials section of the Ministry of Foreign Affairs] (ed.), *Nihon senryō oyobi kanri jūyō bunsho shū (dai I kan kihon hen)* [A compendium of the important materials relating with Japanese occupation and rule] (Tokyo: Tōyō keizai shinpōsha, 1949), p. 1.
41 Irie, *Nihon kōwa jōyaku no kenkyū*, p. 61.

42 Yun Cheng, *Fangyan guoji: lingtu diwei bianqian yu Taiwan* [Taking an international perspective: Territory transfer and Taiwan] (Taipei: Jingyiqiye youxian gongsi, 2007), pp. 19, 127.

43 L. Oppenheimer and H. Lauterpacht, *International Law*, vol. 1, *Peace* (London: Longman, 1967), p. 303.

44 Lin Jinjing, *Zhanhou ZhongRi guanxi yu guojifa*, pp. 80–81.

45 Yoshida Shigeru, *Shijie yu Riben* [The world and Japan], trans. by Yang Junli (Taipei: Zhongguo wenhua xueyuan chubanbu, 1963 for original Japanese work, 1965 for Chinese translation), pp. 79–80.

46 Xiao Yao, "Xianfa yu Zhongri heyue suo zhishe Zhonghua minguo lingtu zhi fanwei bijiao" [A comparison of the territory of ROC in its constitution and the Taipei Treaty], term paper for Chinese Economic History course of National Taiwan Normal University in 2005, cited from Miao Quanji, *Zhongguo zhixian shi ziliao huibian* [A collected series of materials on China's process for stipulating the constitution] (Taipei: Academia Historica, 1992).

47 Cui Shuqin, *Guoji fa* [International law] (Taipei: Taiwan Shangwu, 1961), vol. 1, p. 272; Charles G. Fenwick, *International Law*, 4th edn. (New York: Appleton-Century-Crofts, 1965), p. 519; Chen Zhishi, "Taipeng de falu diwei [The legal status of Taiwan and the Pescadores]," *Dongfang zazhi* [Oriental magazine], revived journal, 4, no. 12 (June 1, 1971): 37.

48 Lin Jinjing, *Zhanhou ZhongRi guanxi yu guojifa*, p. 149.

49 AMOA (Asia-Pacific section), archive No.: 062.4-89001, translation about ROC government's response towards the termination of diplomatic relations between ROC and Japan. AMOA (Asia-Pacific section), archive No.: 062.4-89001, about the overseas ROC nationals' passport and visa issuance.

50 Lin Jinjing, *Zhanhou ZhongRi guanxi yu guojifa*, p. 215.

51 G. Starke, *Introduction to International Law*, 10th edn. (London: Butterworth, 1989), pp. 132–3, and "Montevideo Convention," www.jus.uio.no/.../1.../rights-duties-states.xml.

52 Wang Wenlong, "Waijiao xiaxiang, nongye chuyang: Zhonghua Minguo nongji yuanzhu Feizhou de shishi han yingxiang [Diplomacy at the farms and the move overseas of agriculture: The reality and influence of the aid of agriculture technology of the Republic of China to Africa] (1960–1974)" (Taipei: MA thesis, History Department, National Chengchi University, 2002), p. 235.

53 The photographs with the final ratification dates are shown on the website of the Academia Historica (www.drnh.gov.tw).

54 *United Nations Treaty Series, 1952* (http://treaties.un.org/doc [accessed June 4, 2014]).

55 Grand Justice's Interpretation notes No. 329, based on the Constitution of the Republic of China, Articles 38, 58(2), 63, 141 (www.judicial.gov.tw/constitutional-court/P03_01 [accessed March 22, 2008]).

56 Guoshiguan (Academia Historica), *Zhonghua minguo shishi jiyao* [Key events of the Republic of China] (Taipei: Zhongyang wenwu gongyingshe, 1999), the year 1952, p. 162.

57 *Taiwan nichi nichi shimpo* [New Taiwan daily], April 1, 1931, and https://zh.wikipedia.org/zh-tw (accessed June 4, 2014).

58 The most recent face-to-face talks held since 2008 did not touch upon the Taiwan sovereignty issue.

59 *Zhongyang ribao* [The central daily] (October 14, 1998).

60 AMOA (Central and South America section), Category No. 514.2/90001, 144820, MOFA's explanations for the ROC's participation in the United Nations (July 1996). See also the MOFA website (www.mofa.gov.tw [accessed March 23, 2008]); Bureau of Information, *Taiwan nianjian* [Taiwan almanac], 2004 (Taipei: Bureau of Information, 2004).

61 Chen Yishen *et al.*, *Ziyou Zhongguo xuanji 7: guoji qingshi yu zhongguo wenti* [Collections of the Free China: International situation and Chinese issues] (Taipei: Daoxiang, 2003), p. 28.

62 Chen Yishen *et al.*, *Taiwan guojia dingwei de lishi yu lilun* [History and theories for Taiwan's legal status] (Taipei: Yushanshe, 2004), p. 27, note 38.

63 Ibid., p. 96. Note 69 on p. 38 also points out that Lee Teng-hui's view along this line is presented in his "Understanding Taiwan," *Foreign Affairs* 78, no. 6 (December 1999).

64 Lin Heming, "Paoda rulian: Lee Teng-hui [Lee Teng-hui's criticism against entering the UN referendum proposal]," *Lianhebao* (United Daily) (September 13, 2007).

65 Guoli bianyiguan, *Gaoji zhongxue lishi jiaokeshu* [History textbook of the senior high school], 15th edn. (Taipei: Guoli bianyiguan, 1999), vol. 3, p. 165.

66 See the textbooks published, respectively, by Longteng, Taiyu, Kanxi, Nanyi, and Sanmin bookstores. Some just mention that the ROC did not attend the SFPT; some move forward to the TPT, but claim that it did not transfer Taiwan clearly to the ROC; some say the TPT became invalid in 1972.

67 Zhou Hongtao, *Jianggong yu wo-jianzheng Zhonghua Minguo guanjian bianju* [Chiang Kai-shek and I: Crucial changes for the ROC] (Taipei: Tianxia Yuanjian, 2003), pp. 284–5.

68 "Directives issued by Chiang Zhong-zheng for Engaging Peace Treaty with Japan," President Chiang Kai-shek's archive, held by Academia Historica, No. 002020400053029.

69 The website for Taiwan's history education for junior and senior high-schools (http://203.68.236.92/epaper/epaper2/13epaper122006.htm [accessed March 20, 2010]).

70 Martin W. Lewis and Karen E. Wigen, *The Myth of Continents: A Critique of Metageography* (Berkeley, CA: University of California, 1993), p. ix.

71 For example, Matthew H. Edney, *Mapping an Empire: The Geographical Construction of British India, 1765–1843* (Chicago, IL: University of Chicago Press, 1997), p. 340; Thongchai Winichakul, *Siam Mapped: A History of the Geo-Body of a Nation* (Honolulu: University of Hawaii Press, 1994); Gearoid O' Tuathail, *Critical Geopolitics: The Politics of Writing Global Space.* (Minneapolis, MN: University of Minnesota Press, 1996), p. 2.

72 Du Zhengsheng, "Gushi zuanyan ershinian [Deploring ancient history for twenty years]," *Zhongguo lishixuehui huixun* [Newsletter for Chinese historical association] 47 (June 1994): 7.

73 Cf. Lu Lizheng and Wei Dewen (eds.), *Jingwei Fuermosa* [Taiwan's longitude and latitude] (Taipei, 2006), pp. 82–3 for the shape of the map.

74 Chen *et al.*, *Taiwan guojia dingwei de lishi yu lilun*, pp. 78–9.

75 About the concept of partial succession, see Lin Man-houng, *Wanjin shixue yu liangan siwei*, p. 78.

76 Chen Longzhi, "Reappraisal of US Policies Toward Taiwan and China," Formosa Association for Public Affairs, Westminster Presbyterian Church, Sacramento, September 9, 2006, and the website about Chen Longzhi at www.worldcat.org/identities/lccn-nr96-15933.

77 Chen Zhishi, "Taipeng de falu diwei," p. 41.

78 Yunshan jushi, "Taiwan quanti zhumin ke yi guojifa toupiao jueding 'zhongzhi Zhonghua minguo' [The whole Taiwan population could 'terminate the Republic of China' by vote based upon the international laws]," *Taisheng bao* 497 (issued in Tokyo), May 25, 2007.

79 Zou Nianzu, "Lianheguo huiyuan gaihuan guohao yu huiji de guanxi [Change of national titles and memberships for the members of the United Nations]" *Wenti yu yanjiu* [Issues and research] 36 (June 1997): 29–38.

80 AMOA (East Asian Pacific section), category No.: 035.012/6 (Original No.: 0988-3).

81 *Zhongguo shibao* [China times] (November 28, 1992), p. 6.

82 "Zhiyou Zhonghua Minguo youquan daibiao Zhongguo renmin [The free Republic of China is eligible to represent the Chinese people]," *Zhongguo shibao* [China times], May 2, 1971. "Mei Ri liangguo dui wo daibiaoquan yulun jianbao [A summarized report of the public opinion of the US and Japan on the ROC's representation right in the UN]," AMOA (International Organizations Section), category No. 640.4, volume No. 90003.

83 Masahiko Asada, "The 1952 Treaty as a Peace Treaty between Japan and China," paper presented in the International Conference on Taiwan's status in sovereignty, April 18–19, 2008, Taipei, Taiwan, pp. 83–99, especially pp. 89–91.

84 AMOA (East Asian Pacific Section), category No.: 012.1/89001, W-5.

85 Nancy B. Tucker, "John Foster Dulles and the Taiwan Root of the Two China Policy," in *John Foster Dulles and the Diplomacy of the Cold War*, edited by Richard H. Immerman (Princeton, NJ: Princeton University Press, 1990), pp. 235–62. Tu Chengji, *Zhonghua minguo zai Lian Heguo de zuihou rizi* [The final days of the ROC at the UN] (Taipei: Xiuwei, 2008), p. 32.

86 Tu Chengji, "Yijiu qiyi nian meiguo sheji lianheguo Zhongguo shuangchong daibiaoquan zhi yanjiu [A study on the dual representatives design of the US in 1971]," MA thesis, American Graduate Institute, Tamkang University, 2003, pp. 28–30. "Meiguo dui hua zhengce de jiantao [A review of the American policy toward ROC]," *Xinsheng bao* [Renaissance daily], June 12, 1971. AMOA (International Organizations Section), category No.: 640.4, volume No.: 90004. McCarthyism denotes the anti-communism movement initiated by Senator Joseph Raymond McCarthy (1908–1957) in the early 1950s.

87 AMOA (International Organizations Section), category No.: 640/90013. In the Central News Agency's secret information on the United Nations twenty-fifth general assembly's discussion about Taiwan's representatives, vol. 2.

88 AMOA (International Organizations Section), category No.: 640.4, vol. 90004, 240784–240785.

89 "The Mutual Discussion Among ROC, Japan, and the US on ROC's Representatives," AMOA (International Organizations Section), category No.: 640/90073.

90 Wu Renbo, "Zhonggong jinru Lianheguo zhi celue (Strategies of the PRC's entering UN)," term paper for the world economy and China course in National Taiwan Normal University, 2007.

91 AMOA (International Organizations Section), category No.: 640.4, vol. 90001, vol. 1, 240290.

92 Wu Renbo, "Zhonggong jinru Lianheguo zhi celue."

93 AMOA (International Organizations Section), category No.: 640.4, vol. 90001, vol. 1. The newspaper clips are on the public opinions in the United States and Japan on Taiwan's representative.

94 Section 4b1 of the Taiwan Relations Act states: "Whenever the laws of the US refer or relate to foreign countries, nations, states, governments, or similar entities, such terms shall include and such laws shall apply with such respect to Taiwan." Section 4d states: "Nothing in this Act may be construed as a basis for supporting the exclusion or expulsion of Taiwan from continued membership in any international financial institution or any other international organization."

95 Tu Chengji, *Kelaien yu Taiwan: fangong lixiang yu lixing zhi chongtu han tuoxie* [Cline and Taiwan: Conflict and compromise of the anti-communist ideal and rationality]" (Taipei: Xiuwei, 2007), Appendix, pp. 288–388, covering Ray S. Cline's communications with John K. Fairbank and the US Congress about the one-China policy and the Taiwan Relations Act.

96 E.g., Ramon H. Myers and Jialin Zhang, *The Struggle Across the Taiwan Strait: The Divided Problem* (Stanford, CA: Hoover Institution Press, 2006); Alan M. Wachman, *Why Taiwan? Geostrategic Relations for China's Territorial Integrity* (Stanford, CA: Stanford University Press, 2007).

97 For previous research on the TPT, a more complete bibliography has been listed in Lin Man-houng, *Wanjin shixue yu liangan siwei*, pp. 110–14.

98 *Shang shiji shishi niandai yilai de ZhongRiguanxi* [The Sino-Japanese relation since the 1940s of the last century], 18: 39 (http://news.sina.com [accessed March 20, 2008]).

99 *Renmin ribao* [The people's daily], May 7, 1952.

100 Grand Justice's Interpretation No. 328, November 26, 1993 (www.judicial.gov.tw/constitutionalcourt/p03_01.asp?expno=328 [accessed February 24, 2007]).

101 Lin Man-houng, *Liewu jiaohun yu rentong weiji: Taiwan dingwei xinlun* [A new historical perspective on Taiwan's legal status] (Taipei: Liming Press, 2008).

102 This author led these two exhibitions in his role as president of the Academia Historica.

103 This author was on the committees for textbook guidelines and review.

104 Tong Qian, "Could the Economic Performance be Maintained?" in *Forty Years since the Diplomatic Establishment between the PRC and Japan* series, BBC Chinese network, September 27, 2012.

105 Chen Zhishi, "Taipeng de falu diwei," p. 45.

106 Chi-tai Feng, "The Share of Mutual Benefit among ROC, Japan, and PRC," *Japan's Economic Daily*, June 14, 2010. Feng was the former representative of Taiwan in Japan, 2008–2012; Chi-tai Feng, "Taiwan is Neither Pro-China, nor Anti-China, but Keeping Peace with China," *Mainichi Shinbun*, June 3, 2010. Both are originally in Japanese, Mr. Feng gave this author the original Chinese version.

107 Lin Man-houng, *Wanjin shixue yu liangan siwei*, pp. 205–40.

108 AMOA, Department of International Organizations, category No.: 640, vol. 90059 (September 12, 1970–September 18, 1971), 452777.

109 The injustice of the Albania Resolution toward Taiwan is detailed in Thomas Grant, "Taiwan's Status in International Law: Participation in the UN and Other International Organizations," paper presented at the International Conference on Taiwan's Status in Sovereignty, April 18–19, 2008, Taipei, Taiwan, pp. 53–76, especially pp. 53–62.

7 The San Francisco System at sixty

The Okinawa angle

Gavan McCormack

The San Francisco System and Pax Americana

The question of Okinawa goes to the heart of the United States–Japan relationship and the order established in East Asia following the China and Pacific wars that ended in 1945. For Japan, the system really comprised two treaties: the multilateral peace treaty signed in San Francisco on the morning of September 8, 1951, and the bilateral security treaty signed on the afternoon of the same day. Together, they constituted the post-war settlement imposed by the conqueror upon the defeated enemy in the wake of cataclysmic war and a six-year occupation. The two treaties coming into effect in April the following year constituted the "San Francisco System," which not only formally ended the war but also established the basic structures of the peace that followed. Six decades later, in its essential respects, it remains intact.

How is this sixty-year era to be evaluated? Looking back on it from the long lens of history and in the frame of the past millennium, it may be seen as a Pax Americana, whose stamp upon the region (1952–2012) marks it as successor regime to the Pax Mongolica (1206–1368), the Pax Sinica (1368–1911), and the Pax Nipponica (1931–1945). Like those that came before it, however, the Pax Americana today is plainly in the throes of transition. Retreating from decades of folly and failure in the Middle East and attempting to shore up US hegemony over the perceived crucial center of world power in Northeast Asia, President Obama in January 2012 announced a major policy shift, which has become known as the "Pacific Tilt." More would be expected of allies, but US military pre-eminence would continue to carry the right to hegemonic dominance. Whether the promised concentration on the Western Pacific and Northeast Asia can produce better outcomes than the concentration on the Middle East and West Asia that it follows is not clear, but there is no question that the United States suffers from a collapsing reputation, fiscal exhaustion, and imperial overreach.

The US attempt to construct what might be called a San Francisco System, Mark 2, has been subject to two major challenges. On the one hand, the Hatoyama government in 2009 declared its intent to re-negotiate the relationship on equal terms and to work toward construction of an East Asian Community, but almost immediately abandoned the attempt under fierce pressure. On the other hand, over almost two decades the people of Okinawa have mounted a challenge that becomes ever more serious. Okinawa, a peripheral element in the system as it was constructed six decades ago, has morphed into an axis of pressure, weighing upon the system as a whole and pressing it toward change. The "Okinawa problem" is commonly seen simply as the question of the construction of a new base for the US Marine Corps, but involves much more: it challenges fundamental precepts of the San Francisco System. Its demand for a renegotiation of the terms of its subjection within the system points beyond the hegemonic orders of the past millennium toward a concert of states – a true commonwealth, a Pax Asia.

This chapter considers first the general quality of the United States–Japan relationship as molded and modified by the treaty system and the implications for Okinawa, and looks briefly at key moments in the evolution of the system: 1952–1960 (its inception, the division of Japan, and consolidation of the system), 1969–1972 (Okinawan "reversion" and the secret agreements or *mitsuyaku*), 1990–2009 (post-Cold War phase 1, under the Liberal Democratic Party, or LDP), and 2009–2012 (post-Cold War phase 2, the Democratic Party of Japan, or DPJ, era), concluding with a brief consideration of the outlook, in 2012 and beyond, and of the potential for a Pax Asia.

Japan grew enormously in stature, wealth, and power under the treaty system. Yet the relationship remains marked by the circumstance from which it was born: a conqueror imposing subordination, ruling out the possession of Japanese armed forces, and retaining its own substantial military forces to ensure its will continues to be reflected in Japanese policy. The economic superpower Japan remains to a marked degree still occupied by its former conqueror. Yokosuka is home port for the Seventh Fleet and Sasebo a major secondary facility for the US Navy; Misawa in Aomori and Kadena in Okinawa are key assets for the US Air Force; as for the US Marine Corps are Camps Kinser, Foster, Futenma, Schwab in Okinawa, and Iwakuni in Yamaguchi Prefecture. Much of the airspace above Japan's capital remains controlled by the US Air Force (from its Yokota Base). Scattered throughout Japan are the housing, hospital, hotel, school, golf course (two in Tokyo alone), and other facilities paid for by an annual Japanese subsidy of billions of dollars. As a former administrative vice-minister for defense recently put it, "it is called an alliance, but is really an alliance without substance," and "in practice the U.S. side just decides things unilaterally."[1] Nominally a system for the defense of Japan, it is in effect a system for the defense (and expansion) of the United States. Some go so far as to say that

> As a strategic base, the Japanese islands buttress half of the globe, from Hawaii to the Cape of Good Hope. If the U.S. were to lose Japan, it could no longer remain a superpower with a leadership position in the world.[2]

Nor is the subordination confined to strategic matters. No other country has the sort of relationship with the United States in which every year Washington sends Tokyo a detailed list of the matters it wishes to see reformed so as to remove "impediments" to US penetration of the Japanese market. The initial list of US demands (*nenji yobosho*) in 1989 covered 200 items – everything from the budget, tax system, joint stockholding rules, to the request that Japanese stop working on Saturdays – and was described at the time by one senior Japanese official as tantamount to a "second [US] occupation."[3] The program for massive public works spending, adopted in the time of the Kaifu government in 1989 with a target of 430 trillion yen over ten years, was raised to 630 trillion under the Murayama government in 1994, with, as slowly became apparent, devastating fiscal consequences for both national and local regional governments. Murata Ryohei, Japanese ambassador in Washington between 1989 and 1992, commented later that during his term of office the point of the structural impediment initiative, as it was then known, was to press Japan for "system change" on behalf of US banks, investment banks, and insurance businesses, and to facilitate merger-and-acquisition access to Japan's finance sector. Japan tended simply to accept the US demands in a "clientelist spirit" (*zokkoku konjo*).[4] Economist Uzawa Hirofumi goes even further, saying "Looking at such a policy, isn't Japan a complete colony ... and wouldn't it be better if it were a client state?"[5]

The "master–servant" quality of the relationship that I wrote about in 2007 (*Client State: Japan in the American Embrace*) endures; the twenty-first-century relationship sees a deepening of dependence. The steady dismantling, at US insistence, of elements of the Japanese "system" in the interests of neo-liberalizing it reached a high point under Prime Minister Koizumi (2001–2006), whose popularity in Washington was correspondingly high. It was suspended under Prime Minister Hatoyama (2009–2010), but resumed again (under a slightly different name) from 2011.[6] I use the term "client state," or *zokkoku*, to characterize the twenty-first-century Japanese relationship to the United States, meaning a relationship so structured that Japan, though nominally sovereign, attaches priority to US over Japanese interests.[7] Recently, even Japanese conservatives write of Japan as a "client state" of the United States.[8] In comprehensive terms, Japan can be captured only by an oxymoron: as a "subaltern superpower."[9]

Since the post-1945 United States–Japan relationship was set in place by the San Francisco Peace Treaty (SFPT), at each time when Japan might have taken the opportunity to press for increasing its autonomy and its independence from the United States, it chose instead to deepen it. This was the case notably in 1959–1960, 1969–1972, 1990–1994, and 2009–2011. Especially in the last two of these phases, since the end of the Cold War, military preparations and cooperation have been steadily stepped up and the frame widened from bilateral and regional (in "the Far East") to the world. The transformation has been accomplished by executive choice, not parliamentary or public debate.

The inception of the San Francisco System, Japan divided

Part of the price of "independence" under the SFPT was the division of the country into "peace state" (demilitarized and constitutionally pacifist mainland

Japan) and "war state" (American-controlled Okinawa), the former under strong, indirect American influence and the latter under direct US military rule. Mainland Japan became a semi-independent "protectorate," lacking foreign and defense powers and with only qualified economic and social policy powers. Okinawa, "Nansei Shoto south of the 29 degree North latitude (including the Ryukyu Islands and the Daito Islands)" became a UN-authorized "trusteeship," "with the U.S. as the sole administering authority."[10]

In at least two significant respects, the same emperor who had led Japan through the war played the key role in determining its structure and role in the post-war period. First, despite having assumed office deprived of political powers and defined as a "symbol of the state and unity of the people," he called for the United States to extend its occupation, telling General MacArthur that he believed Japan's security depended on "initiatives taken by the United States, representing the Anglo-Saxons," and to that end the United States should maintain its military occupation of Okinawa "for 25, or 50 years or longer, under the fiction of a long-term lease."[11] The imperial pledge is rarely mentioned today. It meant the emperor approved the division of Japan and the long-term US occupation of Okinawa. The heart of the Pax Nipponica was transferred to and continued to beat in the Pax Americana. In fact, General MacArthur's first demand of the drafters of the new Japanese constitution in 1946 was that "the emperor is at the head of the state."[12]

Second, when President Truman's special envoy, John Foster Dulles, conveyed the American request for the right to maintain military bases in Japan even after the peace treaty, and Prime Minister Yoshida refused, the emperor sent a message via his aide saying that he favored the idea; despite his reluctance, Yoshida bowed to the imperial will.[13] While all six Japanese delegates to San Francisco signed the peace treaty on the morning of September 8, it was he alone who, that same afternoon at Sixth Army Headquarters, signed the accompanying (and much more controversial) Security Treaty.[14] Under this latter treaty, Japan granted to the United States the right to station land, air, and sea forces in and about Japan, and to use them

> to contribute to the maintenance of international peace and security in the Far East and to the security of Japan against armed attack from without, including assistance given at the express request of the Japanese Government to put down large scale internal riots and disturbances in Japan.

The effect was that the US occupation did not end, but was henceforth legitimized. The forces who until April 28, 1952 were part of the "occupation" were from April 29 stationed in the same bases and doing the same things, but they were *Ampo* (US government) treaty-based forces. The national polity (*kokutai*), built around the emperor in pre-war times, was recast along lines determined in significant measure by that same emperor. The *kokutai* was bipolar, with emperor as one pole and *Ampo* as the other.

Three years later, the domestic political arrangements appropriate to the dependent and US-directed Japanese state (the so-called 1955 system of entrenched conservative party rule under the LDP that lasted to 1993) were set in place. The separation of Okinawa (then Ryukyu) and the functional division into "peace-state" mainland and "war-state" Okinawa continued.

1959–1960: the San Francisco System consolidated

America's favored agent through the early San Francisco years was Kishi Nobu-suke, released from Sugamo Prison in December 1948 and rising quickly through the LDP ranks to become prime minister in 1957. The LDP had been set up in 1955 with CIA funds, and in character and inclination owed much to American patronage. Maintaining its close US affiliation, it ran the country, cozily and corruptly and with only one brief interruption, until it was ousted in 2009.[15] However, in 1959–1960, facing major judicial and political challenges to the continuing Japanese military and political subordination to the United States, it not only successfully overcame the challenge but managed to use the occasion to deepen and consolidate Japan's dependency. A constitutional challenge to the continued presence of US forces in Japan on grounds of incompatibility was first beaten off, then a legislative revision of the security treaty was rammed through the Diet.

A Tokyo district court judge (in the 1959 "Sunagawa Incident" case concerning the projected appropriation of land just outside Tokyo for base expansion) held that US forces in Japan were "war potential" and therefore forbidden under the constitution's Article 9 (the peace commitment clause). US ambassador Douglas MacArthur II intervened quickly and decisively. After he warned Foreign Minister Fujiyama of the possible disturbance of public sentiment that the judgment might cause if allowed to stand, the appeal process was cut short by direct referral to the Supreme Court. MacArthur met with the chief justice to ensure that he too understood what was at issue. In December 1959 the Supreme Court duly ruled that the judiciary should not pass judgment on matters pertaining to the security treaty with the United States because such matters were "highly political" and concerned Japan's very existence. The judgment had the effect of elevating the Security Treaty above the constitution and immunizing it from any challenge at law, thus entrenching the US base presence and opening the path to the revision of the Security Treaty (and the accompanying secret understandings) a month later.[16]

The system was modified only once by public debate and parliamentary ratification, the 1960 "Treaty of Mutual Cooperation and Security" (commonly known, from the Japanese abbreviation, as *Ampo*).[17] The 1960 adoption of the treaty was tumultuous. The revised treaty continued to allow the presence of the US bases and to endorse a subordinate Japanese role in the Cold War order that had crystallized around the treaty. Kishi rammed the bill through the House of Representatives in the pre-dawn hours of May 20, in the absence of the opposition, amid such turmoil that President Eisenhower had to cancel his planned visit for fear of a hostile reception, and Kishi had to resign immediately afterwards. The US ambassador at the time, Douglas MacArthur II, reported to Washington on Japan as a country whose "latent neutralism is fed on anti-militarist sentiments, pacifism, fuzzy-mindedness, nuclear neuroses and Marxist bent of intellectuals and educators."[18]

The memory of that 1960 crisis has ever since deterred both governments from submitting the relationship to parliamentary or public review. Secure against constitutional challenge behind the defenses erected by the Supreme Court, and carefully defended against public or political debate by being removed from parliamentary scrutiny, the *Ampo* treaty relationship came through the challenge of 1960 reinforced. Never subsequently revised as to the letter, it has been hugely revised in substance.

Despite the treaty's purpose being stated as "the maintenance of international peace and security in the Far East" – and its reference to settling

> any international disputes in which they may be involved by peaceful means in such a manner that international peace and security and justice are not endangered and to refrain in their international relations from the threat or use of force against the territorial integrity or political independence of any state, or in any other manner inconsistent with the purposes of the United Nations

(Article 1) – in practice it became a global agreement for the pursuit and threat of war, in cases where there has been no threat to Japan or in the "Far East," against successive states in Asia and Africa.

Okinawa, excluded from the constitution that came into force in Japan in 1947, from the SFPT of 1952 and the revised security arrangements of 1960, remained under direct military rule, its continuing war orientation contrasting sharply with the mainland Japanese "peace state."

1969–1972: Okinawa "reversion" and the *Mitsuyaku*

A decade later, under the government of Kishi's brother, Sato Eisaku, the relationship was further developed by a combination of open political agreements under which Okinawa was "restored" to Japan and secret agreements, known as *Mitsuyaku* (literally, "secret agreements") under which Japan agreed to support US war preparations and nuclear strategy. The "return" of Okinawa from US military rule to Japanese rule was arranged in such a way as to prioritize continued US prosecution of the war on Indochina and grant it free use of the nuclear option, should it be deemed necessary (under "conditions of great emergency"). Prime Minister Sato agreed with Nixon that priority should attach to the effective US prosecution of its Indochina War, so therefore the United States would retain its bases in Okinawa and freedom to fight wars from them, and that it could continue bringing nuclear weapons into Japanese ports when thought necessary. No Japanese government could have survived if it had announced public support for the Indochina War and the legitimation of nuclear weapons, so governments then and subsequently (to 2009) persisted in denying the existence of any such agreements.

In 2008–2009, however, faced with public statements from four former Foreign Ministry vice-ministers of the existence of the secret agreements and the deception surrounding them, the Hatoyama government ordered a search of the archives for relevant materials. The committee's findings, published in March 2010, confirmed the main understandings to do with free passage of Japanese posts by nuclear-weapon-carrying vessels.[19] While the public stance was one of the Three Non-Nuclear Principles (1967) – non-possession, non-production, non-introduction – covertly Japan assured the US government that it could ignore the third principle. Privately, Sato told US Ambassador Alexis Johnson that he thought the policy was "nonsense,"[20] while accepting the 1974 Nobel Peace Prize for having declared those very principles. Sato's government paid the United States a huge sum, somewhere in the vicinity of US$650 million (far more than it paid in 1965 supposedly to compensate South Korea for four decades of colonial subjugation), essentially buying the Ryukyu/Okinawa islands back, while at the same time promising the United States that it could continue to hold and enjoy free use of its base assets. While the official construction of the event was that "reversion" was *kakunuki hondonami* (without nuclear weapons and on a par with the rest of Japan), in fact the deal was one of *kaku-kakushi kichikyoka* (nukes concealed and bases reinforced). Furthermore, it was a deal in which Japan actually *bought* the return – thereby establishing a principle that was thereafter continued to this day. US forces remain in Okinawa, to significant degree because they are compensated for being there by payment of "consideration" or "sympathy" (*omoiyari*).[21] The "sympathy" payments were the visible tip of the iceberg, but beneath it deceit and secrecy permeated the core of the relationship. All Japanese governments from 1969 to 2009 persisted in lying to parliament and people about the nature of the US relationship; the attachment to nuclear weapons (the American "nuclear umbrella" as the sine qua non of Japanese defense) was gradually reinforced.

When Okinawa was "returned" to Japan in 1972, what Okinawans sought was a demilitarized, peace-oriented constitutional order, but Chief Minister Yara's submission to the Diet setting forth that vision was left unread. The government pushed the bill through while he was still en route to the chamber. As the two governments worried about the possible consequences of allowing democracy to take hold in Okinawa, Ambassador Edwin Reischauer (1961–1966) spelled out his recommended formula: Use bribery to sway elections, but do so with care, avoiding the risk of exposure by channeling the funds through the LDP. One of those who performed this channeling role was Kaya Okinori, finance minister in Tojo's wartime government and released – along with Kishi – from Sugamo Prison in December 1948.[22]

When the actual day of reversion came, one prominent slogan at the meetings in Naha was "May 15: Day of Humiliation." Those who attempted to tell the truth, although they were aware only of relatively small aspects of it at the time, were savagely hounded. The *Mainichi Shimbun*'s Nishiyama Takichi is still today, after more than forty years, struggling in the courts to restore his reputation and his life from the brutality he endured for having blown the whistle on a small aspect of the secret deals of which he had become aware. He said recently that what Sato and Nixon negotiated was the "prototype of the current alliance" and that the problem for the Japanese state was that "admitting to the secret pacts would be to admit that the United States–Japan alliance strategy was built on illegal grounds."[23]

1990–2009: post-Cold War, Phase 1, the LDP

In the early 1990s, with the Cold War suddenly over and with a brief lapse in LDP hegemony from 1993, a window of possibility opened again in Japan. The Hosokawa government commissioned a report into Japan's desirable post-Cold War posture. That commission, headed by Asahi Beer's Higuchi Yotaro, recommended a renegotiation of the US relationship and greatly enhanced Japanese autonomy.[24] The report alarmed Washington.[25] A response, in opposite vein, was soon drawn up by Joseph Nye: 100,000 US troops would have to remain in Japan and Korea, and the two countries had to be tied even closer to American designs. Ever since then, successive US administrations, Democrat and Republican alike, have held to the Nye formula. Powerful US delegations, one after the other, were dispatched to Tokyo to dictate the role that was expected of it: boots on the ground in Iraq, diplomatic and financial support for US wars and for its global posture, and more recently for "containment" of China and for gradual militarization of Okinawa's frontier southwestern islands.

The Okinawan crisis that continues today began on September 4, 1995, when three US servicemen abducted and raped a twelve-year-old Okinawan schoolgirl. The incident shocked and outraged Okinawans to such a degree as to profoundly shake the prefecture and the United States–Japan relationship. After seventeen years, it remains unassuaged.

The prime concern of the two nation-states was to counter the threat posed by Okinawan anger, rather than to protect Okinawan society from such future outrages. Characteristically, the governments resorted to deception to contain the threat. After crisis talks, a bi-national Special Action Committee on Okinawa (SACO) announced, in December 1996, that Futenma Marine Corps Air Station (which sits incongruously and dangerously amid the bustling city of Ginowan) would be returned to Japan "within five to seven years." However, the deception was in the small print. Where in 1972 "reversion" (of Okinawa) had meant "retention," in 1996 "reversion" (of Futenma) meant "substitution": the construction of a new, enlarged, multi-service facility to substitute for the inconvenient, dangerous, and obsolescent Futenma. Several "five to seven year" periods have passed. Early in 2012, the government of Japan authorized very substantial repair and renovation works to Futenma, evidently on the understanding that it was not going to revert to Okinawans any time soon.

The substitute site was one that had been preferred by the Pentagon since the peak years of the Vietnam War in the late 1960s, the fishing village of Henoko in northern Okinawa. From 1996, however, the FRF (Futenma Replacement Facility) plan was repeatedly either rejected by an angry citizenry or, between

1999 and 2002, reluctantly accepted by local government authorities under conditions – civil–military joint use, limited (fifteen-year) term, environmental assurances – that were tantamount to rejection. But the more Okinawans rejected the project or subjected it to impossible conditions, the more it grew, the floating, temporary heliport of the 1996 designs slowly shedding its conditions and expanding in scale into something comparable in size to Kansai International Airport. The designs for an "on sea" approach were abandoned by Prime Minister Koizumi in 2005, in the face of implacable opposition. A new design was adopted in 2006 for a land-based, dual-runway, comprehensive high-tech air-, land-, and sea-base project centered on the existing Camp Schwab base on the shores of Oura Bay, to be built and handed over to the Marine Corps in 2014, but the 2014 deadline of 2006 was stretched in 2011 to "as soon as possible after 2014," then dropped altogether in 2012. Japan's consistent principle was to do everything possible to ensure the US forces remain in Okinawa.[26] It was deaf to the rising crescendo of Okinawan protest.

In 2009, as the collapse of the LDP loomed in Japan, the 2006 agreements were cemented in place by a formal international agreement, the Guam Agreement, adopted by the LDP-led Diet and therefore binding on any future government of Japan. It was designed to evade the democratic process and was also a classic "unequal treaty," since it was binding only on one side – in due course, with minimal apparent consultation, the US side fundamentally revised it in 2012. Arasaki Moriteru, author of the authoritative modern history of Okinawa, wrote:

> What is exposed, all too vividly and in concrete detail, in the [WikiLeaks] diplomatic cables is just how pathetic and decadent are Japan's political and elite bureaucratic circles. We have seen what we did not want to see: the behaviour of politicians and elite bureaucrats who, while talking all the time of "national interest" and spouting chauvinistic nationalism, were serving the United States and had assimilated to the American "national interest."[27]

Contemplating the transformation that took place under several security agreements with the United States in 2005–2006 (cemented in place by the Guam Agreement), Magosaki says the *Ampo* treaty became "in effect, a dead letter."[28]

The negotiations over the FRF and, more broadly, the *Beigun saihen* or "realignment of US Forces in Japan," were characterized by the same deception as the "reversion" of 1972 and the SACO "Futenma return" of 1996. Under the 2006 agreement, Japan would not only build the FRF, but it would pay US$6.1 billion for the cost of relocating 8,000 marines and their 9,000 dependents to Guam. However, diplomatic dispatches published by Wikileaks in mid-2011 exposed the deception implicit in this deal. As a US embassy dispatch put it in 2008, "Both the 8,000 and the 9,000 numbers were deliberately maximized to optimize political value in Japan," since there were at the time in the whole of Okinawa only "on order of 13,000 marines" and "less than 9,000" dependents. The Guam expenditure was further inflated by the inclusion of one billion dollars for the construction of a military road on Guam, which was simply "a way to increase the overall cost estimate." The road was neither necessary nor ever likely to be built.[29]

2009–2011: post-Cold War, Phase 2, the DPJ

The Hatoyama DPJ government that took office following the elections of August 30, 2009, promised a clean break with LDP politics and, in principle, with the San Francisco System (though it was not so bold as to spell that out). It was committed to a more independent national posture, an East Asian Community, a distancing from US neo-liberal economic policies, an end to bureaucratic rule, and the shifting of US marines from Futenma base in Okinawa to somewhere "outside the prefecture."

However, Hatoyama's election on such a platform triggered an unparalleled outpouring of American abuse and intimidation that saw him resign less than a year later. Along with the intimidation that he faced from across the Pacific, Hatoyama was also betrayed by his senior bureaucratic staff. So eroded by clientelism had the inner core of government in Japan become that the more senior the official, the more likely it was that their loyalty was to the government of the United States rather than that of their own country. They maintained clandestine, even conspiratorial, liaison and cooperation with their opposite numbers in Washington and called on the government of the United States to stand firm and "refrain from demonstrating flexibility" to Hatoyama. The common Japanese media and political response to the barrage of American abuse, focused especially on Okinawa and the FRF, was to reinforce the pressure on Hatoyama to yield. Hemmed in by faithless – if not traitorous – bureaucrats and lacking the courage or clarity of purpose to confront them or to resist the pressures from Tokyo, Hatoyama's political position was untenable.

Hatoyama's own account is that officials in his Departments of Foreign Affairs and Defense had "scornfully dismissed" his ideas, until he reached the point where "anything else was futile, I could go no further and I came to doubt my own strength." So he made a public statement to the effect that he had been persuaded by the needs of "deterrence" that there was no alternative to the FRF at Henoko, but six months later confessed that that had simply been a pretext (*hoben*), which he had been persuaded by his advisers to use to justify the betrayal of his election pledges.

Hatoyama's capitulation has commonly been described as the outcome of his confused and irresolute leadership. It was that, but it was also much more. It was the failure of an attempt, however feeble, to renegotiate the client-state relationship in the direction of autonomy and equality. For political scientist Shinohara Hajime, it was even a pivotal event in modern Japanese history, a surrender of sovereignty of such moment as to warrant being described as "Japan's second defeat" (alongside that of 1945).[30] Since then, Hatoyama's successors seem to have learned the lesson that "deepening" the alliance – making it more subservient and unequal – has to be their top priority.

In 2012 the Obama government was engaged in a comprehensive re-think of its global and Pacific strategy, in the course of which it unilaterally revisited the Guam Agreement package, slashing the number of marines in Guam to 4,700 (sending other contingents to Australia, Hawaii, and the Philippines). Despite the reduction in the number of marines set for Guam, Japan was expected to increase by about one billion dollars its share of the cost.[31] The government of Japan reiterated its commitment on Henoko and Guam, added an as-yet-unspecified pledge to cooperate in a new joint military project on the Northern Marianas, and promised to move toward construction of two new bases, an "International Emergency Center" on Shimojishima (part of the Miyako Island group in southern Okinawa), and a possible "night takeoff and landing" site for carrier-based planes on Mage Island in the Osumi island group, just south of Kagoshima.[32]

As US Defense Secretary Leon Panetta put it, "they [the government of Japan] have been very generous in saying that whatever moves that have to be made they'll support, they'll give us a lot of the funds to try to support that."[33] A more explicit statement of the client-state relationship, and of the priority placed on "sympathy" for the Pentagon (in terms of readiness to pay it many billions of dollars), would be hard to find.

But while the Japanese state's clientelist character slowly deepened, so too did the opposition movement in Okinawa, becoming by 2010 a prefecture-wide *resistance*, something unprecedented in modern Japanese history. As the national government struggled to neutralize, split, or defy the democratic mobilization that began with the Nago City plebiscite of 1997 against the base project, pouring funds in to buy-off local business interests and create fiscal dependency on the part of local governing bodies so that they would have no alternative but to comply with Tokyo demands, the contest escalated. It became, in my view, the defining struggle within the Japanese state. Its outcome was unclear until 2010. In that year, however, the mayor and city assembly of Nago City, the governor, the entire prefectural assembly (the Okinawan parliament), and the heads of virtually all local governing bodies in the prefecture all came out decisively rejecting the Henoko project. The nation-state had cultivated no city (or prefecture) so assiduously and so long as it did Nago (and Okinawa), and yet its politics of deception and secret diplomacy was decisively rejected. In the process, the opposition became a resistance.

The confrontation between prefecture and nation is accompanied by an increasing tendency on the part of the nation-state to prioritize the US alliance to the extent of setting aside, or even flouting, the law. Going beyond the principle affirmed by the Supreme Court in 1959, that Japanese courts had no jurisdiction to interfere in matters pertaining to the security treaty with the United States, they enter new territory in which positive illegalities are warranted in order to fulfill obligations entered into under the alliance.

For a recent example, an environmental impact (EI) study into the projected Futenma Replacement Facility at Henoko was required by law and carried out in due course. The outcome, however, has been a travesty, determined before the process began in the sense that the Japanese government was formally committed by the international agreements of 2006 and 2009 to construct and hand over the base in 2014. Clearly, the EI was seen simply as a necessary (and irksome) formality. The various studies that made up the EI process were contracted out by the Department of Defense, that is, the government itself rather than an independent body, to companies staffed with freshly appointed officials of that same department. Key evidence was withheld from the proceedings, such as that concerning the Pentagon's intention to substitute the MV22 Osprey VTOL aircraft that would replace the present generation of helicopters in use at the marine bases. Indeed, the study was in a sense farcical, as it was a study of the environmental impact of something to which the tribunal was not privy – once the base was handed over to it, the Marine Corps would use it at its own unfettered discretion. As for the internationally protected dugong, the statement estimated that there might be a single creature in the base site vicinity, because it saw only one, ignoring the widely believed Okinawan view that the disturbance created by the survey had driven them away from their favored feeding grounds. The multiple objections launched by the Okinawan governor and parliament (the prefectural assembly) and the evidence of massive prefecture-wide opposition to the construction project were brushed aside.

The statement was delivered to the governor at 4 a.m. on the morning of the last working day of 2011 (December 28), in order to meet the pledge to the US government to do so before year's end. Governor Nakaima, in his February and March responses to the Ministry of Defense on the EI, filed a total of 579 separate and particular objections, which he also resumed by insisting that protection of the livelihoods of people or of the natural environment would be "impossible" if construction went ahead. Environmental law specialists declared it the worst EI study in Japanese history – unscientific, illogical, illegal[34] – but, as had so often been the case since the Supreme Court ruling in the Sunagawa case of 1959, the SFPT trumped law or constitution.

Parallel with the Henoko process, the Japanese state also resorted to so-called SLAPP (Strategic Lawsuit against Public Participation)[35] measures to intimidate the citizens engaged from 2007 in the sit-in protest against the construction of helicopter bases for the Marine aircraft in the forest of northern Okinawa, in the village of Takae. In both the Henoko and Takae cases, the Japanese government manipulated the law to enforce a state agenda in the face of widespread, popular, non-violent opposition. The quiet advance of rights-denying procedures by the state under the law in its treatment of Takae protesters reminded Ryukyu University's Hiyane Teruo of the early advances of fascism in Japan and Nazism in Germany.[36]

As of mid-2012, courts in Naha and in San Francisco deliberate on the legality of the assessment process, and the United Nations Committee on the Elimination of Racial Discrimination sought a response from the government of Japan to NGO allegations about neglect of the human rights of Okinawans in pressing ahead with Henoko construction plans in blatant defiance of Okinawan opinion.[37] Despite Ospreys falling inexplicably from the skies in Morocco (April) and in Florida (June), and an emergency landing in North Carolina (July), the government of

Japan continued to insist that they were safe and that there would be no change to the plan to deploy them to Okinawa (and, from there, throughout Japan). An opinion poll survey found opposition in Okinawa running at 90 percent.[38] Declarations or resolutions of opposition came from the governor, the prefectural assembly, the heads of all forty-one of Okinawa's cities, towns, and villages, and a mass meeting of the 5,000 citizens of Ginowan (site of Futenma Marine base, where the Ospreys were destined to be located). In July, the national Association of Prefectural Governors, meeting in Takamatsu City, adopted unanimously an "emergency declaration" saying that they could not, under the circumstances, "accept the deployment."[39]

It was confrontation of a level of intensity unimaginable elsewhere in the country. At the Ginowan City meeting in June to oppose the deployment, one prominent local citizen used the Okinawan expression "*Nijitin, Nijitin, Nijira-ran*" ("Enduring and enduring again, until it becomes unendurable").[40] Perhaps the best known of Okinawan writers, the novelist Medoruma Shun, referred to the Osprey as a "symbol of discrimination against Okinawa."[41] It was discrimination that Okinawans had tasted time and time again since the San Francisco settlement, and indeed goes back far beyond that to the act of punishment by which the islands were incorporated in the Japanese state in 1879. Belittling law and democracy, the government of Japan seemed determined to deliver what it had promised the Pentagon.

The outlook in 2012: beyond the San Francisco System?

According to the joint statement issued by President Obama and Prime Minister Noda Yoshihiko in April 2012, the official story of the treaty system has it that "The U.S.–Japan Alliance is the cornerstone of peace, security, and stability in the Asia-Pacific region. This partnership has underwritten the dynamic growth and prosperity of the region for 60 years."[42] Beneath the soaring rhetoric, the document was essentially a statement of commitment "to further enhance our bilateral security and defense cooperation," with Japan committing to develop its "dynamic defense force under the 2010 National Defense Program Guidelines and the U.S. strategic rebalancing to the Asia-Pacific ... to achieve a more geographically distributed and operationally resilient force posture in the region." Japan would build the bases it had promised, step up the absorption of its forces under integrated US direction, confront China militarily by expanding those forces into the southwestern islands, and cooperate with the United States in "the high seas, space, and cyber-space." The United States would do what it could to retain its hegemony.

The prospect, however, was for extension throughout Japan of the military base burden borne so unequally by Okinawa for more than a half-century. In April 2012, the US Marine Corps revealed that it was not only planning to bring Ospreys to Okinawa but to deploy them regularly in low-level flights over much of "Japan proper," flying as low as 152 meters above ground in regular training exercises in Tohoku, Hokuriku, and Kyushu. As Burnham Wood once came to

Dunsinane, so "Okinawa" inexorably comes to Japan. On June 29, the US government gave Japan formal notice of its intention to proceed with the deployment, so that the Ospreys would be operational by October. The following day, Defense Minister Morimoto Satoshi headed straight to Iwakuni and Okinawa to convey the news. He was greeted as a "messenger boy." The Okinawan opposition quickly spread. No sooner had the governor of Yamaguchi Prefecture (site of Iwakuni Base) and the mayor of Iwakuni been given formal notice of the coming of the Ospreys than they both protested, along with the governor of Hiroshima Prefecture, while governors of all the regions designated for low-level Osprey flights also made clear their opposition.[43]

In the San Francisco System, as it was created sixty years ago, Japan was incorporated in the regional and global order in such a way as to entrench US hegemony. Japan's continuing submission serves therefore as a barrier to the realization of any Pax Asia. As Ryukyu University's Shimabukuro Jun puts it, Japan has been a "pseudo-sovereign state," in which "US military privilege is paramount and the constitution merely subordinate."[44] When Prime Minister Noda told Fuji TV in July, in the context of the Pentagon plan to deploy the controversial Ospreys to Okinawa despite almost universal opposition, that "when the American government has already decided something, there is no point in us talking about doing this or that," it was an admission of unprecedented candor concerning Japan's subordinate status.[45] Until it becomes an independent state, there cannot be a solution to the so-called Okinawa problem, nor can there be a stable regional order. Constructed in the treaty as a half-state, Japan has been carefully cultivated since then as less than sovereign; its dependent character is deeply embedded in contemporary East Asia's problems. What is commonly called the "Okinawa problem" is really the "Japan problem" and the "US problem"; unaddressed, it also becomes the East Asian problem and the global problem.

A Japanese minority, albeit evidently a growing one, traces the distortion back to the San Francisco settlement, but only in Okinawa is that concern shared by a majority, not for any abstract reason but because the burden of the abnormality weighs excessively upon it and has done so ever since Okinawa was severed from Japan six decades ago and then restored to it by subterfuge four decades ago. When the San Francisco System established the basic outlines of the regional security system, based on Cold War polarities between the Free and Communist worlds, the United States accounted for around half of global GDP; and the respect in which it was held for having played a key role in the defeat of fascism and militarism was still high. Now, though it still maintains a remarkably high share of global GDP (about one-quarter), the corruption and cronyism of its financial and banking system threw the world into chaos in 2008 and the global respect it once enjoyed has been eroded by militarism, wars, and attempts to dictate to the world. China has become the number one trading partner of Japan and the United States, in addition to being the United States' indispensable banker; various schemes proliferate for a new kind of order to substitute for the outdated one. The US design for an economic sphere without China and a security system directed at China is essentially a design for prolonging the SFPT, or Pax Americana, order. The Japanese military, at 240,000-strong and nominally a "self-defense" force, becomes steadily incorporated into a single US-led East Asian military force, merged at the level of tactics and strategy, logistics, and training, with "inter-operability" as the key word. Until the United States–Japan relationship can be straightened into something based on equality and mutual respect, Japan's sense of selfhood and identity is diminished, and its role in the evolution of a regional East Asian or Asian order distorted or blocked.

As the United States sinks under the burdens of empire and debt, loses its way in war and speculation, and sucks much of the world into a vortex of violence and lawlessness, China rises, beset by its own structural problems but already surpassing Japan in GDP and almost certain to surpass the United States, perhaps by around 2016. William Blum estimates that, since 1945, the United States has crushed or subverted liberation movements in twenty countries, attempted to overthrow more than fifty governments, many of them democratic, dropped bombs on thirty countries and attempted to assassinate more than fifty foreign leaders.[46] It intervenes regularly – and more on the side of dictators than of democratic movements. It went to war on dubious legal grounds in Afghanistan and plainly in breach of international law in Iraq, devastating both countries and committing many probable major war crimes. In and around its current wars in Afghanistan and Iraq and semi-wars in/on Pakistan, Yemen, Somalia, and elsewhere, especially in oil-rich countries such as Iran, the United States has extended a global web of spies, drones, bases, assassins, and prisons; it conducts covert operations in eighty countries, from South America to Central Asia and Africa.[47] It has "murdered, maimed or made homeless over twenty million people since the end of World War II (over five million in Iraq and sixteen million in Indochina according to official US government statistics),"[48] and no longer is, if it ever was, the benign, democratic super-state that much of the world looked up to in 1951. Instead, Andrew Bacevich plausibly describes it today as a permanent warfare state: a state that is convinced the world must be shaped; that only the United States is capable of doing that; that it has such a right because it is fundamentally good; and that only rogue states and evil empires could possibly resist it.[49] Its global military presence underpins the ability to project power anywhere and the penchant to do so often.

As a supporter of all such wars, open and covert, and in principle supporter of all the various measures (torture and assassination, robotic, drone, cyber, and space warfare included) adopted in them, Japan, along with all other allied "democratic" countries, shares responsibility. The Japanese attachment to the San Francisco System rests on turning a deliberate blind eye to the way in which the US global role has been radically transformed since the system was inaugurated, and to the way in which Japan's subjection has qualitatively deepened over the decades. Okinawans are more sensitive to the injustice of the system because they are, commonly, its victims.

Modern Japanese history has no precedent for the phenomenon of an entire prefecture united, as is Okinawa today, in saying "No" to the central state authorities of the world's two great powers, so as to block implementation of agreements made between them in 1996, 2006, 2009, 2010, and 2011. They continue to resist a system that prioritizes US strategic and military ends and economic interests over democratic and constitutional principle. Any serious attempt to resolve the "Okinawa problem" would have to begin by setting aside the series of "agreements" to militarize Oura Bay, reached during the high tide of LDP client-state rule, and putting an end to the many vain attempts to impose upon Okinawa something its people consistently say that they will not accept. But to do that would be to revisit the formula on which the post-war Japanese state has rested and to begin to renegotiate its dependence on the United States.

Because of these struggles, Okinawa, at Japan's geographical periphery, becomes Japan's political core. If the San Francisco System is eventually to be transcended and a Pax Asia substituted for the Pax Americana, it would seem most likely to follow from an extension of the Okinawan resistance and the Okinawan model of engaged, citizen-centered civil democracy to the rest of the country and the region.

Notes

1 Moriya Takemasa (vice-minister between 2002 and 2006), quoted in Sunohara Tsuyoshi, *Domei henbo – Nichibei ittaika no hikari to kage* (Tokyo: Nihon keizai shimbunsha, 2007), p. 64.
2 Military analyst Ogawa Kazuhisa, quoted in Mitsumasa Saito, "American Base Town in Northern Japan: US and Japanese Air Forces at Misawa Target North Korea," *Asia-Pacific Journal: Japan Focus*, October 4, 2010 (http://japanfocus.org/-Saito-Mitsumasa/3421 [accessed April 5, 2013]).
3 Gavan McCormack, *Client State: Japan in the American Embrace* (New York and London: Verso, 2006), chapter 3; Gavan McCormack, *Zokkoku – Amerika no hoyo to Ajia de no koritsu* (Tokyo: Gaifusha, 2008); Gavan McCormack, *Jongsokguk ga Ilbon – Miguk ui pumaneseo yokmang hanum jiyok paikwon* (Seoul: Changbi, 2008); Gavan McCormack, *Fuyongguo: Meiguo huanbao zhong de riben* (Beijing: Social Science Academic Press of China, 2008).
4 Murata Ryohei, *Doko e iku no ka, kono kuni wa* (Kyoto: Minerva, 2010), p. 161.
5 "So iu seisaku o mite iru to Nihon wa kanzen ni shokuminchi to iu ka – zokkoku nara mada ii desu," in Uzawa Hirofumi and Uchihashi Katsuto, *Hajimatte iru mirai* (Tokyo: Iwanami, 2009), pp. 41–5.
6 Under the title "Nichibei keizai chowa daiwa" [Japan–U.S. economic harmonizing dialogue], Embassy of the United States, Tokyo, February 2011 (http://japanese.japan.usembassy.gov/j/p/tpj-20110304-70.html [accessed April 12, 2012]).
7 The actual definition of the term appears only in the introduction to the three East Asian editions of McCormack, *Client State*.
8 The term is one that I borrow from the prominent Japanese conservative political leader of the 1970s and 1980s, Gotoda Masaharu. For its recent use, see, for example, Murata, *Doko e iku no ka, kono kuni wa*, pp. 88, 161. (In a forty-two-year-long career in the Japanese Foreign Ministry, Murata was at various times ambassador to Australia, the United States, and Germany, as well as administrative vice-minister for foreign affairs.)
9 See my "The Realm of the Postwar: Where are the Boundaries of the Countervailing Voices in Modern History?" Unpublished paper given at the conference on "Negotiating the Boundaries of Postwar Japan," Sheffield University, March 15–17, 2007.

10 Article 3, Treaty of Peace with Japan, signed at San Francisco, September 8, 1951 (www.taiwandocuments.org/sanfrancisco01.htm [accessed April 5, 2013]).

11 Gavan McCormack and Satoko Oka Norimatsu, *Resistant Islands: Okinawa Confronts Japan and the United States* (Lanham, MD: Rowman and Littlefield, 2012), p. 6.

12 Paragraph 1 of the Secret Memo of February 3, 1946, headed "Copy of pencilled Notes of C-in-C handed to me on Sunday 3 February 1946 to be basis of draft constitution," now held in the library of the University of Maryland (reproduced in full in John Dower, *Embracing Defeat: Japan in the Wake of World War II* [New York: W.W. Norton and Company/New Press, 1999], pp. 360–1.)

13 Toyoshita Narahiko, *Ampo joyaku no seiritsu – Yoshida gaiko to tenno gaiko* (Tokyo: Iwanami shinsho, 1996); and see Ito Narihiko, "Towards an independent Japanese Relationship with the United States," n.d., *Japan Focus* (http://japanfocus.org/-ito-Narihiko/2015?rand=1330143835 [accessed April 5, 2013]).

14 Ministry of Foreign Affairs, "Nihon gaiko bunsho, Sanfuranshisuko heiwa joyaku, choin, hakko" (www.mofa.go.jp/mofaj/annai/honsho/shiryo/bunsho/h20.html [accessed April 5, 2013]). For the text of the 1952 Security Treaty, see http://en.wikipedia.org/wiki/Security_Treaty_Between_the_United_States_and_Japan (accessed April 5, 2013).

15 See, for example, Haruna Mikio, *Himitsu no fairu*, 2 vols. (Tokyo: Shincho bunko, 2003).

16 The US intervention only became known more than fifty years later, from materials discovered in the US archives in April 2008 and confirmed by thirty-four pages of Japanese documentation, released in April 2010 to the surviving defendants of the 1959 action. Further details in McCormack and Norimatsu, *Resistant Islands*, pp. 53–4.

17 Treaty of Mutual Cooperation and Security between Japan and the United States of America, January 19, 1960 (http://en.wikisource.org/wiki/Treaty_of_Mutual_Cooperation_and_Security_between_Japan_ and_the_United_States_of_America [accessed April 5, 2013]).

18 Ambassador MacArthur to Department of State, Cable No. 4393, June 24, 1960 in US Department of State, *Foreign Relations of the United States*, 1958–1960, vol. 18, pp. 377–84, at p. 380.

19 For details, see McCormack and Norimatsu, *Resistant Islands*, pp. 53–67.

20 "Peace Prize Winner Sato Called Nonnuclear Policy 'Nonsense'," *Japan Times*, June 11, 2000.

21 For details, see McCormack and Norimatsu, *Resistant Islands*, pp. 193–6.

22 Details in ibid., p. 82.

23 Ibid.

24 Ibid., p. 64. See also Magosaki Ukeru, *Nichibei domei no shotai, meiso suru anzen hosho* (Tokyo: Kodansha gendai shinsho, 2009), pp. 107–10.

25 Washington was clearly unhappy that the LDP had been shunted aside. Though its response to the Hosokawa government is scarcely to be compared in savagery to that with which it responded sixteen years later to the election of Hatoyama, it did, according to Magosaki, demand the dismissal of chief cabinet secretary Takamura Masayoshi – Hosokawa complied. (Magosaki, *Nichibei domei no shotai*, pp. 141–2.)

26 McCormack and Norimatsu, *Resistant Islands*, passim.

27 Ibid., p. 106.

28 Magosaki, *Nichibei domei no shotai*, p. 117.

29 McCormack and Norimatsu, *Resistant Islands*, p. 104.

30 Ibid., p. 130.

31 "Bei, Nihon ni 8 hyakuoku cho no futanzo yokyu, kaiheitai no guamu iten de," *Ryukyu shimpo*, March 24, 2012.

32 McCormack and Norimatsu, *Resistant Islands*, p. 192.

33 Quoted in Sabrina Salas Matanane, "Congress reviewing DoD Plans," *Kuam News*,

February 15, 2012 (www.kuam.com/story/16946890/2012/02/15/lada-estates-project-moves-forward?clienttype=printable [accessed April 5, 2013]).

34 Governor Nakaima submitted two separate documents in response to the EI statement, in February on the projected airport construction and in March on the projected large-scale reclamation, raising 175 specific objections in the former and 404 in the latter. For accounts of the former, see Sakurai Kunitoshi, "Japan's Illegal Environmental Assessment of the Henoko Base," *The Asia-Pacific Journal – Japan Focus*, February 27, 2012 (http://japanfocus.org/events/view/131 [accessed April 5, 2013]) and "The Henoko Assessment Does Not Pass," *The Asia-Pacific Journal – Japan Focus*, March 4, 2012 (http://japanfocus.org/-John-Junkerman/3701 [accessed April 5, 2013]), and for an account of the latter, "Okinawa gov. blasts base relocation environment report again," *Mainichi Daily News*, March 28, 2012.

35 SLAPP is defined (by Wikipedia) as "strategic lawsuit against public participation, a suit designed to censor, intimidate, and silence critics by burdening them with cost of a legal defence until they abandon their criticism or opposition."

36 "Kisei no ami senzen no soki," *Okinawa taimusu*, March 18, 2012.

37 "UN Panel on Racial Discrimination to Question Japan Over Okinawa Policy," *Mainichi Daily News*, March 14, 2012.

38 "Fukki seron chosa, fubyodo no ue utsu toki da – shin kichi kobamu min-i no hanei o," editorial, *Ryukyu shimpo*, May 10, 2012.

39 "Osupurei: zenkoku chijikai ga hantai ketsugi," *Okinawa taimusu*, July 20, 2012.

40 Kinjo Yoshitaka, president of the City Assembly, quoted in editorial, "Osupurei hantai, shimagurumi no kofun shimesu toki da," editorial, *Ryukyu shimpo*, June 19, 2012.

41 Medoruma Shun, "Osupurei haibi wa nani ka – kiken ninshiki yue no inpei," *Ryukyu shimpo*, June 15, 2012.

42 "United States–Japan Joint Statement: A Shared Vision for the Future," White House, Office of the Press Secretary, April 30, 2012 (www.whitehouse.gov/the-press-office/2012/04/30/united-states-japan-joint-statement-shared-vision-future [accessed April 5, 2013]).

43 "Base-Hosting Governors, Mayor Oppose Osprey Plan," *Japan Times*, July 2, 2012. Also "Osupurei: Zenkoku 15 chiji ga 'anzensei no ken'en," *Okinawa taimusu*, July 10, 2012.

44 "'Okinawa shinko kaihatsu taisei' e no chosen," in Shimabukuro Jun, *Sekai* (Tokyo: Iwanami shoten, 2012), pp. 45–53, at p. 46.

45 See Medoruma Shun, "NO to ienai seijika tachi," Uminari no shima kara, July 17, 2012 (http://blog.goo.ne.jp/awamori777/e/502c985fd40d724097ced833f225038d [accessed April 5, 2013]).

46 William Blum, *Killing Hope: US Military and CIA Interventions since World War II*, updated edition (Monroe, ME: Common Courage Press, 2008) and, by the same author, *Rogue State* (Monroe, ME: Common Courage Press, 2005). For Blum's table of US bombings and assassination plots around the world, see "US Military and CIA Interventions since World War 11," Z-Net, February 23, 2012 (www.zcommunications.org/cntents/184787 [accessed April 5, 2013]).

47 Ron Suskind, *The One Percent Doctrine: Deep Inside America's Pursuit of its Enemies since 9/11* (New York: Simon and Schuster, 2007).

48 Fred Branfman, "When Chomsky wept," Z-Net, June 18, 2012 (www.zcommunications.org/when-chomsky-wept-by-fred-branfman [accessed April 5, 2013]).

49 Andrew Bacevich, *Washington Rules: America's Path to Permanent War* (New York: Henry Holt and Company, 2011). *Pace* Australia's second-longest serving prime minister, John Howard, who told a group of graduating students in Sydney in April 2012 that "we have a very big and enduring relationship with the most peaceful and remarkable country mankind has seen – the United States" (David Humphries, "Dr Howard sees nothing but opportunity in emerging world order," *Sydney Morning Herald*, April 11, 2012).

8 The Japanese military "comfort women" issue and the San Francisco System

Hirofumi Hayashi

Introduction

The purpose of this chapter is to examine how the Japanese military "comfort women" issue has been dealt with under the San Francisco System. After having been ignored for years, in 1991 the "comfort women" issue suddenly became an object of public concern among the international community. In August of that year, Korean former "comfort woman" Kim Hak Sun broke nearly half a century of silence and made her story public. She was followed by several more women, not only in South Korea, but in several other Asian nations and the Netherlands as well. They had been obliged to keep their silence for over forty years.

The courage and dignity of the former "comfort women" who came forward and gave testimony of their own painful experiences had an extraordinary impact on the public, particularly on women. One reason may be that the "comfort women" system was one of the most appalling sexual crimes to be committed against women in the twentieth century.

Although many issues left by World War II remain unsettled, it is reasonable to suppose that the "comfort women" issue is regarded as a symbol of Japan's refusal to acknowledge its war responsibility, and of the international community's lack of regard for women's human rights.

Although the Japanese government has taken certain measures to settle this issue, it is still severely criticized because it has neither accepted its legal responsibility nor paid individual compensation to the victims. In addition, the fact that right wingers who justify Japanese military conduct during the war have considerable influence in the Japanese government and in society as a whole cannot be ignored.

As is commonly known, Japan's war responsibility and its colonial legacy have been major issues in its disputes with other East Asian countries. Resolving these issues is, accordingly, of crucial importance for the harmonious coexistence of countries in East Asia and the Pacific region.

How did the Allies deal with the Japanese military "comfort women" issue after World War II?

The Japanese military fully deployed the military "comfort women" system during the Fifteen Years War, 1931–1945. The first comfort stations were set up in Shanghai, when Japan began its push into China following the Manchurian Incident of 1931 and the establishment of Manchukuo. From 1937, when Japan embarked on full-fledged war with China, the Japanese army began setting up comfort stations in other parts of China. In 1940, when Japanese troops advanced into Indochina, the first comfort stations in Southeast Asia were established. The landing of troops on the Malay Peninsula and the attack on Pearl Harbor in December 1941 mark the outbreak of the Asia-Pacific War. By May 1942, Japanese-occupied territory reached its maximum extension throughout Asia and the Pacific. From Burma and the Andaman–Nicobar islands in the west, to the Indonesian islands in the south, and the Solomon and Marshall Islands group in the east, large parts of the Pacific were brought under Japanese rule.

The comfort station system expanded throughout the war. The "comfort women" consisted of many different nationalities and ethnicities. They included Mainland Chinese, Taiwanese, overseas Chinese, Malays, Thais, Filipinas, Indonesians, Burmese, Vietnamese, Indians, Eurasians, Dutch, Timorese, Japanese, Koreans, and natives of the Pacific islands. There may also have been Laotians and Cambodians.

If one plots the geographical distribution of the comfort stations set up by the Japanese military on a map of the occupied territories, it immediately becomes clear that they spanned more or less the whole occupied area. Toward the end of the war, as Japan started to prepare for a decisive battle in the homeland against the Allied offensive, more and more Japanese troops were stationed on the islands of the Japanese archipelago. Comfort stations were therefore also set up at that time in Okinawa and other parts of Japan. In total, about 20,000 women in the Asia-Pacific region were victimized by the "comfort women" system.[1]

During World War II the Allied nations were already aware of, and had begun to collect information on, Japanese military "comfort women." Some investigators among them regarded the Japanese military's "comfort women" system and other crimes against women as war crimes. So how did the war crimes trials deal with this issue?

Some prosecutors submitted exhibits as evidence to the International Military Tribunal for the Far East (the Tokyo War Crimes Trial), showing that the Japanese military had kidnapped women to work as sex slaves. One exhibit submitted by the Dutch prosecution reads "they arrested women on the streets and after a medical examination placed them in the brothels," as was the case in Pontianak in Borneo. Another exhibit relating to a case in East Timor reads:

> I know of a lot of places where the Japanese forced the chiefs to send native girls to Japanese brothels, by threatening the native chiefs, telling them that if they did not send the girls, the Japanese would go to the chiefs' houses and take away their near[est] female relatives for this purpose.

The French prosecutor submitted an exhibit of a case in Vietnam. The affidavit of a Vietnamese woman reads,

> I was arrested in the town by the Japanese and taken to their Military Police H.Q. situated behind the hospital of the Indo-China Guard.... In the course of their investigation at Lang Son, the Japanese forced several of my fellow-countrywomen who were living with French soldiers, to follow them to a brothel which they had set up at TIEN YEN. By means of a trick I was able to escape them.

It has thus far been confirmed that exhibits of seven cases in which the Japanese military forced women to become "comfort women" were submitted to the court by the prosecution from three countries: the Netherlands, France, and China.[2] As a result of the prosecution's efforts, the findings of the Tokyo Trial made the following reference to "comfort women":

> During the period of Japanese occupation of Kweilin, they committed all kinds of atrocities such as rape and plunder. They recruited women laborers on the pretext of establishing factories. They forced the women thus recruited into prostitution with Japanese troops.

In this case, the victims were Chinese.

Prosecutors from several countries regarded forced prostitution or the coercion of women into such a position as a war crime, but did not regard the Japanese military "comfort women" system, also known as military sexual slavery, as a war crime.

In Class-B and -C war crimes trials, the Dutch prosecuted several cases on suspicion of forced prostitution in Java and Kalimantan. The manager of one comfort station in Guam was also indicted at the US Navy war crimes trial. Although Nationalist China prosecuted three cases, the details are still sketchy.[3]

Nevertheless, the Tokyo Trial neither found the military "comfort women" system to be a war crime nor defined such a system as sexual slavery; we had to wait for the year 2000, when the Women's International War Crimes Tribunal on Japan's military sexual slavery delivered a judgment that pronounced the "comfort women" system as military sexual slavery by Japan, and as a crime against humanity. Although recognition of these issues at the Tokyo Trial was extremely limited and remained at an elementary level, we might say that this early post-war trial laid the groundwork for punishing wartime sexual violence.

Rape was undeniably regarded as a war crime: many cases were brought before both the Tokyo Trial and Class-B and -C trials. According to documents of the Ministry of Justice, Japan, rape was referred to as a war crime in 143 indictments among 5,700 Class-B and -C Japanese accused.[4] However, most of them were handled together with other atrocities, not as a separate crime. As for the Tokyo Trial, 2,282 exhibits submitted by the prosecution were accepted by the court. Among them, more than 100 exhibits referred to rape or other types of sexual violence.[5]

Some war crimes trials did deal with Japanese military "comfort women" cases, most of which resulted in convictions, yet the number was very small in comparison with the gigantic scale of the "comfort women" system. We can therefore say that most of the perpetrators, including high-ranking military officers and bureaucrats, escaped punishment.

The Tokyo Trial was brought to completion in November 1948. Even before it ended, the United States had already lost interest in setting up a second major war crimes trial. In addition, most of the Class-B and -C war crimes trials had been concluded by 1949, while those in Australia continued until April 1951.[6]

War crimes in the San Francisco Peace Treaty and the attitude of the Japanese government

The first paragraph of Article 11 of the San Francisco Peace Treaty (SFPT) reads: "Japan accepts the judgments of the International Military Tribunal for the Far East and of other Allied War Crimes Courts both within and outside Japan, and will carry out the sentences imposed thereby upon Japanese nationals imprisoned in Japan."

The original draft prepared by the United States did not include this paragraph. During negotiations the Japanese government made the following requests to the United States: (1) No more new arraignments; (2) an amnesty on the occasion of the conclusion of the peace treaty; and (3) transfer to Japanese authorities of the execution of sentences.[7] However, the British government asserted that clear notification of war responsibility was needed.[8] In addition, Australia demanded that the United States specify the war responsibility of the Japanese military regime in the preceding sentence.[9] A draft paper prepared by the British government referred to Japan's war of aggression and its responsibility in the preceding sentence. The Japanese government raised strong objections to the British draft, saying that "it would inevitably cause great disappointment to the entire Japanese people."[10]

Consequently, this war crimes clause was added as the result of a compromise between the United States and the United Kingdom/Australia, while a passage referring to war responsibility was dropped.[11] Soon after the final draft was released, Prime Minister Yoshida Shigeru expressed his approval to the US government, noting that this peace treaty bore no reference to Japan's war responsibility.[12]

There is some ambiguity as to how the phrase "accepts the judgments" should be interpreted. A controversy still continues today as to whether "the judgments" includes the legitimacy of the trials themselves, their factual findings and other procedures, or whether it refers only to the judicial decision. Those who want to deny the legitimacy of the war crimes trials try to interpret this phrase in as narrow a sense as possible.

At present, the Japanese Ministry of Foreign Affairs states:

> The Government of Japan acknowledges that there are various arguments regarding this judgment. However, Japan has accepted the judgment of the

International Military Tribunal for the Far East under Article 11 of the San Francisco Peace Treaty. Therefore, in the state to state relationship, the Government of Japan believes that it is in no position to raise any objections regarding this judgment.[13]

Yet this explanation is still ambiguous.

The fact that South Korea, North Korea, China, and Taiwan were not invited to the San Francisco Conference posed another problem. According to the results of our research, the majority of Japanese military "comfort women" were Korean or Chinese.[14] In other words, the key victimized nations whose presence should have been indispensable had no chance to be involved in negotiating or signing the peace treaty.

The United States did try to invite South Korea to the conference. On April 23, 1951, the Japanese government submitted a memorandum entitled "Korea and the Peace Treaty" to the United States, in which it expressed its opposition to South Korea's attendance on the grounds that "this country, not having been in a state of either war or belligerency with Japan, cannot be considered an Allied Power." In addition, Japan showed its discriminatory sentiments by stating that "it should be noted that the majority of Korean residents in Japan are Communists." The Japanese government was afraid that Koreans "would acquire and assert their rights as Allied Nation nationals regarding property, compensation, etc." if Korea were to become a signatory to the peace treaty. At a meeting with John Foster Dulles, consultant to the secretary of state, Yoshida expressed Japan's objections to the participation of South Korea, saying that he wanted to repatriate Koreans because most of them were communists and caused social disruption in Japan.[15] This clearly shows discriminatory sentiments toward Koreans, as well as the anti-communist stance of the Japanese government and Prime Minister Yoshida. The United Kingdom also opposed the invitation of South Korea on the grounds that Korea was a colony and not one of the Allied nations. In the end, the South Korean government was not invited to the San Francisco Conference. Although it had prepared to take part in negotiations for the peace treaty, the South Korean government had no chance to make its demands heard. Yet even so, it is reasonable to suppose that even the South Korean government was not overly concerned with the suffering of the Japanese military "comfort women."

As for China, the United Kingdom supported inviting the People's Republic of China (Communist China), while the United States wanted to invite the Republic of China (Nationalist China or Taiwan). In the end, neither China nor Taiwan was invited. Meanwhile, pressure from the United States obliged Japan to form ties with Taiwan. On April 28, 1952, the day Japan recovered its independence, Japan and Taiwan signed a Japan–China Peace Treaty. This meant that Japan did not recognize Communist China. Such factious relations with China continued until 1972.

The Nationalist government conducted all Class-B and -C war crimes trials in China, concluding its war crimes trials by January 1949. Soon afterward, Nationalist

China escaped to Taiwan. On October 1, 1949, the founding of the People's Republic of China (PRC) was declared.

In the 1952 peace treaty with Japan, Nationalist China waived its right to claim war compensation because the Nationalist government had been expelled from mainland China by the Communists, and support from Japan was imperative for survival.[16] All Japanese prisoners under sentence by Nationalist China were released in August 1952, when the Japan–China Peace Treaty came into effect.

This neglect of the war crimes issue came about because of the situation in East Asia at that time. The United States had already lost interest in the war crimes issue, and was now more interested in utilizing Japan as an ally in the fight against communism. The SFPT was prepared and ratified in the midst of the Korean War. As Japan was an important military and economic partner for the West, it was integrated into the Western camp by the SFPT.

Despite Article 11, as soon as Japan regained independence its government began to appeal to the Allied governments for clemency, and for the release of war criminals serving sentences in the Sugamo Prison in Tokyo. Both the House of Representatives and the House of Councilors adopted several resolutions demanding the release of all war criminals. In May 1952, the Senpan Jukeisha Sewanin kai (Association of Couriers for War Criminals) was founded by former leaders of military, political, and economical circles. They claimed that war criminals were actually victims who had devoted themselves to the nation. An all-out campaign for the release of war criminals had begun. With few exceptions, Japanese society as a whole supported this appeal for clemency; a distorted notion of war criminals as victims rather than as perpetrators of inhumane acts prevailed throughout Japan during the 1950s.[17]

One method employed by the Japanese government to achieve its aim was to use Japan's position in the Cold War. In the mid 1950s, China and Russia began to encourage Japan to restore diplomatic relations. To this end, both countries released and repatriated Japanese war criminals. In turn, the Japanese government and politicians utilized this policy of leniency to gain the release of other war criminals. For example, in October 1953, Ikeda Hayato, an aide to Prime Minister Yoshida who later became prime minister himself, suggested to Assistant Secretary of State for Far Eastern Affairs Walter S. Robertson that the release of war criminals should be an essential condition for the promotion of Japanese rearmament that the United States was then demanding. In addition, on November 11 of that same year, a bureaucrat from the Ministry of Foreign Affairs stated at talks with the US State Department's Office of North East Asian Affairs that he was afraid anti-American feelings might arise among the Japanese if the United States continued to refuse to release war criminals while Russia was repatriating the Japanese war criminals it had held in custody.[18]

Kishi Nobusuke, who became prime minister in 1957, also appealed to the US government for the release of war criminals, including Class-A war criminals. He himself had been arrested on suspicion of Class-A war crimes, and was released at the end of 1948. If the Allied nations had conducted a second Tokyo war crimes trial, he would undoubtedly have been prosecuted.

At that time, the anti-American base movement in Japan had intensified; sympathy for neutralism was growing, not only among leftists, but among conservatives as well. Securing Japan as an ally was imperative for the US government, which decided to support the Kishi administration. One measure for showing its support was the withdrawal of ground combat troops from the Japanese mainland; another was the release of war criminals.

Secretary of State John Foster Dulles stated in a memorandum to President Eisenhower:

> the continued incarceration of these war criminals almost twelve years after the termination of the war is an important source of political and psychological friction between this Government and the Government of Japan. The Japanese consider such detention as inconsistent with our close alignment with them and again and again have requested that we act to alleviate the situation.[19]

By early 1958, US ground combat forces, including the Marines and the Army, had retreated from the mainland of Japan. In addition, by the end of that year, the last war criminals were released from Sugamo Prison. As a category of person, war criminals thus completely disappeared from Japan.[20]

Shortly afterwards, in April 1959, 346 war criminals who had been executed or died in prison were enshrined in Yasukuni Shrine. To achieve this, the Japanese government secretly passed lists of war criminals to the Yasukuni Shrine; the decision to enshrine each war criminal was made cooperatively. In addition, the remaining executed war criminals were enshrined in October 1959 and October 1966.[21] As there were no war criminals in prison at that time, the Allied nations could do nothing about it. In addition, the impending revision of the Japan–United States Security Treaty threw Japan into political turmoil. Faced with a mounting campaign against revision of the treaty, the Japan– United States alliance was itself held in the balance. The war criminals issue was dropped as a matter of concern by the US government and its allies.

We may note in passing that the Ministry of Health and Welfare had already begun planning to enshrine executed war criminals early in 1952, before Japan recovered its independence. They examined the issue in secret, keeping an eye on public opinion and international circumstances. According to a series of documents mentioned here, war criminals were regarded as victims of the war whose honor should be redeemed.[22]

In 1967, a war criminal who had been convicted and sentenced to ten years' imprisonment by the Dutch war crimes trial on a charge of forced prostitution was enshrined at Yasukuni because he had died of illness while serving his sentence. He had managed a comfort station and canteen for Japanese officials in Java.[23] This enshrinement was conducted through an agreement between the Yasukuni Shrine and the Ministry of Health and Welfare. That it honored a man convicted of war crimes suggests that the Japanese government did not regard forced prostitution as a war crime, and, further, that it substantively ignored Article 11 of the SFPT.

Article 11 was not originally written by the United States, but was inserted as a result of a compromise between the United States and nations of the British Commonwealth. The British feared the re-emergence of Japanese militarism. Nevertheless, the Cold War was given top priority in the Western camp.

War compensation in the SFPT

Provisions for war compensation in the SFPT were extremely limited and generous to Japan. Article 14 reads:

> It is recognized that Japan should pay reparations to the Allied Powers for the damage and suffering caused by it during the war. Nevertheless it is also recognized that the resources of Japan are not presently sufficient, if it is to maintain a viable economy, to make complete reparation for all such damage and suffering and at the same time meet its other obligations.
>
> Therefore,
>
> 1. Japan will promptly enter into negotiations with Allied Powers so desiring, whose present territories were occupied by Japanese forces and damaged by Japan, with a view to assisting to compensate those countries for the cost of repairing the damage done, by making available the services of the Japanese people in production, salvaging and other work for the Allied Powers in question. Such arrangements shall avoid the imposition of additional liabilities on other Allied Powers, and, where the manufacturing of raw materials is called for, they shall be supplied by the Allied Powers in question, so as not to throw any foreign exchange burden upon Japan.

Compensation for "those members of the armed forces of the Allied Powers who suffered undue hardships while prisoners of war of Japan" – in other words, former POWs – is referred to in Article 16. This provision was included at the demand of the United Kingdom and Australia. According to Article 16, Japanese assets "in countries which were neutral during the war, or which were at war with any of the Allied Powers" shall be transferred to

> the International Committee of the Red Cross which shall liquidate such assets and distribute the resultant fund to appropriate national agencies, for the benefit of former prisoners of war and their families on such basis as it may determine to be equitable.

A total of about 4.5 million pounds, or about 5.9 billion yen, was transferred to the International Committee of the Red Cross, which delivered it to 203,599 ex-POWs in fourteen countries during 1956 and 1961.[24]

The Netherlands government, furthermore, demanded Japanese compensation for Dutch detainees in Indonesia under the Japanese occupation, because about 27,000 had perished and many were suffering from the after-effects, both physical and mental, of what they had endured during their internment. After several years of negotiations, the Netherlands and Japan reached an agreement that Japan should pay ten million US dollars. This amounted to an average of ninety-one US dollars per person.[25] As this compensation to POWs and internees was not sufficient to satisfy the victims, they again demanded compensation from Japan, taking legal action against the Japanese government during the 1990s. However, their demands were dismissed by Japanese courts.[26] Through all of this, the former "comfort women" victimized by Japanese war crimes were ignored by both the Japanese and Allied governments.

After recovering its independence, the Japanese government conducted negotiations and concluded war compensation conventions by 1960 with Burma, the Philippines, Indonesia, and South Vietnam. In addition, Japan concluded several economic assistance conventions with five countries in Southeast Asia as a gesture of apology. Yet Japanese money did not go to the victims of Japanese atrocities. Instead, Japanese compensation made allocations for marine vessels, various kinds of machinery, and construction of dams, railways, roads, factories, and so on. In Indonesia, some of the money was spent on the construction of hotels and department stores.[27] Needless to say, the "comfort women" issue was not a topic in these negotiations, at least as far as we know.

War compensation provided a good chance for Japan to expand its business network in Southeast Asia, where it had lost its export market after defeat in the war. Furthermore, after mainland China was taken over by the Communists, Japan lost its most important trading partner and site for overseas investments. The compensation method prescribed by the SFPT became a tool for integrating Japan's economy into the Western camp by cutting off economic ties between Japan and China.

On the other hand, newly independent countries in Southeast Asia were trying to recover from the legacy of colonialism and working to establish their economies on the road to nation-building. They needed economic and technological assistance from advanced countries. The leaders of these countries gave precedence to nation-building – in particular, economic development – over compensation to individual war crimes victims. This is one reason why the victims of Japanese war crimes, in particular "comfort women," were not able to speak out or to begin making demands. They had to wait until these dictatorships had collapsed.

South Korea and Japan finally concluded a Treaty of Basic Relations, in addition to other agreements; normalization of diplomatic relations was realized in 1965. Japan provided 300 million dollars, or 108 billion yen, without charge, and a further 200 million dollars, or 72 billion yen, for profit, in accordance with an agreement on the settlement of problems concerning property, claims, and economic cooperation between Japan and the Republic of Korea. This was not an agreement for compensation, but for economic assistance. In short, Japan offered economic assistance in return for South Korea's waiver of its right to claim compensation.

The South Korean government put economic development first, because President Pak Jeong-hui, who had seized power by military *coup d'état* in 1961 and assumed the presidency in 1963, wanted to consolidate his position with the assistance of the United States and Japan. As the United States was beginning military intervention in Vietnam at that time, it requested that Japan provide economic assistance to South Korea in its stead. Thus, economic assistance from Japan was delivered without charge for the importation of raw materials, the development of agricultural water, the construction of steel plants, and so on. Economic assistance for profit was also allocated to the construction of the social infrastructure.[28]

In the 1970s, the Korean government used money from Japan to pay reparation of 2.5 billion won to 8,552 victims' families and 6.6 billion won to those whose assets had suffered damage. The total was 9.1 billion won, or 5.8 billion yen, which was just 5 percent of the total amount of economic assistance without charge from Japan.[29] In the former case, the beneficiaries were limited to families of victims who were conscripted as soldiers, civilian employees, or laborers, and who had died before August 15, 1945. These beneficiaries were only a tiny proportion of war victims. Furthermore, victims who had managed to survive were precluded from the start.

According to documents recently declassified by both governments, the "comfort women" issue was again not mentioned during negotiations between South Korea and Japan. In any case, former "comfort women" have been excluded from all compensation or economic assistance.

Most of Japan's negotiation partners were under autocratic or authoritarian rule. Some, such as South Korea, were under the control of a military dictatorship.

The People's Republic of China and Japan finally resumed diplomatic relations in 1972, but the Chinese Communist government also waived its right to claim war compensation because China needed Japan's political and economic support in order to compete with Russia during a new phase of the Cold War. War victims were ignored by both Chinese governments. International circumstances once again made it possible for Japan to escape its war compensation responsibilities.

Former "comfort women" survivors were forced to keep silent under the San Francisco System until 1991. One reason was that they lived in countries whose governments ignored or oppressed victims' desires. The democratization of these countries, which began during the 1980s and was further strengthened during the 1990s, made it possible for them to speak out in public. In the case of China it was not democratization but economic liberalization that increased people's freedom, despite the continuance of one-party rule.[30]

As a number of feminists have pointed out, an additional reason was prejudice and discrimination against victims of sexual violence by the patriarchal society in which they lived. To take the case of South Korea, the "comfort women" issue was originally dealt with from the perspective of male-dominated nationalism, rather than from that of women's human rights. While blaming Japan for the atrocities it perpetrated, many Koreans ignored the suffering of the victims themselves. Indeed, the victims were regarded as a shameful disgrace to the nation.

To a certain extent, this was also the case in communist countries, although with a different slant. In China, for instance, former "comfort women" were sometimes accused of being "counterrevolutionaries." One woman in Shanxi Province had been abducted and confined in a house as a sexual slave for Japanese garrison troops. Tragically, in the early 1950s she was charged as a "counterrevolutionary" because she had lived with Japanese soldiers for a long time, and given birth to a Japanese soldier's child. She was sentenced to three years' imprisonment. At the time of the Cultural Revolution, she was publicly shamed and forced to wear a sign with the message "Historical Counterrevolutionary" around her neck. She committed suicide.[31]

Thus the women involved were doubly victimized, by the Japanese during the war and by the social prejudice and discrimination they suffered in their own societies afterward.

Progress in and achievements of research

Although there had previously been some interest in Japanese aggression and atrocities in the Asia-Pacific region, the controversy over this issue really began during the 1980s. Before the 1980s, most books published in Japan about the war had dealt with Japanese suffering, such as in Hiroshima and Nagasaki, and with the US air raids against Japanese cities. However, the history textbook dispute of 1982, when the Ministry of Education ordered that references to Japan's aggression and military atrocities be deleted from history textbooks, had a considerable impact on Japanese society. With fierce criticism coming from other Asian countries, many Japanese were made aware of the nature and extent of Japan's wartime aggression.

Moreover, this issue took on new urgency due to the fact that Japan, which had already become a major economic power, was trying to become an important military power as well. Of particular significance was the fact that many veterans, who until then had remained silent about their inhumane conduct, began to speak out both about their own wartime actions and against Japan's new push for military strength.[32] Historians began to look into war crimes such as the Nanjing Massacre and the biological warfare experiments of Unit 731. Even so, the "comfort women" issue still received little attention, although most historians knew about it.

As I noted at the beginning of this chapter, this situation changed dramatically in 1991. The bravery of the former "comfort women" in speaking out has encouraged not only supporting campaigns, but also researchers. There is not enough space here for a detailed account of the research, but I will summarize the main findings so far.[33] First, it has been demonstrated that the Japanese government and military were fully and systematically involved in planning, establishing, and operating the "comfort women" system. Japanese officials involved were Home Ministry personnel, including prefectural governors and police of all ranks, Foreign Ministry officials, and the governors-general of Korea and Taiwan.

Second, the Japanese military set up so-called "comfort stations" in almost every area they occupied. In addition to Korean, Taiwanese, and Japanese women, local women in the occupied areas were victimized.

Third, the "comfort women" system was clearly sexual slavery, organized and controlled by the military, and constituted sexual, racial, ethnic, and economic discrimination and the violation of the women's human rights. The notion of women's human rights finally entered the discussion on war crimes and war responsibility issues in the 1990s. At the time of the SFPT, individual human rights, in particular women's human rights, were not considered important.

Fourth, although one of the reasons given by the Japanese military for introducing the "comfort women" system was to prevent the rape of local women by soldiers, rape was not eliminated. In areas under Japanese military occupation, the systematic organization of military comfort stations was established in urban areas. Women from Korea, Taiwan, and other parts of the empire, as well as from Japan, were sent as "comfort women" to these stations, set up by the quartermaster corps. This type of comfort station was most common in areas where Japanese military rule was relatively well established and the rape of local women was kept in check by military police in order to win the support of the local population. However, in rural areas, where the army encountered strong anti-Japanese resistance, the local population as a whole was considered to be anti-Japanese. In these areas, not only were massacres, ill treatment, and looting rampant, but the rape of local women by soldiers went unchecked. The appalling acts of sexual violence perpetrated by the Japanese army in Shanxi Province in North China and the Philippines during the last phase of the war can be regarded as representative of this pattern. There, Japanese troops routinely abducted, confined, and repeatedly raped women. Japanese troops frequently forced village leaders to provide them with women. In other words, sexual violence against women at comfort stations took place alongside the rape of local women.[34]

Fifth, it has been proven that the Japanese system of military "comfort women" violated numerous international laws, including laws against enslavement and the transportation of minors across national borders. There is overwhelming evidence that the "comfort women" system constituted a war crime and a crime against humanity. In addition, overseas transport of women from Japan proper for prostitution was banned by the Japanese criminal code of the time. The police authority of Japan realized this; however, the Police Bureau of the Home Ministry decided to give tacit approval to such conduct and gave instructions to that effect to each prefectural governor and chief of police for the convenience of the military.[35] The "comfort women" system was therefore not only an international but a domestic crime as well.

Finally, the suffering of the women involved did not end with liberation. Many "comfort women" were unable to return home. Some still remain where they were abandoned. They have suffered after-effects such as disease, injury, psychological trauma, and post-traumatic stress disorder, as well as social discrimination for their past.

It may be worth considering whether the "comfort women" system was or is unique to Japan, or something common to all militaries in the twentieth century. As there is no space here for an extended discussion, I will give only a brief summary.[36]

During World War II, the two nations that employed a systematic method of providing soldiers with "comfort women" or something similar were Germany and Japan, as far as has been established by proof. As mentioned previously, the Japanese government and military were fully and systematically involved in planning, establishing, and operating the "comfort women" system.

On the other hand, some US troops dispatched to various places throughout the world often made use of brothels, and military doctors sometimes conducted medical checks of prostitutes. American officers and soldiers commonly associated with prostitutes or local lovers. However, the military authority in Washington, DC has generally adopted an official policy of repression of prostitution. Detached troops therefore tried to get the local authorities to control prostitution so the US military could pretend they had nothing to do with it. Although the United States and Japan have some points in common, we may say that the Japanese "comfort women" system was unique.

It should also be added that the development of research on Japanese military "comfort women" provided an impetus to research on German military prostitution under the Nazi regime. It has come to light that the Nazi regime set up brothels in concentration camps, while the German armed forces made use of military brothels.[37] Comparative studies between the cases of Germany and Japan should be further expanded in the future.

Survivors' campaigns

We may note that Korean women took the lead in the campaign to publicize the "comfort women" issue in the 1980s. The Korean Council for Women Drafted for Military Sexual Slavery by Japan was set up in November 1990 and demanded that the Japanese government reveal the truth about the "comfort women" system, make formal apology to the women, and pay reparations to the victims. This campaign encouraged former "comfort women" to speak out.[38] With the support of non-governmental organizations (NGOs), lawyers, and researchers, the surviving victims began to file lawsuits against the Japanese government. The first of these was filed by Kim Hak Sun and other Koreans in December 1991.

The Japanese government denied any involvement by the military in the organization of the "comfort women" system and refused not only to apologize or provide reparations, but even to conduct an investigation of any kind.

However, the government was unable to sustain this position, when, in January 1992, historian Yoshimi Yoshiaki unearthed official documents in the Defense Agency's National Institute of Defense Studies that proved conclusively that the military had played a key role in the establishment and control of "comfort stations." As a result, Prime Minister Miyazawa Kiichi publicly admitted that the Japanese military had been involved; he issued the first apology concerning the "comfort women" issue.

The issue then came into the popular consciousness not only in Japan but also throughout Asia and the world. Research on the issue began and popular movements demanding a formal state apology and reparations to the victims appeared. I will not here go into the campaign in Japan in detail, but I will mention the campaign to support lawsuits brought by former "comfort women."

Including Kim Hak Sun's case, a total of ten cases have been filed by Korean, Korean-Japanese, Chinese, Taiwanese, Filipina, and Dutch survivors of Japan's military sexual slavery. Among these, in only one case did the plaintiffs enjoy a partial victory, which was later denied by the High and Supreme Courts, thus finalizing the dismissal of all of the plaintiffs' claims. In all of the decisions, the core of the plaintiffs' claims were rejected on grounds of domestic and/or international law, such as statute of limitations, the immunity of the state at the time of the act concerned, and the non-subjectivity of the individual under international law. However, it is important to note that, in eight out of the ten cases, the courts acknowledged the fact that the plaintiffs had endured great suffering and admitted that the human rights of the former "comfort women" had been seriously violated.[39] As all of the lawsuits mentioned above have been finalized, recent campaigns in Japan have focused on gaining compensation for each victim.

Let us now turn to international campaigns.[40] In August 1992, the first Asian Solidarity Conference, sponsored by the Korean Council, was held in Seoul. Representatives from South Korea, the Philippines, Taiwan, and Japan concluded that the issue of "comfort women" was a prime example of how the patriarchal system, militarism, and war had come together to violate women and trample their human rights. Furthermore, the conference determined that resolving this issue would be a crucial step toward building a peaceful world and preventing the recurrence of war crimes. Since this gathering, cooperation among organizations in the victimized areas and those in Japan has increased. By 2011, this conference had been held ten times.

Steps toward democracy in South Korea, the Philippines, Taiwan, Indonesia, East Timor, and China, facilitated by the end of the Cold War, have made it possible for groups in these and other nations to organize and to publicize the plight of the former "comfort women." And as women have brought a gender-specific viewpoint to the issue, victims and their supporters in various countries have joined in solidarity to criticize nationalist attempts to conceal information about the "comfort women."

The "comfort women" issue first came before the UN Commission on Human Rights in 1992. Since then, it has repeatedly been taken up, despite objections by the Japanese government, which claims that the UN has no jurisdiction over events that took place before the organization came into being. The commission accepted a report by Special Rapporteur Rhadika Coomaraswamy in January 1996, which made six recommendations to the Japanese government. These included acknowledgment of legal responsibility, payment of compensation to individual victims, the making of a public apology, and the identification and punishment of perpetrators to the extent possible.

The UN Sub-commission on Human Rights welcomed a final report by Special Rapporteur Gay J. McDougall in August 1998: "Systematic Rape, Sexual Slavery and Slavery-like Practices during Armed Conflict." The report's appendix is entitled "An Analysis of the Legal Liability of the Government of Japan for 'Comfort Women Stations' Established during the Second World War." One of the major aims of this report was to end the cycle of impunity for slavery, including sexual slavery, and for sexual violence, including rape. The report states,

> One significant impetus for the Sub-commission's decision to commission this study was the increasing international recognition of the true scope and character of the harms perpetrated against the more than 200,000 women enslaved by the Japanese military in "comfort stations" during the Second World War.

And, in conclusion: "Sadly, this failure to address crimes of a sexual nature committed on a massive scale during the Second World War has added to the level of impunity with which similar crimes are committed today." Resolving the "comfort women" issue has been regarded as an important item on the agenda of international movements against acts of sexual violence and slavery that continue to occur in contemporary armed conflicts.

In addition to recommendations for individual compensation, the UN report recommended that responsible government and military personnel be prosecuted for their culpability in establishing and maintaining the rape centers. It also stressed the need for mechanisms to ensure criminal prosecution and to provide compensation.

Thus, the "comfort women" issue can be regarded not only as one of war crimes and war responsibility, but also as one aspect of sexual violence and discrimination in male-dominated societies. In other words, settling the "comfort women" issue is an essential move toward redressing sexual violence and deprivation of the rights of women in contemporary societies. The international solidarity achieved among women in victimized countries and Japan is an important step toward these goals.[41]

Despite pressure from various international movements and organizations, the Japanese government continues to deny legal responsibility for war crimes and crimes against humanity committed against women before and during World War II. It also refuses to pay individual compensation.

The Japanese government did establish the Asian Women's Fund in July 1995. According to the official description of the fund, "the Fund will raise funds in the private sector as a means to enact the Japanese people's atonement for former wartime comfort women." This "atonement" fund was raised through direct donations from the Japanese public. Note that this "atonement" fund is paid for not by the government but by public subscription, and that it offers not compensation, but a form of charity. This approach demonstrates the Japanese government's refusal to accept legal responsibility, even after tacitly acknowledging moral responsibility for atrocities committed against the "comfort women."

When the Japanese government refuses individual compensation, it always makes the following claims: Japan concluded the SFPT, bilateral peace treaties, agreements and instruments with countries concerned, and in accordance with them carried out payment of reparations and other items in good faith. In this way, issues of claims concerning the war have been legally settled with the countries of the parties to these treaties, agreements, and instruments. In other words, the SFPT and its subordinate treaties and conventions have been used as an excuse to reject claims for individual compensation. The Asian Women's Fund was set up in accordance with this line. As a result, the fund has been condemned by most former "comfort women" and by their support groups around the world.

In contrast to the German government, Japan has never prosecuted a single Japanese war criminal or any person responsible for military sexual slavery. Nor has it provided even one yen of government funds in individual reparations to victims. The international war crimes tribunals for the former Yugoslavia and Rwanda, which are prosecuting sexual violence as a crime against humanity for the first time, provide close parallels to the issues posed by the "comfort women." The establishment of the International Criminal Court is also of great significance.

After a 1997 international conference in Tokyo on violence against women in war and armed conflict situations, VAWW-NET Japan (Violence Against Women in War Network, Japan) was organized in January 1998. VAWW-NET Japan proposed to other related organizations that a war crimes tribunal be held. An international organizing committee (IOC) was set up jointly by the Korean Council, the Asian Center for Women's Human Rights (ASCENT)-Philippines, and VAWW-NET Japan. The committee was eventually composed of representatives from North and South Korea, China, Taiwan, the Philippines, Indonesia, and Japan. Three other countries took part in the tribunal that was held in Tokyo in December 2000: the Netherlands, Malaysia, and East Timor. The grand sum of campaigns and research during the 1990s was the Women's International War Crimes Tribunal 2000 in Tokyo. Although the tribunal would have no legal power to punish those found responsible for war crimes, the hope was to clearly establish that the system of military sexual slavery implemented by the Japanese military and government constituted a war crime against women and a crime against humanity.

In preparing for the tribunal, victims, legal experts, historians, and other participants from each country cooperated to prepare evidence and testimony. The five tribunal judges were selected from among internationally renowned experts in international law, including a former head of the international war crimes tribunal for the former Yugoslavia, who was chosen to preside. The IOC planned to run the tribunal as closely as possible to the workings of an actual court. The Japanese government was asked to attend, but no reply was ever received.

The tribunal took place December 8–12, 2000, with judgment delivered on the final day. More than 1,000 people, including over sixty former "comfort women" from various countries, attended each day. The tribunal found Emperor Hirohito guilty of responsibility for rape and sexual slavery, a crime against humanity, and determined that the government of Japan was responsible for establishing and maintaining the "comfort women" system. Verdicts on twenty other military and political leaders accused of crimes against humanity were presented in the final judgment in December 2001 in The Hague, Netherlands.

For the first time, the emperor has been found guilty of war crimes. Since the impunity from prosecution enjoyed by the emperor has led to impunity for the Japanese government and high-ranking government officials, this finding is highly significant, albeit lacking legal authority as the judgment of a citizens' tribunal. In a sense, this is the culmination of ten years of work, as the tribunal made full use of the accumulated historical research and drew on the progress of the moment.

In concluding this chapter, the Wednesday Demonstrations are worth a mention.[42] Since January 1992, a demonstration has been held without exception every Wednesday at noon in front of the Japanese Embassy in Seoul for the restoration of the dignity and human rights of the former "comfort women." This series of demonstrations marked its 1,000th protest on December 14, 2011, when solidarity demonstrations were held worldwide in eight countries, including Korea and Japan, to resolve the "comfort women" issue. These demonstrations in Seoul are the best opportunity to show international solidarity, because people from various countries take part in them every week. Nothing like this happened during the Cold War era. This is one of the new realities that has arisen since the end of the twentieth century.

As stated above, the "comfort women" issue has been understood and interpreted in an increasingly broader context. To give one example, the Korean Council for Women Drafted for Japan's Military Sexual Slavery has recently been dealing not only with Japan's past behavior, but also with South Korean sexual violence against Vietnamese women during the Vietnam War, and ongoing sexual violence against Korean women by US soldiers stationed in South Korea. This broadening of the scope of "comfort women" issues is also taking place in Japan and other countries. It suggests an agenda for action that takes into account acts of sexual violence perpetrated by the military, and by individual soldiers in many other societies that engage in military action and/or maintain military forces abroad.[43] This has provided the impetus, not only for a reappraisal of the way we view military sexual violence, but also for a new movement aimed at dealing with military sexual violence on a global scale.

In addition, supporters of the former "comfort women" criticize not only wartime sexual violence by the military, but that which occurs in everyday life in patriarchal societies. Human trafficking, in which many women from developing countries are brought to countries such as Korea or Japan for prostitution is an important issue on their agenda.

Feminist perspectives have raised awareness of these issues among women internationally. Needless to say, feminists hold a variety of views. For instance, some feminists assert that the military "comfort women" issue should be solved in parallel with the issue of regulated prostitution, and that compensation should be paid both to former "comfort women" and victims of regulated prostitution. Others tend to identify the Japanese "comfort women" system with sexual exploitation by the US military. It seems to me that feminist viewpoints may increase in complexity. In any event, it is reasonable to say that feminists have done much to advance the movement toward the settlement of this issue by bringing more and more people, particularly women, into the movement.

Conclusion

During the war crimes trials, the Allied nations regarded forced prostitution or the coercion of women into such a position as a war crime. Although a war crimes clause was inserted into the SFPT, it has not been adhered to by the Japanese government. In addition, war compensation clauses in the treaty were modified in accordance with US policy during the Cold War. The "comfort women" issue was set aside in the process of negotiations and the implementation of compensation for victims of the war.

The former "comfort women" were forced to keep silent until the 1990s under the repression of undemocratic regimes that held power in East Asian countries within the framework of the Cold War. Since then, campaigns that support former "comfort women" and that demand a formal apology and individual compensation from the Japanese government have developed. Such campaigns have fostered grassroots international cooperation for the first time in East Asia. Although people and countries in East Asia were long divided under the framework of the San Francisco System, this international cooperation should be an important factor in helping them move toward a new era.

It seems reasonable to suppose that the resolution of this issue will proceed concurrently with the creation of a new framework in the East Asia-Pacific region. Settling this issue could contribute to promoting the formation of a new community across this entire region that would be less militarized and less aggressive.

Notes

1 For the development of the Japanese military "comfort women" system, see Yoshimi Yoshiaki, *Comfort Women: Sexual Slavery in the Japanese Military During World War II* (New York: Columbia University Press, 2000). Also see Yoshimi Yoshiaki and Hayashi Hirofumi (eds.), *Nihongun Ianfu* [Japanese military comfort women] (Tokyo: Otsuki Shoten, 1995) and Yoshimi Yoshiaki (ed.), *Jugun Ianfu Shiryo-shu* [Documents on military comfort women] (Tokyo: Otsuki-Shoten, 1992).

2 The three exhibits mentioned here are Exhibit No. 1702, 1972A, and 2120. Also see Nihon no Senso Sekinin Shiryo Senta [The Center for Research and Documentation on Japan's War Responsibility], "Tokyo Saiban de Sabakareta Nihongun 'Ianfu' Seido" [The Japanese military "comfort women" system adjudicated by the Tokyo War Crimes Trial], *Senso Sekinin Kenkyu* [The report on Japan's war responsibility], 56 (June 2007), pp. 11–17; Yoshiaki Yoshimi, Rumiko Nishino, and Hirofumi Hayashi, *Koko made wakatta Nihon-gun Ianfu Seido* [Clarified picture of the Japanese military "comfort women" system] (Kyoto: Kamogawa Shuppan, 2007), pp. 33–7, and Yuma Totani, *The Tokyo War Crimes Trial* (Cambridge, MA: Harvard University Press, 2008), pp. 176–8.

3 Hirofumi Hayashi, *Bi-Shi-kyu Senpan Saiban* [Class B & C war crimes trials] (Tokyo: Iwanami Shoten, 2005), pp. 144–7. On the Guam case, see Hirofumi Hayashi, *Senpan Saiban no Kenkyu* [A study on war crimes trials] (Tokyo: Bensei Shuppan, 2010), chapter 6.

4 Hayashi, *Bi-Shi-kyu Senpan Saiban*, p. 64.

5 Yoshiaki Yoshimi (ed.), *Tokyo Saiban: Sei Boryoku Kankei Shiryoshu* [Tokyo War Crimes Trial: Documents relating to sexual violence] (Tokyo: Gendaishiryo Shuppan, 2011), pp. 13–37.

6 On the Australian case, see Hayashi, *Senpan Saiban no Kenkyu*, pp. 171–4.

7 "Suggested Agenda" prepared by the Ministry of Foreign Affairs and submitted to the US government on January 30, 1951, in *Process Verbal on Conclusion of the Peace Treaty* 4: 24 (The Diplomatic Archives of the Ministry of Foreign Affairs of Japan).

8 CAB134/290 (National Archives of the UK). See Yoichi Kibata, "Tainichi Kowa to Igirisu no Ajia Seisaku" [The peace treaty and British policy for Asia], in *Sanfuranshisuko Kowa* [San Francisco Peace Treaty], edited by Akio Watanabe and Seigen Miyazato (Tokyo: Tokyo Daigaku Shuppankai, 1986), pp. 172–3.

9 Tsutomu Kikuchi, "Osutoraria no Tainichi Kowa Gaiko" [Australian peace diplomacy to Japan] in Watanabe and Miyazato (eds.), *Sanfuranshisuko Kowa*, pp. 203–4.

10 *Process Verbal on Conclusion of the Peace Treaty* 5: 244–53.

11 Kentaro Awaya, *Tokyo Saiban-ron* [A study of Tokyo War Crimes Trial] (Tokyo: Otsuki Shoten, 1989), pp. 182–91.

12 Yoshida's speech at the National Diet on August 16, 1951. See Kumao Nishimura, *Sanfuranshisuko Heiwa Joyaku* [The San Francisco Peace Treaty] (Tokyo: Kashima Kenkyujo Shuppankai, 1971), pp. 178–9.

13 Website of the Ministry of Foreign Affairs of Japan (www.mofa.go.jp/policy/qa/faq16.html#q9 [accessed June 16, 2012]).

14 "Ianfu nisareta Josei wa dorekurai irunoka" [How many women were forced to be comfort women?], website of the Women's Active Museum on War and Peace (www.wam-peace.org/index.php/ianfu-mondai/qa#q05 [accessed June 16, 2012]). There is no indication of an author of this article on the website, but I wrote it at the request of the museum.

15 *Process Verbal on Conclusion of the Peace Treaty* 5: 288, 315.

16 Yin Yanjun, "Nihon no Sengo Shori" [Post-war Japan's treatment of war issues] in *Nenpo Nihon Gendaishi* [Annual on Japanese modern history] 5 (1999): 90–99.

17 Hayashi, *Bi-Shi-kyu Senpan Saiban*, pp. 190–1, and Aiko Utsumi, "Heiwa Joyaku to Senpan no Shakuho" [The peace treaty and the release of war criminals] in *Nenpo Nihon Gendaishi* [Annual on Japanese modern history] 5 (1999): 159–66.

18 *Kowa Joyaku Hakko-go ni okeru Honpojin Senpan Kankei Zakken* [Miscellaneous documents on Japanese war criminals after the effectuation of the peace treaty], vol. 2 (Diplomatic Archives of the Ministry of Foreign affairs of Japan).

19 US Department of State, *Foreign Relations of the United States, 1955–1957*, vol. 23, Part 1 Japan (Washington, DC: United States Government Printing Office, 1991), p. 356.

20 Hayashi, *Bi-Shi-kyu Senpan Saiban*, chapter 6, and Hirofumi Hayashi, *Beigun kichi no Rekishi: Sekai Nettowaku no Keisei to Tenkai* [History of US military bases: The

formation and development of a worldwide network] (Tokyo: Yoshikawa Kobunkan, 2012), pp. 134–43.

21 Hayashi, *Bi-Shi-kyu Senpan Saiban*, p. 198, and Nihon no Senso Sekinin Shiryo Senta [Center for Research and Documentation on Japan's War Responsibility], "Senpan no Yasukuni Jinja Goshi" [Enshrinement of war criminals at Yasukuni Shrine], *Senso Sekinin Kenkyu* [The report on Japan's war responsibility] 57 (September 2007): 76–87.

22 *Senso Saiban Sanko Shiryo* [Reference materials on war crimes trials] preserved in the National Archives of Japan. For the summary of these documents, see *Asahi Shinbun*, January 21 and April 28, 2012.

23 Aiko Utsumi, "Senpan toshite Sabakareta Ianjo Keieisha" [Manager of comfort station convicted of war crimes], *Senso Sekinin Kenkyu* [The report on Japan's war responsibility] 56 (June 2007): 18–19, and Yoshimi, Nishino, and Hayashi, *Koko made wakatta Nihon-gun Ianfu Seido*, p. 39.

24 Aiko Utsumi, *Sengo Hosho kara Kangaeru Nihon to Ajia* [Japan and Asia from the viewpoint of post-war reparation] (Tokyo: Yamakawa Shuppansha, 2002), pp. 28–31.

25 Ibid., pp. 32–34.

26 Ibid., p. 31.

27 For details on compensation by Japan, see Baisho Mondai Kenkyukai [Study group on compensation] (ed.), *Nihon no Baisho* [Compensation by Japan] (Tokyo: Sekai Journal, 1963) and Shin-ichiro Nagano and Masaomi Kondo (eds.), *Nihon no Sengo Baisho* [Post-war compensation by Japan] (Tokyo: Keiso Shobo, 1999).

28 Nagano and Kondo (eds.), *Nihon no Sengo Baisho*, chapter 2.

29 Utsumi, *Sengo Hosho kara Kangaeru Nihon to Ajia*, p. 59.

30 Hayashi, *Sengo Heiwashugi wo Toinaosu* [Redefining post-war pacifism] (Kyoto: Kamogawa Shuppan, 2008), chapter 3.

31 Testimonies of her daughter and villagers can be found in Yoneko Ishida and Tomoyuki Uchida (eds.), *Kodo no Mura no Seiboryoku* [Sexual violence in a village with yellow ocher] (Tokyo: Sodosha, 2004), pp. 49–55, 72–5.

32 Yutaka Yoshida, *Heishitachi no Sengoshi* [Post-war history of veterans] (Tokyo: Iwanami Shoten, 2011), pp. 205–14.

33 Hirofumi Hayashi, "Government, the Military and Business in Japan's Wartime Comfort Woman System," *Japan Focus* (January 2007) (http://japanfocus.org/-Hayashi-Hirofumi/2332 [accessed April 5, 2013]), Hirofumi Hayashi, "Japanese Imperial Government Involvement in the Military 'Comfort Women' System," in *Forced Prostitution in Times of War and Peace: Sexual Violence against Women and Girls*, edited by Barbara Drinck and Chung-noh Gross (Bielefeld: Kleine Verlag, 2007), pp. 145–55, and Yoshiaki Yoshimi, *Comfort Women: Sexual Slavery in the Japanese Military during World War II* (New York: Columbia University Press, 2000).

34 Hayashi, "Government, the Military and Business." *Japan Focus*. For details on sexual violence in various areas by the Japanese military, see Kim Puja and Song Yo Ok (eds.), *Ianfu, Senji Seiboryoku no Jittai: Nippon, Taiwan, Chosen Hen* [The actual state of comfort women and wartime sexual violence: Japan, Taiwan, and Korea] (Tokyo: Ryokufu Shuppan, 2000); Nishino Rumiko and Hayashi Hirofumi (eds.), *Ianfu, Senji Seiboryoku no Jittai: Chugoku, Tonan-Ajia, Taiheiyou Hen* [The actual state of comfort women and wartime sexual violence: China, Southeast Asia, and the Pacific] (Tokyo: Ryokufu Shuppan, 2000).

35 Hirofumi Hayashi, "Nihongun Ianfu Seido to Beigun no Seiboryoku" [The system of Japanese military comfort women and sexual violence by the US military] in *Boryoku to Jenda* [Violence and gender], edited by Hirofumi Hayashi, Momoko Nakamura, and Makoto Hosoya (Tokyo: Hakutakusha, 2009), pp. 201–6.

36 For the details of my discussion, see Hirofumi Hayashi, "Nihongun Ianfu Seido to Beigun no Seiboryoku," and Hirofumi Hayashi, "Kankoku niokeru Beigun no

Siekanri to Seiboryoku" [Sex control and sexual violence by the US military in South Korea] in *Guntai to Seiboryoku: Chosen Hanto no 20 Seiki* [The military and sexual violence: The twentieth century on the Korean Peninsula], edited by Yonok Song and Puja Kim (Tokyo: Gendai Shiryo Shuppan, 2010), pp. 247–50.

37 Christa Paul, *Zwangsprostitution: Staatlich errichtete Bordelle im Nationalsozialismus* (Berlin: Hentrich, 1994) (the Japanese translation was published in 1996 by Akashi Shoten). And also see Barbara Drinck and Chung-noh Gross (eds.), *Forced Prostitution in Times of War and Peace: Sexual Violence against Women and Girls* (Bielefeld: Kleine Verlag, 2007), part 1.

38 For Korean women's effort, see Yun Jong Ok (ed.), *Chosen Josei ga Mita Ianfu Mondai* [The comfort women issue from the viewpoint of Korean women] (Tokyo: San-ichi Shobo, 1992) and Yun Jong Ok, *Heiwa wo Kikyu shite* [Looking for peace] (Tokyo: Hakutakusha, 2003). Emeritus Professor Yun Jong Ok was the first president of the Korean Council for Women Drafted for Japan's Military Sexual Slavery.

39 Hiroko Tsubokawa and Noriko Omori, *Shiho ga Ninteishita Nihongun Ianfu* [Factual findings on Japanese military comfort women] (Kyoto: Kamogawa Shuppan, 2011).

40 For the campaigns since the 1990s, see Hirofumi Hayashi, "The Japanese Movement to Protest Wartime Sexual Violence: A Survey of Japanese and International Literature," *Critical Asian Studies* 33, no. 4 (December 2001): 572–80 (http://japanfocus.org/-Hayashi-Hirofumi/2332 [accessed June 20, 2012]), and Hirofumi Hayashi, "Disputes in Japan over the Japanese Military 'Comfort Women' System and Its Perception in History," *The Annals of the American Academy of Political and Social Science* 617 (May 2008).

41 Hayashi, "The Japanese Movement to Protest Wartime Sexual Violence."

42 On the twenty years of the Wednesday Demonstrations, see Yoon Mee Hyang, *Nijunenkan no Suiyobi* [Twenty Years' Wednesday] (Osaka: Toho Shuppan, 2011) (originally published in Korea).

43 One example is the Korea–Japan Joint Workshop on "US Military Bases Issue in East Asia and Women's Human Rights" in Seoul on December 16, 2011. In the workshop, I also presented a paper on the US military's policy regarding the sex trade and sexual violence. The Korean Council also took part in the workshop as one of the host organizations.

9   The Cold War, the San Francisco System, and Indigenous peoples

Scott Harrison

The Cold War emerged from the ashes of World War II.[1] This new global order was based on military, economic, ideological, and cultural competition between the two remaining superpowers, the United States and the Soviet Union. While not always pervasive or obvious in local or national histories, the Cold War impacted the world on many levels, not just that of inter-state relations. Cold War exigencies also significantly shaped non-state peoples such as Indigenous peoples.[2] By looking at Indigenous peoples' history through a Cold War lens, we can better understand the history and the contemporary situations of Indigenous peoples and add a new dimension for understanding the last sixty years of the San Francisco System (SFS).

This chapter addresses two themes that historically connect the SFS to Indigenous peoples, both of which relate to the United States' Cold War policies of containment and integration, exemplified in the ambiguity of Japan's disposition of several territories as outlined in the treaty.[3] The first looks at how the San Francisco Peace Treaty (SFPT) contributed to post-war US consolidation of Indigenous lands in the Asia-Pacific for military use. Briefly exploring examples from the Marshall Islands and Okinawa highlights how US militarization, embodied in policies of containment and integration, fostered the politicization and growth of Indigenous identities.[4] The second highlights the relationship between the SFPT, development programs, border solidification, and historical experiences from the Ainu and Taiwanese Aborigines. In both of these cases, Japan's territorial dispositions in the emerging Cold War contributed to fast-track development programs to help maintain, negotiate, and solidify state borders. This in turn influenced post-war national government and Indigenous identity rebranding in both Taiwan and Japan.

Militarization

The SFPT aided in dividing the Asia-Pacific between capitalist and communist blocs. For the United States, it contributed to containing communism along the western Pacific. "Containment" gave a certain amount of freedom to the Soviet Union, the People's Republic of China, and North Korea to act without US interference. The treaty also allowed the United States to integrate non-communist areas into its political, economic, strategic, and cultural sphere of influence, including many former League of Nations mandates in the Pacific and Okinawa.

Pacific Islands

The United States used the SFPT as one step to legally justify the maintenance of the "American lake" in the Pacific that it had created with its military island-hopping during the offensive against Japan in World War II.[5] The United States subsequently maintained military bases and performed military tests on many of the islands in the region.[6] One of the most notable of the many cases is that of Bikini Atoll in the Marshall Islands.

Bikini Atoll is one of twenty-nine atolls and five islands, spread over close to two million square kilometers, which make up the Marshall Islands, located north of the equator in the Pacific Ocean. The Marshallese have had close contact with Europeans since the Spanish arrived on their shores in the sixteenth century. Passing from one colonial power to the next, the area was permeated by foreign presence, trade, and religion. The Cold War era, however, brought a new twist with the presence of US military bases, missile testing, and radioactive fallout from the testing of atomic bombs.

In August 1945, President Truman declared that the United States would not profit from or take advantage of the war to increase its territory, but that it would maintain and acquire lands thought essential to their own protection.[7] In the following months, the United States moved aggressively to secure thousands of military posts throughout the Pacific that it had built or occupied by the end of the war. One Sunday after church on Bikini Atoll in February 1946, Commodore Wyatt spoke with biblical analogies, giving the Native islanders a sense of global importance, and asked the religious Bikini people if they would temporarily relocate so that the United States could use their atoll to test bombs "for the good of mankind and to end all world wars." After talking as a group, Juda, the leader of the Bikinians, replied, "We will go believing that everything is in the hands of God."[8] Given the local people's experience during World War II of being caught between Japan and the United States, a short-term move appeared a small price to pay for world peace. In retrospect, this formal dialogue between Wyatt and the Bikini people was merely a formality given the military superiority over the islanders and the fact that President Truman had already approved Bikini as the test site for Operation Crossroads, an experiment partially born out of rivalry between the Army and Navy, which would detonate one-third of the US nuclear stockpile to test their effect on warships.[9]

The following month, the US Navy transported the Bikinians to Rongerik Atoll, 200 kilometers to the east of their atoll. On July 7, 1946, four months before the United States submitted its trusteeship proposal regarding the Pacific Islands to the United Nations, the first of twenty-three atomic and hydrogen bomb tests took place on Bikini Atoll. Due to radioactive fallout and the inadequacy of some islands for supporting human communities, the Bikinians went through five relocations, becoming "nuclear nomads."[10] Radioactive fallout from these and the forty-four other nuclear bombs dropped elsewhere in the Marshall Islands over the next eleven years had grave health and social consequences for many of the Indigenous inhabitants.

In the process of petitioning the United States for health services, aid, and compensation related to the atomic tests, the Bikinians – and Marshallese in general – organized to deal with US bureaucracies and litigation. The Bikinians, frustrated by the negotiations and slow-moving clean-up efforts, took the US government to court in 1981. Individual volunteers from the US Peace Corps and organizations such as Cultural Survival and the Pacific Concerns Research Center magnified the local islanders' efforts from the 1980s onward, as they documented and disseminated their findings on the impact of the nuclear arms race in the Pacific.[11] Opinions and positions between US government departments and their personnel were far from homogeneous, but Henry Kissinger, the national security advisor, summed up the overriding position with his 1969 comment that "There are only 90,000 people out there. Who gives a damn?"[12] In other words, in a broader Cold War picture, a small Indigenous population was inconsequential, next to the importance of the arms race and ensuring that the United States kept one step ahead of the Soviets in nuclear technology.

The Republic of Marshall Islands is now a member state of the United Nations, making its people somewhat different from other Indigenous peoples, but even though they have their own state, their sovereignty is neither full nor complete. In 1983, 60 percent of Marshall Islanders' votes favored the Compact of Free Association, which took effect three years later. The compact recognized the sovereignty of the Republic of Marshall Islands and provided a US$150 million compensation trust fund in exchange for the dismissal of then current legal action against the United States. The compact also guaranteed US military and strategic use of the islands, including a thirty-year lease of Kwajalein Island as a missile range. The combination of continued health claims associated with radiation sickness, and the Department of Energy's release of thousands of classified documents that confirmed the extent of fallout contamination and use of the Marshallese in radiation experiments, contributed to a new Marshallese effort to rethink the circumstances in which they had agreed to the original compact.[13] The Marshallese claims in relation to Cold War-era weapons testing continue to the present. It was not only the vast US military presence, but also Japan's renunciation of the former League of Nations Trust territories in the Pacific, as stipulated in the SFPT, that helped to legitimize the US presence in the region during the Cold War and beyond.

Okinawa

Devastated by the war, Okinawa became both pawn and benefactor of the two-pronged US military strategy of containment against both communism and future Japanese militarization. The war destroyed the islands' ecology and caused the death of a significant portion of the population. The United States movement to make Japan its strongest collaborator in the region to contain communist expansion complicated the structural and subjective identity of Japan's southern frontier.[14] With Japan's unconditional surrender to the Allies, the United States moved to secure direct power over Okinawa during the emerging Cold War in East Asia. This ended the status of Okinawa as a second-class prefecture and left the population stateless. Emperor Hirohito and the Japanese politicians in Tokyo aided in the process of detaching Okinawa from Japan in an effort to bring a quick surrender and to safeguard the emperor's post-war position. The Diet abolished Okinawan voting rights in late 1945 along with those of the Taiwanese and Koreans.[15] Following surrender, Emperor Hirohito showed willingness to release Japan's control over Okinawa in order to end the US occupation.[16] Mao Zedong's victory in China in 1949 and the outbreak of the Korean War less than a year later fueled US fears, in its eyes justifying the creation and maintenance of numerous military bases in Okinawa. These bases came to occupy approximately 11 percent of all Okinawa and around 20 percent of the main island.

The islands became the military "keystone" in the US defense line announced by Secretary of State Dean Acheson in 1950, which ran through the Pacific from the Aleutian Islands to the Philippines, not including Korea or Formosa.[17] Shortly after North Korea attacked the South, President Truman moved to include South Korea and Formosa within US defenses. Throughout the Korean War, US military bases on Okinawa proved invaluable for the US-led United Nations military operations. Slightly less than two years after that war broke out, the SFPT took effect, further securing the US occupation.[18]

During the US occupation of Okinawa, authorities encouraged the use of Ryūkyū as opposed to Okinawa in reference to the archipelago and its peoples, as one way of encouraging a non-Japanese identity for the islanders.[19] The uncertain status of Okinawa under US leadership lasted almost thirty years. Although Okinawa was "returned" to Japan in 1972, the Cold War structure continued, with US military occupation of a significant portion of Okinawan land, sea, and air space.

Cold War exigencies, as reflected in the SFPT, largely silenced the Okinawan history of ambiguous and changing identities, identities that were not always externally forced upon the people, as is often associated with colonial annexations. As a trading partner with both China and Japan, the Ryūkyū Kingdom had adopted both Chinese and Japanese culture. In 1609, after the Satsuma domain of Tokugawa Japan annexed the Amami Islands, the northern part of the Okinawan archipelago, the Satsuma stressed differences between them and the Ryūkyūans to gain status within the Tokugawa worldview. The complex Okinawan dual relationship with Beijing and Satsuma ended in 1879, when the Meiji government unilaterally declared Okinawa a Japanese prefecture.[20] As a Japanese prefecture, Okinawans reacted flexibly to Japanese assimilation policies in the nineteenth century, even to the point of enthusiastically adopting Japanese names and customs.[21]

Despite the difference in status between Hokkaido, as an area for pioneers to develop and extract resources, and Okinawan prefectural status, the Japanese capital treated Okinawa differently from mainland Japan.[22] A historical look at Okinawan identity demonstrates an appreciation of the importance of retaining a unique language and culture, while at the same time maintaining flexible and malleable identities. Okinawan identity fluidly changed along with historical circumstances.

When debate on Okinawan reversion to Japan increased from the late 1960s, discussion about Okinawan identity came to the fore. Most Okinawans favored a return to Japan, as they saw that option as superior compared with subordination to the US military. This is understandable because Cold War exigencies limited and restricted Okinawan options. Their hope was that, through reversion to Japan, Okinawa could rid itself of US military bases. In Article 3 of the SFPT, Japan did not renounce its claim to Ryūkyū as it did other islands specified in Article 2, allowing for flexibility on the status of the islands during the turbulent Cold War.[23] After the return, many Okinawans realized that showing such support did little to change the situation of US bases – the return movement morphed into growing public protests and insistence on a unique identity.

The post-war Japanese search for and rebranding of its own identity as homogenous allowed for other identities within Japan to challenge and speak out against the state.[24] The Japanese government's abandonment of Okinawa, and the experience of a period of statelessness during the US occupation from 1945, contributed to the growth of the concept of indigeneity for a small number of Okinawan activists.

Connections with Ainu and an NGO aided the spread of the concept of indigeneity within Okinawa. Starting in 1981, the Utari Association of Hokkaido (UAH) began performing annual memorial services in Okinawa for the Ainu who had died there during the last major battle of World War II.[25] In 1984 a prominent Ainu activist and an Okinawan poet in favor of separate Okinawan identity met in Kyoto at a conference on minority peoples' discrimination. Ainu increasingly traveled to Okinawa after this.[26] Increased contact with the Ainu led to the Okinawans' first appearance at the United Nations Working Group on Indigenous Populations in 1996, with the help of the Citizens' Diplomatic Centre for the Rights of Indigenous Peoples (Shimin gaikō sentā), the same non-partisan NGO that has helped Ainu attend such events since 1987.[27] Okinawans have attended United Nations forums ever since. It is important to note that concerned citizens and students, not Indigenous peoples, created this NGO, although Ainu, Okinawans, and other Indigenous peoples have greatly influenced its direction.[28] Many of the arguments the Okinawans have presented at international forums about their identity are related to the US Cold War presence that still exists on their islands. The concept of indigeneity in Okinawa is one aspect of the historically flexible and ambiguous Okinawan identity that emerged because of the Cold War, one of many "nationalisms" present in the islands.

Bringing Okinawa into the discussion of indigeneity, the SFPT, and the Cold War highlights the complex, variable, political, and often internally disputed nature of identity, which is important and very much a part of the process of "becoming" Indigenous, through both internal and external imagining. Just as in the case of the Ainu, there are many Okinawans who view themselves as more Japanese than "Indigenous"; others, now a small minority, see it the other way around. Through a new relationship with the United States and Japan, the Cold War helped to shape the post-war understanding of Okinawan identity, both externally and internally, and provided the backdrop on which some Okinawans have attempted to reformat their identity as "Indigenous peoples" as a means to express their interests.

Development, borders, and sovereignty

The territorial divisions reinforced by the SFPT provided opportunities for governments in Formosa (Taiwan) and Japan to focus on economic development. Such projects took the form of large development projects in a variety of milieus, including industry, energy, and food production. Tensions from border disputes contributed to state hegemonies that encouraged a silencing or "forgetting" of the presence of the Ainu in Japan and Aborigines in Taiwan.

Northern Territories

Ainu now live throughout Japan, but the northernmost island of Japan, Hokkaido, is the only Ainu homeland recognized by the Japanese government. This Tokyo-centric view supports the official national history and understanding of the state's northern boundaries while simultaneously limiting the boundaries of Ainu history, culture, and identity. In addition to Hokkaido, the Ainu traditionally lived in Sakhalin, the Kurile Islands, and northern Honshu.

Unlike the situation in Germany, which came under split four-power control at the end of the war in Europe, the United States had sole responsibility for the postwar occupation of Japan. The United States quickly set up the Supreme Commander for the Allied Powers (SCAP) under the direction of General Douglas MacArthur. In an attempt at democratization, SCAP relaxed the hold on previously persecuted socialists. Some Ainu in Hokkaido, including a few men from Sakhalin and the Kuriles, took advantage of this fairly liberal post-war atmosphere and became politically active while pressing for social equality. Most Ainu energies at this time were focused on an eventually unsuccessful protest by the Ainu Association of Hokkaido against land reforms being initiated by SCAP that would directly affect Ainu provisional land-holding, as directed by the outdated 1899 Hokkaido Former Aborigines Protection Act. After two years of unsuccessful petitioning to the Hokkaido-chō and SCAP, SCAP implemented the land reform and over 1,000 Ainu lost land.[29] Emerging Asian Cold War tensions, combined with an already anti-communist General MacArthur, created conditions for SCAP to clamp down on socialist movements in Japan, directly impacting Ainu leftist movements.[30] Strangled by Cold War prerogatives, the Ainu Association was suffocated and remained inactive for a dozen years.

Not all Ainu ceased protesting and petitioning the government, however. One case where Ainu movements continued was in relation to Soviet-captured territories at the end of the war. The Soviet Union broke the Japanese–Soviet Neutrality Pact with its movement into Manchukuo in early August 1945, approximately eight months before the pact's expiration.[31] By early September, it had occupied Sakhalin and the entire Kurile archipelago. Between 1946 and 1948, the Soviets relocated most of the Ainu in Sakhalin and the Kuriles, along with all the Japanese, to Hokkaido.[32]

The SFPT is the latest in a long historical line of documents relating to state boundaries in the Okhotsk region.[33] The ambiguities in the treaty contributed to the newest version of Soviet/Russo-Japanese territorial dispute in the Okhotsk. The highly politicized debate over the four islands to the northeast of Hokkaido reinforced the boundaries of post-war Ainu argumentation, identity, politicization, and internationalization.[34]

Official recognition by either the Soviet or Japanese governments of Ainu still living in Sakhalin, or of an unassimilated Ainu identity, would have complicated claims to the islands by both sides. The Japanese had to show that the lands in question were not taken by force, from another state, or even from peoples traditionally with no state. Cold War tensions and the SFS contributed to the speed with which Japan moved to rebrand its national identity, from multiethnic to homogenous. The early post-war years were important for the structural shift of the process, such as limiting citizenship, but the decades that followed proved more important for the changing of social consciousness through the *nihonjinron* movement.[35] This in turn made it easier to downplay, ignore, and/or forget the historical and then contemporary Ainu presence in the region.

During the 1950s some Kurile Ainu took part in a grassroots movement that presented the Ainu as "living witnesses" to prove that Japan had singlehandedly developed the Kurile Islands. This was a direct defense against the 1943 Cairo Declaration, which stipulated that the Allies would expel Japan from all "territories which she has taken by violence or greed."[36] In aiding this movement, some Ainu could have benefited through a return to the islands, recognition of their history in the region, or monetary compensation. By the late 1960s, however, Ainu participation in the "return" movement ended and mention of the Ainu disappeared from the dialogue. The two main reasons for this are both related to Cold War exigencies. First, scholars who focused on the Ainu became more involved with the return movement in an attempt to supply the government with their opinions on the Yalta agreement, in which the "Big Three" had agreed to "hand over" the Kurile Islands and "return" southern Sakhalin to the Soviets if the Soviets joined the war against Japan.[37] Takakura Shin'ichirō, a prolific writer on Ainu history, contributed to the silencing of the Ainu in the movement as he increasingly wrote in support of the government's position on the islands, opining that the Ainu were either relics of the past who had died out or been fully assimilated.[38] Japan's 1953 Report to the International Labour Organization epitomized the government's position on the matter when it stated that there were no Indigenous populations in Japan, because "Japan lost all its dependent territories."[39] This statement reinterprets Hokkaido and Okhotsk regional history to support the Cold War stance against the Soviet Union. Ironically, Okinawa was not under Japanese control at this time.

Mention of the Ainu disappeared completely from the main dialogue of the return movement when it gained more steam after the United States stated in 1969 that it would "return" Okinawa to Japan. The Japanese government quickly made a conscious connection between Okinawa and the islands to the north of Hokkaido. With this shift, the government took more control of the return movement and, consequently, grassroots movements, such as those including the Ainu, had less room to act on their own accord.

Within the dialogue of the "Northern Territories" problem and the SFPT, Hokkaido became a forgotten internal colony and was internationally recognized as an inherent territory of Japan. The Cold War helped solidify the borders of northern Japan on this island, even though it continued to have a semi-colonial administration. This, in turn, influenced the predominant Japanese national understanding of the Ainu by limiting Ainu history to the boundaries of Hokkaido. Recognizing Indigenous peoples in the Northern Territories or other areas in the Okhotsk was counter to Japan's interest in maintaining unquestioned sovereignty of the island and claim to the four islands; it was also counter to US goals of strengthening Japan's hold on Hokkaido so as to limit Soviet movement in the Okhotsk region.

Early UAH and other Ainu organizations' visits to and studies on other minority and Indigenous peoples fueled a resurgent Ainu movement during the 1970s. In 1960 the UAH re-emerged after twelve years of inactivity. It continued to be a left-leaning organization: many Ainu continued to interpret their status not as a racial, but as a socio-economic condition.[40] From the early 1970s, UAH leaders had ties with the Socialist Party of Japan, which in turn had contacts with the Chinese Communist Party (CCP). These ties facilitated in 1974 the first of four official overseas exchanges with Communist China, as part of the Japan–China Friendship Association. These exchanges with China's minority peoples encouraged broader Ainu interest in Communist China's minorities and international Indigenous peoples.[41]

Several Cold War developments allowed Japan to move closer to China in the early 1970s. In an attempt to work out a resolution on the Vietnam War, isolate the Soviet Union's increased expansion into the Third World, and (reluctantly) deal with the burgeoning trade deficit with Japan, President Richard Nixon and National Security Advisor Henry Kissinger sought closer ties with Communist China. Likewise, Mao Zedong and Zhou Enlai thought closer ties with the United States could work to their advantage, while their relationship with the Soviets continued to sour in the Sino-Soviet split.[42] These visits could be seen as strictly a local Ainu initiative, with no Cold War connection. While this is not entirely incorrect, as historically speaking many Ainu did take the initiative to make these trips happen, it does oversimplify the matter. If the visits were strictly due to local developments, then it would have made more sense for the Ainu to visit the Soviet Union, where Ainu had prior homelands and cultural connections to the Aborigine peoples in the Amur River region, Sakhalin, the Kuriles, and Kamchatka. The Cold War and the issues around the SFPT ensured that this was not a possibility. Without developing relations between the United

States and Communist China as part of Cold War grand strategies, Japan could not have moved closer to China, and any Ainu visit to China would have been very difficult to implement.

The official Ainu exchanges in the 1970s with minorities in China added to the internationalization of the Ainu indigeneity movement.[43] Ainu visits to Canadian and US Indians and Eskimos and attendance at international Indigenous conferences began shortly after the trips to China. With such international contacts and influence, an increasing number of Ainu began moving against the state, proudly redefining their identity as Indigenous peoples in language shared by the global Indigenous peoples' movement.[44] From the early 1980s, the UAH, other Ainu organizations, and individual Ainu and non-Ainu moved to assert the Ainu component of the Northern Territories problem, but were largely unsuccessful in gaining recognition by any state governments or by most academics.[45]

Taiwan

Domestic US politics, the CCP's rise to power, the Kuomintang (KMT) retreat to Taiwan and border regions in Southeast Asia, and the outbreak of the Korean War all provided important backdrops to decision-making behind the SFPT. The Cold War and the SFPT directly influenced the post-1951 economic and political developments in Taiwan.[46] Subsequently, these significantly altered the political and economic atmosphere from which the numerous Taiwanese Aboriginal groups emerged onto domestic and international arenas as Indigenous peoples.

The KMT attempted to reincorporate Taiwan back into mainland China shortly after the end of the war.[47] They increased their control over the island after they retreated there, but major post-war political, educational, and land reforms on the island did not occur until after the implementation of the SFPT. In March 1949, Acheson suggested using the "Formosan autonomy movement" to US advantage,[48] but the United States did not initially place Taiwan within the limits of its containment policy. Acheson and others in the Truman administration did not want an independent Taiwan, because they hoped to develop relations with the CCP and wanted to halt rumors that suggested the United States would intervene on behalf of Taiwan.[49]

With the outbreak of the Korean War, US thinking on the strategic importance of Taiwan quickly changed. The war scared the United States into thinking that Communist forces were on the verge of spreading throughout the region. Truman responded by deploying the Seventh Fleet of the US Navy to the Taiwan Strait and by providing continued economic and military support to the KMT. The implementation of the SFPT, in which Japan renounced rights and claims to Formosa, contributed to the KMT's survival and allowed it to solidify its hold in Taiwan by focusing on internal reform.[50]

The KMT replaced Japanese with Mandarin for the upper class and as the educational language of instruction for both the Indigenous population and the Taiwanese. Neither of these communities were native speakers of Mandarin, but it took the Indigenous population longer to make the transition because of the larger difference between their languages and Mandarin, and because many continued to associate Japanese with political and social prestige. By the late 1950s, after the KMT implemented a more thorough Mandarin education system, the Aborigine population realized that, without skill in Mandarin, they had little hope for social or political mobility. They began to make quick progress in learning the language, while simultaneously emphasizing the Chinese aspects of their identity. The flexibility that many Aboriginal communities showed in reshaping their external identity did not developed long before the post-war era. For example, before Japan took control of the island in 1895, many Aborigines near the western coast had used both their Chinese and Aboriginal identities to maximize political control, trade, and relations between mountain tribes and Chinese traders. After Japan took control of the island they downplayed their Chinese connections and highlighted their connection to Japan. They studied the Japanese language; some Aboriginals went to Japan to study and work. During the late 1950s, they switched emphasis once again, not entirely giving up identifiers of prestige such as the Japanese language, but focusing on Mandarin, because without it there was little chance for social mobility.[51]

Martial law, combined with rapid economic development, helps explain the peculiarities of the Taiwanese Indigenous movement. The KMT initiated martial law in 1947 in response to a Taiwanese uprising that "epitomized the collision between decolonization and reintegration."[52] Aborigine and Taiwanese petitions for self-government abruptly ended. Two years after the implementation of the SFPT, the KMT concluded a Mutual Defense Treaty with the United States. This, along with the CCP's bombing of Quemoy (Jinmen) and Matsu (Mazu) in 1958, moved the KMT closer to the United States and increased the need for martial law to maintain control of the island. The government specifically targeted Aboriginal groups because of their distinctly non-Han identity – the Han idea of Aborigines was that they were warriors – and the potential for guerilla warfare launched from the mountain regions.[53]

It took about thirty years from the implementation of the SFPT for economic development on the island to create a large enough middle class from which Taiwanese and Aboriginal peoples began pushing for their own political interests, democratic reform,[54] and state recognition of Aboriginal nations. The more the government focused on economic and development projects the more the Aboriginal population became alienated from their lands. This was particularly the case for those living in the mountain regions of the island, where many government projects were sited. The subsequent influx of Aborigines into the cities in search of work had two important corollaries. First, it reinforced their familiarity with the Chinese language and Chinese way of life as taught in the education system. This enabled many of the migrant workers to better liaise between their communities and the Chinese. Second, urbanization provided more opportunities to network with people from other Aboriginal communities. They began to notice similarities in social dislocation across different Aboriginal groups. These convergences set the stage for the birth of the Formosan pan-Indigenous social movement that emerged with the establishment of the *Mountain Greenery* newspaper (1983) and the Alliance of Taiwan Aborigines (1984), the first Indigenous NGO on the island.[55] Partially because it involved sympathetic Taiwanese and church groups, this social movement reinforced the Aborigine reliance on Mandarin and urbanization to successfully operate in the greater Taiwanese society.

After the Nationalist government lifted martial law in 1987, the Indigenous movement grew rapidly. Demonstrations on behalf of Aborigines quickly increased during the late 1980s alongside other political demonstrations.[56] Aborigine people, with frequent aid from the Presbyterian Church, established new publications and NGOs. In the early 1990s, the Alliance of Taiwan Aborigines became involved with the regional NGO, the Asian Indigenous Peoples Pact, and began attending international events such as the UN Working Group on Indigenous Populations. The Aborigines, with the help of non-Indigenous allies, increased their pursuit of indigeneity and recognition.

Cold War nuclear proliferation impacted Indigenous peoples on Taiwan, specifically the Tao on Lanyu Island. In Taiwan the nuclear debate arose from the KMT attempt to solidify its borders and preserve its political organization through development of its economy, military, and identity. The KMT pursued nuclear projects without much local protest because of the secrecy that surrounded them, coupled with martial law and the justifications of defense and economic development. The Cold War and the SFPT helped ensure that the CCP–KMT relationship and their respective borders remained tense. Even though the KMT had signed a Mutual Defense Treaty with the United States in 1954, the KMT feared that, should the United States not protect it from a potential CCP attack, it would need its own nuclear arsenal.[57] If the international community were to prohibit a nuclear Taiwan, then the government could argue that nuclear energy would support their rapid economic growth and offset energy imports.

Immediately after the CCP tested a nuclear bomb in the Lop Nor desert in 1964, the KMT began pursuing a nuclear program. In 1969, the KMT began construction of several nuclear projects, including a Canadian-supplied reactor that became operational three and a half years later.[58] In 1978, the government announced to the Tao that it would build a military harbor near their villages. Three years later Tao villagers began working as laborers for its construction, only to find out later that it was actually a radioactive waste disposal site. The problem of nuclear waste on Lanyu became a key point in the pan-Taiwanese Indigenous movement's petitions to international bodies in its search for rights and recognition as Indigenous peoples.[59]

Japan's disposition of Taiwan in the SFPT created the as yet unresolved problem of which government holds its sovereignty. This problem relies on several assumptions. First, that nation-states are the only normal and natural form of human organization – and, therefore, a prerequisite for operating in international or global frameworks. Second, it presumes that nation-states are unchanging, cohesive structural units identifiable back into linear historical time, therefore reinforcing the legitimacy of contemporary boundaries and the dominant nationalism of particular nation-states. This act of historicizing contemporary modes of human organization and their boundaries makes it difficult to see how frequently they have changed throughout history. In relation to Taiwan, these assumptions have contributed to the growth of a process that high-lights a unique Taiwanese identity separate from the boundaries, and therefore the sovereignty, of Communist China. The Taiwanese government's recognition of Aboriginal nations within its borders is a part of this process.

Government recognition of Indigenous peoples on the island politicizes their identity. Recognition provides some political power, both domestically and internationally, to an increasing number of Aboriginal nations on the island. Recognition, however, is not simply granted by the government, but is dependent on the successful mobilization of Aboriginal groups. These state–Aborigine relations are mutually influencing and, importantly, delineate Taiwan's identity as different from that of mainland China.[60]

Final thoughts

The Cold War and the SFS left behind many legacies both for states and indi-vidual groups such as Indigenous peoples, by complicating regional border demarcation issues, militarization, and development. Indigenous–state relations in the Asia-Pacific have significantly changed since the end of World War II. The assimilationist attitudes and policies that dominated states' relations with Indigenous peoples throughout the region have now moved toward state recog-nition of Indigenous identities and rights. These changes have had much to do with increased collaboration between Indigenous groups and non-Indigenous supporters throughout the region and globe. Governmental attempts to simplify and assimilate Indigenous identities during much of the Cold War helped to fuel a resurgence of Indigenous social activity.

The Asia-Pacific is full of incredibly diverse states and peoples, yet in rela-tion to the Cold War and the SFS there are many similarities in Native–non-Native interactions, notably with regard to militarization, development, borders, and sovereignty. The pervasive presence of the United States throughout the Asia-Pacific since the end of World War II is another important linkage to the Cold War and the SFS. These factors have persisted over the last sixty years of the SFPT as governments aggressively increased their state power, especially in state frontier or border regions. The rise of Indigenous movements in the region coincides with developments emerging from the SFS and the Cold War.

Indigenous peoples are themselves full of regional and local diversity. The question here becomes how to find solutions that are not only fitting for states but flexible enough to account for diversity of the many peoples. In the past, many states, including those in the Asia-Pacific, developed and applied policy models to a wide range of diverse Indigenous peoples. These cookie-cutter models have done little to settle claims between the two sides. Generic models, based on predetermined positions, that presume any settlement will be final, have not solved issues between Indigenous peoples and states; there is no reason to think that such methods would help resolve broader legacies associated with the SFPT.

As the last sixty years have shown, it is easier to write about than to implement methods for resolving issues related to the SFS. Historical reconciliation is an initial step required for any meaningful settlement to outstanding regional issues. A depoliticized and denationalized understanding of the region's history is not only important but also necessary for clarifying the past. This includes understanding the relationship of Indigenous peoples to domestic and inter-state relations, as Indigenous peoples were and are intricately connected to international issues. Academic studies, while only one part of the equation, can contribute to dialogues based on non-partisan, non-political, and non-nationalistic understandings of the multifaceted complexities of both the historical and contemporary situations. Any settlement on issues related to the SFS will depend on the ability of all concerned parties to develop relationships, clear and effective means of communication, mutual understanding of each side's interests, options, and alternatives to settlement. To ensure that settlements remain in place and outlast shifts in political winds they will require flexibility and fairness for all sides, and mechanisms that ensure accountability to settlement commitments.

Notes

1 The author would like to thank the conference committee for the invitation to prepare and present an earlier version of this chapter, the conference participants, especially Mark Selden, for their questions and comments, and Kimie Hara for her important feedback.

2 Indigenous peoples share characteristics of "small size, attachment to the land, value system and culture rooted in the environment, commitment to sustainable lifestyle, mobility, and cultural conservatism." Shared historical circumstances include "economic and political domination by outsiders, selected integration/participation with non-Indigenous societies, limited or non-existent power within the nation state, emerging involvement in a local or international process of decolonization" (Ken Coates, *A Global History of Indigenous Peoples: Struggles and Survival* [New York: Palgrave Macmillan, 2004], pp. 13–15).

3 Kimie Hara, *Cold War Frontiers in the Asia-Pacific: Divided Territories in the San Francisco System* (New York: Routledge, 2007).

4 On integration and containment, see Christina Klein, *Cold War Orientalism: Asia in the Middlebrow Imagination, 1945–1961* (Berkeley, CA: University of California Press, 2003).

5 On connections between Micronesia, the trusteeship system, and the SFPT, see Hara, *Cold War Frontiers*, pp. 100–23. On the "American lake" see Hara, *Cold War Frontiers*, and John Dower, "Occupied Japan and the American Lake, 1945–1950," in *America's Asia: Dissenting Essays in Asia–American Relations*, edited by Edward Friedman and Mark Selden (New York: Vintage, 1971), pp. 146–206.

6 David Vine, *Island of Shame: The Secret History of the U.S. Military Bases on Diego Garcia* (Princeton, NJ: Princeton University Press, 2009), pp. 41–55, and Hal Friedman, *Creating an American Lake: United States Imperialism and Strategic Security in the Pacific Basin, 1945–47* (Westport, CT: Greenwood Press, 2001).

7 "President Truman's Report to the Peoples on War Developments," *New York Times*, August 10, 1945, p. 12.

8 Quotes from Jack Niedenthal, *For the Good of Mankind: A History of the People of Bikini and their Islands* (Majoro, MH: Bravo Publishers, 2001), p. 2. Also, see Jonathan Weisgall, *Operation Crossroads: The Atomic Tests at Bikini Atoll* (Annapolis, MD: Naval Institute Press, 1994), pp. 106–15.

9 Friedman, *Creating an American Lake*, p. 67, and Weisgall, *Operation Crossroads*, pp. 13–17, 30.

10 Ibid., p. 4.

11 Micronesia Support Committee, *Marshall Islands: A Chronology: 1944–1983* (Honolulu: 1978, 1981, 1983); Giff Johnson, *Collision Course at Kwajalein: Marshall Islanders in the Shadow of the Bomb* (Honolulu: Pacific Concerns Research Center, 1984); and Catherine Lutz (ed.), *Micronesia as Strategic Colony: The Impact of U.S. Policy on Micronesian Health and Culture* (Cambridge, MA: Cultural Survival, 1984).

12 Walter Hickel, *Who Owns America?* (Englewood Cliffs, NJ: Prentice-Hall, Inc., 1971), p. 208.

13 Embassy of the Republic of Marshall Islands, "Nuclear Issues," (www.rmiembassyus. org/Nuclear%20Issues.htm#History [accessed April 3, 2013]). The Bush administration reclassified many of these documents; Barbara Johnson and Holly Barker, *Consequential Damages of Nuclear War: the Rongelap Report* (Wallnut Creek, CA: Left Coast Press, 2008), p. 32.

14 Glen Hook and Richard Siddle (eds.), *Japan and Okinawa: Structure and Subjectivity* (London: Routledge, 2003).

15 Herbert Bix, *Hirohito and the Making of Modern Japan* (New York: HarperCollins, 2000), pp. 626–7.

16 John Dower, *Japan in War and Peace* (New York: New Press, 1993), p. 171, and Koji Taira, "Okinawa's Choice: Independence or Subordination," in *Okinawa: Cold War Island*, edited by Chalmers Johnson (Cardiff, CA: Japan Policy Research Institute, 1999), p. 174.

17 Department of State Bulletin, 22, January 23, 1950, p. 116.

18 The base became important for US military missions in Southeast Asia and the Himalayas. S. Mahmud Ali, *Cold War in the High Himalayas* (New York: St Martin's Press, 1999); John Kenneth Knaus, *Orphans of the Cold War: America and the Tibetan Struggle for Survival* (New York: Public Affairs, 1999); Kenneth Comby and James Morrison, *The CIA's Secret War in Tibet* (Lawrence: University of Kansas Press, 2002); and Joe Leeker, "Mission to Tibet," *The History of Air America* (last updated March 4, 2013) (www.utdallas.edu/library/specialcollections/hac/cataam/ Leeker/history/Tibet.pdf).

19 Chalmers Johnson, "The 1995 Rape Incident and the Rekindling of Okinawan Protest Against the American Bases," in Johnson (ed.), *Okinawa: Cold War Island*, p. 129, and Steve Rabson, "Assimilation Policy in Okinawa: Promotion, Resistance, and 'Reconstruction'," in ibid., pp. 144–5.

20 For pre-war Okinawan history, see George Kerr, *Okinawa: The History of an Island People*, revised edition (Rutland, VT: Tuttle Publishing, 2000).

21 Rabson, "Assimilation Policy in Okinawa," pp. 136–42, and Scott Harrison, *The Indigenous Ainu of Japan and the Northern Territories Dispute* (Saarbrücken: VDM Verlag, 2008), pp. 34–5.

22 For example, in 1903, Okinawans protested against the idea of being grouped with Taiwanese Aborigines and Ainu at the Osaka Industrial Exposition (Rabson, "Assimilation Policy in Okinawa," pp. 133–48; Richard Siddle, "Colonialism and Okinawan Identity before 1945," *Japanese Studies* 18, no. 2 (1998): 117–33; and Hiraoki Fukichi, "Issues Arising from Historical and Current Perspectives on Okinawa," Buraku Liberation Human Rights Research Institute [http://blhrri.org/blhrri_e/NGO-infomation/007.htm; accessed April 3, 2014]).

23 Koji Taira, "Troubled National Identity: The Ryukyuans/Okinawans," in *Japan's*

Minorities: The Illusion of Homogeneity, edited by Michael Weiner (London: Routledge, 1997), p. 161; and Hara, *Cold War Frontiers*, pp. 158–84.

24 On the change from the pre-war multi-ethnic to post-war mono-ethnic Japanese identity, see Oguma Eiji, *A Genealogy of "Japanese" Self Images* (Melbourne: Trans Pacific Press, 2002).

25 "Kimun utari tō mae de no icharupa," *Senkusha no Tsudoi* 29, January 1, 1982, pp. 1, 5–6, in *Ainu Shi: Hokkaidō Ainu Kyōkai/Hokkaidō Utari Kyōkai katsudō shihen*, edited by Hokkaidō Utari Kyōkai (Sapporo: Hokkaidō Utari Kyōkai, 1994), pp. 471, 475–6.

26 Richard Siddle, "Return to Uchinā: The Politics of Identity in Contemporary Okinawa," in *Japan and Okinawa: Structure and Subjectivity*, edited by Glen Hook and Richard Siddle (London: Routledge, 2003) p. 138.

27 For the first Okinawan position paper to the Working Group, see Matsushima Yasukatsu, "Dai 14 Kai Kokuren Senjūmin Sagyō Bukai Sanka Kanren Shiryō" (www.7b. biglobe.ne.jp/~whoyou/bunkenshiryo3.htm#senzyuminzoku [accessed April 3, 2014]).

28 Citizens' Diplomatic Centre, "What is SHIMIN GAIKOU CENTRE (SGC)?" (www.005.upp.so-net.ne.jp/peacetax/e1.html [accessed April 3, 2014]).

29 Richard Siddle, *Race, Resistance and the Ainu of Japan* (London: Routledge, 1996), pp. 147–53; Harrison, *Indigenous Ainu*, pp. 72–75; Eiji Takemae, *Inside GHQ: The Allied Occupation of Japan and its Legacy* (New York: Continuum International, 2002), pp. 439–40.

30 Michael Schaller, *Altered States: the United States and Japan since the Occupation* (Oxford: Oxford University Press, 1997), pp. 12–18; Yoshihisa Masuko, "Moboroshi no Ainu dokurituron o omou: choro ni shikin o okutta GHQ no shin'i," *Asahi Jānaru* 31 (1989): 87–90.

31 Boris Slavinsky, *The Japanese–Soviet Neutrality Pact: A Diplomatic History 1941–1945* (London: RoutledgeCurzon, 2003).

32 On Uilta and Nivkh relocation to Hokkaido in the post-war years, see Tangik Itsuji, "Aru Nibufu jin no senzen to sengo," *Wakō daigaku gendai jinken gakubu kiyō* 4 (2011): 129–43; and Tanaka Ryō and Gendānu Dāhinien, *Gendānu: Aru hoppō shōsūminzoku no dorama* (Tokyo: Gendai Shuppankai, 1978).

33 For the regional history, see John J. Stephan's *The Kuril Islands* (Oxford: Clarendon Press, 1974) and *Sakhalin: A History* (Oxford: Clarendon Press, 1971).

34 This section draws on Harrison, *Indigenous Ainu*, pp. 71–83.

35 Oguma, *A Genealogy*; John Lie, *Multiethnic Japan* (Cambridge, MA: Harvard University Press, 2001); and Harumi Befu, *Hegemony of Homogeneity* (Melbourne: Trans Pacific Press, 2001).

36 Department of State Bulletin, 9 (December 4, 1943), p. 393.

37 Department of State Bulletin, 14 (February 24, 1946), p. 282.

38 Harrison, *Indigenous Ainu*, pp. 75–6.

39 Ainu Association of Hokkaido, *Statement Submitted to the International Labour Conference, 75th Session*, June 1988, Material 4, in *Kokusai kaigi shiryōshū 1987nen – 2000nen*, edited by Hokkaidō Utari Kyōkai (Sapporo: Hokkaidō Utari Kyōkai, 2002), pp. 127–8.

40 To help minimize discrimination, they changed the organization's name to the Utari Association of Hokkaido, where *Utari* means comrade or fellow (Harrison, *Indigenous Ainu*, p. 91).

41 Mongkjargal, "Ainu no kaigai kōryū to minzoku no fukken – 1970 nendai no Ainu Chūgoku hōmon ga motarashita mono," *Wakō daigaku gendai jinkenbu kiyō* 3 (2010): 117–35. Kayano Shigeru, *Our Land was a Forest* (Boulder, CO: Westview Press, 1994), pp. 151–2.

42 Schaller, *Altered States*, pp. 210–44; Michael Schaller, "Japan and the Cold War, 1960–1991," in *Cambridge History of the Cold War*, Vol. 3, edited by Melvyn Leffler

and Odd Westad (New York: Cambridge University Press, 2010), pp. 156–80; Sergey Radchenko, "The Sino-Soviet Split," in *Cambridge History*, Vol. 2, pp. 349–72; Lorenz Lüthi, *The Sino-Soviet Split: Cold War in the Communist World* (Princeton, NJ: Princeton University Press, 2008); Chen Jian, *Mao's China and the Cold War* (Chapel Hill, NC: University of North Carolina Press, 2001), pp. 238–76; Chen Jian and David Wilson, "All Under the Heaven is Great Chaos: Beijing, the Sino-Soviet Border Clashes, and the Turn toward Sino-American Rapprochement, 1968–69," *CWIHP Bulletin*, 11 (Winter 1998–99): 155–75.

43   The 1978 twelve-member Ainu delegation to the North Slope Autonomous Region in Alaska upon invitation from Barrow Mayor Eben Hopson was also important for directing future Ainu internationalization as Indigenous peoples ("Whalers Face-off Opponents in Tokyo for IWC Showdown," *The Arctic Coastal Zone Management Program* 8, part 1 [December 1977]; *Senkusha no Tsudoi*, 19 [October 1, 1978], supplement, in *Ainu Shi*, pp. 384–6; and Kayano, *Our Land*, p. 153).

44   On Ainu internationalization, see Harrison, *Indigenous Ainu*, pp. 84–116.

45   For the UAH's position on this dispute, see Hokkaidō Utari Kyōkai, *Chishima rettō no Ainu minzoku senjū ni kan suru shiryō* (Sapporo: Shadanhōjin Hokkaidō Utari Kyōkai, 1983).

46   Taiwan's rapid and successful economic development was an anomaly rather than a norm in places where the United States intervened during the Cold War; Odd Westad, *The Global Cold War: Third World Interventions and the Making of Our Times* (Cambridge: Cambridge University Press, 2007), p. 404.

47   Stephen Phillips, "Between Assimilation and Independence: Taiwanese Political Aspirations Under Nationalist Chinese Rule, 1945–1948," in *Taiwan: A New History*, edited by Murray Rubinstein (Armonk, NY: M.E. Sharpe, 2007), pp. 275–319.

48   Stephen Phillips, *Between Assimilation and Independence: The Taiwanese Encounter Nationalist China, 1945–1950* (Stanford, CA: Stanford University Press, 2003), p. 192, n. 54.

49   Ibid., p. 193, n. 69.

50   On reform, see Peter Chen-main Wang, "A Bastion Created, A Regime Reformed, An Economy Reengineered, 1949–1970," in *Taiwan: A New History*, edited by Murray Rubinstein (Armonk, NY: M.E. Sharpe, 2007), pp. 320–38. Dean Acheson, *Present at the Creation: My Years in the State Department* (New York, W.W. Norton & Co., 1969), pp. 349–52.

51   Henrietta Harrison, "Changing Nationalities, Changing Ethnicities: Taiwan Indigenous Villages in the Years after 1946," in *In Search of the Hunters and Their Tribes: Studies in the History and Culture of the Taiwan Indigenous People*, edited by David Faure (Taipei: Shung Ye Museum of Formosan Aborigines, 2001), pp. 50–78.

52   Phillips, "Between Assimilation," p. 292.

53   Harrison, "Changing Nationalities."

54   Phillips, "Between Assimilation," p. 302.

55   Scott Simon, "Writing Indigeneity in Taiwan," in *Re-Writing Culture in Taiwan*, edited by Shih Fang-long *et al.* (New York: Routledge, 2009), p. 57. On the increase of Indigenous literature since the 1980s, see Tao Tao Liu, "The Quest for Identity in the Writings of the Indigenous Peoples of Taiwan," in *In Search of the Hunters and Their Tribes: Studies in the History and Culture of the Taiwan Indigenous People*, edited by David Faure (Taipei: Shung Ye Museum of Formosan Aborigines, 2001), pp. 173–201.

56   Liu, "The Quest for Identity," p. 176.

57   David Albright and Corey Gay, "Taiwan: Nuclear Nightmare Averted," *Bulletin of the Atomic Scientists* (January 1998): 54.

58   Ibid., p. 55.

59   Howard R. Berman, "Taiwan: Statement on the Situation of Indigenous Peoples in Taiwan," *IWGIA Newsletter* 62 (December 1990): 111; Alliance of Taiwan

Aborigines, *Report of the Alliance of Taiwan Aborigines to the United Nations Working Group on Indigenous Populations, August 1993*.

60 On government recognition and non-recognition, see Bruce Miller, *Invisible Indigenes: The Politics of Nonrecognition* (Lincoln, NE: University of Nebraska Press, 2003).

10 From the margins and beyond

Racism, the San Francisco System and Asian Canadians

John Price

Introduction

On November 28, 2007, the Canadian Parliament passed Motion 291, to

> encourage the Government of Japan to abandon any statement which devalues the expression of regret from the Kono Statement of 1993; to clearly and publicly refute any claims that the sexual enslavement and trafficking of the "comfort women" for the Japanese Imperial Forces never occurred; to take full responsibility for the involvement of the Japanese Imperial Forces in the system of forced prostitution, including through a formal and sincere apology expressed in the Diet to all of those who were victims; and to continue to address those affected in a spirit of reconciliation.

This motion reflected an ongoing campaign by many, including groups such as ALPHA (Association for Learning and Preserving the History of World War II in Asia) as well as partners in the Korean and Filipino communities, to help obtain justice for the many women forced into sexual slavery by the Japanese imperial forces. The campaign was also endorsed by the National Association of Japanese Canadians. For many people, the elderly survivors among the "comfort women" are a living emblem of unresolved issues from the war. And in Canada, where today Asian Canadians constitute a large proportion of the population in major cities, political parties could ill afford to ignore the movement; and thus the resolution gained all-party support in the Canadian parliament. Such actions, however, have not been without controversy.

In 2009 Harper Collins published a book, *Nest of Spies*, written by journalist Fabrice de Pierrebourg and Michel Juneau-Katsuya, a former CSIS (Canadian Security Intelligence Service) official. The two authors accused ALPHA (although not named specifically, the group was clearly identified by the description) of being "agents of the Chinese government." Such characterizations harken back to an earlier era, when people of Asian heritage were racialized as alien others and potential fifth columnists. ALPHA launched a libel suit against the authors, the publisher, and newspapers that repeated the claim. Harper Collins quickly folded their tent, as did the newspapers. The book was withdrawn and the newspaper printed retractions. This anecdote highlights the fact that, for some in Asian Canadian communities, the legacies of World War II in Asia remain a concern and that racism, ostensibly overcome with Canada's official adoption of multiculturalism in the 1980s, remains a potent force.

In a similar vein, John Dower's recent work, *Cultures of War: Pearl Harbor/ Hiroshima/9–11/Iraq*, frequently alludes to racist attitudes on the part of US officials involved in waging war on Iraq.[1] That Dower should mark these instances is not surprising, given his previous work on racism in the Pacific War.[2] What is surprising is the persistence, decades after the civil rights movement, of "the imagined dichotomy between rational Westerners and irrational hordes of people of color that, for most Caucasians, never ceases to be gospel."[3]

These accounts underscore two themes that I apply to this discussion of the San Francisco System. First, many people in Asian Canadian communities had an abiding concern about the peace treaty and post-war arrangements in East Asia – an interest that continues to this day. Second, the rise of the post-war San Francisco System was closely linked not only to the geostrategic politics of empire but also to racism. How we associate or dissociate racism from other factors in a system of unequal relations is a continuous challenge, but no more so than in other questions, including the interrelationship between class and gender, for example. In this chapter I use the term *race* to talk about the social construction of categories of people based on physical appearance, ethnicity, or culture that reflect power relations. *Racialization* refers to the process of constructing "race." *Racism* is defined as racialization organized into exclusions that have significant negative consequences for the excluded.[4] I argue that our understanding of the 1951 peace treaty and the post-war system that evolved out of it must take into account racism, not as the sole or necessarily the determining factor in every instance, but rather as an ideological and systemic formation that those in power both reflected and influenced, and that shaped political and strategic outcomes in the post-war era. White supremacy was not land-locked, but arose in tandem with the modern age of imperialism; it found clear expression in the cataclysm of World War II.

By looking at the treaty from the position of those whom the treaty marginalized or who were rendered invisible in the process, including Asian Canadians or other diasporas, we gain a fuller understanding of the politics of power and domination. What is quite remarkable in the case of the peace treaty is how the majority, both of people and countries of Asia, were excluded by the politics of empire and race at San Francisco. Thus, this account provides a different yet complementary lens to the more traditional geostrategic perspective and renders visible the multiple and intersecting layers of race and empire that were at work in the making of the post-war order in East Asia. Including the diasporas in our account of the post-war system also provides new ideas regarding redress and reconciliation, a matter in which a number of Asian Canadian communities now have considerable experience.

Marginalizing the majority

Chinese communities in Canada were deeply concerned with developments in Asia before, during, and after the Pacific War. Thus, it should come as no surprise that Vancouver's daily *Chinese Times* (大漢公报, *dahangongbao*), published by the Freemasons (Hongmen, later Chee Kung Tong) from 1914 until 1992, would provide extensive coverage of the San Francisco Peace Treaty (SFPT) talks at the time. For the three-month period August to October 1951, the paper ran over 100 articles related to the peace treaty. Drawing on reports from wire services as well as newspapers in Hong Kong and radio reports out of Beijing, the coverage ranged from short updates to feature articles and editorials. On August 17, for example, it reported that the People's Republic of China (PRC) had rejected the US-drafted terms of the peace treaty and was not being invited to the conference.[5] Its editorial on August 22 reported on the extensive opposition to the treaty in Asian countries and concerns about Japanese remilitarization.[6] It suggested that somebody had to take responsibility for preventing a resurgence of Japanese militarism. On August 29, its editorial pointed to the opposition to the treaty by Burma, India, and the Soviet Union. It suggested that, from the point of view of justice, it was not clear which side was in the right.[7] During the peace conference itself, the newspaper provided a translation of Truman's speech, but then criticized the process as one-sided, representing only the anti-Soviet camp. Even during the conference, it stated, the Communists were given only a few minutes and then shouted down. By September 8, the editors had had enough and stated that "the peace treaty is an instrument to further the interests of the U.S. empire."[8] The editors also pointed out that the effect of the treaty was to create a wall between Japan and China that would prevent constructive economic relations between the two. While Japan might benefit in the short term, its long-term economic prospects were comprom-ised without ties to East Asia.

Fifty years later, as I began to research the peace treaty, I failed to incorporate the insights offered by this source. On the surface, this failure reflected simply a language issue – I did not read Chinese well and thus wanted to avoid the extra time and effort necessary to search for materials that might not be that helpful. This was, however, a failure to understand the importance of transnationalism in research and the foundational role of Asian Canadians in both Canadian and trans-Pacific history. It was in many ways a reflection of the legacy of racism in Canada. As it turned out, the *Chinese Times* proved remarkably accurate in its assessment of the peace treaty. Of all the feats of the San Francisco System, the most remarkable was the transformation of the peace process in Asia into one that effectively excluded Asia. As I found out, fifty years after the *Chinese Times*:

> Both mainland and Taiwanese China were not even invited to the peace conference. Neither were the Koreas, north and south. India refused to parti-cipate in what it regarded as a rigged affair; so did Burma. Three signatories from Asia (Vietnam, Cambodia, and Laos) were actually representatives of

the French colonial regime and must be excluded from any bona fide count of Asian countries endorsing the treaty. That leaves only four – the Philippines, Indonesia, Ceylon, and Pakistan. Of these four, Indonesia signed the treaty but never ratified it and signed a separate peace treaty with Japan in 1958. The Philippines, although closely allied with the U.S., reserved its signature and did not ratify the treaty until after it had gone into effect. In other words, the only Asian countries that supported the SFPT were Pakistan and Ceylon, both recent colonies of Britain and neither of which had signed the Allied Declaration of 1942.[9]

These exclusions did not happen easily but rather were the outcome of an interchange among the many parties to the treaty process which, when analyzed in detail, reveals the deeply racialized nature of the process. On August 16, 1951, the PRC published Zhou Enlai's statement criticizing the proposed treaty. The PRC, stated Zhou, (1) took particular exception to the clause on reparations for Allied property, because it rendered Japan liable for damages only after December 7, 1941, ignoring that China had been at war with Japan much earlier; (2) refuted the territorial clauses that gave the United States control over Pacific islands and neglected to assign sovereignty for Taiwan and the Pescadores as well as the Kuriles to China and the Soviet Union, respectively; (3) underscored the absence of safeguards to limit Japan's armed forces, to prevent the resurgence of militaristic organizations and to ensure democratic rights; and (4) rejected US predominance over Japan's economy and the exclusion of normal trade relations with the PRC. China, Zhou declared, reserved its right to demand reparations from Japan and would refuse to recognize the treaty.

The US government refused outright to allow the PRC to participate in the peace talks. On the surface, this might seem like a strategic move, based on the fact the United States was at war with China in Korea. Yet the British government was also at war with China, but had recognized the PRC and advocated for its participation in the peace conference. Strong-arm tactics by Dulles in London finally forced the British to back down.[10] What was even more astonishing was that, when the Guomindang (Kuomintang or KMT) also demanded reparations and the return of Taiwan to China as part of the peace settlement, Dulles became convinced that Chinese nationalism was as dangerous as it was "immature" and susceptible to communist manipulation. Thus, for Dulles, excluding even his ostensible allies was preferable to leaving anything to chance at the conference. Dulles had no intention of including the North Korean government in the peace conference and went so far as to disinvite the South Korean government, fearful that Korean nationalism might also upset the US agenda. In response to the ROK's complaints that this would leave Zainichi (Koreans in Japan) defenseless against Japanese discrimination, Dulles emphasized his view

that many of these Koreans were undesirables, being in many cases from North Korea and constituting a center for communist agitation in Japan. He believed, therefore, that probably a legitimate Japanese fear of certain of these Koreans was involved in any action taken against them by the Japanese authorities.[11]

And in regard to Philippine demands for reparations, presented by Elpidio Quirino when Dulles visited Manila in February 1951, Dulles concluded that the only problem was "overcoming the emotional prejudices of the people and explaining to them why the relief to which they have looked forward for so long cannot be had."[12] Finally, when the Indian government filed its protest against the US machinations and announced its decision to boycott the conference, Truman scribbled in the margins of the Indian note "Evidently the 'Govt' of India has consulted Uncle Joe and Mousie Dung of China!" As Noam Chomsky pointed out, in Truman's "joke" Stalin had been humanized but Mao was rendered inhuman, no better than animal excrement. His use of quotation marks around the abbreviated "government" also reveals the contempt he felt for India. Here we see how racism and imperial aspirations intersected to allow Truman, Dulles, and other officials – all white males raised in societies where patriarchy and white supremacy reigned – to caricature and dismiss opposition to their agenda. In that sense, reconstructing the post-war order reflected not only imperial goals but also a deeply racialized view of peoples in Asia as emotional, prone to simplistic nationalism, susceptible to communism, and unable to understand the logic of the rational West.[13]

Beyond the margins: immigration and racial equality

Other issues seldom discussed in relation to San Francisco are immigration and racial equality. Here again, insights from the diaspora provide a unique perspective. In the Japanese Canadian community, *The New Canadian*, the twice-weekly, bilingual journal of the community, tracked the peace treaty discussions very closely. The journal had begun as the English-language voice of the *nisei* (second-generation) community in 1938. After Pearl Harbor, the federal authorities forced all Japanese-language papers to close. On condition that it accept censorship by the federal government, *The New Canadian* was allowed to publish; it began to do so in Japanese as well as English. In the post-war period it continued with this convention, as does the current bulletin, *The Nikkei Voice*. The journal's coverage of the peace treaty process included detailed reports of Commonwealth consultations at the Colombo conference in January 1950.[14] This coverage intensified over the next two years with dozens of articles. It strongly endorsed the September 8 pact with a bitter denunciation of Soviet imperialism.[15] However, it also insisted that the spirit of the treaty would be defeated "if we continue and extend the various forms of exclusion which has discriminated against Japanese immigrants." This article highlights the impact of anti-communism on the one hand, but also raises the issue of racial equality and immigration on the other.

In *Transpacific Racisms*, Koshiro Yukiko described the establishment of the Committee on Problems Concerning a Peace Treaty in Japan in November 1945 and the subsequent studies calling for a peace treaty that affirmed the principle of racial equality and the inclusion of immigration clauses.[16] However, these intentions soon disappeared as the Occupation prohibited any discussion of race or racism; the peace treaty followed suit, excluding all issues relating to racism and immigration. This was another example in which victor's justice reflected not only the strategic goal of making the Pacific an American lake, but also the goal of restricting immigration to the United States. This was a goal that found strong support among the white dominions of the British Empire. Canada, for example, completely barred Japanese immigration into the 1960s, whereas the United States provided for only a small quota of Japanese immigrants in 1949.

The marginalized Zainichi

If the peace treaty completely eliminated racial equality and immigration issues, it also managed to marginalize the largest racialized group in Japan. Caught in the crossfire between racism and anti-communism, Koreans in Japan, or Zainichi (在日朝鮮人), stood up for their rights, but, in the rarefied atmosphere of high politics, they became pawns manipulated from many directions. John Foster Dulles visited Japan four times in the course of consulting about the peace treaty; during his visit in early 1951, he met with Yoshida Shigeru, Japan's prime minister, at which point they came to a meeting of minds regarding Koreans in Japan. Yoshida told Dulles that "the Government would like to send almost all Koreans in Japan 'to their homes' because it had long been concerned by their illegal activities."[17] Dulles stated that he could see the wisdom that "Korean nationals in Japan, mostly Communists, should not obtain the property benefits of the treaty." As a result of these discussions, the treaty excluded hundreds of thousands of Koreans in Japan from the treaty benefits that other Allied civilians received under the SFPT. This specific example, hardly a centerpiece in most discussions of the peace treaty, allows us to perceive the crossover of marginalizing discourses: Yoshida's racializing caricature of Zainichi as "criminals" intersects effectively with Dulles' representation of Koreans as "communists." This double "othering" suggests that anti-communism was not only a generic form of demonization but was also a specific form of racialization in a context in which a more vulgar racism was being repudiated. This intersection deserves far greater exploration than it has received to date.

Racism and Japan's double identity

Japan, ostensibly the winner in the peace treaty, was also racialized in this process, although in a manner radically different from other Asian countries. While in Japan, Dulles met with the British representative Sir Alvary Gascoigne and engaged in an extraordinary exchange regarding the creation of an "elite Anglo-Saxon club." Gascoigne mentioned seeing the phrase in a diplomatic note, to which Dulles replied "that phrase is I think quite possibly one that I used."[18] Dulles went on to explain that he felt that

the Japanese have felt a certain superiority as against the Asiatic mainland masses ... that the Western civilization represented by Britain, more latterly the United States, is perhaps sharing in that, represents a certain triumph of mind over mass which gives us a social standing in the world better than what is being achieved in terms of the mainland human masses of Asia, and that they think they have also achieved somewhat the similar superiority of mind over mass and would like to feel that they belong to, or are accepted by, the Western nations.

Dulles stated that it was important to "encourage that feeling" in order to offset the economic attraction of developing bonds with the mainland, that is, China. As Koshiro has pointed out, this was overt racialization and manipulation of Japanese identity, with the goal of cultivating Japanese notions of superiority over other Asians. The implications of such a dual identity revealed themselves in San Francisco, when Yoshida agreed to open the door to reparations for Dutch citizens while refusing this type of private reparations for citizens of Asian countries.[19] That this alternative was not offered to Asian countries such as the Philippines or Indonesia, whose representatives were vociferous in their demands for reparations at the conference, illustrates the double standard in operation at the time. The Japanese government was willing to offer the nationals of a white country an alternative process in order to ensure the Netherlands would sign the treaty, whereas no such concession was given to Asian signatories.[20]

This manipulation of the Japanese identity did not imply that Dulles had actually accepted Japan as part of the "West." Indeed, the imposition of the security treaty and its administrative regulations, not to mention his blackmailing of Yoshida into recognizing Taiwan as the cost of Senate ratification of the peace treaty, had all the hallmarks of an inequality associated with race and empire that differed only in form from the US veto of the racial equality clause in Versailles in 1919, the uprooting of Japanese-Americans during the war, or the racist immigration laws kept in place into the 1960s.

How, then, we might ask, was the United States able to market the peace treaty with Japan as a "just" peace, when so much opposition existed to its terms in Asia? On the international level, it was able to do so because it marshaled the support of its Latin American allies; more importantly, it consulted and grew its agenda in tandem with its principal allies – the white, Anglo states of Great Britain, Canada, Australia, and New Zealand. This was not by accident nor was it simply a question of ease of consultation through a common language. As early as 1907, Theodore Roosevelt had recognized the necessity of building a global Anglo-American alliance in order to contain Japan. This was a race-based alliance that arose in reaction to Japanese immigration and that came to fruition in the next decades. It was one that Churchill, renowned for his racism, reiterated in his now famous "Iron Curtain" speech of 1946, with Truman sitting on the stage with him in Fulton, Missouri:

Now, while still pursing the method of realizing our overall strategic concept, I come to the crux of what I have traveled here to say. Neither the sure prevention of war, nor the continuous rise of world organization will be gained without what I have called the fraternal association of the English-speaking peoples. This means a special relationship between the British Commonwealth and Empire and the United States.... If the population of the English-speaking Commonwealth be added to that of the United States, with all that such co-operation implies in the air, on the sea, all over the globe, and in science and industry, and in moral force, there will be no quivering, precarious balance of power to offer its temptation to ambition or adventure. On the contrary there will be an overwhelming assurance of security.[21]

Couched in terms of language, this was nothing less than a renewed call for a white, imperial alliance with which to police the world.[22] US policy would eventually respond to this call: the change marked an important point of departure in the politics of empires. In contrast to the conventional analysis that characterizes pre-war US foreign policy as isolationist, John King Fairbank has pointed out that, in fact, "We actually had three policies at once: east toward Europe, no entangling alliances, 'we keep out'; south toward Latin America, the Monroe Doctrine, 'you keep out'; and west across the Pacific, the Open Door, 'we all go in.'"[23] In the post-war world, the United States would, at the behest of the declining British Empire, break with its pre-war policies of select and limited global engagements and instead embark on the road to becoming the global sheriff. It took up this position not unilaterally but rather at the urging of its white, Anglo allies, as well as others.

Underpinning this dramatic and enduring change was the massive cultural production of World War II as the "good war" in the United States. As Dulles put it, when asked by the French ambassador to London if the peace treaty might not be best delayed,

I referred to the preponderant role played by the U.S. in winning Japanese war and conducting occupation and said in fact that in my opinion U.S. [would] not now publicly take a cowardly role in Japan which [would] almost surely lose all we have struggled for past ten years.[24]

In Dulles' mind, and in the minds of many Americans, the war had begun only in 1941 with the attack on Pearl Harbor. The production of this "good war" in US memory was one in which it had "saved" Asia from itself and which would reinforce notions of cultural superiority for decades to come. This situation was further entrenched during the Occupation, when, as John Dower has noted,

the Asian peoples who had suffered most from imperial Japan's depredations – the Chinese, Koreans, Indonesians, and Filipinos – had no serious role, no influential presence at all in the defeated land. They became invisible. Asian contributions to defeating the emperor's soldiers and sailors were displaced by an all-consuming focus on the American victory in the Pacific War.[25]

In emphasizing racism in this chapter, I want to avoid the creation of a simplistic binary of "bad white guys" and "poor victimized Asians." Racism was one important dynamic, but it intersected and at times conflicted with other variables, including class, gender, and the necessity of building an anti-communist coalition. Thus, in more than one instance, Asian leaders actively participated in the process with their own agendas. For example, Japan's prime minister, Yoshida Shigeru, who had vigorously assailed the Zainichi as aliens, also revealed the basis for Japan's reintegration into the world comity:

> As I have stated, and history confirms, ever since the opening of Japan's doors to the Western world more than a century ago, the basic principle of Japanese policy has been the maintenance of close and cordial political and economic ties with Great Britain and the United States. That Japan departed from this basic principle, and became allied with Germany and Italy, was the prime cause for my country being pushed headlong into a reckless war.[26]

In other words, Japan's error was not in invading China but rather in entering into the Axis in 1941. Thus, Yoshida was willing to put up with bullying by Dulles and other US officials because what he sought was re-entry into the "West," even though what was required was reconciliation with the Asian neighbors that Japanese imperialism had so devastated during the war. Was not Yoshida's placing of Asia into a subservient position a renewed instance of the racist contempt toward Asia and its peoples that had arisen in Japan from the time of the First Sino-Japanese War (1894–1895)?

The Philippine president, Quirino, was also willing to tolerate Dulles' paternalism and a peace treaty that undermined his quest for reparations but, unlike with Yoshida, this was not racism projected but rather tolerance of racism with the aim of obtaining the arms and military alliance necessary to put down his left-wing opponents. The difference in these two examples underscores the complex and varied strands of perceived interests, but do not in the least imply that racism, such a factor in the war itself, was somehow suddenly overcome. As Naoko Shibusawa has illustrated in her remarkable work, *America's Geisha Ally*, the racism in the United States that caricatured Japanese as sub-human or beasts during the war was replaced by more subtle caricatures, informed by race, gender, and maturity, all of which "continued to promote an international racial hierarchy."[27]

Diasporas and redress: then and now

The San Francisco System that emerged exacerbated differences in Asia and also created serious problems for diasporas abroad. The US/Canadian refusal to even recognize China meant huge challenges for families already divided and kept separate by racist immigration laws that were to continue for many years. Anti-communism created great fear; political factionalism became rife. Nevertheless, fifty years ago, representatives of the Chinese Canadian Association and the

Japanese Canadian Citizens' Association met to discuss common problems, including "the bitter animosity between these two races, especially with the older folks."[28] At times, representatives of the two communities worked together to overcome racist restrictions on immigrants from Japan and China, policies that were not overcome until the 1970s. But, for the most part, the war had driven a deep divide between the communities, with many Japanese Canadians supporting Japan's invasion of China and many Chinese Canadians agitating for the uprooting of Japanese Canadians. Neither community has seriously addressed this past. The San Francisco settlement of the Pacific War instead gave rise to new cleavages and a serious disjuncture, in which China, a beacon of hope in the war of resistance against Japan and a symbol around which most Chinese Canadians could unite, suddenly became the new enemy, while Japan, the former enemy, became a new ally. Neither community benefited much from the new juxtapositioning. Political divisions plagued the Chinese Canadian community; the Canadian government's refusal to recognize post-1949 China exacerbated family separation. On the other hand, Japan's transformation from enemy to ally did not initially much benefit Japanese Canadians. Immigration from Japan remained taboo; even those Japanese Canadians who had been exiled in 1946 now found themselves stranded in Japan. For the most part, Japanese Canadians had been dispersed across the country and remained intent on assimilating into their new surroundings. Canada had become a country not of two but of many solitudes.

Only in the 1970s did this begin to change. The war in Vietnam put the United States on the defensive, eventually leading to the rapprochement with China. The civil rights movement in the United States and the movement toward multiculturalism in Canada created new space, from which emerged the Asian American movement in the United States and the movement for redress for Japanese Canadians in Canada. As this space opened up, some people in the communities began once again to reinforce ties with the homeland; as the issue of redress related to the Pacific War surfaced in East Asia, actions abroad also occurred. In the United States, local actions date back at least to 1982, when the revision of Japanese textbooks (in which the term "invasion" was replaced by the term "advance" in a number of history textbooks) became an international issue. In response, Korean and Chinese communities in the United States began to organize protests.[29] In Canada there were small demonstrations in the 1970s; in 1996 Chinese Canadians organized a major demonstration outside the Japanese embassy in Ottawa regarding the Diaoyu/Senkaku Islands dispute. This was followed by the formation of Canada ALPHA in 1997.[30] In many ways, these actions are very much part of the legacy of Chinese Canadian identification with the old country, which dates back at least to the first arrivals in Canada.

Japanese Canadians, too, have a long history of identifying with their ancestral homeland, although their experience has been much more difficult because of the war and the uprooting, dispossession, and exile that occurred at that time. During the 1970s and 1980s, the movement for redress consumed Japanese Canadian communities, culminating in the landmark settlement of 1988, in which the government of Canada acknowledged its wartime actions as an injustice and a reflection of "discriminatory attitudes" at the time.[31] The redress settlement included individual compensation as well as funds for community rebuilding. During the struggle for Japanese Canadian redress, a historical narrative took shape in which, "as a racialized minority, they had to maintain an expected model minority role as loyal subjects of Canada."[32] The redress settlement, however, opened a new chapter in Japanese Canadian identity formation, in which historical ties to Japan, hitherto buried as part of the model minority narrative, could once again be articulated. This has led to contention, since some parts of the community desire to stay within the bounds of what we might call the post-war rehabilitated image of Japan as the land of cherry blossoms and geisha, while others have tried to grapple with the complexities of Japan, including its historical role as an aggressor in Asia. In regard to the latter, Roy Miki, scholar, activist, and poet, has done much to promote transnationalism in the emerging field of Asian Canadian studies. He contends that, even though Japanese Canadians are connected to the Canadian state through citizenship, "the achievement of redress can henceforth function as a critical frame that brings into relief the politics of memory in Japan around the question of responsibility for the massive injustices the Japanese state inflicted on others."[33] Miki proposes that redress in Asia will involve compensation, but that acts of acknowledgment and remembrance are "also crucial for those directly affected, just as these acts were for Japanese Canadians in their redress struggle." In drawing direct connections between the struggle for redress in Canada and that in Asia, Miki has issued a challenge to privilege justice over the politics of narrow nationalism.

Recently, Joy Kogawa, the author of *Obasan*, an internationally acclaimed, award-winning novel depicting the Japanese Canadian internment and its aftermath, has also strived to define her relationship with her ancestral homeland. Her most recent work, *My Road to Nagasaki Goes through Nanjing*, recounts her experiences in trying to link the atomic bombing in Nagasaki to the atrocities committed in Nanjing. This experience is based on a trip to Japan in 2010, which gave rise to serious challenges and deep reflections on the author's part about the relationship between Japanese Canadians' experiences in the war and the atrocities committed by Japanese imperialism. Kogawa, who has collaborated on redress with activists in the Chinese Canadian communities, has come under attack from numerous quarters, both in Japan and Canada. Other Japanese Canadians, including Tatsuo Kage and Satoko Norimatsu of Vancouver, have also done important work in building bridges among the communities in Canada and overseas. The challenges encountered by Kogawa and others reflect the complex politics in which the present has failed to catch up to the past.

Conclusion

Japan's economic rise, recognition of China, the ostensible end of immigration restrictions, the ascent of multiculturalism, and the end of the Cold War have all had important repercussions for Asian Canadians. Indeed, recent studies suggest that by 2031 historically racialized minorities will have become the majority in cities such as Vancouver and Toronto, with Asian Canadians forming the largest component in each city.[34] In such a context, empire-building and racism seem almost anachronistic. Yet Canadian foreign policy remains deeply aligned with US policy, including militarily. The Canadian navy regularly participates in RIMPAC war games in the Pacific. Also, institutionalized racism remains a constant problem – witness the recent apology by the governor of the Bank of Canada for air-brushing out the "Asian" features of a scientist on the new $100 bill to make the person appear more "neutral," that is, white.

Senkaku/Diaoyu, Takeshima/Dokdo, Yasukuni, "comfort women," Okinawa – as the chapters in this book illustrate, these terms and many others evoke a legacy of continuing conflict in Asia, bequeathed by the 1951 San Francisco System. Reconciliation and inclusive community-building have proven elusive, even sixty years after the signing of the peace treaty. Not surprisingly, many scholars continue to analyze the myriad challenges through a geostrategic lens. A noteworthy exception is the recent work *Ends of Empire*, in which Jodi Kim suggests that "the Cold War is not only a historical period, but also an epistemology and production of knowledge, what I call the protracted afterlife of the Cold War."[35] Her fascinating integration of race, gender, and imperial politics – in what she terms the triangulation of Asia, the US empire, and Asian American literature – provides much credence to her contention. Yet, the persistence of many problems related to the war in the Pacific suggests that the triangulation she describes must take into account earlier epistemologies; that not only the post-war, but the war itself has claimed a protracted afterlife. Not to recognize this interconnection is to erase Japan's colonial past and the inter-imperial rivalries that culminated in the fifteen years of the Pacific War.

Notes

1 John Dower, *Cultures of War: Pearl Harbor/Hiroshima/9–11/Iraq* (New York: W.W. Norton, 2010).
2 John Dower, *War without Mercy: Race and Power in the Pacific War* (New York: Pantheon, 1986).
3 John Dower, *Cultures of War*, p. 391.
4 Timothy J. Stanley, *Contesting White Supremacy* (Vancouver: University of British Columbia Press, 2011), pp. 7–8.
5 *Chinese Times*, August 17, 1951, p. 1. I am grateful to Andrew Wong for assistance in finding and translating these articles.
6 *Chinese Times*, August 22, 1951, p. 7.
7 *Chinese Times*, August 29, 1951, pp. 7, 8.
8 *Chinese Times*, September 8, 1951, p. 7.
9 John Price, "A Just Peace? The 1951 San Francisco Peace Treaty in Historical Perspective," *JPRI Working Paper No. 78*, June 2001 (Japan Policy Research Institute), p. 8. Other previous work on the treaty is to be found in Price, "Cold War Relic: The San Francisco Peace Treaty and the Politics of Memory," *Asian Perspectives* 25, no. 3 (fall 2001): 31–60, and in chapter 11 of his *Orienting Canada: Race, Empire and Transpacific* (Vancouver: University of British Columbia Press, 2011).

10 *Foreign Relations of the United States*, 1951, Vol. 6, Part 1 (Washington, DC: US Government Printing office), p. 1110 (hereafter cited as *FRUS*).

11 *FRUS*, 1951, Vol. 6, Part 1, p. 1204.

12 *FRUS*, 1951, Vol. 6, Part 1, p. 901.

13 Most recently in *Orienting Canada*, particularly chapters 9 and 12.

14 早期対日講和に一致、英連邦外祖会議で討議 [Agreement reached on early peace treaty with Japan at Commonwealth foreign ministers' consultations], January 14, 1950, *New Canadian* 13, no. 4, p. 6.

15 "It's a Job for Us," *The New Canadian*, September 12, 1951.

16 Yukiko Koshiro, *Transpacific Racisms and the Occupation of Japan* (New York: Columbia University Press, 1999), pp. 24–5.

17 "Memorandum of Conversation," April 23, 1951, *FRUS* 1951 Vol. 6, Part 1, p. 985.

18 "Editorial Note," *FRUS* 1951, Vol. 6, Part 1, p. 825.

19 For details and contemporary repercussions, see Kinue Tokudome, "POW Forced Labor Lawsuits Against Japanese Companies," *JPRI Working Paper No. 82*, November 2001 (www.jpri.org/publications/workingpapers/wp82.html [accessed August 30, 2012]). The Yoshida–Stikker correspondence before the peace treaty is contained in Stikker to Yoshida, September 7, 1951. National Archives and Records Administration, Record Group 59, General Records of the Department of State, Central Decimal File 1955–1959, 294.1141/9-459 through 294.5641/4-1995.

20 For the public statement of Netherlands representative Dirk U. Stikker on this question at the conference, see *Verbatim Minutes, Conference for the Conclusion and Signature of the Treaty of Peace with Japan, Record of Proceedings* (Washington, DC: Department of State, 1951), p. 197.

21 Cited in Robert Rhodes James (ed.), *Winston S. Churchill: His Complete Speeches, 1897–1963*, vol. 7, *1943–1949* (New York: Chelsea House Publishers, 1974), p. 7285.

22 For further discussion of this "racial and cultural alliance," see Thomas Borstelmann, *The Cold War and the Color Line: American Race Relations in the Global Arena* (Cambridge, MA: Harvard University Press, 2001), p. 47.

23 John King Fairbank, *Chinabound: A Fifty-Year Memoir* (New York: Harper Colophon, 1983), pp. 162–3.

24 *FRUS* 1951, Vol. 6, Part 1, p. 1104.

25 John Dower, *Embracing Defeat: Japan in the Wake of World War II* (New York: W.W. Norton, 1999), p. 27.

26 Yoshida Shigeru, *Japan's Decisive Century, 1867–1967* (New York: Praeger, 1967), p. 81.

27 Naoko Shibusawa, *America's Geisha Ally* (Cambridge, MA: Harvard University Press, 2006), p. 6.

28 As cited by Patricia Roy, *The Triumph of Citizenship: The Japanese and Chinese in Canada, 1941–67* (Vancouver: University of British Columbia Press, 2008), p. 255.

29 See Takashi Yoshida, *The Making of the "Rape of Nanking": History and Memory in Japan, China, and the United States* (Oxford: Oxford University Press, 2006), particularly chapter 7.

30 This information is based on private correspondence with Dr. Joseph Yu-Kai Wong, founder of the Chinese Canadian National Council and Canada ALPHA.

31 See www.japanesecanadianhistory.net/GuideExcerptsForSocialStudies5.pdf for a full copy of the acknowledgment.

32 Roy Miki, *In Flux: Transnational Shifts in Asian Canadian Writing* (Edmonton: NeWest Press, 2011), p. 89.

33 Ibid., p. 215.

34 Statistics Canada, *Projections of the Diversity of the Canadian Population* (Ottawa: Minister of Industry, 2010), p. 28. In Toronto, South Asians will form the largest component and, in Vancouver, Chinese Canadians will form the largest group.

35 Jodi Kim, *Ends of Empire: Asian American Critique and the Cold War* (Minneapolis, MN: University of Minnesota Press, 2010), pp. 3–4.

11 The San Francisco System

Past, present, future in United States–Japan–China relations[1]

John W. Dower

Legacies of the past are never far from the surface when it comes to present-day controversies and tensions involving Japan, China, and the United States.

Take, for example, a single day in China: September 18, 2012. Demonstrators in scores of Chinese cities were protesting Japan's claims to the tiny, uninhabited islands in the East China Sea known as Senkaku in Japanese and Diaoyu in Chinese – desecrating the *Hi no Maru* flag and forcing many China-based Japanese factories and businesses to temporarily shut down.

Simultaneously, Chinese leaders were accusing the United States and Japan of jointly pursuing a new "containment of China" policy – manifested, most recently, in the decision to build a new level of ballistic-missile defenses in Japan as part of the Obama administration's strategic "pivot to Asia."

And September 18 in particular? This, the Chinese were keen to point out, was the eighty-first anniversary of the Manchurian Incident of 1931 – the staged event that the Japanese military used as a pretext for seizing the three northeastern provinces of China and turning them into the quasi-colony they renamed Manchukuo.

The disputed islands, the containment-of-China accusations, even the bitter "history issue" involving recollection of imperial Japan's militarism all have toxic roots in the early years of the Cold War. Together with other present-day controversies, they trace back to the San Francisco System under which Japan re-entered the post-war world as a sovereign nation after being occupied by US forces for over six years, from August 1945 to the end of April 1952.

The tensions of September escalated in the weeks and months that followed, and the alarm this generated was occasionally apocalyptic. Pundits spoke of "flash points" – in this case, the Senkaku/Diaoyu confrontation – that could lead to an "accidental war" in which US forces supported Japan against China. This, it was observed, would be consistent with America's obligations under the bilateral security treaty with Japan that lies at the heart of the San Francisco System.

That this worst-case scenario could be taken seriously in 2012 is both surprising and unsurprising. It is surprising because this was taking place forty years after both Japan and the United States belatedly normalized relations with the People's Republic of China (PRC), dramatically abandoning the "containment" policy that had defined Cold War China policy prior to 1972. Over the course of those four decades, the economies of the three countries had become interdependent, seemingly creating a foundation for durable peace.

What makes the crisis of 2012 unsurprising, on the other hand, is the fact that China's emergence as a major economic power has been followed by intense nationalistic pride coupled with resolute commitment to military modernization. This may have been predictable, but it nonetheless came as a shock to those who took the overwhelming military supremacy of Pax Americana for granted.

The San Francisco System and this militarized Pax Americana go hand in hand. They have defined the strategic status quo in the Asia-Pacific area since the early 1950s. They have shaped (and distorted) the nature of the post-war Japanese state in ways beyond measure. They have involved both peace-keeping and war-making.

As the events of 2012 made much clearer, this system and these structures now stand at a turning point.

The contorted origins of the San Francisco System

The San Francisco System takes its name from two treaties signed in San Francisco on September 8, 1951, under which the terms for restoring independence to Japan were established. One was the multinational Treaty of Peace with Japan that forty-eight "allied" nations signed with their former World War II enemy. The second was the bilateral United States–Japan Security Treaty, under which Japan granted the United States the right to "maintain armed forces ... in and about Japan," and the United States supported and encouraged Japanese rearmament.

Both treaties came into effect on April 28, 1952, the day the occupation ended and Japan regained sovereignty.

Two aspects of these agreements are notable. The first is the timing. Japan was still occupied and under US control when the treaties were signed, and the Cold War was at fever pitch. The Soviet Union tested its first atomic bomb on August 29, 1949, triggering the nuclear arms race. The victorious Communists proclaimed the PRC on October 1 of that same year, and a Sino-Soviet Treaty of Friendship and Alliance was concluded on February 14, 1950. On June 25, 1950, war erupted on the divided Korean Peninsula, drawing in US-led United Nations forces immediately. Four months later, in late October, Chinese forces entered the war to counter what China's leaders perceived to be a US threat to advance through North Korea up to – and possibly across – the border with China. The Korean War dragged on until July 1953, and the peace and security treaties of September 1951 were signed during a protracted stalemate in this conflict.[2]

Equally significant but less well remembered, the San Francisco settlement was a "separate peace." The omissions from the list of nations that signed the peace treaty were striking. Neither Communist China nor the Chinese Nationalist regime that had fled to Taiwan were invited to the peace conference, despite the fact that China had borne the brunt of Japanese aggression and occupation beginning a full decade before Pearl Harbor and the US entry into the war. Both

South and North Korea were excluded, although the Korean people had suffered grievously under Japanese colonial rule and oppressive wartime recruitment policies between 1910 and 1945. The Soviet Union attended the peace conference but refused to sign the treaty on several grounds, including the exclusion of the PRC and Washington's transparent plans to integrate Japan militarily into its Cold War policies.

Viewed from the perspective of the separate peace, the San Francisco settlement thus laid the groundwork for an exclusionary system that detached Japan from its closest neighbors. In the months following the peace conference, the United States tightened the screws on this divisive policy by informing a dismayed and reluctant Japanese government that Congress would not ratify the peace treaty unless Japan signed a parallel treaty with the Chinese Nationalist government in Taiwan, thus effectively recognizing that regime as the legitimate government of China. Failing this, the US occupation of Japan would be perpetuated indefinitely. Japan acquiesced to this ultimatum in the famous "Yoshida Letter," dated December 24, 1951 (from the Japanese Prime Minister Yoshida Shigeru to John Foster Dulles, the US emissary in charge of the peace settlement). The ensuing peace treaty between Japan and the "Republic of China" ensconced in Taipei was signed on April 28, 1952 – the same day the peace and security treaties signed in San Francisco came into effect.

Although the Soviet Union and Japan established diplomatic relations in a joint declaration signed on October 19, 1956, they did not sign a formal peace treaty and left territorial issues regarding control of the disputed islands between Japan and the Soviet Union unresolved. Japan and South Korea did not normalize relations until June 22, 1965 (in a Treaty on Basic Relations between Japan and the Republic of Korea). Diplomatic relations between Japan and the PRC were not restored until 1972 (in a joint communiqué issued on September 29), and it was only in 1978 that the two countries concluded a formal Treaty of Peace and Friendship (on August 12).

The corrosive long-term consequences of this post-occupation estrangement between Japan on the one hand and China and Korea on the other are incalculable. Unlike West Germany in post-war Europe, Japan was inhibited from moving effectively toward reconciliation and reintegration with its nearest Asian neighbors. Peace-making was delayed. The wounds and bitter legacies of imperialism, invasion, and exploitation were left to fester – unaddressed and largely unacknowledged in Japan. And ostensibly independent Japan was propelled into a posture of looking east across the Pacific to America for security and, indeed, for its very identity as a nation.

Eight problematic legacies

The conservative Yoshida government that negotiated Japan's acceptance of the San Francisco System faced a fundamentally simple choice in 1951. In return for agreeing to Washington's stipulation that a multinational peace treaty had to be coupled with Japanese rearmament, continued US bases in Japan, and exclusion of the PRC from the peace conference, Japan gained independence plus assurance of US military protection. In the real world of power politics, the alternative that Yoshida's liberal and leftist domestic critics endorsed – namely, to insist on Japan's disarmed neutrality in the Cold War and a non-exclusionary "overall" peace treaty – meant postponing the restoration of sovereignty and submitting to continued US military occupation.

Even Yoshida's staunchly pro-American and anti-communist supporters in Japan expressed anxiety about the price to be paid for agreeing to Washington's demands. Acquiescing in the non-recognition and isolation of the PRC was unpopular, especially in business circles. The uncertain future scale and disposition of post-occupation U.S. bases throughout the nation was worrisome. And Washington's demands that Japan rearm rapidly were deemed short-sighted and foolhardy. Precipitous remilitarization, Yoshida and others argued, would provoke major opposition both domestically and among the recent foreign victims of Japanese aggression.[3]

Despite such reservations, the government and most of the populace welcomed the 1951 treaties and ensuing restoration of sovereignty; by and large, this Cold War settlement continues to be applauded in mainstream Japanese and American circles. The reasons why are not hard to find. The peace treaty itself was non-punitive and generous to Japan. And the United States–Japan military relationship has remained the cornerstone of Japanese strategic and diplomatic policy to the present day. Under the San Francisco System, Japan has established itself as a democratic, prosperous, and peaceful nation.

Rather than viewing the San Francisco System as an unmitigated blessing, however, it is necessary to recognize the many specific ways in which it has become a straitjacket – a system that locked Japan into policies and attitudes that have become more rather than less problematic with the passage of time. The "blessing" and the "straitjacket" are not mutually exclusive. They coexist, and call attention to intractable contradictions that have been inherent in the system since its inception.

Eight of these problematic legacies deserve particular attention: (1) Okinawa and the "two Japans"; (2) unresolved territorial issues; (3) US bases in Japan; (4) rearmament; (5) the "nuclear umbrella"; (6) "history issues"; (7) containment of China and Japan's deflection from Asia; and (8) "subordinate independence."

1 Okinawa and the "two Japans"

One of the tragic legacies of World War II and the early Cold War was the creation of divided countries – notably Korea, Vietnam, Germany, and China. In a perverse way, the San Francisco System made Japan another divided country by detaching Okinawa Prefecture, the southern part of the Ryukyu Islands chain, from the rest of the nation and turning it into a US military bastion.

This was not a tragedy on the scale of the other divided countries. It was, moreover, a territorial partition that involved Tokyo's close and even avid collusion with Washington. In American eyes, Okinawa became an indispensable "staging area" for US forces in Asia from the moment the war ended – a policy that the Soviet atomic bomb, the Communist victory in China, and the outbreak of the Korean War all hardened beyond any possible challenge. To Japanese policy-makers, Okinawa and its residents were simply an expendable bargaining chip. Well before the San Francisco Conference, planners in Tokyo began drawing up proposals to sacrifice Okinawa if this would hasten the restoration of sovereignty to the rest of Japan.[4]

The San Francisco settlement formalized this policy by excluding Okinawa from the "generous" peace terms. The prefecture remained under US administration, with only "residual sovereignty" vested in Japan. During the Korean War, B-29 Superfortress bombers (which only a few years earlier had firebombed the cities of Japan) flew missions to Korea from Okinawa's Kadena Air Force Base. Between 1965 and 1972, Okinawa was a key staging area for the devastating US air war against North Vietnam as well as the secret bombing attacks on Cambodia and Laos. Although administration of Okinawa was restored to Japan in 1972, after twenty-seven years of direct US control, this did not diminish the prefecture's role as the centerpiece of America's forward military posture in Asia.

The ongoing impact of this "two-Japans" policy operates at many levels. Most obvious is the degradation inevitable in any such gargantuan military-base milieu, including GI crimes, noise pollution, and environmental destruction. Less visible is the institutionalized practice of non-transparency, duplicity, and hypocrisy by both the US and Japanese governments – as seen in revelations of secret activities and agreements involving storage on Okinawan soil of both nuclear weapons and chemical weapons such as Agent Orange.[5]

Most pernicious of all, perhaps, is the shameful spectacle of a government that has consigned a specific portion of its land to extensive military use by a foreign power, and simultaneously treated its populace there as second-class citizens.

2 Unresolved territorial issues

Five territorial disputes that plague relations in the Asia-Pacific region today trace back to issues of sovereignty left unresolved in the San Francisco Peace Treaty. Nor was this ambiguity a matter of simple inadvertence or oversight. On the contrary, much of it was deliberately introduced in the final drafts of the peace treaty by the United States, in conformity with Washington's overall strategy of thwarting communist influence in Asia.[6]

Unsurprisingly, these disputes mostly involve countries that did not participate in the separate peace: notably, the Soviet Union (now Russia), South Korea, and China. Three of the disputes involve Japan directly; all of them have become highly contentious issues in the decades following the San Francisco Conference. National pride and strategic concerns naturally underlie these conflicting territorial claims, but in several cases their intensification in recent years also reflects the discovery of maritime resources such as undersea oil and natural gas deposits.

The territorial dispute with Russia involves what Japan calls the "Northern Territories" and Russia "the southern Kurile Islands" – focusing on four islands or island clusters north of Hokkaido. The issue hinges in considerable part on whether these islands are properly regarded as part of the Kurile chain or of Hokkaido, and it is complicated by the Soviet Union's abrupt transformation from ally to enemy in American eyes during the course of 1945 to 1947. At the secret "big three" Yalta conference in February 1945, the United States and Britain agreed that the Kurile Islands would be "handed over" to the Soviet Union following Japan's defeat. This was one of the inducements the Anglo powers used to persuade the USSR to enter the war against Japan; and when the war ended Soviet forces took over the Kuriles, including the now disputed islands. The United States reversed its position as the Cold War took hold and, by the time of the San Francisco conference, essentially viewed the contested islands as Japanese territory under Soviet military occupation. Although the 1951 peace treaty stated that Japan renounced "all right, title and claim to the Kurile Islands," it neither assigned the Kuriles to the Soviet Union nor mentioned the names of the disputed islands.

The Cold War linkage between this territorial dispute and the "two Japans" policy, whereby the United States detached Okinawa from the rest of Japan, emerged in a revealing manner five years after the San Francisco Conference. Prior to the finalization of the peace treaty, both US and Japanese policy-makers gave serious consideration to the argument that the two southernmost of the four islands (Shikotan and the Habomais) were not part of the Kuriles, but that the other two islands (Etorofu and Kunashiri) might reasonably be regarded as such. When high-ranking Soviet and Japanese officials met to negotiate a projected peace treaty in 1956, the former proposed such a compromise "two island return" solution to the territorial dispute, which was initially supported by the Japanese foreign minister, Shigemitsu Mamoru. Such a trade-off was foiled when the US Secretary of State John Foster Dulles informed Shigemitsu that if Japan conceded sovereignty over the Kuriles to the USSR, the United States would regard itself as "equally entitled to full sovereignty over the Ryukyus." Although the 1956 negotiations led to resumption of diplomatic relations between Moscow and Tokyo, this US threat helped prevent conclusion of a formal peace treaty.[7]

Territorial confrontation with South Korea centers on small islets in the Sea of Japan called the Liancourt Rocks in English, Takeshima in Japanese, and Tokdo (also Dokdo) in Korean. Five early US drafts of the Treaty of Peace with Japan explicitly recognized Takeshima/Tokdo as part of Korea, but in December 1949 – immediately following establishment of the PRC, but before the outbreak of the Korean War – US treaty drafts reversed course and assigned the islands to Japan. After Britain and the Commonwealth nations that were contributing to the treaty-drafting process continued to place Takeshima/Tokdo within Korean territory, a compromise was reached whereby US drafts beginning in August 1950 made no specific mention of Takeshima. The final peace treaty vaguely mentioned Korean independence, but did not describe either Japan's territorial limits or offshore islands it was to cede. In August 1951, a month before the San Francisco Conference, the United States informed the government of South Korea that it regarded Takeshima as Japanese.[8]

On January 18, 1952 – three-plus months before the peace treaty went into effect – the president of South Korea, Rhee Syngman, issued a declaration defining his country's maritime borders. He described the purpose of this "Rhee Line," which encompassed Takeshima/Tokdo, as being to protect Korea's maritime resources, referring in this case primarily to fisheries. On May 23, 1952 – roughly a month after Japan regained sovereignty – an official of the Japanese Ministry of Foreign Affairs informed a parliamentary committee that the ministry had approved use of the disputed islands for bombing practice by US forces, the assumption being that this would confirm Japanese sovereignty over the disputed islets. B-29s operating out of Okinawa had in fact used Takeshima/Tokdo as a target as early as 1948, but in practice South Korea succeeded in enforcing the Rhee Line by imposing control over the area with its coast guard. The restoration of relations between Japan and South Korea in 1965 did not resolve the sovereignty issue, although an accompanying fisheries agreement eliminated the Rhee Line, under which South Korea had seized hundreds of Japanese fishing vessels in the intervening years.[9]

The Senkaku/Diaoyu dispute involving China and Japan that erupted with alarming intensity in 2012 involves a small cluster of islets and rocks in the East China Sea, situated between Okinawa and Taiwan and often collectively described in the media as "barren rocks." Here, the territorial issue is entangled not only with the "two Japans" legacy of the San Francisco settlement, but also with "history issues" that date back to the end of the nineteenth century. Japan first laid formal claim to these islands in 1895, following its crushing victory in the first Sino-Japanese War.

Taiwan was the great territorial prize extracted from defeated China in 1895. Although Japan acquired nearby Senkaku/Diaoyu that same year, it did not do so as part of its war spoils. Rather, after declaring these uninhabited rocks to be *terra nullius,* or "land belonging to no one," Japan simply annexed them. They were treated thereafter as part of Okinawa Prefecture – and passed into US hands as such after World War II. The Americans used them for occasional bombing practice. When the United States returned sovereignty over Okinawa to Japan in 1972, Senkaku/Diaoyu was included – albeit under protest from both the PRC and the Republic of China on Taiwan.

In late December 2012 a Chinese-language memorandum surfaced in Beijing that suggests the territorial issue might well have been resolved without great difficulty if the PRC had been able to participate in the peace settlement. Dated May 15, 1950 – before the Korean War, and at a time when China apparently still anticipated being invited to the peace conference – this ten-page memorandum used the Japanese rather than Chinese name (that is, characters) for the islands and reflected ambiguity concerning their sovereignty. At one point the islands were explicitly identified as part of the Ryukyus, but elsewhere in the memo it was noted that their proximity to Taiwan required further examination.[10]

In theory, the Treaty of Peace with Japan that came into effect in 1952 restored all territories seized by Japan between 1895 and the end of World War II to the nations to whom they originally belonged. As the 1950 Chinese memo indicated, the point at issue is whether the Senkaku/Diaoyu islands are properly regarded as part of Okinawa or part of Taiwan – and in the 1970s, when Japan and the PRC established formal relations, it was tacitly acknowledged that this question was too complicated to be resolved at that time. In preparatory talks for reconciliation in 1972, Zhou Enlai told a Japanese politician "There is no need to mention the Diaoyu Islands. It does not count [as] a problem of any sort compared to recovering normal relations." Six years later, when the two countries signed a formal peace treaty, they reached a verbal agreement to postpone discussing the issue. Chinese records quote Deng Xiaoping, the PRC's supreme leader, as telling Japan's foreign minister that issues involving the Diaoyu Islands and continental shelf

> can be set aside to be calmly discussed later and we can slowly reach a way that both sides can accept. If our generation cannot find a way, the next generation or the one after that will find a way.

In his extraordinarily successful October 1978 goodwill tour of Japan – the first such visit ever by a Chinese leader – Deng said the same thing in response to a journalist's question at a huge press conference in Tokyo. The militant confrontations of 2012 made clear that such optimism was misplaced.[11]

The fourth "island" dispute, the greatest of all, pre-dates the San Francisco Conference but was integral to the very essence of the separate peace – namely, the separation of Taiwan from the PRC. This blunt Cold War intrusion into sovereign affairs can be dated precisely to June 27, 1950, two days after the outbreak of the Korean War, when the United States dispatched its Seventh Fleet to the Taiwan Strait to prevent the Chinese Communists from consolidating their victory. The bilateral "treaty of Taipei," which the United States forced Japan to conclude with the government on Taiwan on April 28, 1952, reinforced this intervention. In the eyes of the PRC, this amounted to perpetuating the dismemberment of Chinese territory: first, by Japan's seizure of Taiwan among its spoils of war in 1895 and, now, by Japan and the United States collaborating to thwart Taiwan's return to China.

Although the United States and Japan both recognized the government in Beijing as the sole government of "one China" when relations with the PRC were established in 1972, this did not alter a major premise of US–Japanese military planning under the San Francisco System. To the present day, Pentagon projections have consistently emphasized the threat of conflict between the PRC and Taiwan – and, conversely, China's accelerated military modernization focuses strongly on deterring US intervention should such conflict arise.

The fifth territorial dispute left unresolved at the 1951 peace conference in San Francisco involves the sparsely populated Spratly and Paracel Islands (plus the Scarborough Shoal) in the South China Sea, a strategically situated area that in the 1960s was discovered to be rich in oil and natural gas. Here, sovereignty claims by China were put forth in the late 1940s – first by the Nationalist government and then by the Communists – in the form of a sweeping "nine-dash-line" on a maritime map. This claim is challenged by the Philippines, Vietnam, Malaysia, and Brunei.

At the request of France, which still maintained a colonial presence in Vietnam, the treaty included a clause stating "Japan renounces all right, title and claim to the Spratly Islands and to the Paracel Islands." Although China's claim was ignored, the treaty did not specify to whom the islands belonged. In the words of the leading historian of territorial disputes stemming from the San Francisco Conference, this ambiguity left one more potential "wedge" against China, creating a source of future conflict that it was anticipated would "conveniently serve to contain communism" in Asia.[12]

3 US bases

The original professed rationale for maintaining an extensive network of US military bases in Japan – as elsewhere throughout the world – was defense against a perceived threat of communist aggression directed by Moscow. Following the collapse of the Soviet Union in 1991, the United States vacated around 60 percent of its overseas bases. Following the invasion of Afghanistan in 2001 and Iraq in 2003, it constructed many hundreds of new facilities in the Middle East, before dismantling most of them as it prepared for withdrawal in the 2010s. Still, America's worldwide "empire of bases" is today more extensive than ever before. US military personnel are stationed in around 150 foreign countries, and reasonable estimates place the total number of overseas US military sites at over 1,000 – some of them enormous, some of them small, and increasing numbers of them secret and engaged in covert activities.[13]

US bases in Japan must be seen in this larger context. They are rooted in the occupation of Japan and the ensuing Cold War, with their ongoing presence being formalized in the 1951 security treaty and subsequent bilateral agreements. At the same time, they are but one small part of an American military empire that has taken on a new post-Cold War momentum. In current scenarios, China is a major projected enemy.

From the outset, maintaining a military presence in Japan has served three purposes in the eyes of American planners. First and foremost, it provides an offshore staging area close to continental Asia and Russia. Second, and little remembered today, this presence ensures control over Japan should the country ever be inclined to revert to a more autonomous and militaristic course. (This argument was often heard in the 1950s, when many Americans and other foreigners had reservations about Japan's trustworthiness. It resurfaced in the early 1970s, when the United States normalized relations with China.) Third, and most popular among supporters of the bases, the stationing of US forces in and around Japan contributes – as stated in Article 1 of the 1951 security treaty – "to the maintenance of international peace and security in the Far East and to the security of Japan against armed attack from without."

In the wake of the "3–11" disaster of 2011, when Japan's Tōhoku region was stricken by an earthquake and tsunami, followed by nuclear meltdown at the Fukushima Daiichi power plant, US forces in Japan assumed a new and highly praised role by providing emergency aid and humanitarian relief. Codenamed "Operation Tomodachi" (Operation Friend), this involved input from bases situated throughout the country.

In practice, the most conspicuous use of the bases has been to support US combat operations outside Japan. They were a major staging area for the air war against Korea, where US warplanes dropped more tonnage of bombs than in the air raids that devastated Japan in 1945. (General Curtis Le May, who commanded the firebombing of Japan before moving on to Korea, later observed, "We burned down just about every city in North and South Korea *both* ... we killed off over a million civilian Koreans and drove several million more from their homes, with the inevitable additional tragedies bound to ensue.") Between 1965 and 1972, this use of bases in Japan for deadly combat elsewhere was repeated against Vietnam, Cambodia, and Laos – where US forces dropped more than seven million tons of bombs, well over twice the total tonnage dropped by US and British forces in the European and Asian theaters combined in World War II. Bases in Japan, particularly in Okinawa, also have been used to support the US wars in Iraq and Afghanistan, although not for launching bombing missions per se.[14]

Preserving the peace in Asia and the Pacific through multinational security agreements is obviously an essential endeavor, but past experience under the Pax Americana indicates how destructive this may become in actual practice. It is not plausible that Japan's hypothetical enemies – the Soviet Union and China in the Cold War, China and North Korea today – have ever really posed a serious threat of unprovoked armed attack on Japan, as the rhetoric in the original security treaty implies. On the other hand, there can be no doubt that the continued presence of the bases ensures that in the future, as in the past, Japan will have no choice but to become a participant in America's global military policies and practices, even where these may prove to be unwise and even reckless.

4 Rearmament

When the United States–Japan Security Treaty was signed in 1951, it was clear to both sides that Japan's commitment to rearm was unconstitutional. In 1946, when the new "peace constitution" was being debated in the Diet, Prime Minister Yoshida responded to a question about Article 9 and the charter's "no war" provisions by declaring that this prohibited any remilitarization whatsoever, even in the name of self-defense. As late as January 1950, Yoshida was still talking about "the right of self-defense without force of arms" – vividly evoking an old samurai image to clarify that this meant "self-defense which does not employ even two swords."

The United States began pressuring Yoshida to begin rearming Japan even before the outbreak of the Korean War. When that conflict erupted on June 25, 1950, rearmament was in fact initiated. The United States envisioned deploying Japanese ground forces in Korea, and pushed for extremely rapid remilitarization. Yoshida's policy, by contrast, was to go slow. When the bilateral security treaty endorsing Japanese rearmament was signed, it was with the understanding on both sides that this commitment to rearm was legally precarious and would require constitutional revision in the near future.[15]

Neither Washington nor the conservative government in Tokyo anticipated that popular support for the anti-militarist ideals embodied in Article 9 would block constitutional revision once Japan regained its independence, and would continue to do so for decades to come. The ensuing debate has rattled Japanese politics for over six decades. Failure to revise the constitution has not prevented the government from engaging in "revision by reinterpretation" and creating a technologically advanced military with a continually redefined mission. At the same time, the constitution has retained sufficient influence to place restraints on both the weaponry these "self-defense forces" can acquire and the missions in which they can participate (such as supporting the United States and United Nations militarily in overseas conflicts).

The constitutional crisis is the most widely discussed outcome of Japan's legally dubious rearmament, but it is not the only problematic legacy of this aspect of the San Francisco System. Rearmament has two additional ramifications. First, like the military bases in Japan, it locks Japan into US tactical planning and strategic policy. Second, it goes hand in hand with downplaying, sanitizing, and denying what the Japanese military actually did in its earlier incarnation, when the emperor's soldiers and sailors ran amok in Asia.

Supporters of revising the constitution to remove restrictions on rearmament argue that this will enable Japan to become a "normal nation," to participate in international peace-keeping operations under the auspices of the United Nations, and to develop an autonomous capability to defend itself. In fact, the more Japan rearms, the more it will be placed under irresistible pressure to make ever more substantial contributions to America's war-fighting activities.

5 *"History issues"*

The link between rearming Japan and decontaminating the nation's past becomes clear when we recall how little time elapsed between Japan's defeat and the inauguration of the San Francisco System. Yesterday's militaristic enemy was being rehabilitated as today's peace-loving ally, while at the same time yesterday's World War II ally – China – was demonized as part of a "Red menace" that threatened world peace. Promoting rearmament dictated playing down Japan's transgressions and China's victimization – not only in Japan, but also in the United States and internationally.

This sanitization of imperial Japan's conduct began before the San Francisco Conference. The US-led war crimes trials conducted in Tokyo between mid-1946 and the end of 1948, for example, suppressed atrocities that would poison relations between Japan and its Chinese and Korean neighbors when exposed decades later. One of these crimes was the murderous medical experiments conducted on prisoners by the imperial army's "Unit 731" in Harbin. Another was the abduction of women, mostly Koreans, who were forced to provide sexual services as "comfort women" (*ianfu*) to the imperial forces. Once the Tokyo trials of high-ranking "Class-A" defendants ended in November 1948, moreover, further investigation of war crimes and prosecution of accused high-level war criminals was terminated.

In an ideal world the 1951 peace conference might have been an occasion for forthright historical summation and engagement with issues of war responsibility. Instead, the San Francisco settlement did not just exclude the two countries most deserving of apology and redress, China and Korea, but also became an occasion for spinning history and encouraging amnesia. In the favorite adjective of official Washington, the San Francisco treaty was to be a "generous" peace. When participating countries such as Britain and Canada recommended that the peace treaty include "some kind of war guilt clause," the Americans opposed this idea.[16]

The separate peace did not just endorse exclusion over overall reconciliation and leave the deepest wounds of imperialism and war unaddressed. In Japan, the San Francisco settlement also paved the way for the return of politicians and bureaucrats who had been purged for militarist activities during the occupation and in some cases even arrested for war crimes. By 1957, the prime minister was a former accused (but never indicted) war criminal, Kishi Nobusuke; when the United States–Japan Security Treaty came up for revision and renewal in 1960, it was Kishi who rammed this through the Diet in the face of massive popular protest. (In the final month of 2012, in the midst of the intensifying Senkaku/Diaoyu crisis, Kishi's right-wing grandson Abe Shinzō assumed the premiership for a second time and immediately announced a renewed campaign to promote patriotism and challenge the alleged war crimes of his grandfather's generation.)

Coupled with the many years that elapsed before Japan established formal relations with South Korea and China, the return to power in the 1950s of a largely unrepentant old guard ensured that troublesome history issues would be passed on to later generations. Still, the joint communiqué that restored diplomatic relations between Japan and the PRC in 1972 did state that "The Japanese side is keenly conscious of the responsibility for the serious damage that Japan caused in the past to the Chinese people through war, and deeply reproaches itself." Twenty-six years later, in 1998, another Sino-Japanese declaration of friendship and cooperation similarly included a paragraph emphasizing the importance of "squarely facing the past and correctly understanding history," in which, for the first time, the Japanese government endorsed characterization of Japan's actions "during a certain period in the past" as "aggression."[17]

The anomaly of the "history problem" that blights present-day relations between Japan on the one hand and Korea as well as China on the other is that uses and abuses of the recent past became hugely contentious only after diplomatic ties were belatedly established. Reconciliation and the cultivation of constructive relations went hand in hand with intensification, rather than dissolution, of strident nationalism on all sides. There have been many official Japanese apologies to China and Korea since the 1970s. These expressions of remorse, however, have been undercut with almost metronomic regularity by the whitewashing and outright denial by prominent politicians and influential individuals and organizations of imperial Japan's overseas aggression and oppression.

The escalating Sino-Japanese clash over history issues unfolded in often jarringly tandem steps. Conclusion of a formal peace treaty between Japan and the PRC in 1978, for example, coincided with the secret enshrinement of fourteen Japanese convicted of Class-A war crimes in Yasukuni Shrine, which honors the souls of those who fought on behalf of the emperor; they were entered in the shrine's register as "martyrs of Shōwa" (*Shōwa junnansha*). Visits to Yasukuni by politicians first precipitated intense domestic as well as international controversy when Prime Minister Nakasone Yasuhiro and members of his cabinet visited the shrine in an official capacity on the fortieth anniversary of the end of the war in 1985 – which, as it happened, was the same year the Nanjing Massacre Memorial Hall opened in China. As time passed, Chinese fixation on Japan's wartime aggression and atrocities grew exponentially at every level of expression, from museums to mass media to street protests – while conservative and right-wing denials of war crimes grew apace in Japan.

In part (but only part), "history" became more contested after Japan normalized relations with China and South Korea for a simple reason: interest in the recent past was rekindled on all sides, and historical resources became more accessible. The best scholarship on Japanese war crimes and war responsibility – concerning the Nanjing Massacre, criminal experiments of Unit 731, exploitation of non-Japanese *ianfu*, etc. – dates from the 1970s and after. This investigative work, much of it by Japanese scholars and journalists, was provocative by nature. It triggered patriotic rebuttals in Japan and rage outside Japan. It was tinder for nationalistic sentiments already on the rise on all sides – and grist, as well, for political leaders preoccupied primarily with domestic problems and audiences.

At the same time, it is hardly a coincidence that, in both Japan and China, burgeoning nationalism rode on the back of burgeoning economic growth. In Japan's case, the pride and hubris that accompanied the so-called economic miracle of the 1970s and 1980s spilled over into patriotic campaigns to erase the stigma of the "Tokyo war crimes trial view of history" (a favorite right-wing pejorative phrase). In China, the turn to capitalism introduced by Deng Xiaoping beginning in 1978 displaced prior fixation on Marxism and Maoism and left an ideological gap filled with a new nationalism focusing on victimization by foreign powers, Japan foremost among them. In the several decades following establishment of the PRC in 1949, Communist propaganda had much to say about the military threat posed by the United States and Japan, but relatively little to say about historical grievances against Japan. That changed abruptly after the brief period of amity and goodwill that accompanied reconciliation in the 1970s.[18]

In both China and Japan, this convergence of history and nationalism has turned "memory" into propaganda and "history issues" into history wars that have no end in sight. Denunciation *versus* denial of Japanese war crimes has become a multi-directional and almost ritualistic cycle. In Japan, cleansing the past is integral to attempts to inflate a waning spirit of national pride. In China, manipulating history involves an even more convoluted domestic dynamic. Repetitive attacks on both Japan's war crimes and its alleged post-war failure to show genuine contrition do more than just pump up patriotic ardor. These attacks also provide a distraction from domestic problems and grievances. At the same time, lambasting historical sanitization by the Japanese diverts attention from the PRC's own top-down historical sanitization concerning crimes against the Chinese people inflicted after 1949 by the Chinese Communist Party itself.[19]

6 The "nuclear umbrella"

In becoming incorporated in the San Francisco System, Japan placed itself under the US "nuclear umbrella." This is a seductive euphemism – suggesting that in American hands nuclear weapons are purely defensive. By contrast, the Soviet Union's acquisition of nuclear weapons, following its successful test of an atomic bomb in 1949, was portrayed as provocative and threatening. The same perception was extended to the acquisition of nuclear weapons by China and North Korea (first tested in 1964 and 2006, respectively).

It is challenging to sort out the quirks and contradictions in this "umbrella" argument. The United States was, and remains, the only nation to use nuclear weapons in war; after Hiroshima and Nagasaki, Japan was in a unique position to bear testimony to the abomination of such weapons. When the San Francisco System was being assembled, however, there existed no significant anti-nuclear movement in Japan. Until 1949, US occupation authorities had censored writings or visuals about the atomic-bomb experience, out of fear this could provoke anti-Americanism and public unrest. Only marginal public attention was given to the subject thereafter, until the occupation ended. Astonishingly, the first serious selection of photographs published in Japan of the two stricken cities appeared in a magazine dated August 6, 1952 – the seventh anniversary of the Hiroshima bombing, and over three months after the peace treaty came into effect. Essentially, the Japanese government took shelter under the "nuclear umbrella" before the Japanese people had seriously confronted the horror of their own nuclear experience.[20]

At the same time, however, it was known well before the San Francisco Conference that US planners were considering using nuclear weapons in the Korean War. President Harry S. Truman caused an international uproar when he refused to rule out using atomic bombs in a press conference on November 30, 1950, following China's all-out intervention in the conflict two days earlier. Subsequent fears (and premonitions of "World War III") did not go away. We now know that nuclear scenarios were seriously discussed at various levels within the

US government and military from an early date. On July 24, 1950, almost exactly one month after the war began, for example, General Douglas MacArthur anticipated that Chinese intervention would create "a unique use for the atomic bomb." Five months later, shortly after Truman's inflammatory press conference, MacArthur actually submitted a plan to the joint chiefs of staff that projected using thirty-four atomic bombs in Korea. By the end of March 1951, at the height of the conflict, atomic-bomb loading pits had been made operational at Kadena Air Base in Okinawa, lacking only the nuclear cores for the bombs. The following month, in a significant departure from previous policy, the US military temporarily transferred complete atomic weapons to Guam.[21]

The most harrowing contingency study involving bases in Japan took place in late September and early October of 1951, a few weeks after the peace conference in San Francisco. Codenamed "Operation Hudson Harbor," this secret operation involved flights of B-29s operating out of Kadena and carrying out simulated nuclear attacks on targets in Korea. These trial flights, which did not actually carry atomic bombs, were coordinated from Yokota Air Base, near metropolitan Tokyo.[22]

Although the possibility that America might use nuclear weapons against its latest Asian enemies (China as well as North Korea) was alarming, anti-nuclear sentiment did not gain widespread support in Japan until almost two years after the country regained sovereignty. The catalyst for this popular opposition was the Bikini Incident, in which fallout from a US thermonuclear (hydrogen bomb) test on the Bikini Atoll in the Marshall Islands on March 1, 1954, irradiated over 7,000 square miles in the mid-Pacific. The destructive force of the Bikini explosion was roughly 1,000 times that of the bomb that devastated Hiroshima. Contrary to US denials, radioactive fallout was extensive. And this fallout quickly took on an intimately human dimension when it became known that ashes from the explosion had rained down on the twenty-three-man crew of a Japanese tuna-fishing vessel named *Daigo Fukuryūmaru* (Lucky Dragon #5), which was outside the danger zone declared by the United States in advance of the test. The entire crew was hospitalized with symptoms of radiation sickness upon returning to Japan, and the ship's radio operator died over half a year later, on September 23, 1954.

The Bikini Incident precipitated the greatest crisis in Japan–United States relations since World War II. Public concern over the plight of the fishermen was compounded by fear that fish caught in the Pacific were contaminated, and these concerns in turn spilled into outrage at dismissive or deceptive responses by US officials. By mid 1955, a nationwide petition campaign to ban hydrogen bombs had garnered tens of millions of signatures, and a spectrum of grassroots organizations had coalesced to form Japan's first anti-nuclear organization.[23]

The emergence of this anti-nuclear movement coincided with the secret intensification of US nuclear deployments in the Asia-Pacific area. In December 1954, the United States introduced "complete nuclear weapons" in Okinawa for the first time, and simultaneously approved introducing "non-nuclear components" (bomb casings or assemblies capable of being quickly nuclearized) to bases elsewhere in Japan. In the years immediately following, military planners in Washington gave serious thought to using these nuclear weapons against China on at least three occasions: in September 1954, during the First Taiwan Strait Crisis; in the Second Taiwan Strait Crisis, which erupted in August 1958; and during the Cuban Missile Crisis in October 1962, when Mace nuclear missiles in Okinawa were placed on a fifteen-minute nuclear alert.[24]

Between 1954 and the reversion of Okinawa to Japanese administration in 1972, nineteen different types of nuclear weapons were stored there, mostly at Kadena Air Base and probably totaling close to 1,000 at any given time. At the request of the Japanese government, these were removed when reversion took place. The nuclear-ready "non-nuclear components" on bases elsewhere in Japan appear to have been removed in 1965, but this did not prevent the US military from bringing nuclear weapons into Japan. In 1981, former ambassador Edwin O. Reischauer caused a commotion by acknowledging what he himself regarded as common knowledge: that nuclear-armed US warships regularly entered Japanese waters and ports.[25]

In the aftermath of the Bikini Incident, supporters of the "nuclear umbrella" in and outside Japan lost no time in mounting a multi-front offensive. Then and thereafter, the anti-nuclear movement was both castigated as being manipulated by hardcore communists and belittled as reflecting a "pathologically sensitive" victim consciousness. This is when the pejorative term "nuclear allergy" became attached to the Japanese – as if loving the bomb were healthy, and fearing and deploring it a kind of sickness. At the same time, the United States launched an intense campaign to divert attention from the nuclear arms race by promoting the peaceful use of atomic energy throughout Japan. The success of this "atoms for peace" crusade became widely recognized over half a century later, when the meltdown of the Fukushima Daiichi nuclear power plant in 2011 highlighted the country's great dependence on nuclear energy. The Fukushima disaster also served as a reminder of the extent to which Japan's advanced nuclear technology has made it a "paranuclear state" or "virtual nuclear weapons state," with extensive stockpiles of separated plutonium that make it capable of transitioning to the development of nuclear weapons within a year or so should a decision be made to do so.[26]

From the 1950s on, Japan's conservative leaders have been caught between a rock and a hard place where nuclear policy is concerned. Beginning in the 1960s, they responded to domestic opposition to nuclear weapons with several grand gestures designed to associate the government itself with the ideal of nuclear disarmament. These included the highly publicized "three non-nuclear principles" introduced by Prime Minister Satō Eisaku in 1967 and endorsed in a Diet resolution four years later (pledging not to possess or manufacture nuclear weapons, or permit their introduction into Japanese territory). Japan signed the Nuclear Non-Proliferation Treaty in 1970 (ratifying it in 1976), and Satō shared the 1974 Nobel Peace Prize for his anti-nuclear performances.

At the same time, however, living under the nuclear umbrella has engendered secrecy, duplicity, and unflagging Japanese subservience to US nuclear policy. In the wake of the Bikini Incident, and for years thereafter, Japanese officials accompanied the government's public expressions of concern over US thermo-nuclear tests with private assurances to their American counterparts that these should be understood as merely "a sop to the opposition parties in the Diet and ... primarily for domestic consumption." Their public protests, they explained confidentially, were just "going through the motions."[27]

When the mutual security treaty was renewed under Prime Minister Kishi in 1960, a secret addendum (dating from 1959) referred to consultation between the two governments concerning "the introduction into Japan of nuclear weapons including intermediate and long-range missiles, as well as the construction of bases for such weapons."[28] Similarly, the reversion of Okinawa to Japanese sovereignty in 1972 was accompanied by a prior secret agreement between Satō and President Richard Nixon (in November 1969), stating that the United States could reintroduce nuclear weapons in Okinawa in case of emergency, and also sanctioning "the standby retention and activation in time of great emergency of existing nuclear storage locations in Okinawa: Kadena, Naha, Henoko and Nike Hercules units."[29]

On various occasions during and after the Cold War, influential Japanese politicians and officials have made clear – sometimes privately and frequently publicly – that they themselves do not suffer any "nuclear allergy." In May 1957, for example, Prime Minister Kishi told a parliamentary committee that the constitution did not bar possession of nuclear weapons "for defensive purposes." Four years later, in a November 1961 meeting with the US secretary of state, Kishi's successor Ikeda Hayato wondered out loud whether Japan should possess its own nuclear arsenal. (He was told that the United States opposed nuclear proliferation.) In December 1964, two months after China tested its first atomic bomb, Prime Minister Satō informed the US ambassador in Tokyo that Japan might develop nuclear weapons. A month later, Satō told the US secretary of state that if war broke out with China, Japan expected the United States to retaliate immediately with nuclear weapons. Despite having signed the Non-Proliferation Treaty, moreover, Japanese politicians and planners have secretly examined the feasibility of Japan acquiring tactical nuclear weapons. Over the course of recent decades, various conservative politicians and officials have publicly stated that this would be constitutionally permissible and strategically desirable.[30]

Lost in these charades – and probably lost forever – has been the opportunity for Japan to build on its own tragic nuclear experience and move beyond rhetoric and token "motions" to take a vigorous leading role in promoting nuclear arms control and ultimate abolition.

Lost, too, is any apparent concern that what American and Japanese supporters of the nuclear umbrella present as "deterrence" is, in the eyes of the targets of this arsenal, threatening and provocative.

7 China and Japan's deflection from Asia

It is perhaps inevitable that, nearly seventy years after World War II, Japan and China have still failed to establish what might be called, idealistically, deep peace. Beginning with the intrusion of the Western powers into East Asia in the mid nineteenth century, the respective experiences of the two nations could hardly have been more different. To contemporary Chinese, the narrative of their nation's modern times is in great part a story of humiliation at the hands of foreign powers. In each and every retelling, moreover, it is made clear exactly when this began: in 1840, with the country's shattering defeat in the First Opium War and the subsequent imposition of unequal treaties by Great Britain and other Western imperialist powers.

Japan's response to the Western challenge, by contrast, was in the terms of the times a resounding success, in which rapid "Westernization" was carried out under such provocative slogans as "throwing off Asia." The signal event in this putative success took place in 1895, when Japan joined the imperialist camp by crushing China in the first Sino-Japanese War, imposing its own unequal treaty on the defeated foe and acquiring Taiwan as its first colony. (Korea was annexed in 1910.) In the larger global arena, the spoils of war for Japan included being treated as a great power. Imperial Japan's subsequent depredations in China up to 1945 rested on this 1895 base. In theory, the 1951 San Francisco peace settlement took 1895 as its chronological demarcation point for stripping Japan of an ill-begotten empire and restoring its parts to their rightful sovereigns.[31]

The humiliation of being defeated, dismembered, invaded, and occupied by Japan between 1895 and 1945 has not been expunged in China, and never will be. Nor, on the other hand, has the arrogance of a one-time conqueror (and erstwhile pre-war successful Westernizer as well as post-war economic superpower) been dispelled from Japan. Deeply discordant historical narratives, kept alive by the potent machinery of manipulated memory, thus blight contemporary Sino-Japanese relations in especially harmful ways. At the same time, it should be kept in mind that the historical humiliation that fuels contemporary Chinese nationalism extends beyond Japan to include the Western powers.

The piling up of historical grievances did not, of course, end for China with Japan's defeat in World War II or the Communist victory in 1949. Rather, it was compounded by the exclusion of the PRC from the 1951 peace conference and Japan's subsequent incorporation in the policy of non-recognition and "containment" mandated by Washington. For two decades, ending only in 1972, Japan was deflected from the Asian continent and wrapped in the embrace of its new American partner. The Cold War mindset welcomed and encouraged protracted hostility between Japan and China. Reconciliation and healing were thwarted, while trends detrimental to the process of coming to terms with the past were given time and space to take root.

The proclaimed premise of Washington's containment policy was elemental. An America-led "free world" confronted a monolithic communist bloc directed by Moscow. China was but a puppet or satellite of the Soviet Union. And Japan, with its potential to become again the "workshop" of Asia (like West Germany in Europe), could tip the global balance of power if allowed to interact closely with the communist side of this bipolar divide.[32]

Less openly acknowledged, another premise behind detaching Japan from China was racist, and entailed exploiting the old "throwing off Asia" mentality. John Foster Dulles, who choreographed the drafting of the peace and security treaties (before later becoming secretary of state), conveyed this in a confidential conversation with a British diplomat in Tokyo in January 1951, in which he called attention to how "the Japanese people have felt a certain superiority as against the Asiatic mainland masses," and consequently "would like to feel that they belong to, or are accepted by, the Western nations." (The two Anglo diplomats also referred to affiliation with "an elite Anglo-Saxon Club.") Less than six years after the end of an atrocious war, Japan's recent enemy was envisioning a partnership based on a fusion of Caucasian supremacy with Japan's warped envy of the West and contempt for other Asians.[33]

For largely practical reasons, many Japanese conservatives disagreed with the Manichaean outlook that set Japan against China; where Japan was concerned, the containment policy was never watertight. Between 1952 and 1972, a modest level of trade took place between the two nations, as well as exchanges involving non-governmental or semi-official political, cultural, business, and labor delegations. At the same time, Japan was inhibited from restoring diplomatic relations with Beijing or recognizing the Communist government as the sole government of China.

This changed dramatically in July 1971, when President Richard Nixon unexpectedly announced that the United States was abandoning containment and that he would soon visit the PRC. America's *volte-face* shocked the world and caused particular bitterness in Japan, where the government was informed of the new policy fifteen minutes in advance of Nixon's announcement. Such public humiliation replicated the cavalier manner in which Japan had been forced to participate in the containment of China two decades earlier – only now the spin was in the opposite direction. Nixon's rapprochement with China paved the way for restoration of Sino-Japanese diplomatic relations in 1972.

The full significance of this abandonment of the containment policy lay in its confluence with other developments. These included not only the winding down of the Vietnam War and restoration of Okinawa to Japanese administration, but also early harbingers of Japan's "economic miracle" and the uncertain effect this might have on Japanese remilitarization. Secretary of State Henry Kissinger, who laid the groundwork for rapprochement in top-secret talks with Prime Minister Zhou Enlai in 1971, informed Nixon that "fear of revived Japanese militarism was a major theme throughout our discussions." This same theme carried over to the president's own conversations with Zhou in Beijing the following year. Had Japan's leaders been privy to these exchanges, the mortification they experienced upon being given only a few minutes of advance notice that Nixon would visit China would have seemed negligible by comparison.[34]

As conveyed by Zhou, the PRC feared that Japan's economic boom was bound to lead to expansion abroad, which in turn would inevitably be accompanied by military expansion – especially given "their tradition of militaristic thinking." At one point, Zhou referred to Japan as a "wild horse," making clear that the PRC was particularly apprehensive that Japanese military forces might in the near future be dispatched to Taiwan and South Korea. What China wished to see was abrogation of the United States–Japan Security Treaty and Japan's reversion to a position of unarmed neutrality.

Kissinger and Nixon rejected this unrealistic scenario not by dismissing fears of a resurgent Japanese militarism as irrational, but rather by arguing that (in Kissinger's words) "paradoxically, the presence of U.S. troops on Japan helped to restrain the Japanese rather than the reverse." As Nixon put it, continuing the United States–Japan defense relationship

> can restrain Japan from following a course which the Prime Minister cor-
> rectly pointed out could happen, of economic expansion being followed by
> military expansion.... If we don't have that close relationship they aren't
> going to pay any attention to us.

Such frank acknowledgment that a basic rationale for US bases in Japan was to exercise control over the Japanese was embellished with other statements that would also have made Japan's faithful pro-American leaders cringe. Kissinger argued that Japanese neutralism "would probably take a virulent nationalist form," while Nixon agreed that, without the US defense partnership, the Japa-nese as a people, given their "drive and a history of expansionism," would be "susceptible to the demands of the militarists." At one point, in responding to Zhou's expressed concerns, Kissinger delivered an extended indictment of the Japanese national character. He observed that "China's philosophical view had been generally global while Japan's had been traditionally tribal," described Japan as a nation "subject to sudden explosive changes," and declared that the Americans "had no illusions about Japanese impulses and the imperatives of their economic expansion." When Zhou opined that the US nuclear umbrella tended to make Japan more aggressive toward others, Kissinger declared that the alternative was "much more dangerous. There was no question that if we with-drew our umbrella they would very rapidly build nuclear weapons." Absent the restraint of the bilateral security treaty and US bases in Japan, there was no way of predicting what Japan might do beyond near certainty that it would be destabilizing.

The Americans won this argument hands down, to the extent that the PRC subsequently ceased to criticize the United States–Japan security relationship. Even as America's highest officials were endorsing Chinese mistrust of Japan, Japan and the PRC were separately working out their own joint declaration of reconciliation. In this honeymoon period of United States–Japan–PRC rap-prochement, shared strategic preoccupation with the Soviet Union helped per-suade the three nations to submerge their prior antagonism.[35]

Formally, the reconciliation of Japan and China was affirmed in four joint documents between 1972 and 2008. These pronouncements created and rein-forced a bilateral relationship under which mutually beneficial exchanges flour-ished across the board, with particularly spectacular results in areas such as business, commerce, and technology transfer. Despite these declarations of friendship and concrete manifestations of bilateral integration, however, reconciliation remained fragile and deep peace elusive. The ratcheting up of the Senkaku/Diaoyu islands dispute that took place beginning in September 2012 was the most alarming example of this fragility, but this simply exposed tensions, and fissures that had already become apparent in the 1980s, soon after the normalization of relations.[36]

The parallel but contradictory trajectories of genuine Sino-Japanese reconciliation after 1972 on the one hand and, on the other hand, intensified tensions that trace back to creation of the San Francisco System are both dramatic and disturbing. The Senkaku/Diaoyu dispute is but one example of this. Taiwan is another example. For four decades after Washington and Tokyo recognized "one China" under the sole government of the PRC, Taiwan remains a source of discord and distrust, as the Chinese perceive that neither the United States nor Japan actually desires reunification. On the contrary, much United States–Japan joint military planning remains predicated on responding to a crisis in the Taiwan Strait.[37] "Containment of China" is yet another reminder of the linkage between early post-war policy and present-day affairs. In the second decade of the twenty-first century – six decades after the Cold War containment policy was introduced, and four decades after it was ostensibly repudiated as an "abnormal state of affairs" – the air is blue with American and Japanese strategists and pundits warning about a new China threat and calling for a new policy of military containment.

Perhaps the most corrosive deep legacy of mistrust lies in the contention over "war history" that became so bitter after normalization of relations. Where China is concerned, anti-foreign nationalism was promoted to compensate for the waning of Marxist ideology, as market-oriented reforms gained traction beginning in the 1980s. That Japan became the prime villain in a historical narrative of victimization and humiliation was unsurprising, given its predatory activities in China beginning with the first Sino-Japanese War. This demonization, however, has been abetted in ways beyond measure by the post-war eruption of right-wing nationalism in Japan, in which denial of imperial Japan's aggression and war crimes plays a central role.

In a convoluted way, Japanese neo-nationalists are driven by much the same mixture of pride and humiliation that propels their Chinese counterparts: pride at throwing off adversity and becoming a post-war superpower, and humiliation, in this case, from seeing their erstwhile holy war turned into a criminal and atrocious undertaking. Much of the conservative retelling of Japan's war history reflects an attempt to eradicate, or at least diminish, this stain on Japan's national honor. And much of this revisionism is directed at domestic audiences and a domestic electorate, with scant regard for how negatively it is seen by outsiders.

The onus of defeat, coupled with accusations of criminality, weighs heavily indeed in these circles – more rather than less so as time passes – and this has inflicted Japan with a debilitating malaise. Sanitizing the war years and repeatedly undercutting official apologies and expressions of remorse is widely perceived by others – including not just foreigners, but also many thoughtful Japanese – to be not only dishonest, but also appallingly insensitive to the victims of imperial Japan's expansion and aggression. Certainly among Chinese and Koreans this conveys the impression of an utter lack of empathy, identity, responsibility, guilt, or repentance. It suggests that Japan is once again "throwing off Asia."

No matter how often and how sincerely Japan and China have pledged to work together for the peace and progress of Asia from the 1970s on – and no matter how great their interactions and economic interdependence have become – what matters most decisively to Japan's leaders in the final analysis is continuity of the intimate United States–Japan relationship.

8. "Subordinate independence"

Strategically, materially, and psychologically, Japan's current status in Asia – and in the world more generally – is riddled with ambiguity. In considerable part this reflects China's emergence as a major economic power, coupled with the countervailing spectacle of Japan's relative decline since the 1990s. The labels that were attached to Japan in the 1970s and 1980s – "economic superpower," "miracle," "Japan as number one," and so on – have evaporated where Japan is concerned, but they have not disappeared. They have been more or less transposed to China.

There is a great deal of exaggeration in this role-reversing and relabeling, of course: Japan remains a major power, and China faces daunting economic, political, social, demographic, and environmental challenges. Still, there has been a tectonic shift in stature and influence since the early years of the Cold War, when Americans referred to the Pacific as an "American lake" and Japan was projected as *the* great workshop of Asia. All eyes now focus on China as the mesmerizing rising nation-state in the Asia-Pacific region, and on the uncertain configuration of power politics this portends – especially where the "triangle" of the United States, China, and Japan is concerned.

This is a lopsided triangle, however, for it is composed of two indisputably autonomous nations (the United States and China) and a third, Japan, which still lacks genuine independence. This may be the most intractable legacy of the San Francisco System, and it is especially ironic when one considers the original premise of the Cold War containment policy. Global communism was monolithic, it was argued then, and the newly established PRC but a puppet or satellite of Moscow. China's independence has been clear for all to see since the Sino-Soviet split erupted in the early 1960s, and no one today could possibly question its autonomy. The same cannot be said of Washington's "free world" ally Japan.

Japan's circumscribed autonomy is inherent in the nature of the United States–Japan military relationship. Although the two countries have been at odds on many issues since the San Francisco System was created, especially during the heyday of Japanese economic expansion that began in the 1970s, even the most acrimonious trade disputes were never allowed to disturb the security alliance. With few exceptions, Washington's basic strategic and foreign policies go unchallenged in Tokyo. Even staunch supporters of the alliance acknowledge that it is "inherently and unavoidably asymmetrical." Harsher appraisals employ the language of subordination and subservience, arguing that since the end of the Cold War Japan has become an American "client state" in ever deepening, rather than diminishing, ways.[38]

It can be argued that this unbalanced relationship has brought phenomenal benefits to Japan in the form of peace and prosperity. At the same time, however, it can also be argued that post-war Japan never actually faced a serious external threat from the Soviet Union or so-called Communist bloc, and that the nation's prosperity derives far more from Japanese efforts than from American patronage. Be that as it may, peace and prosperity for Japan has come at the cost of being a cog in an American war machine that has indeed kept the peace at various times and in various places – but that also has squandered resources, precipitated arms races, flirted with "first use" of nuclear weapons, committed atrocities (like targeting civilians and practicing torture), and inflicted enormous destruction and suffering in Korea, Indochina, Iraq, and Afghanistan. Client-state status has also required giving generally unstinting support to less overtly militarized US foreign policies that are often shortsighted and counterproductive. It has inhibited geopolitical flexibility and stifled any real possibility of innovative statesmanship on Japan's part.

To more than a few Japanese, ranging across the full political spectrum, this protracted patron–client relationship is as "abnormal" as the state of affairs Japan and China repudiated when they restored relations in 1972. To some, this poses basic foreign-policy questions about Japan's orientation and identity, particularly as an "Asian" power. To others, the root issue is national pride. In conservative and right-wing circles, agitation to become a "normal" nation focuses on revising the constitution and throwing off constraints on remilitarization. But the notion that accelerated militarization is a path toward more bona fide independence or autonomy is delusory. Japan cannot escape the US military embrace. In fact, the United States desires a more militarized partner, free of constitutional restraints, to support its evolving strategic visions not only in Asia, but globally.

Asymmetry is not exceptional in relations between the United States and its allies. On the contrary, hierarchy is integral to the hegemonic nature of the post-war Pax Americana. Notwithstanding this, it can be argued that no other bilateral relationship between Washington and its allies is more conspicuous and commented-upon in its structural imbalance than the United States–Japan relationship. Even among Japanese who accept the fact that wisdom and restraint have often been wanting in post-war US war and peace policies, it is customary to hear the argument that going along with the dictates of Washington is a small price to pay for maintaining the precious friendship that has been forged between the two countries.

Obviously, especially when one recalls the hatreds and horrors of the Pacific War, that friendship is indeed precious. The price paid for this under the San Francisco System, however, has been higher than is usually acknowledged –

whether measured by the humiliation of being regarded as a client-state, or by Japan's inability to speak with a truly independent and persuasive voice about matters of war and peace. This is an unfortunate legacy to carry into the second decade of the twenty-first century, when power politics are in flux and talk about an impending "Asian century" is more compelling than ever before.

Present uncertainties

It is generally acknowledged that the US restoration of relations with China in 1972 – coupled with the winding down of the Vietnam War – ushered in almost four decades of uncontested US strategic supremacy in the Asia-Pacific region. In return for Washington recognizing its legitimacy, the Communist government in Beijing dropped its criticism of the United States–Japan security alliance and refrained from criticizing or challenging America's overwhelming military superiority. Shared enmity toward the Soviet Union helped cement this Sino-US agreement. So did US assurances to China that Japan would not, and indeed could not, re-emerge as a major military power, so long as the bilateral security treaty was maintained.[39]

This tacit understanding amounted to China's leaders accepting a gross imbalance of power vis-à-vis the United States in the Pacific until their country became more prosperous – and prosperity arrived more quickly than anticipated.[40] Beginning in 1978, reforms introducing capitalist market principles led to annual growth rates averaging around 10 percent. In 2008, China surpassed Japan as the biggest foreign holder of US Treasury securities and became the largest creditor nation in the world. Two years later, the nation's gross domestic product (GDP) surpassed Japan's, making China under "state capitalism" the second largest economy in the world after the United States. Predictions of when China's GDP would surpass America's usually look to a mere two decades or so hence – that is, to around 2030.

One outcome of this stupendous growth was increasing interdependence between China and the rest of the world, including the United States and European Union, not just China's Asian neighbors. China became the world's biggest recipient of direct foreign investment, as well as its biggest trader. The PRC soon emerged as Japan's largest trading partner in both exports and imports, while the United States became China's major export market and its second largest overall trading partner (after the European Union). China's integration into the global economy seemed to signal a materialization of converging interests that could and would become a sound foundation for future peaceful relations.

By the second decade of the twenty-first century, such shared interests seemed imperiled. Economic globalization was accompanied by China asserting its status as a great power more generally – and these great-power aspirations extended to overturning the modus vivendi negotiated forty years earlier and challenging the military status quo. This is the milieu in which so many of the problematic legacies of the San Francisco System resurfaced in disquieting ways

– including not just territorial disputes and contested history issues, but also accelerated Japanese remilitarization. The US response to this unsettled and fluid situation has been to engage in new levels of strategic planning aimed at maintaining an unchallenged Pax Americana in the Pacific.

Given the enormous domestic challenges China will face for many decades to come, the goal of its military transformation is not to achieve strategic parity with the United States. That is not feasible. Rather, the primary objective is to create armed forces capable of blunting or deterring America's projection of power into China's offshore waters – to develop, that is, a military strong enough to dispel what Henry Kissinger has called China's "nightmare of military encirclement."[41] In military jargon, this mission is referred to as China's pursuit of "anti-access/area denial" (A2/AD) capabilities, and the area of particular strategic concern lies within what Chinese (and others) refer to as the "first island chain" or "inner island chain," which includes the Yellow Sea, East China Sea, and South China Sea. Central to this area-denial strategy is developing "asymmetric capabilities" that will enable Chinese forces to offset America's ability to intervene militarily should, for example, a conflict over Taiwan arise.

This accelerated militarization on China's part reflects more than rising economic clout and assertive nationalism. It is also driven by technological imperatives that escalated to new realms of sophistication when the collapse of the Soviet Union in 1991 essentially coincided with the takeoff of digital technology and the revolutionary transformation of precision-guided warfare. The so-called asymmetric capabilities under development in China cover a broad range of weaponry: nuclear warheads;[42] short-range and medium-range ballistic missiles, including a "carrier-killing" anti-ship ballistic missile (the Dong Feng 21D); long-range cruise missiles; "fourth generation" jet aircraft as well as a "fifth generation" stealth fighter (the Chengdu J-20); missile-carrying submarines, warships, and aircraft; an envisioned albeit still far-distant fleet of aircraft carriers; fiber-optic command and control centers; advanced laser and radar systems; satellite surveillance systems; anti-satellite and cyberwar capabilities; and so on. Should conflict with US forces arise, China's response presumably would include missile attacks on US bases in Guam and Okinawa (notably Kadena Air Force Base).[43]

Such an agenda of military modernization by a late-arriving power in a new world of high-tech warfare is predictable. Also predictable is the alarm it has provoked among those who take America's overwhelming military superiority for granted, especially in the United States and Japan. Rhetorically, the American response to the rise of China often calls to mind the early years of the Cold War. Anti-communism no longer defines this rhetoric. What remains relatively unchanged is an assumption of fundamentally adversarial rather than convergent American and Chinese values, interests, and agendas. In 2012 alone, Americans were bombarded with headlines and book titles about "The China Threat," a new "Cold War with China," an impending "Struggle for Mastery in Asia." "Containment of China" was resuscitated as geopolitical wisdom from an earlier generation. More detached commentators called attention to a pervasive "China-bashing syndrome."[44]

"China-bashing" itself carries distorted echoes from a more recent past, notably the 1970s and 1980s when Japan was still being mythologized as a superpower and "Japan-bashing" was all the vogue in America. There is, however, no real comparison. Japan-bashing focused exclusively on economic issues, and Japan's moment in the sun was ephemeral. No one believes China's rise to be a passing phenomenon. This poses an unfamiliar challenge to the United States: the notion of exercising power in the Pacific from a position of other than overwhelming superiority. There is no post-war precedent for this.

In US strategic planning circles, the most widely publicized concept aimed at countering "emerging anti-access/area denial challenges" is called Air–Sea Battle (ASB). First mentioned publicly by the secretary of defense in 2009, this calls for integrated air, sea, space, and cyberspace forces capable of overcoming the "asymmetric capabilities" of adversaries. An Air–Sea Battle Office (ASBO) was established in the Pentagon in August 2011, and an acronym-heavy release from the ASBO explains, in formulaic language repeated in other official statements, that "The Air-Sea Battle Concept centers on networked, integrated, attack-in-depth to disrupt, destroy and defeat (NIA-D3) A2/AD threats." Another official report typically notes that the goal is "to preserve U.S. and allied air-sea-space superiority."[45]

US officials usually take care to declare that ASB does not specifically target China and is a general and still rudimentary projection. In fact, the concept dates from war games initiated around a decade and a half earlier that identify the PRC as the major projected adversary (with Iran a distant second). These scenarios make clear that disrupting, destroying, and defeating China's A2/AD capabilities may involve operations such as destroying surveillance systems and missile defenses located deep inside the country, followed up by "larger air and naval assault."[46]

The ASB projections have provoked criticism in US strategic planning circles concerning costs, risks, and implications for existing US bases and operations in Asia. Much of this debate, however, involves inter-service turf battles and efforts to reconcile ASB with an alphabet soup of other current strategic formulations. These include the Pentagon's overarching JOAC (Joint Operational Access Concept); Army and Marine Corps projections such as the GMAC (Gain and Maintain Access Concept) and JCEO (Joint Concept for Entry Operations); and the Navy's MDBS (Mutually Denied Battlespace Strategy). As summarized by a strategic analyst in Asia, the Army-Marines JCEO strategy focuses on "amphibious, airborne and air assault operations to gain and maintain inland access to the adversary's territory," while the Navy's MDBS plan would "rely on U.S. maritime superiority to deny access to Chinese warships in their own waters and [Chinese] commercial shipping in the surrounding oceans." Consistent with these projections, in 2012 the United States announced plans to shift long-range B-1 and B-52 bombers as well as a fleet of high-altitude surveillance drones from the Middle East to the Pacific.[47]

These strategic guidelines, all easily accessible in declassified form, entered the public domain virtually hand in hand with widely quoted official pronouncements that the United States would "pivot to Asia" or "rebalance toward the

Asia-Pacific region" as it withdraws from its misbegotten wars in Iraq and Afghanistan. The "pivot" term emerged during President Obama's trip to Asia in November 2011, and Secretary of State Hillary Clinton followed with an article on "America's Pacific Century" that same month. This rhetorical offensive was widely interpreted as indicating that the hegemonic Pax Americana would be maintained in the face of proposals to work toward attaining some sort of less confrontational and more balanced multinational power sharing.[48]

The pivot to the Pacific involves two distinct levels of projected integration. One, embodied in the ASB concept, focuses on joint US military operations that optimize cutting-edge weaponry and technology. The other involves promoting greater strategic integration with Asian allies like Japan and South Korea. Although all parties speak with apparent sincerity about restoring the spirit of cooperation and interdependence with China that was initiated in the 1970s, the inherently confrontational and hierarchical aspects of the San Francisco System still define this evolving recalibration of power.

Where Japan is concerned, the concurrence of North Korea's traumatizing development of nuclear weapons and mounting tensions with China has given new direction to the two bedrock policies that date back to inauguration of the San Francisco System: taking shelter under the US military shield and promoting incremental militarization under the still unrevised "peace constitution." Pyongyang's test of a ballistic missile in 1998 triggered a series of policy decisions in Tokyo that prioritized establishing a multi-layered missile defense system in close collaboration with the United States. (Among other things, this involved revising earlier Japanese restrictions on arms exports plus lifting a ban on the military use of space.) Virtually in tandem with this, new "National Defense Program Guidelines" issued in 2004 expressed concern over China's military modernization for the first time.[49]

Revised guidelines issued in December 2010 reaffirm Japan's peaceful goals of defense and deterrence under the US nuclear umbrella, but take note of a "global shift in the balance of power ... along with the relative change of influence of the United States." While acknowledging that Japan faces no serious threat of being invaded, the guidelines call renewed attention to disputes and confrontations that must be prevented from escalating into war. These "gray zone" areas of concern include the Korean Peninsula, the Taiwan Strait, and the spectacle of China "widely and rapidly modernizing its military force" and intensifying its maritime activities in surrounding waters. Essentially, the 2004 and 2010 guidelines reflect the shift in Japanese security focus away from Cold War preoccupation with the Soviet Union toward heightened concern about Korea, China, and the seas and islands to the south. They also reflect the same technological imperatives that drive war planning by the United States and China.

The breakthrough concept in the 2010 guidelines is the creation of a "dynamic defense force" (*dōteki bōeiryoku*) capable of "immediate and seamless response to contingencies." This envisioned force, which replaces prior focus on a more static "basic defense force" (*kibanteki bōeiryoku*), will "possess readiness, mobility, flexibility, sustainability, and versatility ... reinforced by advanced technology based on the trends of levels of military technology and intelligence capabilities." Attaining these capabilities will "further deepen" the security alliance with the United States in areas such as contingency planning, joint training and operations, information gathering (extending to capabilities in outer space and cyberspace), and "technology cooperation," with particular attention to ballistic missile defense. At the same time, the new emphasis on "dynamic deterrence" points to a conspicuously more proactive defense posture on Japan's part.[50]

In November 2011, almost a year after the guidelines were issued, the Japanese government announced that it was loosening restrictions on arms exports that had been introduced in 1967 and reformulated in 1976 as a general ban "regardless of the destinations." One early result of this, it was anticipated, would be selling submarines to countries like the Philippines and perhaps Vietnam – another example of the strategic regional integration envisioned under the "pivot" to Asia. In September 2012, Japan announced that it would host a second US advanced anti-ballistic-missile radar system. Although ostensibly directed against North Korea's nuclear provocations, this was denounced by Beijing as another step toward the containment of China. In December 2012, the *Wall Street Journal* praised Japan for now possessing "the most sophisticated missile-defense system outside the U.S.," describing this as "a system poised for export to other nations."[51]

Sixty years later, containment of China has clearly evolved into something radically different and more complex and contradictory than when this policy was first introduced under the San Francisco System.

Fears and hopes

The thrust of these developments is disturbing. The rise of China challenges the Pax Americana that has prevailed in the Asia-Pacific area since the 1950s. A stepped-up arms race looms – now pitting the United States and Japan against China rather than the Soviet Union, and driven by the impact of the digital revolution on precision warfare and cyberwar. We have entered a new era of strategic escalation without leaving reliance on brute force behind, and without any reason to believe that advanced hardware and software has produced a wiser generation of leaders.

All participants in this arms race naturally claim to champion peace: their militarization is bubble-wrapped in the rhetoric of "defense" and "deterrence." On all sides, however, strategizing shades into paranoia. Chauvinism burns ever more feverishly. The structures of goodwill and interdependence between China and the rest of the world that were painstakingly built up beginning in the 1970s appear brittle. Warnings of "accidental war" hang in the air.

There is no reason to believe that the problematic legacies of the San Francisco System will disappear soon, or that new threats to stability can be held in check easily. Rival nationalisms are here to stay, manipulated by jingoists in and out of public office and passed on to younger generations. History wars will go on unabated, hand in hand with the cynical cultivation of historical amnesia for domestic audiences and agendas. Territorial disputes that were embedded in the peace treaty signed in San Francisco and aimed at thwarting "communism" in Asia will fester for years to come. The American empire of bases will keep contracting and expanding like a shape-shifting monster, as it has done since the end of the Cold War; but the disgrace of Okinawa and the "two Japans" will not change drastically in the foreseeable future. Japan's incremental but now "dynamic" remilitarization under the nuclear umbrella will continue to accelerate – even more dynamically if the constitution is revised, but never to the point of eliminating the material and psychological constraints of subordinate independence under the eagle's wing.

"Asymmetry" is a central concept in commentary on the rise of China and the US "pivot" to Asia. The term has numerous connotations. It calls attention to the patron–client nature of the United States–Japan relationship, for example, and also characterizes China's present and projected military capabilities vis-à-vis the prodigious arsenal of the United States. As America's experience in post-World War II conflicts makes clear, however, asymmetrical capabilities can stymie overwhelming superiority in weaponry. This was the (unlearned) lesson of the Vietnam War, repeated in the US debacles in Iraq and Afghanistan. China's military modernization rests on recognizing the potential effectiveness of materially inferior forces in deterring what American strategists hubristically refer to as "full spectrum dominance." The US response, epitomized in concepts like "Air–Sea Battle" and jargon about "A2/AD" threats and "NIA-3D" in-depth attacks, guarantees that strategists and weapons manufacturers on all sides will never break out of this vicious circle.

There is also asymmetry of a political nature in China's challenge to continued domination of the San Francisco System: the PRC is an authoritarian state, whereas democratic principles underlie governance in the United States and Japan. This is a critical difference. At the same time, it should not obscure the fact that powerful dysfunctional influences are in play in all three states. Transparency is blatantly absent in the PRC, but secrecy and non-accountability are not peculiar to China. Beginning with the onset of the Cold War – and with almost exponential acceleration after September 11, 2001, when terrorism entered the picture as an obsessive security concern – the United States has become a national-security state of unprecedented bloat and clandestine activity. Special interests influence and pervert policy-making in all three nations. So does corruption, and so do delusion and wishful thinking. Time and again, pathologies rather than rational policies and practices influence the course of events.

Where, then, do hopes for a more stable and constructive future lie? They do not lie in fixation on military confrontation, although this is where political resources and media attention tend to be directed. Nothing hopeful can come from perpetuating hateful nationalisms, although this has become addictive in China, Japan, and Korea through ceaseless rekindling of the history wars. Nor can stability be secured by postulating a zero-sum struggle between China and the old Pax Americana for domination over the Asia-Pacific area. The United States is no longer the sole great power in the region, but it maintains an awesome military juggernaut coupled with a sprawling network of alliances consolidated in the early years of the Cold War. China's long-delayed re-emergence as a great power is irresistible – unlike imperial Japan's doomed aggression in the early twentieth century and post-war Japan's short interval as a putative superpower in the 1970s and 1980s – but both domestic and external factors militate against China imposing hegemonic influence over the area.

Future hope lies in returning to the visions of peaceful integration that accompanied the normalization of relations with the PRC beginning in the 1970s, and in strengthening the many concrete areas of cooperation and economic interdependence that gave substance to these optimistic projections. As regional tensions heated up in 2012, "power-sharing" became the phrase of choice for postulating a less confrontational new order. This found expression in formulations such as a "Concert of Asia" or "Pacific Community" or "Pax Pacifica" (as opposed to the Pax Americana).[52]

This is more easily imagined than realized, of course, especially when territorial disputes and military expansion have been elevated to issues of national honor as well as security. "Asia-Pacific" regional organizations have been active since the 1990s and provide an object lesson in the unwieldiness of multinational forums, as well as their potential for promoting constructive engagement.[53] Ultimately, however, the success of power sharing depends on expanding the non-governmental civilian networks that lie at the core of genuine interdependence and mutual understanding. These crisscrossing personal and corporate connections run the gamut from NGOs and multinational corporations to cultural and educational exchanges to tourism and pop culture. They are the bedrock of grass-roots collaboration and integration – and, as such, the antidote to ultranationalism and bellicose confrontation.

These networks are already substantial. The questions that demand attention are: Why have they failed to decisively tip the balance against voices of extremism and unreason? Can they do so? And if so, how?

Notes

1 This chapter is an abbreviated version of the first section in a book co-authored by John W. Dower and Gavan McCormack and published in Japanese translation by NHK Shuppan Shinsho in January 2014, under the title *Tenkanki no Nihon e: "Pakkusu Amerikana" ka – "Pakkusu Ajia" ka (Japan at a Turning Point – "Pax Americana?" "Pax Asia?")*. It also appears in, *The Asia-Pacific Journal*, 12, no. 8, (2014), accessible at www.japanfocus.org.

2 Great Britain, which formally recognized the PRC in January 1950, supported PRC participation in the peace conference before bowing to US pressure in July 1951. The ostensible reason for excluding Korea was that, as a Japanese colony, it had not been a belligerent party against Japan in World War II. On August 16, 1951, Zhou Enlai, serving simultaneously as foreign minister and prime minister of the PRC, released a statement criticizing the treaty and conference. South Korea also expressed outrage when informed it was being excluded. For China and Korea, see John Price, *Orienting*

Canada: Race, Empire, and the Transpacific (Vancouver: University of British Columbia Press, 2011), pp. 245–8.

3 The third distinguishing feature of the San Francisco settlement (alongside the Cold War setting and "separate peace") was the "unequal treaty" nature of the bilateral United States–Japan Security Treaty. As Secretary of State Christian Herter told a Senate committee when the treaty came up for revision in 1960, "There were a number of provisions in the 1951–1952 Security Treaty that were pretty extreme from the point of view of an agreement between two sovereign nations"; US Senate, Committee of Foreign Relations, *Treaty of Mutual Cooperation and Security with Japan*, 86th Congress, 2nd Session (June 7, 1960), esp. pp. 11–12, 27, 30–1. This gross inequality provoked considerable tension between Tokyo and Washington in the 1950s, prompting revision and not just renewal of the treaty in 1960. Various backstage exchanges and commentaries on this issue are included in Department of State, *Foreign Relations of the United States, 1958–1960. Japan; Korea*, vol. 18; see pp. 23–9 for a representative expression by the US ambassador in Tokyo of US apprehension concerning "the stigmas and disadvantages now associated in Japan with the present Security Treaty."

4 Nishimura Kumao, who played a leading role in Japanese planning for the restoration of sovereignty, details the evolution of post-war strategic projections, including Okinawa, in his illuminating *San Furanshisuko Heiwa Jōyaku*, vol. 27 in Kajima Kenkyūjo, ed., *Nihon Gaikō Shi* (Tokyo: Kajima Kenkyūjo, 1971). As early as September 1947, a letter from Emperor Hirohito himself was delivered to General Douglas MacArthur, the supreme commander of Allied occupation forces, proposing that Okinawa be leased to the United States for twenty-five or fifty years, or "even longer," to support the struggle against communism and hasten the end of the occupation. The letter was uncovered by Professor Shindō Eiichi and reported in "Bunkatsusareta Ryōdo," *Sekai* (April 1979): 31–51 (esp. 45–50).

5 The major investigative work on Agent Orange and other toxins in Okinawa has been conducted by Jon Mitchell. See his "US Military Defoliants on Okinawa: Agent Orange" and "Agent Orange on Okinawa – New Evidence," both online in *The Asia-Pacific Journal* 9 (September 12, 2011, and November 28, 2011, respectively). See also Mitchell's articles in *Japan Times*: "Agent Orange 'Tested in Okinawa'" (May 17, 2012); "25,000 barrels of Agent Orange Kept on Okinawa, U.S. Army Document Says" (August 7, 2012); and "U.S. Agent Orange Activist Brings Message of Solidarity to Okinawa" (September 15, 2012). Secret agreements on nuclear issues are discussed and annotated below under "The 'Nuclear Umbrella'." The most detailed and incisive critical commentary on Okinawa in English appears in various publications by Gavan McCormack, including most recently his co-authored (with Satoko Oka Norimatsu) *Resistant Islands: Okinawa Confronts Japan and the United States* (Lanham, MD: Rowman & Littlefield, 2012).

6 The major scholarly study of the origins of these territorial issues is Kimie Hara, *Cold War Frontiers in the Asia-Pacific: Divided Territories in the San Francisco System* (New York: Routledge, 2007, 2012), which devotes separate chapters to each of the disputes. Hara reiterates the thesis of deliberate ambiguity in the San Francisco Peace Treaty concisely in various essays. See, for example, "50 Years from San Francisco: Re-examining the Peace Treaty and Japan's Territorial Problems," *Pacific Affairs* (Fall 2001) and "Cold War Frontiers in the Asia-Pacific: The Troubling Legacy of the San Francisco Treaty," *The Asia-Pacific Journal* (September 2006), accessible at www.japanfocus.org. For another densely annotated treatment, see Seokwoo Lee's online article "The 1951 San Francisco Peace Treaty with Japan and the Territorial Disputes in East Asia," *Pacific Rim Law & Policy Journal*, 2002.

7 For the US response to the 1956 Japan–Soviet negotiations, see Department of State, *Foreign Relations of the United States, 1955–57. Japan*, vol. 23, part 1: 202–5, 207–13. See Hara, *Cold War Frontiers*, pp. 71–99 on the 1945–1951 background, and p. 96 (and accompanying citations) on the thwarted compromise of 1956.

8 Hara, *Cold War Frontiers*, pp. 14–49, esp. pp. 31–5, 47.

9 The densely annotated entry on "Liancourt Rocks dispute" on Wikipedia includes many references to Korean-language sources. The Democratic People's Republic of Korea (North Korea) also declares the islands to be Korean territory.

10 The May 15, 1950 memorandum was reported by Japanese journalists affiliated with the Jiji Press news agency in Beijing; see the December 27, 2012, Beijing Jiji dispatch " 'Senkaku wa Ryūkyū no Ichibu' " online at www.jiji.com, as well as coverage in the *Asahi Shimbun* on December 27 and 28.

11 For Zhou and Deng, see Yinan He, *The Search for Reconciliation: Sino-Japanese and German–Polish Relations since World War II* (New York: Cambridge University Press, 2009), p. 194; M. Taylor Fravel, "Something to Talk About in the East China Sea," *The Diplomat*, September 28, 2012; and Ezra F. Vogel, *Deng Xiaoping and the Transformation of China* (Cambridge, MA: Harvard University Press, 2011), pp. 303–4. Speculation about potential oil and gas resources in the East China Sea dates from the late 1960s, and obviously influenced both China's and Japan's percep-tions of the Senkaku/Diaoyu dispute. The increasingly intransigent Chinese position that developed after Zhou and Deng's downplaying of the dispute in the 1970s is that there is a deep historical record showing that the islands have traditionally been regarded as part of China. The US position is that it is agnostic on the sovereignty issue, but obliged to side with Japan militarily if Sino-Japanese tensions over the Senkakus lead to conflict. For an almost elegiac essay on the early history of the islands between China and Okinawa, see "Narrative of an Empty Space: Behind the Row Over a Bunch of Pacific Rocks Lies the Sad, Magical History of Okinawa," *The Economist*, December 22, 2012.

12 Hara, *Cold War Frontiers*, p. 157.

13 The concept of an American "empire of bases" was introduced by the late Chalmers Johnson in *The Sorrows of Empire: Militarism, Secrecy, and the End of the Republic* (New York: Metropolitan Books, 2004). For an informative recent overview, see David Vine, "The Lily-Pad Strategy: How the Pentagon is Quietly Transforming Its Overseas Base Empire and Creating a Dangerous New Way of War," posted online in July 2012 at www.tomdispatch.com/blog/175568.

14 See Curtis E. LeMay with MacKinlay Kantor, *Mission with LeMay: My Story* (Garden City, NY: Doubleday, 1965), p. 382. LeMay spoke similarly in an April 1966 inter-view for the J.F. Dulles Papers archive at Princeton University; cited in Bruce Cumings, *The Korean War: A History* (New York: Modern Library, 2010), pp. 151–2. He was not taking pride in this devastation, but rather arguing that immediate and massive bombing of key cities in North Korea might have been more effective and less costly in human terms than the devastation wreaked in the protracted air war. The cities in South Korea were bombed when they were occupied by North Korean or Chinese forces. On the air war in Korea in general, see Cumings, *Korean War*, pp. 147–61; Callum A. MacDonald, *Korea: The War Before Vietnam* (New York: Free Press, 1986), pp. 226–48, 259–60; and Taewoo Kim's two-part treatment: "War Against an Ambiguous Enemy: U.S. Air Force Bombing of South Korean Civilian Areas, June–September 1950," *Critical Asian Studies* 44, no. 2 (June 2012) and "Limited War, Unlimited Targets: U.S. Air Force Bombing of North Korea during the Korean War, 1950–1953," *Critical Asian Studies* 44, no. 3 (September 2012). Bombing tonnage varies depending on the source. Cumings (*Korean War*, p. 159) cal-culates that the United States dropped 635,000 tons of bombs (plus 32,557 tons of napalm) in Korea, compared to 503,000 tons in the entire Pacific theater in World War II. Marilyn Young puts the volume of bombs dropped in the Korean War at 386,037 tons (and 32,357 tons of napalm), with a total of 698,000 tons when all types of airborne ordnance are included; "Bombing Civilians: An American Tradition," *The Asia-Pacific Journal*, April 19, 2009, accessible online at www.japanfocus.org. At the peak of the bombing in Korea, US planes were dropping around a quarter-million

pounds (125 tons) of napalm per day – with napalm tanks initially manufactured in Japan; see the "Napalm in War" entry at www.globalsecurity.org, and also Stockholm International Peace Research Institute, *Incendiary Weapons* (Cambridge, MA: MIT Press, 1975), p. 43. The total tonnage of bombs dropped by the British and US Air Forces combined in World War II was slightly over two million tons, of which 656,400 tons were dropped in the Pacific theater. In the US air war that devastated over sixty Japanese cities, the total tonnage dropped was 160,800 tons (24 percent of the Pacific theater total); see United States Strategic Bombing Survey, *Summary Report (Pacific War)*, July 1, 1946, p. 16. In the air war against Vietnam, Laos, and Cambodia, the volume of bombs dropped by US forces escalated to over seven million tons.

15 Yoshida's early arguments in defense of Article 9, and the later shift in policy, are annotated in J.W. Dower, *Empire and Aftermath: Yoshida Shigeru and the Japanese Experience, 1878–1954* (Cambridge, MA: Council on East Asian Studies, Harvard University, 1979), pp. 369–400.

16 See, for example, Department of State, *Foreign Relations of the United States, 1951. Asia and the Pacific*, vol. 6, part 1:831. In the end, Article 11 of the peace treaty simply stipulated that "Japan accepts the judgments of the International Military Tribunal for the Far East and of other Allied War Crimes Courts both within and outside Japan" – a proviso that required the Japanese government to obtain permission of the foreign governments involved in these trials before altering individual sentences that had been imposed.

17 The translations from 1972 and 1998 are from the English renderings released by the Japanese Ministry of Foreign Affairs. The full apologetic phrasing of the 1998 "Joint Declaration on Building a Partnership of Friendship and Cooperation for Peace and Development" reads as follows:

> The Japanese side is keenly conscious of the responsibility for the serious distress and damage that Japan caused to the Chinese people through its aggression against China during a certain period in the past and expressed deep remorse for this.

The 1998 declaration was issued during a state visit to Japan by China's president Jiang Zemin, and accompanied by acrimonious public exchanges over Japan's war responsibility that are not reflected in the text of the declaration itself. See Kazuo Sato, "The Japan–China Summit and Joint Declaration of 1998: A Watershed for Japan–China Relations in the 21st Century?" CNAPS Working Paper Series, Center for Northeast Asian Policy Studies, Brookings Institute, 2000–2001; accessible at www.brookings.edu.

18 The escalating acrimony from the 1980s of "war history" issues on both the Chinese and Japanese sides, including the politics propelling this, is a major theme in He, *The Search for Reconciliation*.

19 The devastating famine that resulted from the Great Leap Forward of 1958–1961, the destructive Cultural Revolution of 1966–1976, and the Tiananmen Square Massacre of 1989, for example, are all taboo subjects in China – ignored in textbooks, censored on the internet, and brushed over in historical exhibitions such as at the recently renovated National Museum of China in Tiananmen Square.

20 On censorship of the nuclear bombing of Hiroshima and Nagasaki, see John W. Dower, *Embracing Defeat: Japan in the Wake of World War II* (New York: Norton/ The New Press, 1999), pp. 413–15, 620–1. The first major collection of photographs appeared in the August 6, 1952 edition of *Asahi Gurafu*.

21 For US considerations concerning the use of nuclear weapons in the Korean War, see Bruce Cumings, "Korea: Forgotten Nuclear Threats," *Le Monde Diplomatique*, December 8, 2004, accessible at http://mondediplo.com and reproduced as "Nuclear Threats Against North Korea: Consequences of the 'Forgotten' War," at www.japan-focus.org; also see Cumings, "Why Did Truman Really Fire MacArthur? The Obscure

History of Nuclear Weapons and the Korean War Provides an Answer," *History News Network* (George Mason University), January 10, 2005, accessible at http://hnn.us/articles/9245.html. See also Malcolm MacMillan Craig, "The Truman Administration and Non-use of the Atomic Bomb during the Korean War, June 1950 to January 1953" (MA thesis, Victoria University, New Zealand, 2009).

22 Operation Hudson Harbor is discussed in Craig, "The Truman Administration and Non-use of the Atomic Bomb," pp. 119–21.

23 The literature on the impact of the Bikini Incident is enormous. For a descriptive overview that places Japanese anti-nuclear protests in a global context, see Lawrence S. Wittner, *Resisting the Bomb: A History of the World Nuclear Disarmament Movement, 1954–1970* (Stanford, CA: Stanford University Press, 1997), vol. 2 of *The Struggle against the Bomb*, esp. pp. 8–10, 42–3, 241–6, 321–4. Wittner also describes the high-level US response to the Bikini Incident, which included identifying the *Lucky Dragon* as a "Red spy outfit" and the ship's captain as being "in the employ of the Russians" (this by the head of the Atomic Energy Commission), denying that the fishing boat had been outside the officially announced danger zone, emphasizing the "high degree of safety" of American nuclear tests in general, and asserting that the vessel's radio operator had died of hepatitis rather than "radiation sickness," as the Japanese government itself reported. In a cable to Washington, the US ambassador to Tokyo described the popular outrage in Japan as "a period of uncontrolled masochism" as the nation "seemed to revel in [its] fancied martyrdom." See ibid., pp. 146–8, 153–4.

24 Robert S. Norris, William M. Arkin, and William Burr, "Where They Were," *Bulletin of the Atomic Scientists*, 55, no. 6 (November/December 1999): 26–35. On mobilization during the Cuban Missile Crisis, see Jon Mitchell, "'Seconds Away from Midnight': U.S. Nuclear Missile Pioneers on Okinawa Break Fifty Year Silence on a Hidden Nuclear Crisis of 1962," *The Asia-Pacific Journal*, July 20, 2012; accessible at www.japanfocus.org.

25 Norris *et al.*, "Where They Were." Reischauer's statement came in an interview with the *Mainichi Shimbun* on May 18, 1981; for an English summary, see "Nuclear 'Lie' Strains U.S. Ties," *Time*, June 8, 1981. Reischauer threatened to resign as ambassador in 1967 when he "discovered that there was a craft at Iwakuni, the Marine base on the Inland Sea, which held a store of nuclear weapons." In his view, this was entirely different from the legitimate transit of nuclear-armed ships through Japanese waters, and violated understandings with the Japanese government. He regarded the uproar that greeted his 1981 acknowledgment of the latter as a "fiasco"; see his memoir *My Life between Japan and America* (New York: Harper & Row, 1986), pp. 249–51, 276–7, 280, 299, 346–7.

26 See, for example, Yuki Tanaka and Peter Kuznick, "Japan, the Atomic Bomb, and the 'Peaceful Uses of Nuclear Power'," *The Asia-Pacific Journal*, May 2, 2011; accessible at www.japanfocus.org. The "paranuclear state" language appears in a lengthy treatment of nuclear development in Japan titled "Nuclear Weapons Program," accessible at www.globalsecurity.org/wmd/world/japan/nuke.htm. As of late 2012, it was calculated that Japan's stockpiles of separated plutonium totaled more than nine metric tons, enough to make "more than 1,000 nuclear warheads"; "Rokkasho and a Hard Place: Japan's Nuclear Future," *The Economist*, November 10, 2012. See also Frank N. von Hippel and Masafumi Takubo, "Japan's Nuclear Mistake," *New York Times*, November 28, 2012. The easy conversion from civilian nuclear programs to weapons projects is addressed in Matthew Fuhrmann, *Atomic Assistance: How "Atoms for Peace" Programs Cause Nuclear Insecurity* (Ithaca, NY: Cornell University Press, 2012); see pp. 221–5 on Japan.

27 The two quotations are from internal Department of State memoranda, both dated May 4, 1956 (DOS file number 711.5611/5-456), but many similar diplomatic notes and exchanges took place beginning in the mid 1950s. See Wittner, *Resisting the*

Bomb, pp. 109, 116–17, 166–7, 388, 505n69, 514n17. For an accessible sample of these apologies (and the patronizing US "understanding" they prompted), see Department of State, *Foreign Relations of the United States, 1955–57. Japan*, vol. 23, part 1:495–98, reporting on a September 1957 meeting in Washington between Secretary of State Dulles and Foreign Minister Fujiyama Aiichirō, who had just delivered a speech at the United Nations calling for an end to nuclear testing. Fujiyama took the occasion of this meeting with Dulles to essentially dismiss what he had said to the United Nations. His apology, as the State Department summarized it, ran as follows:

> The Japanese people, old and young, are very sensitive on this question. It is not merely a question of communists. The Japanese Government was placed in a position where it had to lodge a protest. The handling of this matter is vital for the conservative government. The psychological situation in Japan compels the Government to stand for disarmament, the abolition of war, and the establishment of peace, and against the manufacture and use of all nuclear weapons.

Dulles replied that he understood that "the Japanese Government has a special problem that is more emotional than reasonable. The American people perhaps reason about this, while the Japanese view the problem emotionally, and the Japanese Government must take that into account."

28 Eric Johnson, "Nuclear Pact Ensured Smooth Okinawa Reversion," *Japan Times*, May 15, 2002, quoting from a declassified US document dated June 20, 1959.

29 Many declassified English-language documents pertaining to the 1960 and 1969 secret agreements have been assembled by Robert A. Wampler and made available in two widely separated releases by the National Security Archive at George Washington University. See (1) "Revelations in Newly Released Documents about U.S. Nuclear Weapons and Okinawa Fuel NHK Documentary," May 14, 1997, covering thirteen documents and accessible online at www.gwu.edu/~nsarchiv/japan/okinawa/okinawa.htm; (2) "Nuclear Noh Drama: Tokyo, Washington and the Case of the Missing Nuclear Arrangements," October 13, 2009, covering eleven documents and accessible at www.gwu.edu/~nsarchiv/nukevault/ebb291/index.htm. (3) The November 1969 secret agreement between Satō and Nixon is discussed in Kei Wakaizumi, *The Best Course Available: A Personal Account of the Secret US–Japan Okinawa Reversion Negotiations* (Honolulu: University of Hawaii Press, 2002); Wakaizumi was an aide to Satō, and his book originally appeared in Japanese in 1994. An online copy of the agreement is accessible at www.niraikanai.lwwma.net/pages/archive/wakai.html. Satō's copy of the secret agreement was made available by his son in 2009 and reproduced in *Asahi Shimbun*, December 24, 2009. (4) See also Shinichi Kitaoka, "The Secret Japan–US Pacts," in Research Group on the Japan–US Alliance, *In Search of a New Consensus: The Japan–US Alliance Toward 2010* (Institute for International Policy Studies, December 2010), pp. 15–27. Kitaoka, who headed a Foreign Ministry committee investigating the secret agreements, at one point refers to the Japanese government's "intentional avoidance of clarification." He also quotes Satō, stating, in October 1969, that "the three non-nuclear principles were a mistake." The full Institute for International Policy Studies publication is accessible online. (5) Henry Kissinger discusses the Nixon–Satō agreement (without calling it secret) in *The White House Years* (Boston, MA: Little, Brown, and Company, 1979), pp. 325–36, 1483.

30 For Kishi, see Department of State, *Foreign Relations of the United States, 1955–1957. Japan*, vol. 23, part 1:285; Kishi was following up on a similar statement by the head of the Defense Agency the previous month. For Ikeda, see Jon Mitchell, "Okinawa, Nuclear Weapons and 'Japan's Special Psychological Problem'," *Japan Times*, July 8, 2010. For Satō as well as others on Japan possessing nuclear weapons, see "Nuclear Weapons Program," op. cit., at www.globalsecurity.org. Satō's bellicose statement about attacking China with nuclear weapons is cited in "The U.S. Nuclear

Umbrella, Past and Future," a December 27, 2008, editorial by Hiroshima Peace Media Center, accessible at www.hiroshimapeacemedia.jp; their source is a declassified Foreign Ministry document. Beginning in the late 1950s, US diplomats and planners sometimes anticipated that Japan might acquire nuclear weapons in the near future. See, for example, Department of State, *Foreign Relations of the United States, 1955–1957. Regulation of Armaments; Atomic Energy*, vol. 20:276–7 (minutes of a January 1956 meeting involving the Joint Chiefs of Staff); also *Foreign Relations of the United States, 1958–1960. Japan; Korea*, vol. 18:27 (an April 1958 dispatch from the US ambassador to Tokyo, Douglas MacArthur II).

31 The "throwing off Asia" (*datsu-A*) phrase comes from a famous 1885 essay attributed to Fukuzawa Yukichi. For an extended image-driven treatment covering Meiji Westernization, the Sino-Japanese War, and the Russo-Japanese War, see the three-part online treatment "Throwing Off Asia" at visualizingcultures.mit.edu.

32 For the pivotal role assigned to Japan by US Cold War planners, see John W. Dower, "The Superdomino in Postwar Asia: Japan In and Out of the *Pentagon Papers*," in Noam Chomsky and Howard Zinn (ed.), *The Pentagon Papers: The Senator Gravel Edition*, vol. 5 (Boston, MA: Beacon Press, 1972), 101–42.

33 Department of State, *Foreign Relations of the United States, 1951. Asia and the Pacific*, vol. 6, part 1:825–6. The fuller statement by Dulles explains that the Japanese

> have felt that the Western civilization represented by Britain, more latterly the United States … represents a certain triumph of mind over mass which gives us a social standing in the world better than what is being achieved in terms of the mainland human masses of Asia, and … they think that they have also achieved somewhat the similar superiority of mind over mass and would like to feel that they belong to, or are accepted by, the Western nations. And I think that anything we can do to encourage that feeling will set up an attraction which is calculated to hold the Japanese in friendly association with us despite the fact that the mainland is in possession of the economic means of setting up an attraction which we, perhaps, in those particular terms of economy cannot match.

34 For basic documents covering Nixon's talks with Zhou in February 1972 and declassified for the National Security Archive, see William Burr, "Nixon's Trip to China," posted December 11, 2003 and accessible at www.gwu.edu/~nsarchiv; two long reports from Kissinger to Nixon summarizing his talks with Zhou in July and October 1971 can be accessed through note 4 here. Although these declassified documents are only lightly sanitized, some lines and passages pertaining to Japan have been excised.

35 The strategic considerations underlying the rapprochement are summarized in He, *The Search for Reconciliation*, 182–9. The honeymoon wording is hers.

36 The four key bilateral documents are as follows: (1) The landmark "Joint Communiqué of the Government of Japan and the Government of the People's Republic of China," issued on September 29, 1972, announced termination of "the abnormal state of affairs" and established the basic terms reiterated in subsequent statements. Japan recognized the "Government of the People's Republic of China as the sole legal Government of China," and expressed understanding and respect for the PRC's position that "Taiwan is an inalienable part of the territory of the People's Republic of China." The two nations declared commitment to peaceful coexistence as embodied in the charter of the United Nations, and pledged to "refrain from the use or threat of force" in any disputes that might arise between them. Japan expressed regret for "serious damage" inflicted on the Chinese people in the past, and China in turn renounced its demands for war reparations. Reparations had also been renounced by the Republic of China in 1952 and by South Korea in 1965. (2) The "Treaty of Peace and Friendship between Japan and the People's Republic of China" that followed six years later, on August 12, 1978, was exceedingly brief, consisting of an introduction declaring continued adherence to the principles enunciated in the 1972 communiqué, followed by

five platitudinous articles. (3) On November 26, 1998 – twenty years after the peace treaty was signed, and seven years after the collapse of the Soviet Union and end of the Cold War – the two countries issued a lengthy "Japan–China Joint Declaration on Building a Partnership of Friendship and Cooperation for Peace and Development," accompanied by a list itemizing thirty-three specific areas of proposed collaboration. In addition to apologizing for Japanese aggression in the past, this declaration opposed nuclear testing and proliferation, and called for "the ultimate elimination of nuclear weapons." (4) The fourth joint statement – issued ten years later, on May 7, 2008, and bearing the lengthy heading "Joint Statement between the Government of Japan and Government of the People's Republic of China on Comprehensive Promotion of a 'Mutually Beneficial Relationship Based on Common Strategic Interests'" – took care to emphasize that the two nations "are partners who cooperate together and are not threats to each other."

37 See, for example, Ronald O'Rourke, *China Naval Modernization: Implications for U.S. Naval Capabilities – Background and Issues for Congress* (Congressional Research Service, October 17, 2012); also Jianwei Wang, "Confidence-Building Measures and China–Japan Relations," February 2000 report to the Stimson Center (Washington, DC), accessible at www.stimson.org.

38 For the asymmetry quotation, see Gerald L. Curtis, "U.S. Policy Toward Japan from Nixon to Clinton: An Assessment," in G.L. Curtis (ed.), *New Perspectives on U.S.–Japan Relations* (Tokyo: Japan Center for International Exchange, 2000), 39–40; this forty-three-page overview of United States–Japan relations after 1972 is accessible online. Gavan McCormack develops the client-state argument in detail in two books: *Client State: Japan in the American Embrace* (London: Verso, 2007) and, with Satoko Oka Norimatsu, *Resistant Islands*. For a capsule summary, see McCormack, "The Travails of a Client State: An Okinawan Angle on the 50th Anniversary of the US–Japan Security Treaty," *The Asia-Pacific Journal*, March 8, 2010; accessible at www.japanfocus.org.

39 The power-shift argument has been advanced by Hugh White of Australian National University, among others. For a concise presentation, see his "Power Shift: Rethinking Australia's Place in the Asian Century," *Australian Journal of International Affairs* 65, no. 1 (February 2011): 81–93, esp. 82. For an extended analysis, see his *The China Choice: Why America Should Share Power* (Australia: Black Inc., 2012). White's arguments have generated considerable online discussion and controversy.

40 In 1991, Deng Xiaoping advised colleagues to maintain good relations with the United States while building up China's strength; see Andrew J. Nathan, "What China Wants: Bargaining with Beijing," *Foreign Affairs*, July/August 2011, 154.

41 Henry A. Kissinger, "The Future of U.S.–Chinese Relations," *Foreign Affairs*, March/April 2012; this essay was adapted from the afterword to a paperback edition of Kissinger's book *On China* (Penguin Press, 2011).

42 In December 2012, the newly appointed Chinese leader Xi Jinping took care to make one of his first public events a meeting with the nuclear unit in charge of ballistic and cruise missiles (the Second Artillery Corps), praising it as "the core force of our country's strategic deterrent … a strategic pillar of our great power status, and an important bedrock for protecting our national security"; Jane Perlez, "New Chinese Leader Meets Military Nuclear Officers," *New York Times*, December 5, 2012.

43 For an overview of the revolution in precision warfare plus analysis of China's projected "A2/AD" capabilities, see Andrew F. Krepinevich, *Why AirSea Battle?* (Center for Strategic and Budgetary Assessments, 2010). Fear that China's growing sophistication in ballistic missiles threatens America's hitherto "virtually invincible" Pacific fleet of carriers is typically expressed in a widely circulated Associated Press article: Eric Talmadge, "Dong Feng 21D, Chinese Missile, Could Shift Pacific Power Balance," *Huffington Post*, August 5, 2010. For a concise sampling of current military jargon, see "China's Military Rise," *The Economist*, April 7, 2012.

44 Much of this bellicose rhetoric focuses on economic and financial issues. Its ubiquity can be gleaned by online searches under phrases such as "China threat," "containment of China," and "Cold War with China." Certain books also trigger extended online commentary. See, for example, Aaron L. Friedberg, *A Contest for Supremacy: China, America, and the Struggle for Mastery in Asia* (New York: Norton, 2011); Peter Navarro, *The Coming China Wars: Where They Will Be Fought and How They Can be Won* (Upper Saddle River, NJ: Financial Times Press, 2006; revised and enlarged in 2008); and Peter Navarro and Greg Autry, *Death by China: Confronting the Dragon: A Global Call to Action* (Upper Saddle River, NJ: Pearson Prentice Hall, 2011). *Death by China* became the basis of a full-length documentary film with the same title. China-bashing intensified during the 2012 presidential election, as noted in "The China-bashing Syndrome," *The Economist*, July 14, 2012. The *New York Times* published a selection of opinions under the headline "Are We Headed for a Cold War with China?" on May 2, 2012.

45 See press releases from the ASBO dated November 9 and 10, 2011, and titled, respectively, "Multi-Service Office to Advance Air-Sea Battle Concept" and "The Air-Sea Battle Concept Summary." For another concise summary of the ASB mission by two officers affiliated with this office, Navy Captain Philip Dupree and Air Force Colonel Jordan Thomas, see "Air-Sea Battle: Clearing the Fog," *Armed Forces Journal*, May 2012; accessible at www.armedforcesjournal.com. The Defense Department's *Sustaining U.S. Global Leadership: Priorities for 21st Century Defense*, issued in January 2012, refers to "asymmetric challenges" by states such as China and Iran, and italicizes its mission in this area as follows: "*Accordingly the U.S. military will invest as required to ensure its ability to operate effectively in anti-access and area denial (A2/AD) environments.*"

46 China was targeted as a rising problem by the incoming administration of President George W. Bush in 2001, but this was put aside after the September 11 terrorist attacks and ensuing fixation on the "war on terror." The ASB concept, with primary focus on China, is attributed to Andrew Marshall, the influential long-time head of the Pentagon's Office of Net Assessment. Its articulation is now strongly associated with the Center for Strategic and Budgetary Assessments (CSBA), a Pentagon-supported think tank; see Greg Jaffe, "U.S. Model for a Future War Fans Tensions with China and inside Pentagon," *Washington Post*, August 1, 2012; this includes a map of the "inner" and "outer" island chains where "A2/AD" access is contested. For CSBA reports, see Krepinevich, *Why AirSea Battle?*; also Jan van Tol *et al.*, "AirSea Battle: A Point-of-Departure Operational Concept," May 18, 2010, accessible at www.csbaonline.org. Krepinevich includes chapters on China and Iran, while emphasizing that the former is by far the greater threat to US power projection; he also includes a map of the "first" and "second" island chains. ASB represents a departure from "Air–Land Battle" concepts introduced after the Vietnam War for countering the Soviet threat.

47 Department of Defense, *Joint Operational Access Concept (JOAC)*, Version 1.0, January 17, 2012. Army Capabilities Integration Center, US Army & Marine Corps Combat Development Command, US Marine Corps, *Gaining and Maintaining Access: An Army-Marine Corps Concept*, March 2012. For a brief summary, see Michael Raska, "Air-Sea Battle Debate: Operational Consequences and Allied Concerns," *Defense News*, October 30, 2012; accessible online at www.defensenews.com and other sites. Raska is affiliated with the Rajaratnam School of International Studies in Singapore. On the transfer of long-range bombers as well as Global Hawk drones to the Asia-Pacific area, see Thom Shanker, "Panetta Set to Discuss U.S. Shift in Asia Trip," *New York Times*, September 13, 2012.

48 President Obama himself never used the term "pivot" during his Asia trip, although it was used by his spokespeople. For official presentations, see "Remarks by President Obama to the Australian Parliament," November 17, 2011, accessible at the White

House website (www.whitehouse.gov); Hillary Clinton, "America's Pacific Century," *Foreign Policy*, November 2011; and Department of Defense, *Sustaining U.S. Global Leadership: Priorities for 21st Century Defense*, January 2012. For independent in-depth analyses, see Kenneth Lieberthal, "The American Pivot to Asia: Why President Obama's Turn to the East is Easier Said than Done," *Foreign Policy*, December 21, 2011; Mark E. Manyin *et al.*, *Pivot to the Pacific? The Obama Administration's "Rebalancing" Toward Asia*, Congressional Research Service, March 2012; David J. Berteau and Michael J. Green, *U.S. Force Posture in the Asia Pacific Region: An Independent Assessment*, Center for Strategic and International Studies, August 2012; and Michael D. Swaine *et al.*, *China's Military & the U.S.-Japan Alliance in 2030*, Carnegie Endowment for International Peace, May 2013.

49 Masaki Toki, "Missile Defense in Japan," *Bulletin of the Atomic Scientists*, January 16, 2009. The reference to China in the guidelines issued in 2004 reads:

> China, which has a major impact on regional security, continues to modernize its nuclear forces and missile capabilities as well as its naval and air forces. China is also expanding its area of operation at sea. We will have to remain attentive to its future actions.

Prime Minister of Japan and His Cabinet, *National Defense Program Guideline, FY 2005~*, December 14, 2004. The Japanese government has also released very slightly different translations of this document. The "Basic Space Law" was revised in August 2008 to permit using space for defense purposes.

50 *National Defense Program Guidelines for FY 2011 and Beyond*, approved by the Cabinet and Security Council on December 17, 2010. The official English translation is accessible at www.tr.emb-japan.go.jp.

51 For the 1967 and 1976 policies restricting arms exports, see the report submitted by Japan to the United Nations in 1996 under the title *Japan's Policies on the Control of Arms Exports*; this is accessible on the UN website (www.un.org) and Ministry of Foreign Affairs website (www.mofa.go.jp). As noted in this report, in 1983 excep-tions were made for transferring military technologies to the United States, leading to cooperation in the production of fighter aircraft and missile defense systems. For other exceptions involving small arms and dual-use goods, see Robin Ballantyne, "Japan's Hidden Arms Trade," *Asia Times*, December 1, 2005. On the missile-defense system announced in 2012, see Thom Shanker and Ian Johnson, "U.S. Accord with Japan over Missile Defense Draws Criticism in China," *New York Times*, September 17, 2012; Chester Dawson, "Japan Shows Off Its Missile-Defense System," *Wall Street Journal*, December 8, 2012.

52 "Concert of Asia" is the concept advanced by Hugh White in widely quoted commen-taries following publication of his 2012 book *The China Choice*. For "Pacific Com-munity," see Kissinger, "The Future of U.S.–China Relations." The "Pax Pacifica" concept was promoted in 2012 by commentators like Kevin Rudd, the foreign minister of Australia; see, for example, "Rudd: Asia Needs 'Pax Pacifica' as China Rises," summarizing a talk at the Asia Society of New York, January 13, 2012.

53 ASEAN (the Association of Southeast Asian Nations) dates from modest regional beginnings in 1967; became ASEAN Plus Three in 1997 with the addition of Japan, the PRC, and South Korea, bringing total membership to thirteen; and in 2010 expanded to ASEAN Plus Eight by adding Australia, India, New Zealand, Russia, and the United States. APEC (Asia-Pacific Economic Cooperation), which presently has twenty-one Pacific Rim "member economies," was established in 1989 and held its first summit in 1993. The East Asia Summit (EAS), dating from 2005, added Russia and the United States in 2011; total membership numbers eighteen nations, including Japan, the PRC, and India.

12 Historical legacies and regional integration

Haruki Wada

Northeast Asia is now facing a grave crisis. In order to get out of this crisis we should stare at our historical legacies which have separated us so severely, create common perceptions of the legacies, and find ways of overcoming them in name of true reconciliation.

For those of us living in Northeast Asia or East Asia, historical legacies are multilayered. In this region, three wars have raged. The first was the Japanese Fifty Years' War (1894–1945). The second was the New Asian Thirty Years' War (1946–1975). The third was the Cold War (1946–1987).

Each war left its historical legacies. But not every war was ended with a peace treaty. The San Francisco Peace Treaty (SFPT) was a treaty which closed the Japanese Fifty Years' War. And it was concluded between Japan and a part of the Allied victors which were now participants of the New Asian War. Therefore it was a treaty which could close the past war only partly and at the same time it was a treaty which made it possible to continue the new wars.

The New Asian Wars and the Cold War were not ended with peace treaties. The San Francisco System which was born from the treaty transformed itself through the New Asian Wars and the Cold War. Some parts vanished, but other parts still persist. They form special historical legacies which prevent reconciliation and regional cooperation.

The end of the Japanese War and the start of the New Asian Wars

From the Sino-Japanese War (1894–1895) to Japan's defeat in 1945, an expansive Japan was at war, often aggressive war, for fifty years. The age of the Japanese wars coincided with the age of imperialism in Northeast or East Asia. Japan waged wars most frequently with Russia (four times: 1904–1905, 1918–1922, 1939, and 1945), the longest war with China (1931–1945), and annexed Korea for thirty-six years. Finally, Japan fought with the United States and its allies, including the United Kingdom, China, and the Soviet Union, succumbing to them on August 14, 1945.

Japan's defeat meant not only the end of Japanese military aggression and imperialist expansion, but also the end of the old Western imperialism and colonialism in Northeast or East Asia. The collision of Japanese with Western imperialisms brought forth the demise of the imperialist system in this region.

But at the last moment of World War II, hostilities had already emerged among the Allied Powers. The Cold War started in Europe just after the capitulation of Nazi Germany; it exerted influences on the last phase of the Asia-Pacific War. President Truman wished to finish the war with his atomic bombs, without Soviet participation. When Stalin heard about the atomic bomb in Hiroshima, he rushed to start his attack against Manchuria. Yet in the early years of the post-war period in Northeast Asia, the United States and the Soviet Union, which had begun to collide in Europe, remained faithful to the concluded accord on the post-war management of this region.

Specifically, the US–Soviet accord set forth the following rules: (1) the United States would monopolize the occupation of Japan proper, with the Soviet Union regulating the occupation through its participation in the Allied Council of Japan; (2) in return for forsaking direct involvement in Japan's occupation, the Soviet Union would occupy South Sakhalin and the Kurile Islands; (3) Okinawa would be placed under US control; (4) the Korean Peninsula would be divided into two parts, with the southern half occupied by the United States and the northern half by the Soviet Union; (5) with regard to China, the Soviet Union would accept Chiang Kai-shek's Kuomintang government as legitimate, in exchange for regaining control over former Russian interests in Manchuria and winning recognition of the independence of Outer Mongolia; and (6) China would recover Taiwan.

But an upsurge of nationalist movements, seeking post-colonial state-building as military aggressors and imperialist forces fell, rose everywhere in this region. In these movements, Communist nationalists and anti- or non-communist nationalists came to fight with each other for hegemony over independent states. This was the case in China in 1946. On the Chinese continent, where the Japanese war of aggression had raged for fifteen years, a civil war was resumed between Communists and Nationalists. In Indochina, a war broke out between Communist nationalists and returning French colonists in 1946. The roar of guns shook the air again, from Manchuria to the delta of the Mekong. These wars may be named the "New Asian Wars." Although they became involved in the global East–West conflict, known as the "Cold War," they were not cold, but true hot wars.[1]

In this first phase of the New Asian Wars, the United States and the Soviet Union tried to show that they were not involved. Instead, they continued to cooperate in the occupation of Japan. Stalin made every effort not to produce an impression that the Soviet Union was challenging American hegemony by manipulating the Japanese Communist Party (JCP). From 1946 to 1949, the Communist Party of the Soviet Union had no official relations with the JCP, with all communications between the two parties carried out secretly through contacts between the Red Army's GRU (main espionage department) agents and Sanzo Nozaka.[2]

Japan, defeated, adopted a new constitution that required the abandonment of war and placed a prohibition on armed forces, in obedience to the strict leadership of the occupation forces and on the basis of strong anti-military sentiments held by the people. The Japanese, who had been waging war incessantly for the past fifty years, swore not to fight again. The New Asian Wars developed side by side with Japanese peace under the US occupation.

The second phase of the New Asian Wars and the Cold War: formation of the San Francisco System

When the war in mainland China ended with Mao Zedong's victory in 1949, the situation changed dramatically. Chinese Communists dominated mainland China and kicked out the Nationalists to Taiwan. At this moment, the Cold War between the United States and the Soviet Union began to be one of the real driving factors of the political situation in this region. The North Korean Communist government at last got permission from the Soviet Union to start military action against the South Korean anti-communist nationalist government, in order to build a unified, independent nation-state.

In the early morning of June 25, 1950, North Koreans, supplied with Soviet weapons and led by Soviet military advisers, attacked the ROK outright. President Syngman Rhee, thinking that this crisis presented the best opportunity for settling the Korean problem, decided to retreat in order to return with US forces.[3] Though defeated by the sudden attack, Rhee was glad that at last he had a chance to attack North Korea with Americans, in order to build a unified, independent nation-state.

The United States swiftly decided to help South Korea with all its might. At the same time, the US Seventh Fleet was sent to the Taiwan Straits to prevent an attack by Chinese Communists. This meant that the United States had finally intervened in the Chinese civil war. Supreme Commander for the Allied Powers General MacArthur ordered the Japanese government to provide services to support the US forces in Korea; the United States began to use all its military bases in Japan to wage the Korean War. Four bombardment groups with 100 B-29s in total were ordered from the United States and Guam to Yokota and Kadena, Okinawa. In July those B-29s began to fly from Yokota and Kadena to drop bombs on the North Koreans. Now, the whole of the Okinawa Islands became a US military base.[4]

Japanese Prime minister Yoshida Shigeru, while stating that his government was willing to support the United States spiritually and to cooperate to the extent possible, overtly declared that there was no reason for Japan to take any positive actions in this war. On the other hand, his government complied with General MacArthur's orders and requests for cooperation, by reason that the Japanese government and individuals were obliged to respond to directives of the Supreme Commander for Allied Powers which occupied defeated Japan.

When the ROK–US forces retreated south of River Naktong, Kim Il Sung and Pak Hon Yong's dream seemed to come true rather quickly. But the Korean People's Army could not break the last defense line of the ROK–US forces. And after the landing of the US forces at Inchong, the North Koreans were forced to retreat northward in disorder. Now the ROK–US forces hastily crossed the 38th parallel and rushed toward Pyongyang and Yalu River. It seemed then that Rhee's dream was about to be realized. But at this very moment, 180,000 Chinese soldiers crossed the river to help the North Koreans. The ROK–US forces were crushed, retreating southward in equal despair. From this moment the Korean War transformed itself into a Sino-American War on the Korean Pennisula.[5]

Stalin was pressed by the Chinese to provide air support. He bravely sent Soviet air forces to Andung. Soviet air pilots in aircraft disguised with Chinese markers fought against US air pilots. On the surface, the war was a Sino–American War, but in the air it was a Soviet–American War.

The Korean War was an international war that might be called a Northeast Asian War.[6] It consisted of three factors: the North–South war for unification; a hot war born out of the US–Soviet Cold War; and the Sino-American War.

The SFPT was concluded on September 8, 1951, at the height of the Korean War. Though the negotiation for ceasefire had started in July 1951, the war continued at full strength. This treaty was a settlement to end the Japanese Fifty Years' War, but, with the United States–Japan Security Pact concluded on another day, it served as the settlement defining Japan's position in the US camp for the New Asian Wars and the Cold War. The Soviet Union was the United States' main enemy, but formally a country with which the United States had diplomatic relations. On the other hand, Red China and North Korea were the enemies of the United States, with which it was waging war under the auspices of the UN. Though neither government of China nor Korea were invited to the peace conference, the United States pressed Japan to start separate negotiations with the ROC and ROK immediately.

The SFPT was designed to allow Japan to restore its economy and to keep Japan and Okinawa's position as strategic and logistic bases for US armed forces. Japan was forced to accept US dominance on Okinawa. At the same time, Japan was obliged to abandon her right to South Sakhalin and the Kurile Islands. South Sakhalin and the Kuriles had been annexed by the Soviet Union in 1946. Yoshida Shigeru, the Japanese plenipotentiary, stated that Habomais and Shikotan were not included into the Kurile Islands. The SFPT was supplemented by the Japan–ROC peace treaty in April 1952.[7]

Three important treaties after the end of the Korean War: transformation of the San Francisco System

On July 27, 1953, the Korean War ended in an armistice near the 38th parallel at almost the same place where Korea was divided in 1945. The Korean Peninsula settled into a hostile standoff, both sides being incapable of military action against the other. From the standpoint of Korean nationalists, the war that could not lead to unification was a debacle, but from the standpoint of the Chinese, the war with the United States, which had led to a draw, perfectly accomplished their stated aim, and was equal to a victory.

After Stalin's death, Soviet leaders approved the armistice of the Korean War and sought peaceful coexistence with the capitalist world. They wished to improve relations with West Germany and Japan. In June 1955 negotiations between Japan and the Soviet Union started in London. Japanese plenipotentiary Matsumoto was instructed to demand and get back Habomais and Shikotan. His Soviet counterpart Jacob Malik conveyed to him in August 1955 that the Soviet side was ready to hand over Habomais and Shikotan to Japan. But the United States and the anti-Soviet group of the Foreign Ministry in Japan worked together to adopt a new "four islands" (Habomais, Shikotan plus Kunashiri and Etorohu) demand as the Japanese government's new position. This was a revision to the SFPT, because Kunashiri and Etorohu belonged to the Kuriles, which Japan abandoned in the treaty. The Soviet Union rejected this new demand from Japan and negotiations were stopped. Finally, on October 16, 1956, Japan and the Soviet Union signed a joint declaration, re-establishing diplomatic relations between the two nations. The Soviet Union promised to hand over Habomais and Shikotan after the peace treaty was signed.[8]

In 1960 a true revision of the United States–Japanese Security Pact was realized by Prime Minister Kishi Nobusuke. A new security pact was ratified in the Japanese parliament in the midst of nationwide protests. This cost Kishi the prime minister's post. To compensate for this loss, Kishi's successor, Ikeda Hayato, invented a final rationale for the "four islands" demand, declaring that Kurile Islands did not include the South Kurile islands Etorohu and Kunashiri originally. Now Khurushchev answered that no territorial issue existed between the Soviet Union and Japan. Thus, Japan's Northern Territories demand was born in 1956–1960 in order to keep Japan–Soviet relations hostile and to strengthen Japan–United States relations in the Cold War.

The Japan–ROK Treaty was concluded on June 22, 1965. Japan rejected Korean demands for an apology for its colonial rule and agreed only to provide economic aid of 300 million dollars unconditionally and 200 million dollars at low interest. The Takeshima/Dokdo problem was shelved, while the island was kept under Korean occupation.

Three treaties of 1956, 1960, and 1965 were additional structures to the San Francisco System, tackling the more difficult phase of the New Asian Wars.

The Indochina war had ended in 1954 with the victory of the Vietnamese Communists. Nevertheless, after the French colonists had left, the Americans came to dominate Saigon, blocking the Vietnamese Communist nationalists' total victory. Therefore, in 1960, the National Front for the Liberation of South Vietnam (NFLSV) was formed; armed resistance started in South Vietnam. We can say that the Vietnam War broke out in this year. The United States mobilized all its resources to destroy the Vietnamese Communist nationalists. South Korea was induced to send its ground forces to Vietnam in 1965, just after concluding the Japan–ROK treaty. Fifty thousand Koreans annually joined this war against the Vietnamese. It can be said that South Koreans' participation was supported by the Japan–ROK treaty.

On the other hand, North Korea wished to support North Vietnam by creating a second front in South Korea. Championing the Juche ideology and establishing a "*yuil sasang chegye*" (monolithic ideological system), North Korea started to build a "partisan state" from 1967 and sent an armed partisan unit to Seoul on January 21, 1968, to attack the South Korean presidential palace. The unit was annihilated, with only one survivor. Two days later, the US Navy's intelligence boat *Pueblo* was captured by the North Korean navy. All these actions looked as if they were coordinated with the Tet offensive of the NFLSV which followed them in a week. But the North Koreans were not trusted by the Vietnamese. In August 1967, the Vietnamese charge d'affaires Hoang Muoi told the East German (GDR) ambassador in Pyongyang:

> In foreign policy, the leaders of the DPRK have two faces. They manipulate lying and deception. They say one story to us and say another story to Chinese, and say a third story to Soviet comrades. Such behavior cannot be continued for long.... Rumors about the dangers of war in Korea are sheer propaganda. The situation is utterly different in Korea and Vietnam.[9]

Lacking an understanding of strategy in common with North Vietnam, the North Koreans started actions, but failed hopelessly. Later, they sent pilots to North Vietnam to fight in aircraft disguised with Vietnamese markers. From the standpoint of both South and North Korea, the Vietnam War was a continuation of the Korean War. A peculiar North Korean type of state socialism was born as a byproduct of this fruitless projection.

In this war, Okinawa served as the main base for US forces, with Japan as a permanent logistics base. This was made possible by the new Japan–United States Security Pact concluded in 1960. On the other hand, the Soviet Union and China supplied arms and strategic materials to North Vietnam. The Vietnam War was an East Asian war, but it can be called rather a world war, because people all over the world stood up against the US aggression in Vietnam.

Also in Japan and Okinawa strong anti-war, anti-US base movements of citizens and students arose in 1968. Those people protested against the Japanese government's cooperation with US aggression in Vietnam and the Japan-United States Security Pact. The US President Richard Nixon and Japanese Prime Minister Sato Eisaku deemed this situation as grave and wished to ease it by realizing the return of Okinawa. In 1972 administrative power over Okinawa was returned to Japan, with all US military bases and nuclear arms remaining intact. In the Vietnam War, Japan could not but promise that the position of Okinawa in the US military system would be respected with no change. The Okinawa clause of the SFPT lost its meaning, but here the San Francisco System remained unchanged.

The Vietnam War ended with the fall of Saigon and the defeat of the United States in April 1975. This was the end of the New Asian Wars. But the United States did not face this fact. Therefore, no special international peace conference was convened, nor a special peace treaty concluded. The Thirty Years' War ended silently, without any wholesale review of war on the side of the defeated aggressor. The United States has never extended an apology to the Vietnamese people, nor paid atonement to them.

The management of the post-war situation had started a few years before. In 1971–1972, while the Vietnamese were still fighting against Americans, Communist China and the United States came to a common understanding that their war had ended as a draw. President Nixon visited Beijing to shake hands with Zhou Enlai and Mao Zedong. The United States succeeded in saving face before the coming defeat in Saigon.

Japan rushed to catch up with the United States, establishing diplomatic relations with the PRC while annulling the peace treaty with the ROC. In the joint statement dated September 29, 1972, Japan for the first time recognized its responsibility for the war in China and made an apology to the Chinese people. This was a step towards overcoming the San Francisco System. On September 21, 1992, Prime Minister Tanaka Kakuei established diplomatic relations with the Democratic Republic of Vietnam, presumably to US indignation.

The Vietnamese, knowing the settlement between China and the United States, was enraged and came to lean more towards the Soviet side. In the following years two new hostile alliances were formed in East Asia, China, the United States and Japan on one hand, and the Soviet Union, Vietnam and Afghanistan. In 1979 Vietnam sent troops to Cambodia to fight against Pol Pot and China attacked Vietnam to "punish" the Vietnamese. Finally the Soviet Union sent troops to Afghanistan to kill the unreliable Afghan leader, Amin. It was the beginning of the Afghan War. This period was the darkest years of the crisis. But amidst those tragic events China launched capitalist economic development under the banner "Reform and Opening" in 1978.

After the fall of Saigon, the South Korean government lost face before its own people, who were demanding democracy in spite of all the suppressions. In 1987, a people's democratic revolution broke out in South Korea; at last South Korean people won a democratic regime. After this victory their attitude to Japanese colonial rule changed thoroughly. The end of the thirty-year-long New Asian Wars gave Asian nations a chance to demand apology and atonement from Japan for its Fifty Years War.

In December 1987 the new Soviet leader, Mikhail Gorbachev, declared the end of the Cold War together with US President Ronald Reagan in Washington. By 1991 East European socialist countries and the Soviet Union itself had ceased to exist. After the end of the Cold War, South Korea established diplomatic relations with the Soviet Union and the PRC. But North Korea, losing privileged trade relations with the Soviet Union, experienced a serious economic crisis; also losing its position under the Soviet nuclear umbrella, it chose the path toward independent nuclear armament. In this sense, North Korea proved to be a victim of the end of the Cold War.

Our historical legacies

At the beginning of the twenty-first century, we are experiencing the conclusion of three wars: the Japanese Fifty Years' War (1894–1945); the New Asian Thirty Years' Wars (1946–1975); and the forty-five years of Cold War (1946–1982).

The San Francisco System has considerably decayed, but its main parts have survived to this day. That is to say, we are facing four sets of historical legacies.

Among the legacies of the Japanese Fifty Years' War, presumably the most striking is that Japan–DPRK relations have not been normalized. Japanese colonial rule has not yet been buried in the past in relation to North Korea. No apology has been written in a treaty and no atonement has been paid. And there are problems posed by war victims in China and both Koreas: the so-called former comfort women, drafted laborers, and Korean former war criminals of class B and C are awaiting apology and atonement from the Japanese government and people. Furthermore, there are territorial problems. Among them, the most severe is Okinawa, which is still occupied by the US military. The problems of the Northern Territories, Dokdo/Takeshima and Senkaku/Diaoyu islands are to be solved too. These unsolved territorial issues are presently creating constant unrest and dangerous tensions in the region.

Among the legacies of the New Asian Wars, a central problem is that of remaining hostilities between China and Taiwan, and between the two Koreas. Concretely it is hostilities between the authoritarian party-state system and democratic presidential system. In both cases, solutions should be sought not in forced unification, but in the stabilization of mutual relations and agreement of long-term co-existence. The belligerent countries of the Korean War were the DPRK and PRC on one side, and the sixteen countries of the United Nations forces. The PRC has now established diplomatic relations with all of these sixteen countries, including the United States and the ROK. The DPRK established diplomatic relations with thirteen of the sixteen countries. It does not have normal diplomatic relations with the United States, the ROK, or France. France is a far away country that belongs to a different region, and the ROK forms the other half of the Korean Peninsula. So to the DPRK the absence of normal relations with the United States is the most burning post-war issue, together with the absence of normal relations with Japan. Of course, relations of the two Koreas should be completely stabilized. For that purpose it would be useful to create a common understanding about the Korean War. As far as the Vietnam War is concerned, what is missing is an apology and compensation from the United States. Vietnamese war victims, especially victims of Agent Orange, are awaiting apology and atonement.

Finally, the legacy of the Cold War and the legacy of the San Francisco System are concentrated on the Japan–United States relations, which can be characterized by Japanese dependency on the United States and the US control of Japan. This problem before the people of this region is rising hostilities against the United States–Japan intention to construct a new marine airfield in Henoko, against the protests of the Okinawan people.

The significance of regional integration

In order to overcome the historical legacies and solve various complicated problems, we need a solution that departs from ordinary bilateral negotiations between countries, and a design of peaceful regional cooperation for the future. A wide forum formed of all the countries of Northeast Asia is necessary. There, all problems may be cross-checked, discussed, and solved.

Such a forum already exists: the Six-Party Talks. Representatives of all six countries of Northeast Asia have joined. Though shut down for a long time, it started in August 2003 and has continued to exist until now. Its main task was defined as the denuclearization of the Korean Peninsula, but its joint statement of the fourth round, dated September 19, 2005, showed clearly what great potential this forum possesses. It reads:

> The DPRK committed to abandoning all nuclear weapons and existing nuclear programs.... The United States affirmed that it has no nuclear weapons on the Korean Peninsula and has no intention to attack or invade the DPRK with nuclear or conventional weapons.... The DPRK stated that it has the right to peaceful uses of nuclear energy. The other parties expressed their respect and agreed to discuss, at an appropriate time, the subject of the provision of light water reactor to the DPRK.... The DPRK and the United States undertook to respect each other's sovereignty, exist peacefully together, and take steps to normalize their relations subject to their respective bilateral policies.... The DPRK and Japan undertook to take steps to normalize their relations in accordance with the Pyongyang Declaration, on the basis of the settlement of unfortunate past and the outstanding issues of concern.... The Six Parties committed to joint efforts for lasting peace and stability in Northeast Asia. The directly related parties will negotiate a permanent peace regime on the Korean Peninsula at an appropriate separate forum. The Six Parties agreed to explore ways and means for promoting security cooperation in Northeast Asia.

This is all good. Many important problems arising from our historical legacies are raised here and solutions declared. Of course, there are only promises so far. To deepen discussion of all problems, it is first necessary to take firm steps toward control of North Korean nuclear development by real, effective agreements. But in order to realize these steps we must comprehensively tackle other issues mentioned in the September 2005 statement at the same time. In the next stage, the Six-Party Talks should be reconstructed and expanded. The problems concerning conventional weapons, arms control, and security should be added to the talks' agenda, along with the burning territorial problems of the region. Finally, the Six-Party Talks should take up the problems of history and reconciliation.

In the September 2005 statement, a Northeast Asian security organization was defined as the aim of the Six-Party Talks. A reconstructed and expanded Six-Party Talks would be something like an Association of North East Asian Nations (ANEAN), which might develop into a Northeast Asian Community.

People have long discussed various plans for a regional community.[10] In July 1990, I proposed at the Seoul symposium hosted by Dong-A Ilbo to build "a House of coexistence in Northeast Asia." I said:

A new alliance of the Soviet Union, China, South and North Korea, the United States and Japan in Northeast Asia can be called a house where peoples of the world live together, and rapprochement and merger of South and North Korea on the basis of democracy provides a core of that house.

In 2001 the East Asia Vision Group, established by ASEAN Plus Three, submitted a report, "Towards an East Asian Community: Region of Peace, Prosperity and Progress," at the Kuala Lumpur meeting of the ASEAN Plus Three Summit. This report begins:

We, the people of East Asia, aspire to create an East Asian community of peace, prosperity and progress based on the full development of all peoples in the region. Concurrent with this vision is the goal that the future of East Asian Community will make a positive contribution to the rest of the world.

In February 2003, the then South Korean president Roh Moo-hyun announced that "Northeast Asia" must develop into a "community of peace and prosperity."

The Korean Peninsula is located at the heart of the region. It is a big bridge linking China and Japan, the continent and the ocean. Such a geopolitical characteristic often caused pain for us in the past. Today, however, this same feature is offering us an opportunity. Indeed, it demands that we play a pivotal role in the Age of Northeast Asia in the 21st century.

In December 2005, the ASEAN Plus Three Summit and the first East Asia Summit held at Kuala Lumpur adopted declarations about the necessity for an East Asian Community. On December 13, the ASEAN Plus Three Summit declared:

Reiterating our common resolve to realize an East Asian community as a long-term goal … we are convinced that the ASEAN Plus Three process will continue to be the main vehicle in achieving that goal.

Also, on December 14, the first East Asia Summit meeting, attended by the heads of state of the member countries of ASEAN, Australia, People's Republic of China, Republic of India, Japan, Republic of Korea, and New Zealand, adopted a declaration that "shares the view that the East Asia Summit could play a significant role in community building in this region."

The two different visions of an East Asian community discouraged people's willingness to move forward. Discussions continued, but no real progress was made. In 2009 Prime Minister Hatoyama Yukio, of the new Democratic Party of Japan, which defeated the Liberal Democratic Party in the election, began to talk about an East Asian Community, attracting the attention of neighboring countries. But the US government did not take this well. President Obama declared his position overtly in Tokyo on November 14, 2009.

In addition to our bi-lateral relations we also believe the growth of multi-lateral organizations can advance security and prosperity of the region. I know that the United States have been disengaged from many of these organizations in recent years. So let me be clear. Those days have passed. As an Asia-Pacific nation, the United States expect to be involved in discussions to shape the future of this region and to participate wholly in appropriate organizations as they are established and evolved.

After Hatoyama's failure, the next prime minister, Kan Naoto, ceased to speak about the East Asian Community and sought sympathy from the US government by expressing his willingness to join the TPP (Trans-Pacific Strategic Economic Partnership Agreement). In spite of vehement controversy about Japan's participation, the new LDP prime minister Abe Shinzo finally decided to join the negotiations to start the TPP. Presently, it seems that people do not pay active attention to the arguments about an East Asian Community, though in 2011 the United States and Russia were invited to join the East Asian Summit.

The final form of regional community is still open. I think that a combination of several forms with different kinds of membership is preferable. And, in this situation, the Six-Party Talks, though shut down for the time being, is no doubt already a real entity that provides us with one form of regional community-building. If the Six-Party Talks grew into an Association of North East Asian Nations, this new association could cooperate with ASEAN to create a new form of East Asian community. An East Asian community is conceivable with or without the United States. We need not decide it beforehand. We must make efforts to recover the Six-Party Talks and develop it into a true regional forum.

Conclusion

With the end of World War II the Japanese Fifty Years' War ended. But in Europe the Cold War started and spread outward. In East Asia the New Asian Thirty Years' Wars started from mainland China. And when Chinese Communists gained a victory over Nationalists in their War throughout the Chinese Continent, Korean Communists started a war throughout the Korean Peninsula. Then the New Asian Wars entered into their second phase and the Cold War began in full scale there.

During this second phase of the New Asian Wars a peace treaty was concluded by Japan and the Allies to end the Japanese War. This San Francisco Peace Treaty, together with the United States–Japan Security Pact concluded at the same time, served as the settlement defining Japan's position in the US camp for the New Asian Wars and the Cold War. With Okinawa, Japan was expected to provide permanent strategic and logistic bases for US armed forces. The SFPT could not bury totally the Japanese War.

The San Francisco System was supplemented and partly transformed by two treaties and one joint declaration; the Japan–ROC Peace treaty, the Japan–Soviet Joint Declaration and the Japan–ROK treaty. The San Francisco System with the

Japan–ROK treaty worked well for the United States to wage the Vietnam War. But in 1975 the United States was defeated in Vietnam. This was the end of the New Asian Wars. In 1991 the Cold War ended and Soviet state socialism also fell. But after these events neither peace conferences nor peace treaties occurred. Therefore, at the beginning of the twenty-first century, we are still facing three sets of historical legacies of the past wars: the Japanese Fifty Years' War, the New Asian Wars, and the Cold War. And the main part of the San Francisco System remains in effect. This forms the fourth historical legacy of our region.

In order to overcome the historical legacies and solve various complicated problems, we need a solution that departs from ordinary bilateral negotiations between countries, and a design of peaceful regional cooperation for the future. Such a forum already exists. The Six-Party Talks, though shut down for the time being, is no doubt already a real entity that provides us with one form of regional community-building. If the Six-Party Talks grew into an Association of North East Asian Nations, this new association could cooperate with ASEAN to create a new form of East Asian community.

Notes

1 Kimie Hara wrote in her book as follows: "After the Japanese withdrawal, the postwar liberation and independence movements in some parts of the region turned to civil war over the governing principles for the new states." She is right, but she tends to see these civil wars as surrogates for "a direct clash between the USA and the USSR," or a battle between capitalism and socialism; see Hara, *The San Francisco System and the Regional Conflicts in the Asia-Pacific* (London: Routledge, 2007, p. 4.). I myself would like to emphasize an independent significance of these civil wars, which distinguished them from the Cold War.
2 Wada Haruki, "The Korean War, Stalin's Policy, and Japan," *Social Science Japan Journal* 1, no. 1 (April 1998): 8.
3 President Rhee shared his thinking with Ambassador John J. Muccio at noon on June 25, 1950. *FRUS, 1950*, Vol. 7, p. 131.
4 Robert F. Futrell, *The United States Air Force in Korea 1950–1953* (Washington, DC: Office of Air Force History, 1961), pp. 65, 69–70.
5 See Wada Haruki, *The Korean War: An International History* (Lanham, MD: Rowman & Littlefield, 2014), pp. 144, 299.
6 Wada, *The Korean War*, pp. xxvi–xxvii.
7 Wada Haruki, "Economic Co-operation in Place of Historical Remorse: Japanese Post-war Settlements with China, Russia, and Korea in the Context of the Cold War," in *The Political Economy of Japanese Society*, Vol. 2 (Oxford: Oxford University Press, 1998), pp. 110–19.
8 Ibid., pp. 119–28.
9 GDR Embassy Pyongyang, August 28, 1967, PolArchAA, MfAA, G-A-364.
10 See Wada Haruki, "Envisioning a Northeast Asian Community: Regional and Domestic Factors to Consider," in *Regional Cooperation and its Enemies in Northeast Asia: The Impacts of Domestic Forces*, edited by Edward Friedman and Sung Chull Kim (London: Routledge, 2006), pp. 38–57.

13 Preparing ideas for the future

Envisioning a multilateral settlement*

Kimie Hara

On the sixtieth anniversary since the enactment of the San Francisco Peace Treaty (SFPT) (April 28, 2012), an international conference entitled *Sixty Years of the San Francisco System: Continuation, Transformation, and Historical Reconciliation in the Asia-Pacific* was held in Waterloo, Ontario, Canada. The whole-day conference was devoted to examining key developments of the contentious political and security issues in the Asia-Pacific that share a common foundation in the early post-World War II arrangement with Japan.

The SFPT, together with its associated security arrangements, significantly shaped the post-World War II order and laid the foundation for the structure of the Cold War confrontation in the Asia-Pacific: The San Francisco System is in many ways responsible for continuing tensions in the region. These include both tangible and intangible conflicts, of which the major issues were examined at the conference, where intensive and lively discussions were exchanged among the participants from China (PRC and ROC), Japan, Korea (ROK), Russia, Australia, the United States, and across Canada. Although almost all participants acknowledged the importance of peaceful resolution, they did not necessarily share a common view on the issues examined, such as disputes over territories and "history" problems. Nevertheless, it generated significant inspirations for considering conflict resolutions in the region.[1]

As noted at the conference and in this volume, expanded regional cooperation and interaction since the 1990s paved the way for notable confidence building measures (CBMs) among neighboring states at both government and non-government levels in East Asia. However, as seen in the recent relations between Japan and its neighbors, tensions can easily be reignited once those contentious "unresolved problems" are brought to the centre of political attention. Tangible conflicts, particularly the territorial disputes, tend to be associated with other intangible issues of their unsettled past, and lead to exacerbation of nationalism. No matter how much CBMs are enhanced and relations are improved, as long as the sources of the conflict remain unchanged, there is always a possibility that tensions resurge and conflicts escalate.

The road to peace ultimately requires removal of principal sources of conflict. Yet is it really possible to solve the problems that have been ongoing for such a long time? If so, different and more creative approaches may be necessary. Such may be found in multilateral efforts that reflect on the historical experience and new reality of international relations. This chapter explores some ideas for their future resolution, particularly the tangible territorial problems between Japan and its neighbors.

Why multilateral?

Historical experience suggests that it is extremely difficult to solve those conflicts derived from the post-war disposition of Japan bilaterally or through negotiations confined to the nations directly involved in the disputes. This may be particularly true of contentious territorial issues. In fact, some, if not all, of these issues may be insoluble as long as they remain within such traditional bilateral frameworks. Having been mutually linked and multilaterally disposed of in the context of the post-World War II settlement, it seems worthwhile to return to their common origin and consider their solution within a multilateral framework.

In a multilateral framework, mutually acceptable solutions not achievable within a bilateral framework may be found by creatively combining mutual concessions. Such an approach may also avoid the impression of a clear win–lose situation and an international loss of face. Furthermore, multilateral international agreements tend to be more durable than bilateral ones. The more participating states there are, the stronger restraint tends to be, and the greater the possibility that a country in breach will be internationally isolated. Obtaining wide international recognition for settlements is, therefore, desirable.

In the contemporary context of regionalism, multilateral problem solving may contribute to regional community building and integration. Resolution of long-standing issues will not only help remove political barriers to regional integration, but may also help promote the growth of regional identity, thereby reducing the relative importance of national borders. Resolution of the territorial disputes may be sought in this broader context as well.

Possible frameworks

What kind of multilateral framework is appropriate for dealing with these regional conflicts in East Asia? An existing framework may be used, or a new framework may be created. Today, the International Court of Justice (ICJ) is available for dealing with international disputes. Bringing cases to the ICJ, if disputes arise, was also suggested in the SFPT. Japan, in fact, proposed in 1954, 1962, and 2012 that the case of Takeshima (Dokdo) be brought to the ICJ, but South Korea refused. Bringing individual cases into such a multilateral framework is certainly extremely difficult. Through over half a century of disputes, the positions of all parties are widely known and mutually exclusive. Any settlement produced by an international organization, even within a multilateral framework, could be viewed as a win–lose situation, with a danger of international loss of face. Third-party arbitration runs the same risk of a win–lose situation and potential loss of face – if cases are dealt with individually.

However, if at least some of these issues were examined or negotiated together within a multilateral framework, or along with a number of other outstanding issues, the circumstances might be different. For example, Japan's territorial disputes with its neighbors – Russia, Korea, and China – may be brought to the ICJ together for joint examination and collective settlements, that is, to determine clear post-World War II borders of Japan. If not the ICJ, some existing regional framework may be used. For example, the Japan–ROK–PRC trilateral meetings since the December 2008 Dazaifu summit may have potential for conflict resolution. This trilateral group might add Russia, creating a four-party framework that would consist of Japan and its dispute counterparts that were not signatories to the SFPT. This framework would include Russia and China, the two powers that successfully negotiated and achieved the settlement of the world's longest border demarcation.

The Six Party Talks, with the United States and the DPRK added to the four parties mentioned above, offer another potentially useful framework. US participation may make sense, considering its role in preparing the SFPT as well as its continuing presence and influence in the region. The Six Party Talks have been the particular forum for negotiating issues surrounding the North Korean nuclear crisis. This issue is essentially about survival of the North Korean regime, which has been trying to obtain cooperation and assurances from the United States and neighboring countries. Originally, this problem developed from the question of to which country or government Japan renounced "Korea." Like Takeshima/Dokdo and other conflicts in East Asia, it was an "unresolved problem" originating from the post-war territorial disposition of Japan. The Six Party framework, although stalled since 2008, may also have the potential to develop into a major regional security organization in the North Pacific in the future.

In addition to the above, a broader framework may be possible, such as by adding the ASEAN members to include the South China Sea issues in the negotiations, or even the broader "Asia-Pacific" may be worth considering in the context of stabilizing the regional status quo (which is discussed in the next sections).

When it comes to detailing the conditions or concrete adjustments necessary for a settlement, multilateral negotiations may be supplemented by parallel discussions in a bilateral framework. If initiating such negotiations at the formal governmental (Track I) level is difficult, they may be combined with more informal (Track II) level discussions.

In considering such negotiation frameworks, a key question to be addressed may be whether US involvement would work positively or negatively for the solution of these conflicts. If the United States perceives their settlement as inimical to its strategic interests, its involvement would become detrimental. Historically, US Cold War strategy in the SFPT gave rise to various conflicts among regional neighbors. During the warming of East–West relations of the past, the United States did not necessarily facilitate full recognition or clear settlement of the territorial problems between Japan and its neighbors. It actually intervened in the Soviet–Japanese peace negotiations to prevent their territorial settlement the mid-1950s, and in the early 1970s left the Senkaku/Diaoyu dispute between Japan and China on its reversion of Okinawa's "administrative rights" to Japan. In the post-Cold War world, where the Soviet Union no longer exists and China has become a large capitalist country, however, the Cold War strategy to contain communism no longer seems valid.

Nevertheless, the United States may perceive regional instability as beneficial to its strategy, as long as it is manageable and does not escalate into large-scale war. It is precisely "manageable instability" that helps justify a continued large US military presence in the region, not only enabling the United States to maintain its regional influence, but also contributing to operations farther afield, such as in the Middle East. A solution to East Asian regional conflicts would alter the regional security balance and accordingly influence regional security arrangements, particularly the San Francisco Alliance System. Just as was the case during the Cold War détente and after the so-called "end of the Cold War," considerable pressure would arise for the United States to withdraw from, or reduce its military presence in, the region. This would very likely affect its bases in Okinawa, which still remains the most contentious issue in United States–Japan relations. Although an accommodation between Japan and its neighbors is preferable for regional stability, it would not be viewed as beneficial by US strategists if it was perceived as likely to reduce or exclude US influence. Thus, continued conflicts among regional countries may still be seen as meeting US interests.

On the other hand, if the United States perceives the resolution of disputes as being beneficial, its constructive involvement can be a strong factor in ending them. How will the United States benefit from resolving these disputes? A peaceful and stable East Asia, a region in which the United States is heavily involved in economic development, trade, culture, and other arenas, surely is a significant US interest. Reduction of its military presence will contribute to cutting US defense spending at a time of heavy budget pressure. US leaders may also be convinced of the value of conflict resolution if it can maintain its influence and presence through security arrangements – for example, a multilateral security organization based on the Six Party or other frameworks. The continuing presence and expanded mission of NATO since the Cold War and after the establishment of the EU may present a notable precedent.

Settlement formula: mutual concessions and collective gains

What kinds of concrete settlements can be envisioned in a multilateral framework? A workable settlement formula would include mutual concessions and collective gains. Each party would have to make some concessions, but the gains would potentially be far greater than the concessions if the region is viewed as a whole.

The following are considerations with *hypothetical* examples that may be used as bases for further deliberation. In the trilateral framework, Japan might, for example, make a concession to Korea with respect to Dokdo/Takeshima, while China might make a concession to Japan over Senkaku and Okinawa.[2] Then, in exchange for these, Korea might offer concessions over the naming issues of its surrounding seas by withdrawing its claim for "East Sea," "West Sea," and "South Sea" and accepting "Sea of Japan," "Yellow Sea," and "East China Sea," respectively, as their names. Also, China might receive recognition of its sovereignty over the Paracel Islands in the South China Sea, to which it has strong historical links.

In the four-party framework, with Russia added to these three countries, Japan and Russia might make mutual concessions and return to the two-island transfer of the 1956 Joint Declaration – an international agreement ratified at the time by their legislatures. This might appear as a win–lose situation in a bilateral framework, but such an impression would be softened by combining the agreement with other territorial settlements and additional conditions. These are basically recognition of the status quo, except for the Russia–Japan islands transfer. Accomplishing that much would at least bring the situation closer to the level of the 1975 Helsinki Accords in Europe.

These arrangements may also be combined with mutual concessions in maritime border negotiations, including EEZ delimitations. As mentioned earlier in this volume, introduction of UNCLOS has greatly contributed to complicating territorial problems. Yet it may provide opportunities for dispute settlement by opening up more options for a combination of concessions. For example, instead of using Dokdo (Korea) and Oki (Japan) as base points to draw the EEZ line, Dokdo could be used as the base point for both Korea and Japan, and their median line could be drawn along the 12-nautical-mile territorial waters of Dokdo. The logic here is that the median line would be drawn in ways favorable to Japan in exchange for its recognition of Takeshima (Dokdo) as Korean territory. A similar arrangement may be made for Senkaku/Diaoyu, with the islands used as the base point of both Japan and China for their EEZ. Furthermore, it may be possible to link these problems with other "settlements of the past," including non-traditional security issues. Such mutual concession could pave the way for reducing tensions and greater cooperation in multiple areas with mutual benefits for all parties.

Other settlements might include the demilitarization, international autonomy, or joint development of disputed islands. For those, a historical precedent of conflict resolution in northern Europe – the 1921 settlement of the Åland islands dispute – provides useful lessons, particularly for the Northern Territories/Southern Kuriles where consideration should be given to the residents of the islands. The Åland Settlement, which was achieved in a multilateral framework under the League of Nations, featured settlement of a border dispute through mutual concessions and collective gains. The formula was so mixed that the decision on the islands' ownership could not be interpreted in the usual win–lose terms. The settlement was also positive-sum for all parties, including the residents of the islands. Finland received sovereignty over the islands, Åland residents were granted autonomy combined with guarantees for the preservation of their Swedish heritage, and Sweden received guarantees that Åland would not constitute a military threat. The settlement also contributed to the peace and stability of northern Europe as a whole. The majority of Ålanders originally wanted to reunite with Sweden, and thus were dissatisfied with the settlement. However, as a result of the settlement, Ålanders enjoyed various benefits and special international status, including passports that now read "European Union – Finland – Åland." If these innovative arrangements had not been made and Åland had been returned to Sweden, it might well have become merely a run-down and depressed border region, or a military frontier area – quite a different situation from today. The Åland Settlement presents an attractive model of conflict resolution.[3]

The Åland model, however, cannot be applied to the Northern Territories/Southern Kuriles dispute or any other regional conflicts in East Asia "as is." The model must be creatively modified to be applicable. For example, the Northern Territories/Southern Kuriles, Dokdo/Takeshima, and Diaoyu/Senkaku might all be demilitarized. Also, rather than placing them under a local government jurisdiction, some or all of these territories could become a special administrative region in politics, economy, culture, and environment. Moreover, such arrangements may be guaranteed not only by the governments directly concerned, but also in a wider international framework.[4]

The settlement ideas explored above may be called "status quo *plus alpha*" or "modified (East Asian) version of the Helsinki Accord." Unless there is a clear mutual agreement of territorial transfer, like the 1956 Japan–Soviet Joint Declaration, it is extremely difficult, or nearly impossible, to change the existing borders without waging wars again. However, most nations do not favor wars. People in Europe realized this earlier. The Helsinki Declaration was released in 1975, the year of the thirtieth anniversary since the end of World War II, but Europe by then had a long history of wars and conflicts.

The Helsinki Accord recognized the (then) status quo of the post-World War II international order, the so-called "Yalta System." That there is common recognition, or consensus, about the political status quo and existing borders contributes to regional peace and stability. The European Community (EC) of the Cold War era later developed into the European Union (EU), where regional identity has grown while relative importance of national borders decreased. The Conference on Security and Cooperation in Europe (CSCE), where the Helsinki Accord was adopted, also developed into the Organization for Security and Cooperation in Europe (OSCE), the world's largest security-oriented intergovernmental organization. In retrospect, the Helsinki Accord did not necessarily finalize post-World war II borders in Europe; in the early 1990s, 15–16 years later, borders in Europe moved again, as seen in the reunification of Germany and the independence of the Baltic States.

Asia is different from Europe, as is often pointed out. It is certainly different and behind in terms of dealing with the past. In order to bring stability and create peaceful regional community in Asia, there are important lessons to learn from the European experiences.

Preparing ideas for the future

The SFPT was, after all, a war settlement with Japan. Therefore, it may make sense for Japan to take the initiative in solving the "unresolved problems" derived from that treaty. The United States has been Japan's most important partner throughout the post-war period and will remain important in the continuing San Francisco System for a foreseeable future. However, in the longer term their positions could diverge greatly. The United States, which never colonized Korea or Taiwan, and has no territorial disputes in this region, could withdraw if it so chose, for example, following a peaceful resolution of the Korea and Taiwan problems. Japan, on the other hand, has no option of withdrawal from the region. It may choose to become a "normal country" by revising the anti-war provisions in its constitution, to prepare against future contingencies. Whether or not it does so, it seems necessary for Japan to avert its isolation, open up diplomatic alternatives for its future, and build constructive relations with its neighbors by solving the pending questions and removing the "wedges" or "walls" dividing them. For that purpose, it would be worth Japan's while to take the initiative in solving the "unresolved problems" derived from the post-war peace treaty.

Japan's neighbors, however, may not favor Japan's political initiative, if taken in a multilateral framework, given its record of the pre-war period. The idea of applying the "Helsinki Model," which brought Europe the end of the Cold War or the collapse of the Yalta System, to East Asia has been discussed for some time, particularly in the context of the Korean Peninsula.[5] South Korean President Park Geun-hye has also been advocating the "Seoul Process" as a Northeast Asian version of the Helsinki Process since her inauguration. For the sake of neutrality, Mongolia, which has tended to be ignored in the regional security dialogue, may actually serve better than the other countries that are directly in disputes in the region. If conflict resolution and regional community-building are to be considered in a broader framework of the Asia-Pacific, then a country like Canada may also have the potential to take such an initiative.

In any event, final settlement will require political decisions. Unless politics, not bureaucracy, can predominate in policy-making, the territorial problems will remain deadlocked. Complex threads of international relations cannot be easily disentangled. Yet, while there are clues, solutions to problems should never be impossible. In the long run, positive factors for solving regional conflicts may develop, i.e., domestic and social change in concerned states, changes of existing policies by disputant states, breakthroughs in official and unofficial dialogues, change of political dynamics in the region, etc.

Togo Kazuhiko, a former senior diplomat of Japan who played a leading role in the negotiations with the USSR/Russia from the late 1980s to 2001, identified five opportunities to settle the Northern Territories problem.[6] Yet none of the proposals presented then were mutually acceptable to both Japan and Russia. As with the Northern Territories and many other international disputes, time may again present opportunities for solutions. Scholars may be able to contribute to such diplomatic efforts by providing ideas and information, to prepare for the time when an opportunity does present itself again.

Notes

* This chapter is a revised last section of the author's article "The San Francisco Peace Treaty and Frontier Problems in the Regional Order in East Asia: A Sixty Year Perspective," *The Asia-Pacific Journal* 10, no. 17 (April 23, 2012).
1 The conference also generated a report, *Sixty Years of the San Francisco System: Continuation, Transformation, and Historical Reconciliation in the Asia-Pacific – Conference Report* (Keiko and Charles Belair Centre for East Asian Studies, Renison University College, University of Waterloo, 2012).
2 Since the ROC government in Taiwan has not formally withdrawn its claim to Okinawa/Ryukyu, the PRC could disavow it or promise not to revive it.
3 Kimie Hara and Geoffrey Jukes (eds.), *Northern Territories, Asia-Pacific Regional Conflicts and the Åland Experience: Untying the Kurillian Knot* (London: Routledge, 2009).
4 For details, see Hara and Jukes, *Northern Territories, Asia-Pacific Regional Conflicts and the Åland Experience*, pp. 119–24.
5 For example, See Markku Heiskanen, "The 'CSCE Helsinki Model' and the Security and Cooperation in Northeast Asia," Nordic Institute of Asian Studies, Copenhagen/Helsinki, February 24, 2004 (http://nautilus.org/publications/books/dprkbb/multilateraltalks/dprk-briefing-book-the-csce-helsinki-model-and-the-security-and-cooperation-process-in-northeast-asia/#axzz2sfSQgVdl [accessed December 1, 2013]); Vladimir Petrovsky, "The Helsinki Process Experience as a Model for Northeast Asia" Universal Peace Foundation, May 28, 2005.
6 Kazuhiko Togo, *Hoppo ryodo kosho hiroku: ushinawareta gotabi no kitai* (The Secret Record of Northern Territories Negotiations: Five Missed Opportunities) (Shincho-sha, 2007).

Epilogue

The San Francisco System and geopolitical conflict in the Asia-Pacific in the new millennium[1]

Mark Selden

The San Francisco System not only shaped the post-war international order in the Asia-Pacific, but its influence extends into the new millennium. The unresolved territorial conflicts that were the legacy of a treaty whose signatories included neither the Soviet Union nor China, together with the US-centered alliance-base structure that was set in place with the end of the US occupation of Japan, continue to shape regional and global geopolitics at a time of global instability.

The end of the Asia-Pacific War, the dismantling of the Japanese empire and US occupation, far from bringing peace to the Asia-Pacific, gave way to what Wada Haruki calls the New Asian Wars. These included national independence, liberation and revolutionary wars, as well as protracted international and civil wars. Major participants included China, Korea (DPRK and ROK), Vietnam (DRV and RVN) as well as Indonesia and the Philippines, and of course the Soviet Union and the United States.

The three most important geopolitical conflicts that are the legacy of the San Francisco System, the New Asian Wars, and East–West conflict in the Asia-Pacific, were those between the People's Republic of China (PRC) and the Republic of China (ROC). That is, the Taiwan Question and the future of China, the contestation for power within Korea and Vietnam, each of which extended to wider wars – indeed the exhibited features of world war – as a US-led coalition confronted both the Soviet Union and China. Of the three, only the US–Indochina War would be resolved with US military defeat and national unification under the DRV, while China and Korea remain divided, albeit in quite different circumstances. In each case the United States and China are centrally involved in the conflict and any resolution of the issues will hinge on United States–China agreement. The intertwined character of the issues is illustrated by the fact that the price for ending the US occupation of Japan in 1952 was not only the signing of a United States–Japan Security Treaty that would keep American bases and troops in Japan for the next six decades, but the severing of Okinawa from Japan in the form of a US military colony, a status that continued for two more decades. Japan's "client-state" status is further illustrated by its succumbing to US pressure to sign a 1952 peace treaty establishing diplomatic relations with the Republic of China (rather than the People's Republic).

From the mid-1970s, the Asia-Pacific experienced relative peace for the first time in more than a century. The end of the era of permanent war facilitated the emergence of East Asia as the world's most dynamic growth zone in the wake of the US military defeat in Indochina. Rapid region-wide growth was equally a product of the United States–China opening, which enabled the PRC to reclaim China's place in the United Nations Security Council and to emerge by the 1990s as a world leader in manufactures and exports, while navigating a fundamental shift to Chinese-style state capitalism that preserved the power of the party-state. China consolidated a position as a major regional power, a trade and transportation hub, and a significant participant in shaping the global order. Under these circumstances, the primary locus of global warfare shifted from the Western Pacific to the Middle East, Central Asia and North Africa, where the United States has been embroiled in protracted, unwinnable wars directly in Iraq and Afghanistan, indirectly in Egypt, Syria, Libya, Iran and beyond, wars that will leave the region economically, politically and socially scarred for decades to come. How critical have these costly failures been to the gridlock that now paralyzes American politics, domestic and global?

In the new millennium, while East Asia and the Pacific strengthened their position at the center of world economic growth with the formation of a deeply intertwined regional economy, and dense intra- and inter-regional transportation links, far from easing geopolitical tensions and ushering in a harmonious regional order, precisely the reverse has occurred. Deepening territorial and inter-state geopolitical conflicts have erupted, albeit short of major wars. Some of these have been shaped by divisions rooted in the systemic conflicts of the immediate post-war era, including the US–Korea and US–Indochina Wars. In addition, new conflicts have arisen within the US-led alliance structure.

Four critical factors help to explain the nature and intensity of contemporary conflicts in the Asia-Pacific. First, the United Nations Convention on the Law of the Sea (UNCLOS), which was concluded in 1982 and came into effect in 1994, divided large areas of what had once been open seas into exclusive economic zones (EEZs) extending outward 200 nautical miles, thereby igniting rivalries over even the smallest islands and rocks. Second, the discovery of (perhaps) substantial oil, natural gas, and other resource deposits at sea raised the stakes concerning control over contested insular territories. Third, there is a changing balance of power notable for China's resurgence as the world's second largest economy and a regional power bent on challenging US hegemonic ambitions and establishing its own geopolitical and territorial claims in the Western Pacific. It is notable that the United States, claiming 11,351,000 km^2 as its EEZ in three oceans as well as the Gulf of Mexico and the Caribbean, was by far the largest beneficiary of territory as a result of the UNCLOS treaty (despite not having ratified it), while China, which did ratify it, was among the smallest beneficiaries. Indeed, the old colonial powers, with the United States followed by the United Kingdom and France and including Japan, were the big winners. Thus Japan, at number nine in the size of its EEZ, received five times the ocean area of China, which ranked in thirty-first place.

Third, China's resurgence has occurred at a time of relative decline in US power and credibility, as illustrated by its costly failures in Iraq and Afghanistan, and an even sharper decline in Japanese power as a result of the economic meltdown of the 1990s and subsequent stagnation. The point should not be exaggerated. US military power is without rival, as is its wealth and corporate might. Nor is there a candidate on the horizon for a new hegemonic power. Nevertheless, the bloom is off the rose. It will be more difficult for the United States to dictate the terms of international geopolitical and economic order, above all in the Western Pacific. Finally, we note the continued significance of major historical memory wars centered on Japanese brutality and atrocities – notably the savaging of the Chinese countryside in a war that took twenty million Chinese lives, the massive use of Korean and Chinese coerced labor, the sexual slavery of the military "comfort women" and the Nanjing Massacre, all highlighted by prime ministerial visits to Yasukuni Shrine, the symbol of Japan's emperor-centered nationalism. All of these memory wars, rooted in an earlier era of colonialism, far from being resolved in the seven decades since the end of the Pacific War, have repeatedly surfaced as sources of conflict. The importance of the historical conflicts is that they undermine the possibilities for inclusive regional solutions to the territorial and other conflicts that plague the region.

This epilogue examines four territorial-geopolitical conflicts which have come to the fore in recent years, each involving small islands with few or no inhabitants and each involving a long historical dispute over sovereignty. They span the East China Sea, the East Sea/Japan Sea, the Sea of Okhotsk, and the South China Sea. These are (see Figure 14.1):

1   the PRC, ROC, and Japan: Diaoyu/Senkaku islets (hereafter Senkaku) in the East China Sea with Japan holding effective control;

2   Japan and Korea: Dokdo/Takeshima (hereafter Dokdo) in the East Sea/ Japan Sea with Korea holding effective control;

3   Japan and Russia: Southern Kurile Islands/Northern Territories (hereafter Kuriles) in the Sea of Okhotsk, four contested islands with Russia holding effective control;

4   the PRC and Vietnam/the Philippines, among others in the South China Sea including the Spratly Islands, the Paracel Islands, and Scarborough Shoals, each claimed by multiple nations.

In all but one of these cases, the dispute pivots on virtually uninhabited rocks; in the Kuriles, the Soviets expelled the entire Japanese population in 1946. In 2013 the Kuriles had 19,000 people of multiple nationalities.

In each of these flashpoints, the United States has played a critical role from the framing of the San Francisco Treaty to the present, though it makes no territorial claim in the contested areas. In recent years, not least in response to these disputes, the Obama administration has sought to implement the preliminary stages of a "Pivot to Asia." This has involved reaffirming and strengthening the position of the US as the major ally and treaty partner of Japan, Korea, Australia,

Figure 14.1 The four contested areas and the rival claimants (source: Kimie Hara).

and the Philippines; strengthening the already formidable US geostrategic position resting on a network of bases as well as overwhelming naval, air and nuclear supremacy in the Western Pacific; and, in the Senkaku dispute, directly challenging the PRC on behalf of a US ally, Japan.

The United States is also, of course, a major trade and investment partner not only with its allies throughout the Asia-Pacific, but also with China. The United States–China trade and investment bond is not only among the world's most robust, but is complemented by China's purchase of more than US$2 trillion in US Treasuries, the largest holding of any nation in the service of propping up the US dollar and relieving the pressure of US chronic trade deficits. The result might be described as an antagonistic symbiosis joining China and the United States together at the hip like Siamese twins.

In each of the four cases, since 1968, the stakes have been raised by the possibility of oil and natural gas revenues in the vicinity of the contested territories, albeit to varying degrees.

The Russia–Ukraine military clashes of recent years, as well as general conflict over the expansion of NATO on Russia's borders, have highlighted United States–Russia antagonisms, but it is China that poses the largest potential threat to US hegemony in the Asia-Pacific in the long run, and it is China, encircled by US bases, that is directly challenging US definitions of regional power on its borders and at sea. Stated differently, a resurgent China, historically the dominant power in the Western Pacific prior to the nineteenth century, having clashed with the United States on the battlefield in the US–Korean and less directly in the US–Indochina Wars, is now prepared to challenge the claims of the United States to set the rules for the Asia-Pacific that it established in the early post-war epoch. Times have changed. If China cannot begin to rival the United States in its global reach and ability to establish rules shaping the international order, still less in its air and naval power, base network, or alliances, it has begun to challenge the territorial outcomes structured in the era of US hegemony in the Western Pacific. This comes at a time when Washington is preoccupied with the Middle East and when the luster surrounding the United States has been tarnished by its worldwide use of drones and the surveillance conducted on allies and foes alike as revealed by Edward Snowden. Here we briefly highlight the US role in relation to the disputants in these contemporary conflicts.

It is sometimes forgotten that the Diaoyu/Senkaku conflict involves three claimants: PRC, ROC, and Japan. The United States returned administrative rights to the islands in 1972 at the time of the reversion to Japan of administrative rights to Okinawa, leaving the US base structure intact. In response to the Chinese challenge over Senkaku, the United States has stated explicitly that it will come to Japan's aid should China militarily challenge the status quo in accord with the US interpretation of the Ampo Security Treaty. In this case alone among the four, a direct US action, that is, transfer of administrative rights over Senkaku to Japan in the context of the 1972 reversion of administrative rights to Okinawa, created the basis for the present impasse in which the PRC and ROC challenge Japan's claims to ownership of the islands. The United States was keenly aware of ROC and PRC claims to Senkaku prior to their 1972 return to Japan as revealed in the record of discussions among Nixon, Kissinger, and ROC Ambassador Chow Shukai; the US action virtually coincided with the agreement brokered by Zhou Enlai and Tanaka Kakuei in 1972 in the course of normalizing PRC–Japan relations to shelve discussion of the ownership issue in the interest of reaching agreement on fundamental questions of mutual recognition and trade. China's Deng Xiaoping reiterated that position in 1978. Over the next four decades, both sides strengthened economic, trade, as well as cultural and educational relations. This accord was breached by the Japanese decision in 2002 to register its rental of three of the five disputed islands, a means of highlighting the claim that the islands had been in Japanese possession since the 1890s, and far more provocatively a decade later on September 11, 2012 when the Japanese government purchased the islands from a Japanese claimant. The latter action precipitated the ongoing crisis involving repeated standoffs between Chinese and Japanese ships and aircraft. This took the form of Chinese claims to an exclusive Air Defense Identification Zone (ADIZ) in the contested area, mass protests in China resulting in a setback to Japanese business interests, and a general hardening of relations between the two nations. With both China and Japan strengthening their military positions in the region, among the four conflicts reviewed here, this poses the greatest immediate risk of escalation to war.

The Japan–ROK clash over Dokdo involves two US allies, both of whom have provided indispensable support for the US side in every war since 1950 and host major US bases that played pivotal roles in the US–Korean and US–Indochina Wars. Both are essential to the exercise of American power with respect to China and Russia. The contentiousness of the issues is emblematic of unresolved political and territorial legacies of two centuries of colonialism in East Asia as well as of the post-war territorial disposition of the San Francisco Treaty and the global conflict that it mirrored and defined.

Since 1953, Dokdo has been administered by the ROK, which then seized control of the islets. The Dokdo question has never been resolved, however, by bilateral or multilateral agreement or treaty. And although the issue surfaced at various times, including the 1965 negotiations over Japan–ROK normalization, it was not until 2005 that Japanese claims led to a public standoff over the islets. In contrast to a range of territorial issues that emerged as a result of the Asia-Pacific War and the dismantling of the Japanese empire, issues that were left unresolved in the San Francisco Treaty of 1951, there is no significant security issue or population at stake in the case of Dokdo.

There remains, however, a powerful emotional issue for Koreans. Japan seized Dokdo in 1905 as a prized asset for use in waging the Russo-Japanese War. That year it took major steps to subjugate Korea en route to full-scale colonization in 1910. Again, the United States played an important role. US mediation of the Russo-Japanese War took the form of the Taft–Katsura agreement of 1905 in which the United States recognized Japan's claims to Korea in exchange for Japanese recognition of US colonial rule in the Philippines. For the moment, the two rising colonial powers in the Pacific found common interests.

The issue of Dokdo, for Koreans, remains inscribed in consciousness of Japan's brutal colonial rule, a key factor in the public rage that surfaces at moments of Japanese official statements such as the 1994 claim to the islands at the time when UNCLOS took effect, or the official order that all history textbooks present Japan's historical claims to Dokdo. With both sides digging in their heels, and given continuing Korean anger over such historical memory issues as comfort women and forced labor, there seems little basis for accommodation at present.

The Kuriles provide another instance of a pivotal US behind-the-scenes role in shaping territorial outcomes and clashes in the Asia-Pacific, including territories in which the United States has no direct stake. The Kuriles were a key bargaining chip in the Asia-Pacific War endgame. In February 1945, Roosevelt and Churchill at Yalta promised their transfer to the Soviet Union from Japan in exchange for early Soviet entry into the war. Then, in 1956, with a Soviet–Japan agreement to give Japan two of the four main contested islands as a basis for settlement imminent, US Secretary of State John Foster Dulles informed Japan that if it accepted any territorial compromise with the Soviets, the United States would never return Okinawa. The San Francisco Treaty had announced Japan's renunciation of all claims to the Kuriles but, as in numerous cases, it neither specified their disposition nor named the disputed islands. Nearly six decades later, in the wake of repeated diplomatic efforts to break the impasse, there has been no territorial settlement and no peace treaty between Russia and Japan. The numerous visits by Prime Minister Abe Shinzo to Russia, President Vladimir Putin's apparent openness to a two-island compromise solution along the lines basically agreed to in 1956, and the need for allies by both the Russians (at a time when a US-led response to the Ukrainian–Russian conflict poses the threat of isolation of Russia by the Western powers) and the Japanese (at a time of mounting concern over the China challenge), as well as their common interest in striking a deal for Japanese financing of oil and gas development, suggest that the time could again be ripe for negotiations.

The South China Sea contains hundreds of small islands and rocks of which the Paracel/Xisha, the Spratly/Nansha, and Scarborough Shoal have been hotly contested in recent years, with the most intense clashes pitting China (PRC) against the Philippines and Vietnam. As in the case of the Kuriles, Japan in the San Francisco Treaty renounced claims to the Spratlys and Paracels, but without specification of which islands were included or to whom they belonged: the PRC, ROC, the Philippines, and Vietnam are among the claimants. Again, oil lies behind the tensions which peaked in 2012 when China and the Philippines clashed over Scarborough Shoal and in 2014 when China moved two underwater oil-drilling rigs into territory contested with Vietnam. Attempts to mediate these clashes at meetings of the Association of Southeast Asian Nations (ASEAN) have proven abortive, but they have led ASEAN to develop collective security arrangements. Here, too, US intervention in support of the Philippines and Vietnam in the form of pressure on China to back-off from its aggressive pursuit of South China Sea claims reveal that the immediate conflict masks a deeper United States–China clash.

The April 2014 United States–Philippines Enhanced Defense Cooperation Agreement marks the return of US forces and training in the Philippines two decades after the 1992 termination of US bases and forces. (Discussions under-way would give Japan similar entry to the Philippines in conjunction with the US at a time when Japan is strengthening its military posture with creation of a National Security Council, expanded arms purchases and sales, and forging tighter diplomatic bonds with nations such as the Philippines and Vietnam, which are at odds with China.) Nevertheless, with continued US preoccupation with the Middle East, where an unfolding region-wide crisis raises the prospect of a region-wide war that could encompass Syria, Pakistan, Egypt, and Libya, as well as Israel and Iran, the question arises whether the US, whose military power has no rival, can simultaneously shape outcomes in the South China Sea and the Western Pacific.

We have noted the deepening of tensions in a series of territorial conflicts spanning both the East China and South China seas. These are not simply isolated events. They reflect a strategic shift in the Western Pacific that is the product of growing Chinese strength and power projection, continuing American preoccupation with multiple wars in the Middle East despite moves toward implementing the strategic

Asia pivot, and steps toward an expansive Japanese military presence in Southeast Asia that includes arming Indonesia, the Philippines and (shortly) Vietnam with patrol boats together with a larger Japanese coast guard presence and arms sales. For China, as for the United States and Japan, the East China and South China Seas issues are clearly linked in a wider strategic understanding of changing geopolitical circumstances in the Western Pacific and beyond.

It has frequently been observed that despite the rapid emergence of an East Asian or Asia-Pacific regional economy since the 1970s, nothing comparable to the European Union has emerged to structure the geopolitical order. Europe, however, does not provide the only regional model that merits consideration. Over the last 500 years there have been three different regional models for bringing order to East Asia. The first, longest lasting, most stable and least intrusive of these was the China-centered tributary-trade order. At its apogee in the eighteenth century, China presided over a protracted peace in much of East Asia even as it extended the reach of empire in Inner Asia. It was an order premised on high levels of autonomy for neighboring regions. The second was Japan's short-lived regional order, framed as a Greater East Asia Co-Prosperity Sphere prior to and following the attack on Pearl Harbor and Japan's conquest of much of the Asia-Pacific. In invading China in the years 1931–1945, and in expanding its empire at the expense of the United States and its allies in the years 1941–1945, Japan sought to impose a new order on the region. However, Japan not only challenged more powerful imperialist adversaries but ignited revolutionary forces that would redefine the regional order following Japan's crushing defeat. Finally, like the Japan-centered order that preceded it, the US order was carved out in a series of wars including the Chinese Civil War and the United States–Korea and United States–Vietnam wars that defined the bipolar geopolitics of the post-war era. Unlike Japan's Pacific empire, the US global reach has made it possible to dominate the major international institutions from the United Nations, International Monetary Fund, World Bank, and World Trade Organizations while shaping international norms through the War Crimes Tribunals of the late 1940s and UNCLOS. But in contrast to the protracted peace that China presided over in East Asia in the eighteenth century, the United States has been perpetually at war from 1941 to the present, often fighting multiple wars simultaneously. If the United States presently faces more serious international and domestic challenges than at any time since 1945, it is far from clear whether a new hegemonic order is in the making or a pandemic disorder. Indeed, there is no potential challenger on a global scale in the coming decades.

This epilogue has emphasized the roots of conflict and the material and ideological forces that challenge those who would find peaceful cooperative solutions to territorial conflicts. Yet we note, too, the material foundations for such a new order: the interpenetration of the national economies, the emergence of infrastructure in the form of roads and railroads increasing interchange among nations, and a shared need to find solutions to the increasingly toxic problems associated with global climate crisis that will affect all nations and whose solution cannot be found exclusively or even primarily within the borders of any single nation-state. The future of the region, if it is not once again to be consumed by war, can only lie in mutual recognition of the need for shared development of the territories and seas that give rise to such contentious problems.

Note

1 Thanks to Peter Dale Scott, Marilyn Young, and Kimie Hara for comments and suggestions.

Index

Page numbers in *italics* denote tables, those in **bold** denote figures.